Discover Indian Reservations USA:

Discover Indian Reservations USA:

A Visitors' Welcome Guide

Edited by

Veronica E. Tiller

Foreword by

Ben Nighthorse Campbell

Council Publications
1999 Broadway, Suite 2600
Denver, CO 80202-5726

Discover Indian Reservations USA:

A Visitors' Welcome Guide

Library of Congress Catalog Number: 92-071259

ISBN 0-9632580-0-1

Attention: Corporations, government agencies, professional organizations, and educational institutions: quantity discounts are available on bulk purchases of this book for educational purposes, gifts, or fund raising. Special books or book excerpts can also be created to fit specific needs. For information, please contact Council Publications, 1999 Broadway, Suite 2600, Denver, CO 80202-5726, or call (303) 297-2378.

Table of Contents

Washington (cont)

Wisconsin

Wyoming

Maps

Maps (cont)

Appendix I

Appendix II

Appendix III

Index

FOREWORD

by Ben Nighthorse Campbell

In this year of campaigns to "rediscover" America, I'm pleased to introduce a unique publication that can help you learn more about the "First Americans." With this book, you can easily plan an excursion into vast areas of the United States that are still untouched and virtually unknown. Indian Reservations offer exhilarating vistas and less-explored pathways for your enjoyment and learning. You'll find exciting rodeos, festive tribal fairs, lively pow wows, solemn dances and great fishing and golf.

Indian Reservations USA: A Visitors' Welcome Guide enables you to locate new, exciting vacation opportunities. By exploring Indian country, you will also have the opportunity to see how Indian people live today; to hear their stories, learn about their culture. The attractions described are living testimony of proud and culture-enriched people who have survived adversity while maintaining their independence. All of the events, recreation areas and museums listed in this volume are owned and operated by Indians.

In a clear, simple format, this book provides information about what to see and do in Indian country. This is the first book to focus entirely on what tribes offer at home on their own reservations. All the facts in this publication were contributed by the tribes themselves, and the volume was compiled and edited by a consortium of tribes. The Council of Energy Resource Tribes is well known for its work that brings prosperity and equality to its people.

Use **Discover Indian Reservations USA: A Visitors' Welcome Guide** to help you enjoy the lands of the First Americans.

Good Voyages!

Ben Nighthorse Campbell
Colorado, District Three
United States House of Representatives

PREFACE

Sharing has always been a cornerstone in Indian life since ancient times. Indian societies have taken the concept of welcoming its visitors to heights unknown to the immigrant peoples to this land by institutionalizing the fine art of hospitality with elaborate customs and practices, such as the giveaway, potlatch, feasts, and various other welcome celebrations. In some ways, this spirit of sharing has not always served the best interests of the Indian people. In fact it has led to the loss of their homelands and way of life. Yet, despite the heavy losses, Indians today continue practicing and staging the welcome rites of generosity, often without expectations of remuneration, simply because it is still the right thing to do, the Indian thing to do, and because we are still Indians. What is more important than financial gain are the twin ideas of fostering understanding and respect for all peoples through common decency and sharing. It is within this basic Indian tradition and spirit of sharing that this travel guide is offered to the American and visiting public.

The bringing of the neighbor, visitor, or stranger to the Indian home and hearth has been the proven way of promoting mutually respectful relations, first among Indians, and then between Indians and non-Indians. The value of the firsthand experience and direct contact cannot be underestimated. It is this simple and practical approach that this guide encourages. Direct one-on-one contact between Indians and non-Indians can take away the uncertainty and second guessing that so often form the basis of relations between the two peoples, relations that in the past have been built on second-hand accounts and half-truths. In this way negative racial stereotypes can be replaced with positive images and perceptions. It is our hope that this visitors' guide provides the travelling public with accurate and updated information about the modern day Indian tribes and communities, so that by visiting Indian tribal lands and communities, a greater understanding and appreciation of Indian cultures both past and present, can be garnered.

Discovering Indian Reservations will show that Indian people continue to make positive contributions to American society. One obvious Indian contribution is economic, especially in regions such as the Western United States, where the majority of Indian tribes are located. It is in this region where the Indian presence has become synonymous with tourism and where tourism has become, and still is a growing industry. In the past, the Indian contribution to this anchor industry of the West has been marketed primarily by and for the benefit of non-Indians; little of the tourist dollar has filtered down to the Indians and their communities. The perception that Indians do not welcome visitors and, thus, do not care to share in the benefits of tourism, is totally erroneous. Indians do welcome visitors, not only to share the beauty of their cultures, but to do business with them. Indian tribes, like all other American communities, need revenue to run their governments, their cultural attractions, their recreational industries, to protect their environments, to create jobs, and, yes, their members do pay taxes.

Many Indian tribes are only beginning to assert their presence in the tourism marketplace that their very presence has done so much to support for generations. Not every reservation is equipped with the infrastructure to accommodate large numbers of visitors on a daily basis. Others have already developed sophisticated hospitality industries of their own. What has been missing, it seems, is reliable information about what things to do and see on Indian Reservations, and about what attractions and accommodations are available from the Indians themselves. This guide is compiled of information provided by the tribes themselves, and is designed to fill that information gap.

It is our hope that, by visiting Indian reservations, the traveling public will replace the prevalent image of the "dying race," with a more clear perception of the role that Indian peoples play in modern day America. Viable Indian communities form an important part of the mosaic of American life, pursuing the same goals and dreams of participating in the American way of life. Yet, they continue to maintain their distinctiveness from each other and from the remainder of their American countrymen and women because of the strength of their cultural heritage, their steadfast belief in their rights to self-determination and their "right to be Indian." In this 500th anniversary of Columbus' arrival in the new world, Indians celebrate more than their survival. We celebrate the beauty of our Indian spirituality, the correctness of the Indian view of "living in harmony with nature," and the ways of sharing, caring, and accepting the differences among all peoples of the world, because it is the very differences that makes all mankind one.

This Guide was conceived in the spirit of sharing among Indian peoples by the 49 Indian tribes and four affliated Canadian Indian nations who make up the membership of the Council of Energy Resource Tribes. In modern times Indian tribes continue the ancient tradition of working together to achieve common goals for a better tomorrow. Too often, Indian tribes have been perceived as separate and divided. The Council of Energy Resource Tribes offers this Visitors' Guide for the benefit of all tribes. CERT believes that only though the Indian tradition of sharing of resources and networking can the common goals and visions of Indian peoples be attained.

A. David Lester
Executive Director,
Council of Energy Resource Tribes

ACKNOWLEDGEMENTS

No publication project of this magnitude dealing with contemporary American Indian life could have been completed without the assistance, cooperation, dedication, and contribution of many people. The cooperation of the Indian tribes and communities, particularly those individuals who collected the information at the Indian community level, was essential. Because the basic data was collected primarily at the reservation level, it is the most recent and updated information available. To date there is no one single and reliable source of general information throughout the entire United States that can be tapped for the most recent and reliable information on Indian tribes, and for this reason, the tribal sector cannot be thanked enough for their cooperation and input.

A special thanks goes to the Board of Directors of the Council of Energy Resource Tribes for believing enough in the publication project to give us their endorsement and support. CERT's commitment to self-determination and its belief that Indian tribes have the inherent right to chart their own cultural, economic, and political destinities were reflected in undertaking this publication project. In addition, our gratitude goes out to all CERT member tribes and their leadership for their cooperation in all phases of the data collection.

Contributing valuable photographs were individuals, professional photographers, tribal and state agencies, newspapers, and private businesses who all believed in our project mission and goals. Photographs for the cover were generously provided to us by Gary Robinson, John Running, Sammy Still, and the New Mexico Economic Development and Tourism Office. For their generous consideration, we are grateful. A complete list of individual contributors of photographs can be found in Appendix III. This special group contributed their work as a courtesy to CERT and as a way of promoting Indian tourism. Another group of contributors to whom we are indebted is the state and tribal offices: the Absentee Shawnee Tribe of Oklahoma, the Arizona Office of Tourism, California Tourism Office, the Cherokee Office of Tourism, the Colorado Tourism Board, the Coushatta Tribe of Louisiana, the Iowa Tribe of Kansas and Nebraska, Michigan Travel Bureau, Navajoland Tourism Office, the New Mexico Office of Economic Development and Tourism, the Menominee Tribe, the Nevada Tourism Office, and the Oklahoma Office of Tourism, the Southern Ute Tribe, the St. Regis Mohawk Tribal Council, and the Turtle Mountain Chippewa Tribe. Without all these contributions, the Guide would not be as well illustrated. By allowing us to use his Navajoland Map, Cal Nez, saved us many hours and we appreciate his contribution.

Always willing to promote his Indian brethren and constituency is U.S. Congressional Representative Ben Nighthorse Campbell, who graciously wrote the foreword, and to him we extend a special thanks.

Without the dedication and hardwork of the Council of Energy Resource Tribes' Council Publications Project staff: Jonny BearCub Stiffarm (assistant project director), Christopher J. Norton (computer and desktop publishing coordinator) Raymond W. Loloff, (graphics and map designer), Gail Tsikewa and Clint J. LeBeau (clerical assistance), and Preston Corsa (Controller), this project would still be a dream. For his unwavering support, encouragement, and insights, a very special thanks to our Executive Director, A. David Lester.

The project is also grateful to our consultants. Professional editorial and research services were provided by Susan J. Worthman and Carol S. Clark. Public relations writing services were often provided by Carol Clark. About Books, Inc. of Buena Vista, Colorado, is credited for general book publishing advice and for marketing services.

Discover Indian Reservations USA:

Introduction

How To Use This Guide

Discover Indian Reservations USA is an up-to-date, comprehensive listing of things to do and see on Indian reservations throughout the United States, except Alaska. It provides current and accurate information to help the general traveling public plan visits to Indian reservation lands and communities. Alaska is not included in this guide because the broad extent of travel opportunities to Native Alaskan villages and communities requires its own volume.

This guide is for the adventurous traveler who is interested in visiting an Indian reservation or community. Its focus is the tourist attractions located within the actual physical boundaries of reservations and their communities. There are numerous other guides that deal with off-reservation Indian tourist attractions, mostly in large urban areas.

There is no attempt to recount the histories of the tribes; the Tribal Profiles included in this guide describe the reservations listed, the Indian tribes and bands living on them and the businesses and industries that operate there. The objective is to give travelers an idea of whom and what they will find there and to help visitors get to the Indian reservations where they can learn more about the Indian peoples and enjoy the recreational activities, cultural institutions, and special events and festivals.

We believe that a better, more accurate understanding of tribes and their histories can be had if travelers actually visit Indian reservations; thus we have minimized the information on the cultural and historical background of the tribes.

Indian tribes, for purposes of this guide, are any Indian tribes, bands, or groups who are self-governing, either federally recognized (as are 305) or state recognized (13 in number) and have a land base or recognized community (as some of the tribes of Oklahoma).

Understanding the Alphabetical Listings by States and Reservations:

There are 33 states (Alaska not included) that have Indian reservations and communities within their borders. The states are listed alphabetically beginning with Alabama and ending with Wyoming. For the convienence of the traveler, California has been divided into Northern California and Southern California. Within each state the Indian reservations, rancherias, and communities are also listed alphabetically by reservation, rancheria, or community name. For Indian reservations whose boundaries expand into more than one state, the Indian reservation is listed in the state where the tribe has its headquarters, but it is given a notation within the state in which the Indian reservation is also located. Examples are the Fort Yuma and Fort Mojave Indian Reservation boundaries include Arizona and California, and both are featured in Arizona but cross-referenced in California. There are also Indian reservations and communities, such as in Minnesota, where a tribe has more than one reservation land base. In this instance, the "satellite" reservations or communities are mentioned and cross-referenced to the headquarter reservation.

An example of this is the Deer Creek Reservation in Minnesota. The information is under Leech Lake Reservation, the headquarter reservation.

The Navajo Reservation, which covers parts of three states, is the only exception to our standardized listing approach. The tourism activities for the entire Navajo Reservation are listed in ARIZONA, where it has its tribal headuqarters, but are only cross-referenced in UTAH and NEW MEXICO. Taking our clue directly from the Navajoland Tourism Office, we have divided the Navajo Reservation into three sections: Western, Central, and Eastern, encompassing all Four Corner States. For this reason, a special Navajo Reservation Map is provided to show the three divisions. Our purpose is to present the Navajo Reservation as one unit and for ease-of-use.

In the general listings we attempted to acknowledge the existence of all Indian tribes and communities throughout the continental United States. Numerous tribes and communities, particularly the small rancherias of California and the small tribes and communities of Oklahoma and Washington, who did not respond to our request for information, are simply listed alphabetically in a chart at the end of each State section. Few tribes and communities specifically requested not to be listed and their wishes are respected.

Over 350 Indian tribes, groups, and bands are in some way referenced throughout the guide. A handy cross reference chart, ***Location of Tribes, Bands and Communities by State and Reservation or Community***, is included in Appendix I. It may be useful to refer to this chart if one wants to look up where any particular Indian group is located, especially large tribal groups like the Apaches, Sioux, and Chippewa.

TRIBAL PROFILES:

Each reservation, rancheria, or community is introduced with a brief profile that identifies the tribes and bands located on that reservation, rancheria, or community. The profile details the legal creation of the original land base, the current acreage making up all Indian trust lands, totals for resident population and tribal membership, if known, and the general economic structure of the reservation. All of this information is varied and general. Often tribal historic backgrounds are mentioned.

ADDRESS AND LOCATION:

The main tribal address and phone number is given. These two sources are the beginning and end of all information for any visitor. Since circumstances change over time, we suggest visitors telephone the main number for hours and other needed detail.

The description location for each reservation is for general directional purposes. The maps are intended to help travelers find the general region within each state where Indian reservations are located. It is strongly recommended that travelers consult a standard road atlas or highway map, since only selected Interstates, US highways and state highways are shown and referenced. The legend for all state maps is as follows:

CULTURAL INSTITUTIONS:

Under this heading are visitor centers and museums, as well as schools or institutes devoted to tribal heritage, including arts and crafts centers that offer the visitor the chance to see craftsmen at work. Typically, the visitors center on a reservation can provide detailed information about all the tourist opportunities available; it may house the tribe's museum as well.

Archaeological and Historic Sites:

This heading appears whenever a reservation has such a site open to the public. These sites range from the international recognized historic sites to those listed on the National Register of Historic Places. They can be operated by agencies such as the U.S. National Park Service. Archaeological and historic sites near the reservation will be noted. In every case, remember that artifacts found on such a site belong there. Thieves will be prosecuted.

Special Events:

Here are listed events held regularly on the reservation, including rodeos, pow-wows, festivals and athletic events, as well as those ceremonies that are open to the public. The guide includes only those events you can reliably expect to take place; all have been held for at least three years.

Recreational Opportunities:

This section is devoted to recreational opportunities such as boating, fishing, hunting, hiking, biking, and facilities such as golf courses, ski areas, marinas, and raceways, listing their names and phone numbers. Also listed are undeveloped sites open for boating, hunting, fishing, trails for hiking, biking and riding. Look here for bingo halls and casinos.

Industries and Businesses:

Only the Indian-owned and operated businesses related to recreation and tourism are listed. Of special note are the Indian arts and crafts enterprises, tour operators, and RV facilities. Many tribal businesses offer tours of their facilities, and the scope of their activities is considerable, ranging from floral nurseries to greeting card factories. Such operations and their phone numbers are listed. Call for address information and hours.

Tribal Organizations:

Entries in this section are provided to assist in tribal networking activities as well as to illustrate the variety of interests promoted by the tribes and Indian communities.

Accommodations:

Restaurants, service stations, convenience stores, motels/lodges and camping/RV facilities, especially those that are Indian owned and operated are listed. Where there are no tribally owned lodgings, the nearest town or city is noted.

Restrictions and/or Special Considerations:

This section details tribal rules protecting artifacts, regulation of camera use, effects of climate, et cetera. Remember that on a reservation an unmarked road probably leads to a private home. Avoid driving about unless you have a definite destination.

Appendices and Index

In Appendix I, ***Location of Tribes, Bands, and Communities by State and Reservation or Community***, is a handy reference listing of all Indian tribes and communities under their larger tribal group name (i.e., Apache, Chippewa, Sioux), the states they are located in, and the specific name of the reservation or community. Only those that appear in the guide are listed. Because of the hundreds of proper names and places, the INDEX does not relist the tribal groups and bands and their locations by specific page numbers. Appendix II, ***Pow Wow Directory by State and Month***, is a general Pow Wow Directory consisting mainly of those mentioned in the guide, but there are some off-reservation pow wows listed. Appendix III, is the ***Photo/Map Credits*** listed first by state and by photo or map contributor in alphabetical order, and then by page number where photo or map appears. The ***Index*** is compiled mainly by subject matter and activity such as festival, museum, skiing and boating.

Federal and State Indian Reservations of the United States

WASHINGTON
1. Makah Res.
2. Ozette Res.
3. Quileute Res.
4. Hoh Res.
5. Quinault Res.
6. Shoalwater Bay Res.
7. Lower Elwha Res.
8. Jamestown Klallam Res.
9. Port Gamble Res.
10. Port Madison Res.
11. Skokomish Res.
12. Squaxin Island Res.
13. Chehalis Island Res.
14. Nisqually Island Res.
15. Puyallup Island Res.
16. Muckleshoot Island Res.
17. Tulalip Island Res.
18. Stillaguamish Island Res.
19. Sauk Suiattle Island Res.
20. Swinomish Island Res.
21. Upper Skagit Island Res.
22. Nooksack Island Res.
23. Lummi Res.
24. Colville Res.
25. Kalispel Res.
26. Spokane Res.
27. Yakima Res.

OREGON
28. Grand Ronde Res.
29. Siletz Res.
30. Coos, Lower Umpqua & Siuslaw Res.
31. Coquille Res.
32. Cow Creek of Umpqua Res.
33. Klamath Res.
34. Warm Springs Res.
35. Umatilla Res.
36. Burns Paiute Colony Res.

CALIFORNIA (North)
See state map on page 50 for:
Benton Paiute Res.
Berry Creek Rancheria
Big Bend Rancheria
Big Valley Res.
Blue Lake Rancheria
Bridgeport Indian Colony
Buena Vista Rancheria
Cedarville Rancheria
Cloverdale Rancheria
Cortina Rancheria
Dry Creek Rancheria
Elk Valley Rancheria
Enterprise Rancheria
Greenville Rancheria
Grindstone Rancheria
Hopland Rancheria
Inaja-Cosmit Res.
Jackson Rancheria
Laytonville Rancheria
Likely Rancheria
Lookout Rancheria
Manchester-Pt. Arena Rancheria
Middletown Rancheria
Montgomery Creek Rancheria
Mooretown Rancheria
Pinoleville Rancheria
Pit River Tribe of California
Potter Valley Rancheria
Redding Rancheria
Redwood Valley Rancheria
Rohnerville Rancheria
Sheep Ranch Rancheria
Shingle Springs Rancheria
Smith River Rancheria
Stewarts Point Res.
Sulphur Bank Rancheria (Elem Colony)
Susanville Rancheria
Table Bluff Rancheria
Upper Lake Rancheria
XL Ranch

CALIFORNIA (South)
See state map on page 66 for:
Augustine Res.
Big Pine Res.
Big Sandy Res.
Bishop Res.
Cahuilla Res.
Campo Res.
Cold Springs Rancheria (Sycamore Valley)
Cuyapaipe Res.
Jamul Indian Village
La Posta Res.
Lone Pine Res.
Manzanita Res.
Mesa Grande Res.
North Fork Rancheria
Pauma & Yuima Res.
Pechanga Res.
Ramona Res.
Rincon Res.
San Manual Res.
San Pasqual Res.
Santa Rosa Res.
Table Mountain Rancheria
Timba-Sha Shoshone (Death Valley)
Torres-Martinez Res.
Twenty-Nine Palms Res.

IDAHO
37. Kootenai Res.
38. Coeur D'Alene Res.
39. Nez Perce Res.
40. Fort Hall Res.

NEVADA
41. Duck Valley Res.
42. Fort McDermitt Res.
43. Summit Lake Res.
44. Pyramid Lake Res.
45. Winnemucca Colony Res.
46. Lovelock Colony Res.
47. Te-Moak (Battle Mountain) Res.
48. Te-Moak (Elko Colony) Res.
49. Te-Moak (South Fork) Res.
50. Te-Moak (Ruby Valley) Res.
51. Te-Moak (Odgers Ranch) Res.
52. Ely Colony Res.
53. Duckwater Res.
54. Yomba Res.
55. Walker River Res.
56. Yerrington Res.
57. Washo Res.
58. Carson Colony Res.
59. Dresserville Res.
60. Reno Sparks Res.
61. Moapa River Res.
62. Las Vegas Colony Res.

MONTANA
63. Flathead Res.
64. Blackfeet Res.
65. Rocky Boys Res.
66. Fort Belknap Res.
67. Fort Peck Res.
68. Northern Cheyenne Res.
69. Crow Res.

WYOMING
70. Wind River Res.

UTAH
71. Northwestern Band of Shoshoni Res.
72. Uintah and Ouray Res.
73. Skull Valley Res.
74. Goshute Res.

75-82. Southern Paiute Res.

COLORADO
83. Ute Mountain Ute Res.
84. Southern Ute Res.

ARIZONA
85. Navajo Res.
86. Kaibab Res.
87. Hualapai Res.
88. Havasupai Res.
89. Hopi Res.
90. Camp Verde Res.
91. Yavapai Res.
92. Payson Res.
93. Fort Apache Res.
94. San Carlos Res.
95. Fort McDowell Res.
96. Salt River Res.
97. Gila River Res.
98. Akchin Res.
99. Gila Bend Res.
100. Fort Yuma Res.
101. Cocopah Res.
102. Papago Res.
103. Pascua Yaqui Res.
104. San Xavier Res.

NEW MEXICO
105. Jicarilla Apache Res.
106. Zuni Res.
107. Ramah Navajo Res.
108. Alamo Navajo Res.
109. Acoma Pueblo
110. Laguna Pueblo
111. Canoncito Navajo Res.
112. Isleta Pueblo
113. Sandia Pueblo
114. Santa Ana Pueblo
115. San Felipe Pueblo
116. Santo Domingo Pueblo
117. Cochiti Pueblo
118. Jemez Pueblo
119. Zia Pueblo
120. Nambe Pueblo
121. San Juan Pueblo
122. Taos Pueblo
123. Picuris Pueblo
124. Pojaoque Pueblo
125. Santa Clara Pueblo
126. San Ilde Fonso Pueblo
127. Tesque Pueblo
128. Mescalero Apache Res.

NORTH DAKOTA
129. Turtle Mountain Res.
130. Fort Berthold Res.
131. Devils Lake Sioux Res.
132. Standing Rock Sioux Res.

SOUTH DAKOTA
133. Cheyenne River Sioux Res.
134. Lake Traverse Sioux Res.
135. Crow Creek Sioux Res.
136. Lower Brule Sioux Res.
137. Pine Ridge Sioux Res.
138. Rosebud Sioux Res.
139. Yankton Sioux Res.

NEBRASKA
140. Santee Sioux Res.
141. Winnebago Res.
142. Omaha Res.

KANSAS
143. Sac and Fox Res.
144. Iowa of Kansas Res.
145. Kickapoo of Kansas Res.
146. Potawatomi Res.

OKLAHOMA
147. Osage Indian Reservation
148. See state map on page 258
Absentee Shawnee Tribe of Oklahoma
Alabama-Quassarte of Creeks
Apache
Apache, Ft. Sill
Caddo
Cherokee Nation of Oklahoma
Cherokee, United Ketoowa Band of
Cheyenne Arapaho Tribes
Chickasaw Nation
Choctaw Nation of Oklahoma
Comanche Tribe
Delaware Tribe
Eastern Shawnee Tribe
Kialegee Creek Tribe
Kickapoo Tribe
Kiowa Tribe
Miami Tribe
Modoc Tribe
Muscogee (Creek) Nation
Iowa Tribe of Oklahoma
Kaw Nation
Otoe-Missouri Tribe
Ottawa Tribe of Oklahoma
Pawnee Tribe of Oklahoma
Peoria Tribe of Oklahoma
Ponca Tribe of Oklahoma
Potawatomi Tribe, Citizen Band of
Quapaw Tribe of Oklahoma
Sac and Fox Nation of Oklahoma
Seminole Nation of Oklahoma
Seneca-Cayuga Tribe of Oklahoma
Thlopthlocco Creek Tribal Town
Tonkawa Tribe
Wichita Tribe
Wyandote Tribe

TEXAS
149. Isleta Del Sur Pueblo (Tigua Res.)
150. Texas Kickapoo Res.
151. Alabama-Coushatta Res.

MINNESOTA
152. Red Lake Res.
153. Nett Lake Res.(Bois Forte)
154. Grand Portage Res.
155. White Earth Res.
156. Leech Lake Res.
157. Fond du Lac Res.
158. Mille Lacs Res.
159. Upper Sioux Res.
160. Lower Sioux Res.
161. Prior Lake Res.(Shakopee)
162. Prairie Island Res.

IOWA
163. Sac & Fox Res.

LOUISIANA
164. Coushatta Res.
165. Tunica - Biloxi Res.
166. Chitimacha Res.
167. Houma Nation Res.

MICHIGAN
168. L'Anse Res.
169. Bay Mills Res.
170. Sault St. Marie Res.
171. Lac Vieix Desert Res.
172. Hannahville Indian Community
173. Grand Traverse Res.
174. Isabella Res.
175. Huron Potawatomi Res.

WISCONSIN
176. Red Cliff Res.
177. Bad River Res.
178. La Courte Oreilles Ojibwa Res.
179. St. Croix Res.
180. Lac du Flambeau Res.
181. Mole Lake Res.
182. Forest County Potawatomi Res.
183. Menominee Res.
184. Stockbridge Munsee Indian Community
185. Oneida Res.
186. Winnebago Res.

MISSISSIPPI
187. Choctaw Res.

ALABAMA
188. Poarch Band of Creek Indian Res.

MAINE
189. Houlton - Maliseets Res.
190. Passamaquoddy Indian Township Res.
191. Pleasant Point Res.
192. Penobscot Nation Res.

NEW YORK
193. St. Regis Mohawk Res.
194. Oneida Nation Res.
195. Onondaga Nation Res.
196. Tuscarora Res.
197. Cattaraugus Res.
198. Allegany (Seneca) Res.
199. Tonawanda Seneca Res.
200. Poospatuck Res.
201. Shinnecock Res.

MASSACHUSETTS
202. Hassanamisco Res.
203. Mashpee - Wampanoag Res.
204. Wampanoag Res.

RHODE ISLAND
205. Narragansett Indian Res.

CONNECTICUT
206. Mashantucket Pequot Res.
207. Paucatuck Eastern Pequot Res.
208. Paugussett Golden Hill Res.
209. Schaghticoke Res.

VIRGINIA
210. Pamunkey Res.
211. Mattaponi Res.

NORTH CAROLINA
212. Cherokee Indian Res.
213. Haliwa-Saponi Res.

SOUTH CAROLINA
214. Catawba Res.

FLORIDA
215. Brighton Res.
216. Big Cypress Res.
217. Hollywood Res.
218. Miccosukee Res.

Federal and State Indian Reservations of the United States

Alabama

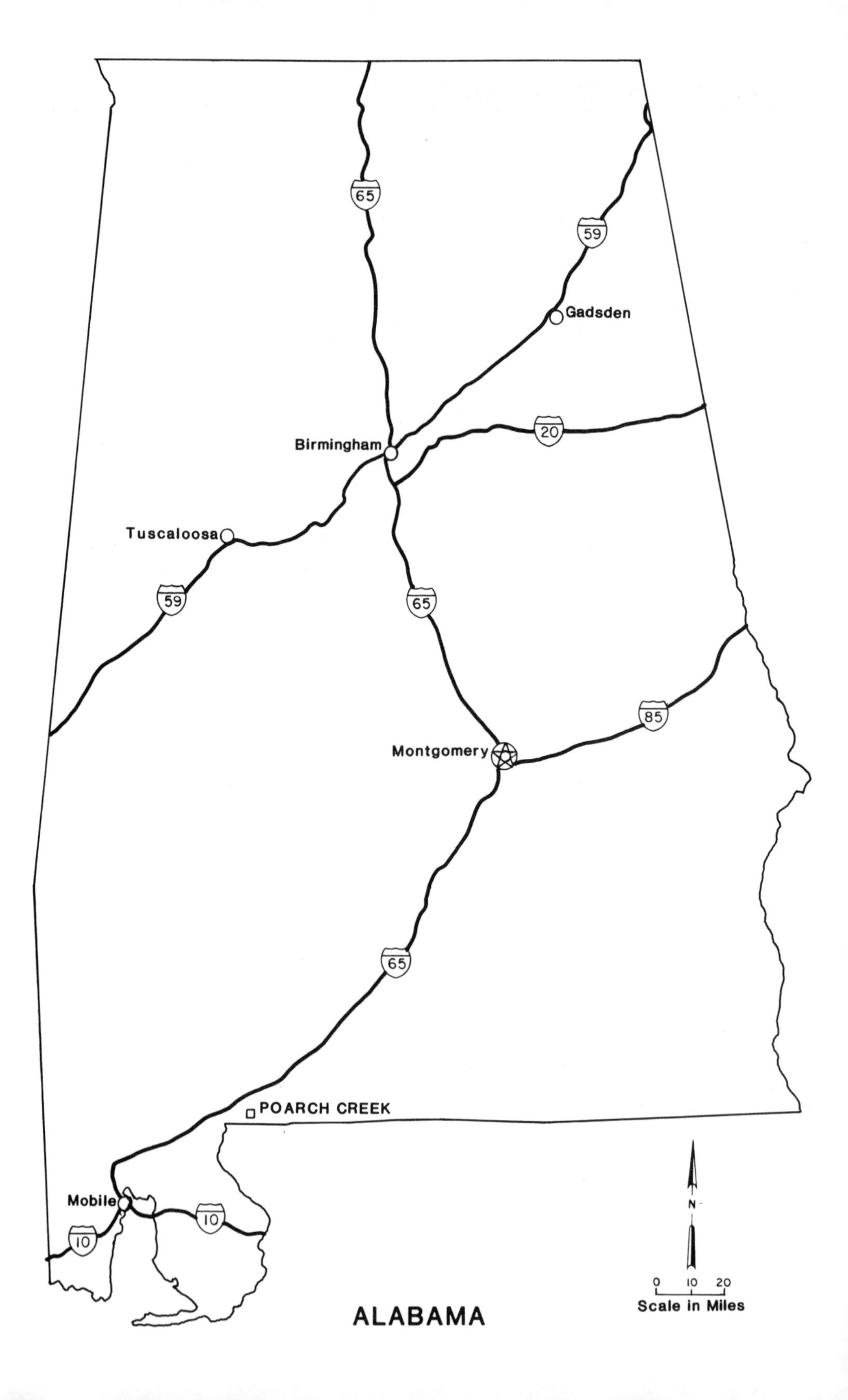
65
59
Gadsden
20
Birmingham
Tuscaloosa
59
65
85
Montgomery
65
POARCH CREEK
Mobile
10
10
N
0 10 20
Scale in Miles
ALABAMA

Poarch Creek Reservation

TRIBAL PROFILE:

Situated in one of the fastest growing regions in the state of Alabama, the Poarch Creek Indian Reservation occupies 600 acres, with its service area spanning 5 counties in Alabama and Florida. This federal reservation, recognized in 1984, is home to approximately 1,850 Poarch Creek Tribe members. The tribe is a segment of the original Creek Nation, indigenous to Alabama and living in this locality since the 1700s. Poarch Creek Tribal government works to deliver essential services and develop community projects designed to improve quality of life without sacrificing the tribe's identity.

LOCATION:

Southwestern Alabama, northeast of Mobile off I-65. Atmore is at the junction of Hwy 21 and US 31.

ADDRESS:

Poarch Creek Indians
Rte. 3, Box 243-A
Atmore, AL 36504
(205) 368-9136

CULTURAL INSTITUTIONS:

A museum is in the planning stages.

SPECIAL EVENTS:

Thanksgiving Day Pow Wow
Poarch Creek Pow Wow Grounds
Poarch, AL
An exuberant and fun-filled celebration of Poarch Creek heritage featuring competition and exhibition singing and dancing by youth and adult groups from throughout the region; princess contests; and opening ceremonies featuring distinguished Indian leaders. Food, arts and crafts, turkey shoot, greased pig chase, and donkey rides available throughout the day. Poarch is north of I-65 off AL Hwy 21. Small admission fee. Held 4th Thursday in November.

RECREATIONAL OPPORTUNITIES:

Creek Bingo Palace
P.O. Box 09
Atmore, AL 36504
(205) 368-8007 or (800) 826-9121
High stakes bingo offering over $50,000 in cash and prizes. The facility can accommodate large groups and offers an in-house deli. Open every Tuesday, Thursday, Friday and Saturday evening, afternoons on Sunday. Off I-65, exit 57 in Atmore.

BUSINESSES & INDUSTRIES:

Red Eagle Paint
Rte. 2, Box 21-A
Atmore, AL 36502
(205) 368-1733
Producing high quality specialty polyurethane coating systems for government and industrial users.

Strader Manufacturing, Inc.
5552 Industrial Blvd.
Milton, FL 32570
(904) 626-2229 or (205) 368-9136
Manufacturing stainless steel identification tags and plates for industrial use.

ACCOMMODATIONS:

Creek Family Restaurant
Hwy 21 & I-65
Atmore, AL
(205) 368-4422
Serving regional and homestyle favorites, plus an all-you-can-eat buffet Wednesday nights; facilities include banquet and conference areas. Bakery on premises. Open daily 6:00 a.m.-9:00 p.m. Relax in the Journey's End Lounge.

Best Western of Atmore
Atmore, AL
(205) 368-8182
Part of the complex that houses Creek Family Restaurant.

Arizona

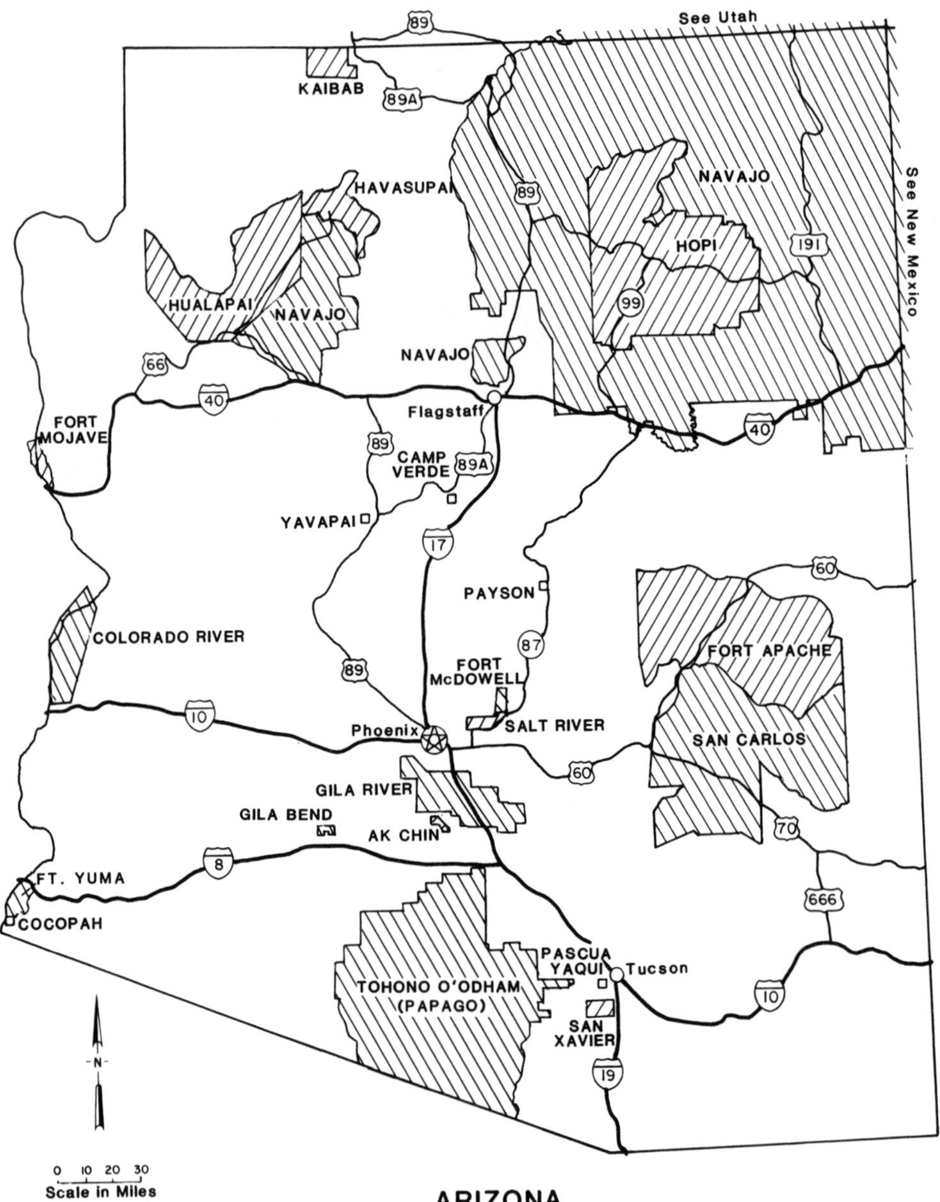
See Utah
See New Mexico
KAIBAB
HAVASUPAI
HUALAPAI
NAVAJO
HOPI
FORT MOJAVE
Flagstaff
CAMP VERDE
YAVAPAI
PAYSON
COLORADO RIVER
FORT McDOWELL
SALT RIVER
Phoenix
FORT APACHE
SAN CARLOS
GILA RIVER
GILA BEND
AK CHIN
FT. YUMA
COCOPAH
PASCUA YAQUI
Tucson
TOHONO O'ODHAM (PAPAGO)
SAN XAVIER
N
0 10 20 30
Scale in Miles

ARIZONA

Ak Chin Reservation

Tribal Profile:

A federal reservation of 21,840 acres, Ak Chin is home to about 625 members of the Tohono O'odham Tribe, who were formerly known as Papago. The Tohono O'odham extend from Ak Chin south to Sonora, Mexico. Ak Chin is governed by the Ak Chin Indian Community Council; tribal income is derived from farming. Annual rainfall is about eight inches; temperatures range from 30 to 110 degrees.

Location:

Ak Chin is directly south of Phoenix (40 miles from the Phoenix airport). A county road connects Ak Chin with I-10 to the northeast and I-8 to the south.

Address:

Ak Chin Indian Community
Route 2, Box 27
Maricopa, AZ 85239
(602) 568-2227

Cultural Institutions:

Ak Chin Him Dak
(602) 568-2221
This "eco-museum" displays valuable artifacts relating to the early Ak Chin people. It is distinguished from a traditional museum in that land and territory replace the museum building, the tribal members being curator and public. The decentralized organization encourages each and every family to create, maintain and enjoy exhibits they have developed.

Special Events:

Ak Chin St. Francis Church Feast/Honoring Past Chairmen Day
A feast and dance honoring St. Francis, who loved nature. Chile, flour tortillas, fry bread and other local foods are served. The afternoon and evening are filled with traditional dances, in which more than 500 dancers usually participate. Held in October.

Businesses & Industries:

Ak Chin Farms
(602) 568-2227
The tribe operates a 10,000 acre farm; ask for the farm manager to arrange a tour. The principal crop is cotton.

Camp Verde Reservation

Tribal Profile:

The Camp Verde Yavapai-Apache Reservation was established in 1875 by President Ulysses S. Grant. The present reservation consists of four separate communities located in Camp Verde, Clarkdale, Middle Verde and Rimrock. Tribal membership is about 1,100.

Location:

Central Arizona, in the Verde Valley. Rimrock, Middle Verde and Camp Verde are on I-17. Montezuma's Castle National Monument lies between them. Clarkdale is to the northwest, on AZ Alternate 89, near Tuzigoot National Monument and the towns of Cottonwood and Sedona. To reach the Yavapai-Apache Visitors Center and Cliff Castle Lodge, exit I-17 at Exit 289 east and follow Middle Verde Road 1/4 mile.

Address:

Yavapai-Apache Tribe
P.O. Box 1188
Camp Verde, AZ 86322
(602) 567-3649

Cultural Institutions:

Yavapai-Apache Visitors Center
P.O. Box 1167
Camp Verde, AZ 86322
(602) 567-3109
Exhibits, including films, present both traditional and modern life styles of the Yavapai and Apache people.

Special Events:

Exodus Days
Yavapai-Apache Visitors Center
(602) 567-3649
A commemoration of the Exodus to San Carlos in 1875, the celebration includes an historic re-enactment, a pow wow, and arts and crafts displays and sales. Held on Saturday, beginning at 7:00 a.m., at the end of February.

Archaeological & Historic Sites:

Contact the Yavapai-Apache Visitors Center, (602) 567-3109, for information about sites open to the public.

Accommodations:

Cliff Castle Lodge and Convention Center
Yavapai-Apache RV Park
At the Yavapai-Apache Visitors Center.

Cocopah Reservation

Tribal Profile:

The Cocopah Reservation was established by Executive Order in 1917 as home for the Cocopah Indian Tribe; it presently encompasses just over 6,000 acres divided into three parcels with a total tribal membership of about 600. The Cocopah Indians are descended from a Yuman tribe that migrated from Baja California, settling along the Colorado River. The main source of tribal income is agricultural leases.

Location:

Near the borders of Arizona with California and Mexico. Southwest of Yuma at Somerton, the Cocopah Reservation is intersected from north to south by US 95.

Address:

Cocopah Tribal Office
P.O. Bin G
Somerton, AZ 85350
(602) 627-2102

Special Events:

Cocopah Pow Wow
(602) 627-2102
Traditional dancing and singing, with contest dancing in 12 categories; plus Gourd and Bird Dancing. Peon tournament. Arts and crafts and food booths. At Cocopah Bingo Hall, 8 miles south of Yuma on US 95. Free admission. Held mid-February weekend.

Recreational Opportunities:

Cocopah Casino and Bingo Hall
Somerton, AZ
(602) 726-8066
Various Las Vegas-style games and high stakes bingo. On US 95; open 24 hours.

Cocopah Bend RV and Golf Park
Yuma, AZ
(602) 343-9300
Large, full-service RV Park with 806 spaces, full hookups. Amenities include large swimming pool, ballroom, planned activities and 18-hole golf course. Open year round.

Businesses & Industries:

EZ Corner Store
Next to the Casino on US 95.

Colorado River Indian Tribes Complex. Far L: Library & Museum, R: Tribal Office. Courtesy of Arizona Office of Tourism.

Colorado River Reservation

TRIBAL PROFILE:

The Colorado River Reservation straddles the Colorado River; it is 45 miles from north to south and boasts 90 miles of river shoreline. Of its 268,900 acres, 226,000 are in Arizona, the remainder in California. The reservation was established in 1865. Of the total tribal membership of just over 3,000, the present resident population of the reservation is about 1,800, mostly Mohave and Chemehuevi tribal members, although some Hopi and Navajo were located here following World War II.

The reservation economy is centered around agriculture, recreation, government and light industry. The fertile river bottom land and available water are used extensively in irrigated agriculture, producing cotton, alfalfa, wheat, feed grains, lettuce and melons. The Colorado River is the basis for well-developed recreation and tourist facilities.

LOCATION:

North of I-10, along the Arizona-California border. The town of Parker is about 40 miles north of I-10, with access from US 60 and Hwy 72 or US 95, and can also be reached by driving south from Lake Havasu City on Hwy 95.

ADDRESS:

Colorado River Indian Tribes
Route 1, Box 23-B
Parker, AZ 85344
(602) 669-9211

CULTURAL INSTITUTIONS:

Tribal Museum/Public Library/Archives
Tribal Administrative Center
2nd Avenue and Mohave Road
Parker, AZ
(602) 669-9211
Museum features collections of local Indian baskets, arts and crafts, a gift shop, and oral history and cultural collections. Tribal museum staff members provide guided tours. The library includes tribal archives available upon application for serious students of tribal history.

SPECIAL EVENTS:

National Indian Days Celebration
Manataba Park
Parker, AZ
(602) 669-9211
Organized by the Irataba Society, festival includes the Miss Indian Arizona Pageant, pow wow, shinny games, peon games, traditional singing and dancing, displays of arts and crafts and a parade. Held Thursday through Sunday, last week of September.

All Indian Rodeo
PIRA Rodeo Grounds
Parker, AZ
(602) 669-9211
Organized by the Parker Indian Rodeo Association; draws participants nationally. Held first weekend in December.

Recreational Opportunities:

The tremendous appeal of the Colorado River for hunting, fishing and boating has been developed by the tribes. Reservation hunting and fishing permits are required. The area is excellent for water sports, including motor boating, water skiing and swimming. Speed boat, motorcycle and off-road vehicle races are held annually in the area.

Blue Water Marina
(602) 669-2433
Boating facilities, 193 RV spaces, restaurant, lounge and club house.

Archaeological & Historic Sites:

Old Mohave Presbyterian Mission: In La Paz; contact the Tribal Museum, (602) 669-9211, for information and to arrange a visit. Ask as well about petroglyphs and pictographs, ancient trails and intaglios.

Tribal Organizations:

All Indian Rodeo Association

Irataba Society

Accommodations:

Various lodgings in Parker; many RV facilities along the river.

Fort Apache Reservation

Typical mountain scenery on the Fort Apache Indian Reservation. Courtesy of Candi L. Stasiek, McHenry, Ill.

Tribal Profile:

The White Mountain Apache Tribe is located on the 1.6 million acre Fort Apache Indian Reservation, established by an Act of Congress in 1897. Forestry is the main source of income on the reservation, followed by livestock and tourist-related businesses. The tribal enrollment is about 9,800, but total resident population is 13,000. The major reservation communities are Whiteriver, Cibecue, Carrizo, Hon Dah, McNary, Forestdale, Seven Mile, East Fork, and Canyon Day. Tribal headquarters is Whiteriver.

LOCATION:

The Fort Apache Indian Reservation is in east-central Arizona. US 60 crosses the reservation. A commercial air shuttle to Phoenix is located 10 miles from the reservation at Show Low.

ADDRESS:

White Mountain Apache Tribe
P.O. Box 700
Whiteriver, AZ 85941
(602) 338-4346, -4453

CULTURAL INSTITUTIONS:

White Mountain Apache Cultural Center
P.O. Box 507
Old Fort Apache, AZ 85926
(602) 338-4625

Old Fort Apache lies within a national historic district, and the cabin erected by General George E. Crook in 1871 during his campaign against the Western Apaches houses the Cultural Center. Collection and exhibits are small but range from the prehistoric through modern times. Apache language and history taught by Director. Facilities include gift shop and picnic area. Offers nature tours during summer that begin at the Indian village along the nearby river. With advance notice, a tour can be taken to Geronimo's Cave, about 10 miles from Fort Apache, south of Whiteriver. Open 8:00 a.m. to 5:00 p.m., Monday through Friday except in summer; from 7:30 a.m. to 4:30 p.m. 7 days a week, Memorial Day to Labor Day. Donations are appreciated.

SPECIAL EVENTS:

Traditional dances are held throughout the summer months; contact the Cultural Center for times, dates, and location.

White Mountain Apache Tribal Fair & Rodeo
Whiteriver, AZ
Festivities include parade, western dances, carnival, Night Dances, arts & crafts, rodeo, and traditional sunrise dances. Held Labor Day weekend.

RECREATIONAL OPPORTUNITIES:

Fishing and Hunting: The White and Black Rivers and many creeks rise in the heart of White Mountain Apache lands. The reservation is also scattered with 32 lakes and reservoirs, many stocked with trout. Some popular fishing spots are Horseshoe, Hawley, and Sunrise Lakes. Camping sites are abundant.

Check with the White Mountain Apache Game & Fish Dept., (602) 338-4385, for details on fishing, hunting, and camping in any area of the reservation. *Permits are required for fishing, backpacking and cross-country skiing.*

Sunrise Park Resort
P.O. Box 217
McNary, AZ 85930
(602)735-7600, -7669 or
(800)55-HOTEL for hotel reservations
Ski more than 60 trails on 3 interconnected mountains designed for all levels of skill, or attend Ski School before hitting the slopes at one of the Southwest's premier resorts. The Sunrise Park Hotel is nearby with a restaurant and lounge, an indoor pool, spa and sauna for relaxation after a strenuous day on the slopes. The hotel offers a wide variety of complete recreation packages and amenities. It also hosts competitions and exhibitions throughout the ski season.

Skiing at Sunrise Park Resort. Courtesy of Sunrise Resort/Chaco Mohlerl Mountain Stock Photo.

Sunrise Resort Hotel. Photo by John Canally. Courtesy of Sunrise Resort.

Salt River Canyon: Recreational activities abound in the Salt River Canyon, including boating, rafting, camping, hiking and fishing. A tribal shop offers arts and crafts, groceries, gasoline, fishing tackle and reservation permits. Fishing and camping permits are required. About 1 hour west of Fort Apache off I-60. For information, call (602) 367-5126, ext. 8573.

Hawley Lake: Offering cabins, motel rooms, trailer spaces and boat rentals; small store with fishing tackle and groceries sells reservation permits. Open seasonally. For information: (602) 335-7511.

Horseshoe Lake: Boat rentals, tackle and groceries. Open seasonally. For information: (602) 338-4417.

Reservation Lake: Amenities include cabin and boat rentals; grocery and tackle shop; gasoline and reservation permits. Open seasonally. For information: (602) 338-4417.

ARCHAEOLOGICAL & HISTORIC SITES:

Kinishba Ruins: South of Fort Apache 3 miles, about 1/2 mile off Hwy 73 and straight into the mountains.

Mt. Baldy: Archeological sites and pictographs are scattered throughout the entire region.

BUSINESSES & INDUSTRIES:

White Mountain Apache Game & Fish Dept.
P.O. Box 220
Whiteriver, AZ 85941
(602) 338-4385, -4386

Fort Apache Timber Company (FATCO)
P.O. Box 1090
Whiteriver, AZ 85941
(602) 338-4931
Established in 1963, the timber company is owned by the White Mountain Apache Tribe and employs more than 300 Apaches in logging, manufacturing and business management. FATCO has yearly lumber sales in excess of $20 million. Tours of its facilities are not encouraged; however, for very interested individuals and small parties, contact main offices for possible tours.

Hon Dah Restaurant
(602) 369-4040
Full service restaurant serving breakfast, lunch and dinner buffets, and all-you-can-eat Sunday brunch.

Apache Service
(602) 338-4315
Carries groceries, gasoline, and fishing tackle.

Carrizo Food Store
(602) 332-2404
Services include cabin and boat rentals, groceries, fishing tackles, gasoline, and reservation permits.

Cedar Creek Food Store
(602) 338-1210
Groceries and gasoline sold here.

Seven Mile Food Store
(602) 338-1100
Groceries and gasoline sold here.

ACCOMMODATIONS:

See Sunrise Park Resort under Recreational Opportunities.

Hon Dah (Be My Guest)
(602) 369-4311
Facilities include cabins, motel rooms, conference hall, and trailer spaces. Sells reservation permits.

RESTRICTIONS AND/OR SPECIAL CONSIDERATIONS:

Check with the White Mountain Apache Game & Fish Department for recreational activity regulations.

Archaeological sites are tribally protected properties that must be left intact.

Fort McDowell Reservation

TRIBAL PROFILE:

Fort McDowell Reservation is 24,680 acres; tribal government was established in 1936. The reservation population of just over 630 includes Yavapai, Mohave and Apache Indians. Tribal income derives primarily from recreation fees and rental incomes.

LOCATION:

The reservation is adjacent to Fountain Hills, along the western shore of the Verde River, northeast of the Gila River Reservation and Phoenix. Hwy 87 runs east-west through the reservation.

ADDRESS:

Fort McDowell Mohave-Apache Indian Community
P.O. Box 17779
Fountain Hills, AZ 85268
(602) 990-0995

RECREATIONAL OPPORTUNITIES:

Fort McDowell Baja Bingo
Rte. 1, Box 798
Scottsdale, AZ 85264
(602) 837-1424
Off Hwy 87 on Fort McDowell Road, in Fort McDowell, AZ.

Fort Mojave

see Southern California

Fort Yuma Reservation

TRIBAL PROFILE:

The Fort Yuma Indian Reservation straddles the Colorado River and the Arizona/California border in the southern desert. The Quechan, one of the Yuman tribes, are traditionally farmers and live on a portion, approximately 44,400 acres, of ancestral lands. The reservation, established by Executive Order in 1884, is home to about 2,500 tribal members.

LOCATION:

Adjacent to the Mexican border, in the southeastern corner of California and southwestern corner of Arizona, off I-8. Take Hwy 80 to Picacho Road.

ADDRESS:

Quechan Indian Tribe
P.O. Box 11352
Yuma, AZ 85366
(619) 572-0487

CULTURAL INSTITUTIONS:

Quechan Museum
(619) 572-0661
Featuring Quechan and Spanish culture and military history. Admission fee charged. Open week days 8:00 a.m.-5:00 p.m.

SPECIAL EVENTS:

Yuma Crossing Day
Winterhaven, CA
(619) 572-0661
This annual event, a commemoration of the history of Yuma Crossing, is held at the Quechan Museum, Fort Yuma Indian Reservation, and at other historic and cultural sites in Yuma. Programs include Native American demonstrations and sales of beadwork, arts and crafts, and foods, as well as living history demonstrations. Free admission. Held the last Saturday in February.

Native American Organization Pow Wow
San Pasqual High School
Route 1, 676 Baseline Rd.
Winterhaven, CA
(619) 572-0222
Visitors have come from all over the U.S. and from foreign countries to this Indian Pow Wow that features intertribal dancing and singing, arts and crafts, food booths, barbecue and raffles. Admission fee charged. Held the 1st weekend in March.

4th of July Celebration
Features a wide variety of Indian dance events; similar to a pow wow in content and structure.

Indian Day
Indian dances.
Held in September.

RECREATIONAL OPPORTUNITIES:

Quechan Bingo
604 Picacho Road
Winterhaven, CA
(619) 572-0848

Laguna Dam RV Park
1975 Imperial Road
Winterhaven, CA 92283
(619) 572-0798
Clean, quiet; fishing and a mountain view.

Sleepy Hollow RV Park
369 Algodones Rd.
Winterhaven, CA 92283
(619) 572-5101
Offers a club house, restrooms, fishing, shade trees, utilities. Within walking distance of Algodones, Mexico. Fee – monthly and summer rates.

Trailer Village Mobile Home & RV Park
400 Picacho Rd.
Winterhaven, CA 92283
(619) 572-0313
Permanent spaces available; facilities, club house, utilities, and security. Fee – monthly rates.

ARCHAEOLOGICAL & HISTORIC SITES:

Yuma Crossing National Historic Landmark
Winterhaven, CA
(619) 572-0487

Fort Yuma
Yuma, AZ
(619) 572-0487
The site of the Quechan Museum and tribal offices, St. Thomas Mission built circa 1858, and various fort buildings. Ask at the museum for

directions to petroglyphs, geoplyghs, pot holes, and other areas of interest scattered throughout the reservation.

Businesses & Industries:

Pipa Market – convenience store
Fort Yuma Reservation

Gila River Reservation

Gila River Indian Arts and Crafts Center. Courtesy of Gila River Arts & Crafts Center.

Tribal Profile:

The Gila River Pima-Maricopa Indian Community is located on the 372,000-acre Gila River Indian Reservation. The reservation was established by the Act of February 28, 1859, and Executive Orders between 1876 and 1915. It is located in the "Golden Corridor" between metropolitan Phoenix and the communities of Chandler, Casa Grande and Tucson. This prime location enables the tribe to develop educational, cultural and industrial centers to serve the tribes and public.

Location:

On I-10, approximately 15 miles south of Phoenix.

Address:

Gila River Pima-Maricopa Indian Community
P.O. Box 97
Sacaton, AZ 85247
(602) 562-3311 or 963-4323

Cultural Institutions:

Gila River Arts & Crafts Center
P.O.Box 457
Sacaton, AZ 85247
(602) 963-3981
Complex includes museum, gift shop, restaurant and heritage park. Patio with seating for 500 is site for dance groups, crafts demonstrations and other activities. Gift shop features jewelry, baskets, pottery and other handmade crafts. Restaurant serves authentic, regional Native American cuisine along with traditional American food. Heritage park features displays representing the history of all the Indian tribes of the area. 20 minutes south of Phoenix, via I-10 at Exit 175; the complex is right off the freeway. No admission is charged. 9:00 a.m. - 5:00 p.m., 7 days a week, except federal holidays.

SPECIAL EVENTS:

St. John's Indian Fair
Indian Mission School
Route 2, Box 752
Laveen, AZ 85339
(602) 550-2400
Indian-style barbecue, cultural dance performances, handicrafts, and a midway. At the western end of the reservation, 6 miles south of Baseline. Held 1st Sunday in March, 10 a.m to 6 p.m.

Mul-Chu-Tha Tribal Fair
Presenting a rodeo, parade, arts, crafts, music, Indian foods and dancing. Held in early April.

Christmas Sale and Fair
Gila River Arts & Crafts Center
(602) 963-3981
Indian dancers, raffle, children's activities and craft sale. Held in late November.

RECREATIONAL OPPORTUNITIES:

Firebird International Raceway
P.O. Box 5023
20000 N. Maricopa Road
Chandler, AZ 85226
(602) 268-0200
Modern, versatile motor-sport park featuring 3 race circuits, a drag strip and a lake built for water races. In addition to a wide variety of competitions and a high-performance driving school, Firebird offers a conference center with an assortment of facilities appropriate for many business and social purposes. Catering available. Call for race schedule or to arrange facility use.

Casa Blanca RV Park
P.O. Box 176
Sacaton, AZ
(602) 562-3205
Next to the museum. Full service, pull-through lots; laundromat and market. Nightly and weekly rates.

RESTRICTIONS AND/OR SPECIAL CONSIDERATIONS

Visitors are requested not to enter reservation communities, which are private.

Havasupai Reservation

TRIBAL PROFILE:

The Havasupai live on their ancestral lands at the bottom of Havasu Canyon. On a major tributary of the Grand Canyon, 3,000 feet deep, the 188,077-acre reservation is home to 430 tribal members. Traditionally a peaceful and agrarian tribe, the "People of the Green Waters" still farm, recently adding a trading company and a tourist enterprise to welcome visitors. Accessible by air or trail, this area of sparkling waterfalls, towering plateaus, and minimal development is a back country sojourner's dream.

LOCATION:

60 miles north of Hwy 66 just east of Peach Springs, almost in the center of the Grand Canyon area; reached solely by helicopter and horse or foot trails.

ADDRESS:

Havasupai Tribe
P.O. Box 10
Supai, AZ 86435
(602) 448-2961

Havasupai Tourist Enterprise
Supai, AZ 86435
(602) 448-2121

CULTURAL INSTITUTIONS:

Tribal Museum
Supai, AZ
(602) 448-6211
In the Tribal Arts Enterprise building.

BUSINESSES & INDUSTRIES:

Havasupai Trading Company
Supai, AZ
(602) 448-2951
General store.

Tribal Arts Enterprise
(602) 448-2611
Museum and curio shop.

SPECIAL EVENTS:

Havasupai Peach Festival
Supai, AZ
Held in late August.

RECREATIONAL OPPORTUNITIES:

Havasu Canyon: South of the Village; water, toilets. Fee charged for use.

ACCOMMODATIONS:

Havasupai Lodge
Supai, AZ
(602) 448-2111

Hopi Reservation

TRIBAL PROFILE:

The 1.5 million acre Hopi Reservation, created on the tribe's ancestral lands by Executive Order in 1882, features areas of vivid color and contrast, rising dramatically from the lower desert. It is completely surrounded by the Navajo Reservation. There are 12 Hopi villages on three mesas – First Mesa, Second Mesa, and Third Mesa – that are home to the majority of the 9,000 member Hopi Tribe.

Coal and oil deposits provide some income to the tribe, but many Hopi commute to jobs off the reservation. The Hopi are well known for beautifully crafted basketry, polychrome pottery, carved Kachina figures, and jewelry, as well as for the elaborate costuming and intricate movements of their religious ceremonial dances.

LOCATION:

Northeastern Arizona; the Hopi Reservation is reached via Hwy 264, which runs through the heart of the reservation from east to west. From I-40, Hwy 77 north at Sun Valley, or from US 89 north of Flagstaff, enter the reservation on Hwy 264.

ADDRESS:

Hopi Tribe
P.O. Box 123
Kykotsmovi, AZ 86309
(602) 734-2445

CULTURAL INSTITUTIONS:

Hopi Cultural Center closed '92
P.O. Box 67
Second Mesa, AZ
(602) 734-2401
East of Mishongonovi, off Hwy 264, on Second Mesa.

Hopi Arts &Crafts -Silvercraft Cooperative Guild
P.O. Box 37
Second Mesa, AZ 86043
(602) 734-2463
Hopi crafts cooperative and retail store offering jewelry, basketry, pottery, Kachina dolls, and textiles. Off Hwy 264. Call for tour information; visitors can speak directly with the artisans.

SPECIAL EVENTS:

The Hopi have a rich variety of dances and ceremonies that serve religious and community needs. These are held throughout the year. Best known are the Kachina Dance, Snake Dance, and Flute Ceremony. Contact the Hopi Cultural Center on Second Mesa for ceremonies and their dates and exact location. Because all of the dances are held outdoors and at times are quite lengthy, folding chairs and protection from the sun are recommended.

Kiva Buffalo Dances
Hopi Villages, AZ
First Kachina Dance of the year. Held in January. Kiva Buffalo Dances are also held every weekend May through July.

Carved Hopi Indian Kachina Dolls. Courtesy of Arizona Office of Tourism.

Powamu Ceremony or Bean Dance
Hopi Villages
A fertility ritual to ask for a plentiful crop. Held in February.

Snake Dance
Hopi Villages
This dance is performed with poisonous sidewinders, showing the people are pure of heart and asking the spirits to bring rain. Held in late August.

Flute Ceremony
Hopi Villages
An enactment of Hopi beginnings and history. Only the final day of the sacred ceremony is open to the public.

Hopi Rodeo
Polacca, AZ
Held in early July.

Niman Festival
Hopi Villages
A celebration of the summer solstice. The Hopi bless the Kachinas before they depart for their home in the San Francisco Peaks, and ask for blessings from the Kachinas for all humanity. Held in late July.

RECREATIONAL OPPORTUNITIES:

Pumpkin Hill: Camping. New Oraibi; no facilities.

New Oraibi Campground: New Oraibi; 1 mile east of the village. No amenities.

Second Mesa Picnic Area: No amenities.

Keams Canyon Park: Camping; water and toilets. Keams Canyon. Fee.

Hopi Trailer Park: Camping; water and toilets. Keams Canyon.

ARCHAEOLOGICAL & HISTORIC SITES:

There are a total of 12 Hopi villages, many of them built or re-constructed in the mid-1600s. Old Oraibi and Walpi, on First Mesa, are most notable.

Old Oraibi Village: Built by 1150 and believed one of the oldest continuously inhabited towns in the U.S., Old Oraibi is composed of stone and log structures, some 3 or 4 stories high. Just south of Hwy 264 on Third Mesa.

Third and Second Mesas on the Hopi Reservation from the south. Courtesy of Susan J. Worthman.

Inscription Rock: Two miles up Keams Canyon from the town of Keams Canyon, Inscription Rock bears the name of Kit Carson chiselled into it.

Businesses & Industries:

Hopi Industries, Inc.
P.O. Box 100
Polacca, AZ 86042
(602) 737-2536
Building electronics for buses and airplanes. Call ahead to schedule a tour.

Hopi Silvercraft Cooperative Factory
(602) 734-2463
West of the Hopi Cultural Center on Second Mesa.

Craft work can be purchased directly from artisans in the villages, as well from the following groups.

Badger Indian Arts & Crafts
Hopi Cultural Center
P.O. Box 503
Kykotsmovi, AZ 86039
(602) 734-9266

Calnimptewa's Gallery
P.O. Box 37
Kykotsmovi, AZ 86039
In Old Oraibi Village.

Dawa's Hopi Arts and Crafts
P.O. Box 127
Second Mesa, AZ 86043
(602) 734-2430
Specializing in Hopi overlay jewelry. In Shungopavi Village.

Hohnani's Gallery
P.O. Box 221
Second Mesa, AZ 86043
(602) 734-2238
Offering a variety of Hopi crafts by Hopi artisans.

Hopi Gallery
P.O. Box 316
Second Mesa, AZ 86043
(602) 737-2211

Kalemsas
P.O. Box 754
Second Mesa, AZ 86043

Kiva Arts & Crafts
P.O. Box 96
Kykotsmovi, AZ 86039
Specializing in Hopi overlay jewelry.

Monongya's Gallery
P.O. Box 287
Kykotsmovi, AZ 86039
In Old Oraibi Village

Native Images
P.O. Box 217
Keams Canyon, AZ 86034
(602) 737-2703
In Polacca Village

Old Oraibi Crafts
P.O. Box 193
Kykotsmovi, AZ 86039
(602) 734-9375
In Old Oraibi Village

Shalako Arts & Crafts
Hopi Cultural Center
P.O. Box 146
Kykotsmovi, AZ 86039
(602) 734-2384

Tsakurshovi
P.O. Box 234
Second Mesa, AZ 86043

Kykotsmovi Village Store
(602) 734-2456
General store.

ACCOMMODATIONS:

Hopi Cultural Center
P.O. Box 67
Second Mesa, AZ
(602) 734-2401
Tribally owned hotel and restaurant. Ask about available campsites.

Keams Canyon Motel
Keams Canyon, AZ
(602) 738-2297

RESTRICTIONS AND/OR SPECIAL CONSIDERATIONS:

Before photographing, sketching, or tape recording on the reservation, obtain permission from the village chief or governor.

Hualapai Reservation

TRIBAL PROFILE:

The Hualapai occupy a naturally diverse tract of land that covers almost 1 million acres south of Grand Canyon National Park. The reservation was created by executive order in 1883 and is now home to about 1,675 Hualapai.

Crafts, cattle raising, farming, forestry, and tourism are all part of the Hualapai economy. Wildlife abounds, making this area popular for fishing and hunting, and the proximity of the Colorado River offers many opportunities for river rafting and other water sports.

LOCATION:

West of Flagstaff and east of Kingman, the Hualapai Reservation can be reached via Hwy 66. Access from I-40 by exiting at Seligman, heading west, or Kingman, travelling east, onto Hwy 66.

ADDRESS:

Hualapai Tribe
P.O. Box 168
Peach Springs, AZ 66434
(602) 769-2216

SPECIAL EVENTS:

Sobriety Festival
Peach Springs, AZ
Indian festival and pow wow. Activities include 5-K run, stick games, beauty pageant, baby contest, rodeo, and booths with food, arts and crafts. Held in May.

RECREATIONAL OPPORTUNITIES:

Hualapai Wildlife Conservation Dept.
Box 249
Peach Springs, AZ 86434
(602) 769-2227
Contact for information on camping, fishing and hunting. The Hualapai Wildlife Conservation Dept. oversees trophy game hunting in a 108-square mile area on the South Rim. A limited number of licenses is issued; each hunter is provided an experienced guide and vehicle. Two hunts conducted yearly, September and October; fees include cabin lodging and all meals. Contact Conservation Dept. for details or further information.

Grand Canyon West
(602) 769-2216
Small visitors center near the rim at the west end of the Grand Canyon. Headquarters for guided bus tours along the rim that include sightseeing

Grand Canyon - West view from Hualapai Reservation. Courtesy of Sharon L. Phelps, Shingle Spgs. CA.

permit and a barbecue lunch. Per-person fee charged. Private vehicles are not allowed past the visitors center. From Hwy 66, turn north at the Buck & Doe sign (3 miles from Peach Springs) to Grand Canyon West.

Hualapai River Runners
P.O. Box 246
Peach Springs, AZ 86434
(602) 769-2210, -2219 or (800) 622-4409
Offering 1- and 2-day Colorado River raft trips in the spectacular Lower Granite Gorge from Diamond Creek to Pierce Ferry. Reservations recommended; special packages available. May through October, at very reasonable prices.

Tribal Organizations:

Peach Springs Livestock Association
(602) 769-2216

Accommodations:

Both Truxton, about 7 miles west, and Grand Canyon Caverns, about 7 miles east of Peach Springs, have motels.

Best Market
Peach Springs
(602) 769-2435
Grocery & deli.

Kaibab Paiute Reservation

Tribal Profile:

The Kaibab Paiute Reservation is in remote northwestern Arizona, just across the Utah/Arizona border from the incredible Zion National Park, and north of the Grand Canyon. Members of the Paiute tribal group, the 270 member Kaibab Paiute Band inhabits about 120,000 acres. Traditional leather beadwork is still an important art.

Location:

Accessible from I-15 in southwestern Utah. Exit at Hwy 17 south, or Hwy 9 east, just north of St.

George. Hwy 389 crosses the reservation from east to west.

ADDRESS:

Kaibab Band of the Paiute Indians
HC65 Box 2
Fredonia, AZ 89022
(602) 643-7245

SPECIAL EVENTS:

Cultural Fair
Kaibab Paiute Reservation
(602) 643-7245
Held Memorial Day weekend.

RECREATIONAL OPPORTUNITIES:

Heart Canyon Campground
Kaibab Paiute Reservation
(602) 643-7245
Trailer park near Pipe Springs National Monument headquarters. Facilities: campsites, RV hook-ups, showers, restrooms.

ARCHAEOLOGICAL & HISTORIC SITES:

Pipe Springs National Monument: Fort built in 1870 by Mormons, now called Windsor Castle. Features re-enactment of settler life in the West. Visitors center, museum, and gift shop near the monument. Open daily 8:00 a.m. - 5:30 p.m. summer months only; 8:00 a.m.- 4:00 p.m. the rest of the year. Closed New Year's Day, Thanksgiving, and Christmas. Small fee for adults.

"Welcome to the Navajo Nation" sign. Courtesy of Navajoland Tourism Office.

Navajo Reservation

TRIBAL PROFILE:

"The Dineh" ("the People"), or Navajo, are world-renowned for their silver crafting, sand painting, and rug making. Their reservation holds some of the most spectacular geographic features in the Southwest and offers a wide variety of attractions, events, and recreation opportunities. Today the Navajo number around 260,000; the Navajo Reservation is the largest in the U.S., covering 17.5 million acres, an area larger than New England.

Established by treaty in 1868, the Navajo Nation is rich in culture, history, and natural resources. In 1923, following the discovery of rich oil deposits on the reservation, the Navajos created a tribal government to aid resource development. Currently the Tribal Council handles timber, mineral, energy, and agricultural development, and the Navajo Nation maintains offices to actively encourage arts and crafts, tourism and other industries.

LOCATION:

In the Four Corners region, portions of the reservation are in Utah, Arizona, and New Mexico. Major north-south routes through the reservation are US 666, US 191 and US 160. I-40 runs east-west, south of the reservation.

Unlike the rest of the state of Arizona, the Navajo Nation observes daylight savings time. Due to the extent of the Navajo Reservation, information is divided into three sections: **Western**, **Central** and **Eastern**, which is in New Mexico and includes chapters assigned to smaller reservations. Please refer to the map and look in the section indicated to find details about the area you expect to visit. The Navajoland Tourism Department is an excellent source of detailed information.

ADDRESS:

Navajo Nation
P.O. Box 308
Window Rock, AZ 86515
(602) 871-4941

Navajoland Tourism Department
P.O. Box 663
Window Rock, AZ 86515
(602) 871-6659, -6436

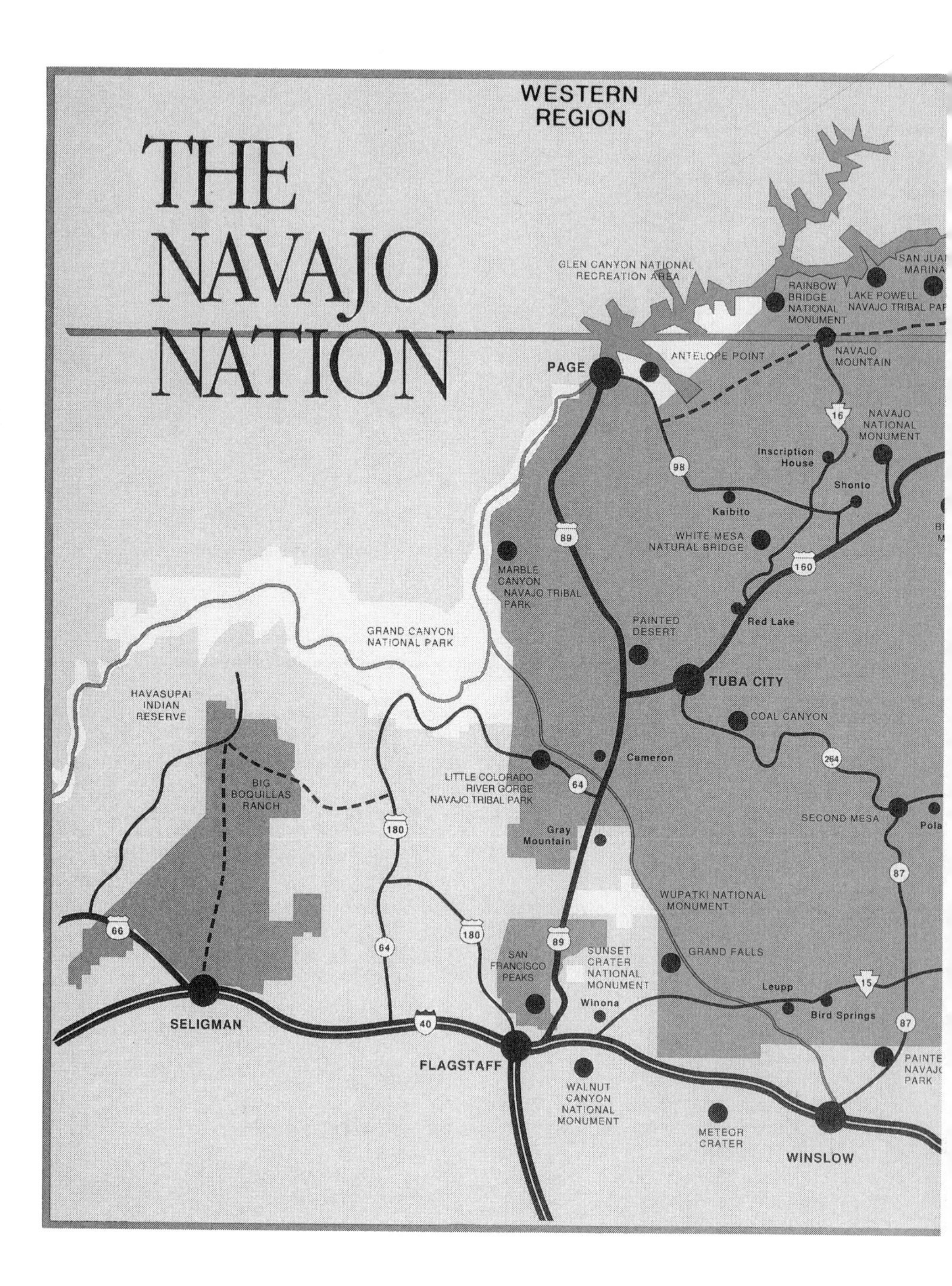
WESTERN
REGION
THE
NAVAJO
NATION
GLEN CANYON NATIONAL
RECREATION AREA
RAINBOW
BRIDGE
NATIONAL
MONUMENT
LAKE POWELL
PAGE
ANTELOPE POINT
NAVAJO
MOUNTAIN
16
NAVAJO
NATIONAL
MONUMENT
Inscription
House
98
Shonto
Kaibito
WHITE MESA
NATURAL BRIDGE
89
160
MARBLE
CANYON
NAVAJO TRIBAL
PARK
PAINTED
DESERT
Red Lake
GRAND CANYON
NATIONAL PARK
TUBA CITY
HAVASUPAI
INDIAN
RESERVE
COAL CANYON
Cameron
264
BIG
BOQUILLAS
RANCH
LITTLE COLORADO
RIVER GORGE
NAVAJO TRIBAL PARK
64
SECOND MESA
180
Gray
Mountain
87
WUPATKI NATIONAL
MONUMENT
66
180
64
89
SAN
FRANCISCO
PEAKS
SUNSET
CRATER
NATIONAL
MONUMENT
GRAND FALLS
Leupp
15
Winona
Bird Springs
87
SELIGMAN
40
FLAGSTAFF
WALNUT
CANYON
NATIONAL
MONUMENT
METEOR
CRATER
WINSLOW

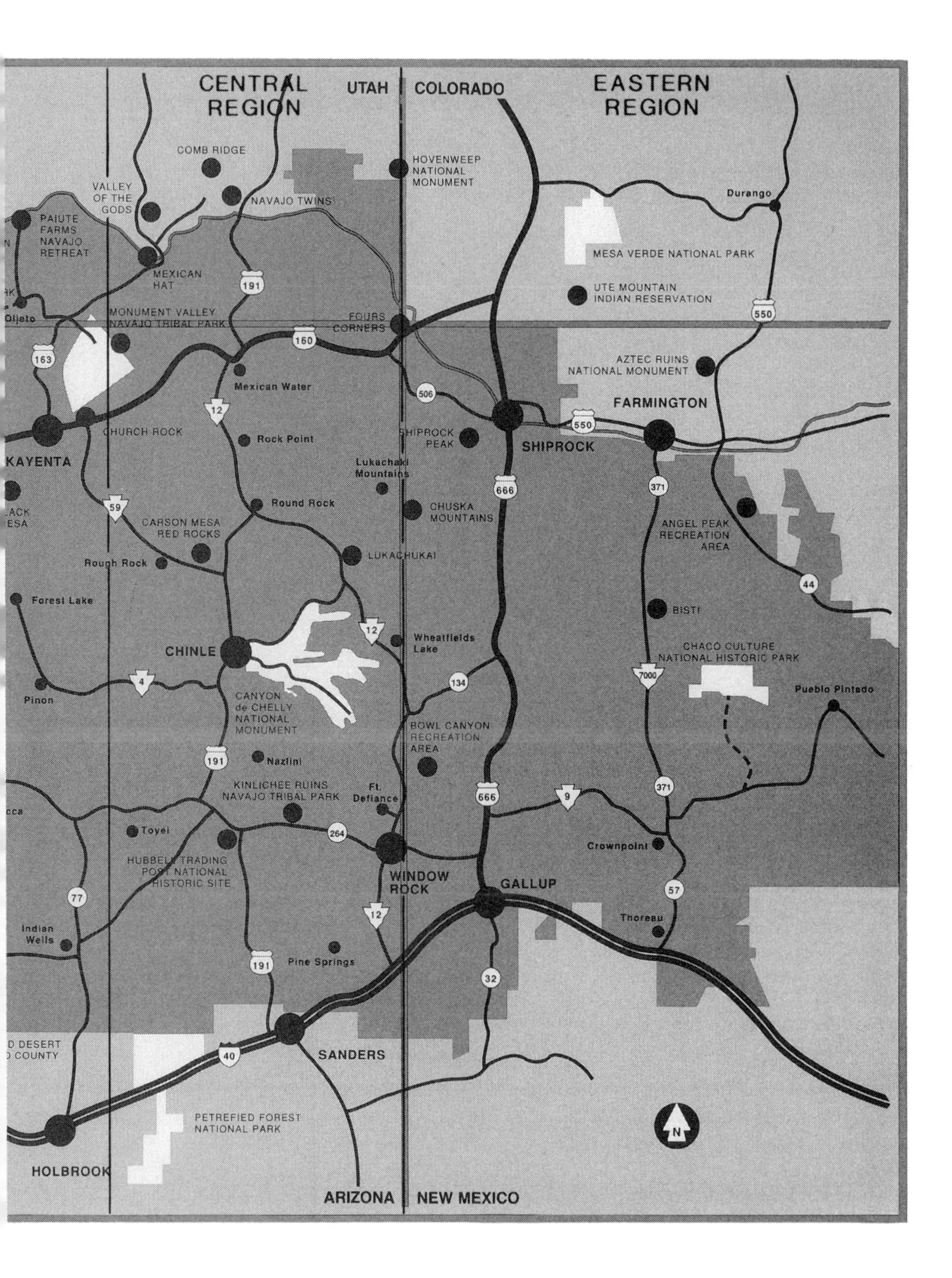

Courtesy of Cal Nez, Salt Lake City, UT.

SPECIAL EVENTS:

For more information about any Navajo Nation event contact the Navajoland Tourism Department. The tribal radio station, KTNN, AM 660 (602) 871-2582, has listings of ceremonies, dances and other cultural events held throughout the reservation.

Navajo Nation Free Fishing Day
All Navajo Reservation Lakes
(602) 871-6451, -6452
Held in June.

Coyote Calling Contest
(602) 871-6451, -6452
Various locations in January and November.

KTNN Song and Dance Festival
Location varies. Held in May.

TRIBAL ORGANIZATIONS:

For phone numbers and leaders' names for these groups, contact the Tribal Office.

All Indian Rodeo Cowboys Assn. (AIRCA)
St. Michael's, AZ 86511

Navajo Nation Rodeo Cowboys Assn. (NNRCA)
Tohatchi, NM 87325

Very popular with the Navajos, more than 80 rodeos are held on the Navajo Reservation during rodeo seasons. Contact the current association secretary for information and schedule of rodeo events.

Navajo Medicine Man Association: Formerly called Navajo Practitioners, established in the early 1970s. Dedicated to developing and promoting the science of Navajo healing.

WESTERN REGION

SPECIAL EVENTS:

Annual Tuba City Spring Round-Up Rodeo
All-Indian Rodeo Cowboy Association
Tuba City, AZ
Held in April.

Navajo Area Native American Festival
Many Farms High School
Many Farms, AZ
(602) 781-6226
Held in April.

Monument Valley Cycling Classic Road Race
Monument Valley
Kayenta, AZ
(602) 697-3732
Held in June.

Thunderbird Pow Wow
Tuba City Boarding School
(602) 283-5214
Held in July.

Horseshoe Canyon Mountain Bike Race
Dilcon, AZ
Held in July.

Southwestern Navajo Fair
Dilcon, AZ
(602) 657-9244 or 3376
Held in September.

Western Navajo Fair
Tuba City, AZ
(602) 283-5452
Held in Mid-October.

RECREATIONAL OPPORTUNITIES:

Antelope Lake: 9 miles north of Pine Springs, Arizona.

Cameron Picnic Area: Cameron, AZ, near the junction of Hwy 89 and 64.

Dinosaur Tracks Scenic Area: Tuba City, AZ, 5 miles west of Tuba City off Hwy 160.

Elephant Feet Scenic Area: Red Lake, AZ, just east of Red Lake on Hwy 160.

Mitten View Campground: Monument Valley, UT, in Monument Valley Tribal Park, 23 miles east of Kayenta, AZ on US 165.

ARCHAEOLOGICAL & HISTORIC SITES:

Antelope Creek Canyon: Twisted rock formations, a maze of underground canyon walls – in places only a yard in width – and a 2,000 foot descent make Antelope Creek Canyon a hiker's delight. For hiking permit information contact:

Window Rock Tribal Park. Courtesy of Billie D. Rogers.

LeChee Chapter House, Box 1257, Page, AZ 86040, (602) 698-3272.

Rainbow Bridge National Monument: Rainbow Bridge, the world's largest natural bridge, overlooks beautiful Lake Powell. Visitors will cover 14 miles of rough canyon country, accessible only by foot, boat or horseback. Obtain required hiking permit from Navajo Tribal Parks and Recreation Department, P.O. Box 308, Window Rock, AZ 86515; (602) 871-6645, -6646, -6647. Boat tour concessions and other services offered in Page, AZ.

Marble Canyon National Park: On the east side of the Colorado River, off Hwy 89, adjoining the Grand Canyon National Park. Marble Canyon is an undeveloped area with limited camping.

Navajo National Monument: The Anasazi, the Ancient Ones, thrived here more than 700 years ago in 2 of Arizona's largest complexes –Betatakin and Keet Seel. In the north-central area of Arizona, just 10 miles north of US 160 on Hwy 564. Take US 160 north from Tuba City, or south from Kayenta, AZ, to Hwy 564. For more information: Navajo National Monument, HC 71, Box 3, Tonalea, AZ 86044; (602) 672-2366, -2367.

Monument Valley Navajo Tribal Park: A 14 mile drive through breathtaking stone monoliths and spires standing hundreds of feet above the floor of Monument Valley. Small fee charged. For more information: Monument Valley Navajo Tribal Park, Box 93, Monument Valley, UT 84536; (801) 727-3287.

Agathla Peak and Owl Slim Rock: Agathla Peak, 1,500 feet high, and Owl Slim Rock gateway to Monument Valley, are the remains of ancient volcanic activity in the region. Approximately 8 miles east of Kayenta on US 163.

Dinosaur Tracks: Dinosaurs left their tracks in the mud flats of this once lush tropical area some 200 million years ago. Road comes within 100 feet of the tracks. 5 miles east of US 89 and 1/4 mile north of US 160 on the unpaved road to Moenave, AZ.

BUSINESSES & INDUSTRIES:

Navajo Tour Operators: Individual and group tours, both standard and custom packages. Contact individual operators for detailed information.

Genevieve Augustine
Golden Sands Tours
P.O. Box 458
Kayenta, AZ 86033
(602) 697-3684

Dick W. Bigman
Bigmans Horseback Tours
Kayenta, AZ 86033
(602) 677-3219

Navajo Arts & Crafts Enterprise
P.O. Box 645
Cameron, AZ 86020
(602) 679-2244

Monongya's Indian Jewelry
Tuba City Mall
Tuba City, AZ 86045
(602) 283-4637

Oljato Trading Post
P.O. Box 738
Kayenta, AZ 86033
(801) 727-3210

ACCOMMODATIONS:

Greyhills Inn
Tuba City, AZ
(602) 283-6271 ext. 36
A project of Greyhills High School; hostel style lodgings using dormitory space on the campus; open year round. Call ahead for reservations.

Holiday Inn
Kayenta, AZ
(602) 697-3221

CENTRAL REGION

CULTURAL INSTITUTIONS:

Navajo Arts and Crafts Enterprise
P.O. Drawer Window A
Window Rock, AZ 86511
(602) 871-4090, -4095
Established in 1941 to promote traditional Navajo crafts, improve workmanship quality, and assist Navajo artisans. Also runs 2 non-profit stores in Window Rock and Cameron; carries crafts from other tribes. Accessible from I-40, Hwy 264, and Indian Route 12, on Hwy 264.

Navajo Community College
Tsaile, AZ
(602) 724-3311
The first Indian-owned community college in the U.S. On site are a 6-story hogan-shaped cultural center and the Hatathli Medicine Man Museum. Near the beautiful Lukachukai and Chuska Mountains. Off Indian Routes 64 and 12. Hatathli Gallery: Open Monday-Friday, 9:00 a.m.-4:00 p.m.

Navajo Nation Council Chambers
Window Rock, AZ
The tribal council meets and enacts legislation for the Navajo Nation in this chamber designed in the form of a traditional hogan. Murals painted by the Navajo artist Gerald Nailor portray the early history of the Navajo Nation.

Navajo Tribal Museum
P.O. Box 308
Window Rock, AZ 86515
(602) 871-6673, -6675
Displays objects relating to Navajo history and culture. Includes artifacts from pre-historic cultures of the Four Corners. Fields of interest include: natural history, archaeology, ethnology, history, and fine arts. Featured artist exhibits change monthly. Also houses a re-created trading post of 1870-1930 vintage. In the Navajo Arts and Crafts Enterprise building on Hwy 264. Winter: Monday-Friday 8:00 a.m. - 5:00 p.m. Summer: Monday-Saturday 8:00 a.m. - 5:00 p.m. No admission fee.

St. Michael's Historical Museum
St. Michael's, AZ
(602) 871-4171
Small museum looking at the influence of the Franciscan friars on the early Navajo. 3 miles west of the Arizona-New Mexico border. April to Labor Day: Monday-Friday 9:00 a.m. - 5:00 p.m. No fee.

Navajo Nation Zoological Park
Window Rock, AZ
(602) 871-6573
The collection consists of animals native to the area and culturally important domestic animals. The park includes an exhibition center, trails, Navajo dwellings. Group tours offered. Open year round, except Christmas and New Year's Day, 9:00 a.m. to 5:00 p.m.

Rodeo is one of the favorite sports events on the Navajo Reservation. Courtesy of Navajoland Tourism Office.

SPECIAL EVENTS:

Chinle Agency Navajo Song and Dance Pow Wow Festival
Chinle, AZ
(602) 674-5201, ext. 201
Held in March.

Fort Defiance Native American Festival
Fort Defiance Agency
(602) 729-5041, ext. 251
Held in April.

KTNN Song and Dance Festival
Window Rock, AZ
(602) 871-2582, -4487
Held in May.

Navajo Nation Treaty Day
Window Rock, AZ
(602) 871-6436
Held in June.

4th of July PRCA Rodeo and Pow Wow
Window Rock, AZ
(602) 871-6702, -6478
Event includes a pow wow, rodeo and carnival, as well as ceremonial dances. Week long; held in early July.

Big-T Bike Race
Hunters Point to Bowman Park
(602) 871-2367
Held in July.

Central Navajo Nation Fair
Chinle, AZ
(602) 672-2857
Held in August.

Navajo Nation Fair
Window Rock, AZ
(602) 871-6478, -6702, -6282, -6659
A 5-day gala festival that draws well-known musicians, top riders in the All Indian Rodeo, world-renowned Indian artisans, and over 100,000 people who walk the midway and carnival, sample Indian foods, and watch the pageants and parade. Held in early September.

Utah Navajo Ahoohai Days
P.O. Box 311
Bluff, UT 84512
(801) 678-2285
Held in September.

Labor Day Bike Race
Fort Defiance
Sawmill, AZ
(602) 729-2434
Held in September.

Fishing on Tsaile Lake. Courtesy of Navajoland Tourism Office.

Annual Christmas Arts & Crafts Fair
Window Rock, AZ
(602) 871-6376

Recreational Opportunities:

Cottonwood Campground: Offers restrooms, picnic tables, water, and dump station April to October; November to March offers portable toilets and picnic tables. 1/2 half mile from Canyon de Chelly Visitor Center. Open year round, no camping fees.

Many Farms Lake Campground: Open year round, RVs not recommended. No facilities. 1 mile south of Many Farms, AZ, Trading Post near the Junction of Hwy 191 and Rte. 59; dirt road.

Monument Valley Tribal Park: Camping & picnic; small fee. 4 miles north of Hwy 160.

Summit Campground Area: Open year round. RVs welcome. 8 miles west of Window Rock, AZ on Hwy 264.

Tsaile Lake Campground: RVs not recommended. 1/2 mile south of the Navajo Community College in Tsaile, AZ, and 2 miles off Rte. 12.

Tse Bonito Park: Limited camping; RVs allowed. 1/4 mile west of the New Mexico/Arizona state line on Hwy 264. Open year round.

Window Rock Navajo Park: Camping, picnic, water, restrooms. On the northeast outskirts of Window Rock.

Archaeological & Historic Sites:

Canyon de Chelly National Monument: 26 miles of red sandstone canyon harbor 5 periods of Indian culture dating from A.D. 348 to 1300. White House, Antelope House, Standing Cow, and Mummy Cave are the most notable of the ruins. 3 miles east of Chinle off Indian Route 64. Tours available. The visitor center is open year round, except Thanksgiving, Christmas, and New Year's Day. Summer (late May - September 30): 9:00 a.m. - 6:00 p.m.; October - April: 8:00 a.m. - 5:00 p.m. No fee. Rim Drive and Trail: dawn to dusk. For information: Canyon de Chelly, P.O. Box 588, Chinle, AZ 86503, (602) 674-5436,-5213

Hubbell Trading Post National Historic Site: Navajo people have been purchasing goods from this trading post, the oldest on the reservation, since 1878. 1 mile west of Ganado, AZ, on Hwy 264. Offers rug weaving and silver smithing demonstrations, and guided tours through the Hubbell House. No admission fee. For more information: P.O. Box 150, Ganado, AZ 86505, (602) 755-3475, -3477.

Spider Rock at Canyon de Chelly. Courtesy of Navajoland Tourism Office.

Hubbell Trading Post. Courtesy of Billie D. Rogers.

Tse Bonito Park: Approximately 8,500 Navajo camped here before their "Long Walk" to Fort Sumner, NM. Red sandstone monoliths, called "haystacks", guard the park. Open year round, except Christmas and New Year's Day. Limited camping facilities, Small admission fee. In Window Rock, AZ, (602) 871-6647.

Window Rock Tribal Park: For decades the Window Rock stone formation has been integral to Navajo spiritual tradition. Trails, restrooms, and picnic tables available. No camping; always open.

BUSINESSES & INDUSTRIES:

Navajo Nation Inn Tours
P.O. Box 1687
Window Rock, AZ 86515
(602) 871-4108

Tours of the Big Country
P.O. Box 309
Bluff, UT 84512
(801) 672-2281

Frederick Cly
Fred's Adventure Tours
P.O. Box 310308
Mexican Hat, UT 94531
(801) 739-4294

Vergil Bedoni
Totem Pole Guided Tours
Box 360306
Monument Valley, UT
(602) 626-3227

Bennett Guiding Tours
P.O. Box 360285
Monument Valley, UT
(801) 727-3283

Tsegi Stables
P.O. Box 881
Chinle, AZ 86503
(602) 674-5678

Navajo Nation Transit System
P.O. Drawer 1330
Window Rock, AZ 86515
(602) 729-5457, -5458, -5449

Crownpoint Rug Auction at Crownpoint, NM.. Courtesy of New Mexico Economic and Tourism Department.

Western Indian Tours
11431 N. 23 St.
Phoenix, AZ 85028
(602) 992-4845

Teec Nos Pos Arts & Crafts
P.O. Drawer Z
Teec Nos Pos, AZ 86514
(602) 871-4090, -4095

Navajo Arts & Crafts Enterprise
P.O. Drawer A
Window Rock, AZ 86515
(602) 871-4090, -4095

ACCOMMODATIONS:

Navajo Nation Inn
48 West Hwy 264
P.O. Drawer 2340
Window Rock, AZ 86515
(602) 871-4108
(800) 662-6189 for reservations.
Features 56 rooms, conference facilities; tours available. Restaurant open 6:30 a.m. to 9:00 p.m.; offers traditional Navajo and American style dishes. Off Hwy 264, 26 miles west of Hwy 666 Junction, and easily accessible from I-40.

Willie Tsosie, Jr.
Coyote Pass Hospitality (Bed & Breakfast)
P.O. Box 91
Tsaile, AZ
(602) 724-3383 or 674-9655
Specialty is the chance to live in traditional Navajo style; providing authentically furnished hogans, traditional Navajo breakfast. Readily combined with customized "Off the Beaten Path" tours, also operated by Mr. Tsosie.

EASTERN REGION

SPECIAL EVENTS:

Crownpoint Rug Auction
P.O. Box 1630
Crownpoint, NM 87313
(505) 786-5302
Monthly auctions, January through December.

Tse National Challenge Road Race
Smith Lake to Red Rock State Park
(505) 863-2746
Held in June.

Eastern Navajo Fair
Crownpoint, NM
(505) 786-5841, -5244
Held in late July.

Chaco Canyon in New Mexico. Photo by Mark Nohl. Courtesy of New Mexico Economic & Tourism Dept.

Washington Pass Cycling Classic Road Race
Wheatfields Lake - Washington Pass
(602) 871-5757
Held in August.

Crystal Mountain Bike Classic
(602) 729-3224
Held in August.

Inter-Tribal Indian Ceremonial
Red Rock State Park
Gallup, NM
(505) 863-3396 or (800) 233-4528
Held in August.

Shiprock Navajo Fair & Rodeo
P.O. Box 1893
Shiprock, NM 87420
(505) 368-5108
Held for 60 years, the Shiprock Navajo Nation Fair is the oldest of the Navajo traditional fairs. The community of Shiprock, with the largest population on the Navajo Nation, celebrates the year's harvest and traditionally holds an ancient healing ceremony, a 9-day chant called "YEI BEI CHEI." The public is welcome to parts of the ritual; however, NO PHOTOGRAPHS MAY BE TAKEN. Events at the Fair include a free barbecue, a rodeo, carnival, a 10-K run, dancing, and pageants. Native arts and crafts and produce are offered at the Indian Market. Held in early October.

RECREATIONAL OPPORTUNITIES:

Angel Peak Recreation Area: Breathtaking 5-mile tour along the rim road, looking out over badlands, mesas, and buttes. Overlook. 19 miles southeast of Bloomfield, NM.

Berland Lake Campground: Open all year, road conditions permitting. Primitive campground, no RVs. 13 miles north of Crystal, NM.

Camp Asaayi Lake Campground: Open all year. RVs not recommended. 11 miles east of Navajo, NM on rough dirt road.

Morgan Lake: Camping; primitive facilities, no RVs, fee. South of Fruitland, NM.

Shiprock Campground: Water & toilets, fee. Near Shiprock, NM.

Washington Pass Campground: Open year round, depending on road conditions. RVs welcome. 5 miles east of Crystal, NM.

Wheatfields Lake: An opportunity for fishing and camping; 44 miles northeast of Window

Shiprock, New Mexico. Courtesy of Navajoland Tourism Office.

Rock, AZ, on Indian Route 12. For information: (602) 871-6647.

ARCHAEOLOGICAL & HISTORIC SITES:

Aztec Ruins National Monument: Pueblo Indian ruins dating from around A.D. 1300, with a fully restored kiva. Just north of Aztec, on Hwy 550. For more information: (602) 334-6174.

Bisti Badlands: Geologic display of remarkable rock sculptures of delicate hue and tortuous design, formed from clay deposited 65 million years ago. Bisti, Navajo for "badlands," displays history of the dinosaurs. Northwest of Chaco Culture National Historic Park, near the junction of Hwy 371 and Indian Rte. 5.

Chaco Culture National Historical Park: Peppered with Anasazi ruins, Chaco National Park history dates back to A.D. 800. Here a sophisticated society developed awesome buildings, basketry, pottery, irrigation ditches, roads and trade routes to distant lands. The largest of the structures, Pueblo Bonito, consists of 800 rooms. Self-guided tours, visitor center with several activities offered; museum, library and campground. On unpaved Rte 57, accessible from Hwy 44 or Indian Route 9. For more information: Star Route 4, Box 6500, Bloomfield, NM 87413, (505) 988-6716, -6727.

El Morro National Monument: The sandstone cliffs of El Morro National Monument guarded precious water and sheltered migrants and explorers. The Monument offers a self-guided trail, visitors center, campground, and picnic area. Southeast of Gallup: take Hwy 602 south to Hwy 53, east. Easily accessible from I-40, Hwy 53 at Grants. Ramah, NM 87321, (505) 783-4226.

Four Corners National Monument: 5,000 feet above sea level, Four Corners Monument is the only place in the U.S. where one can stand in 4 states at one time. Near the San Juan River, Anasazi occupied this area as early as A.D. 1300. 1/4 mile west of Hwy 160, 6 miles north of Teec Nos Pos, AZ, in Navajo Tribal Park. Open year round. Summer (May-October) 7:00 a.m. - 8:00 p.m. Winter (November-April) 8:00 a.m. - 5:00 p.m. Fee.

Shiprock Peak: The remains of an ancient volcano, Shiprock Peak rises dramatically 1,500 feet from the desert floor. Important in Navajo legend, the peak is called Tse' Bitai', or "Rock with Wings." Roadside picnic area.

BUSINESSES & INDUSTRIES:

Navajo Agricultural Products Industries (NAPI)
P.O. Drawer 1318
Farmington, NM 87499
(505) 327-5251, ask for Personnel Office
By appointment. No vehicles to accommodate large groups, but can take groups in their own vehicles.

Navajo Forest Products Industries(NFPI)
P.O. Box 1280
Navajo, NM 87328
(505) 777-2211
A tour of the entire milling operation of the company is offered. Call ahead to schedule.

Beclabito Trading Post
Shiprock, NM 87320
(505) 656-3455

Shiprock Trading Post
P.O. Box 906, Hwy 550
Shiprock, NM 87420
(505) 789-3270

Two Grey Hills Trading Post
Tohatchi, NM 87325
(505) 789-3270

Pascua-Yaqui Reservation

TRIBAL PROFILE:

The Pascua Yaqui Reservation occupies 892 acres just south and west of Tucson and is home to about 2,760 members of the tribe, which has an enrollment of approximately 7,600.

LOCATION:

Near Picture Rocks, Old Tucson, and Saguaro National Monument, the Pascua Yaqui Reservation is south of Tucson off I-19. Take the Valencia exit, west; 5 miles to the reservation.

ADDRESS:

Pascua Yaqui Tribe
7474 S. Camino De Oeste
Tucson, AZ 85746
(602) 883-2838

SPECIAL EVENTS:

Yaqui Easter Ceremonies
Christo Rey
7500 S. Camino Benem
Tucson, AZ
(602) 883-2838, ext. 39
An Indian Festival and the most important event of the year to the Yaqui. Both Catholic liturgy and ceremonial dramatization of the crucifixion of Jesus take place throughout Lent and Easter week. Begins on Ash Wednesday; lasts a week. Visitors are asked not to photograph or record the ceremonies.

RECREATIONAL OPPORTUNITIES:

Arizona Club (Bingo)
7406 S. Camino de Oeste
Tucson, AZ
(602) 883-1700
Open Tuesday-Sunday; matinee 2 p.m.; bingo goes to 11 p.m., video games until 2 a.m.

RESTRICTIONS AND/OR SPECIAL CONSIDERATIONS:

No photographs of cultural activities; special permission by tribal council only, arrangements should be made well in advance. No liquor allowed.

Yaqui Indians of Pascua village's re-enactment of 17th Century Easter ceremony. Courtesy of Arizona Office of Tourism.

Salt River Reservation

Tribal Profile:

The Salt River Pima-Maricopa Indian Community lives on the 52,729-acre Salt River Indian Reservation. The reservation was established by Executive Order of 1879 and is organized under the provisions of the Indian Reorganization Act. Tribal enrollment in 1991 was 4,620, with the reservation population estimated at 5,120.

Location:

30 miles east of Phoenix, adjoining Scottsdale on the west, Mesa on the south and the Fort McDowell Reservation on the north. The major road into the reservation communities of Salt River and Lehi is McDowell Road, through Phoenix and Scottsdale.

Address:

Salt River Pima-Maricopa Indian Community
Route 1, Box 216
Scottsdale, AZ 85256
(602) 941-7277

Cultural Institution:

Salt River Pima-Maricopa Tribal Museum
10000 East Osborn Road
Scottsdale, AZ 85256
(602) 941-7379
Focuses on the culture and history of the Pima and Maricopa tribes. Open to the public Tuesday through Friday 10 a.m. to 4:30 p.m. and on Saturday from 10 a.m. to 2 p.m. Small admission fee, except for persons enrolled in Native American tribes, who are free, as guests of the Pima and Maricopa tribes.

Special Events:

For times of specific festivals, call the tribal community relations department at (602) 941-7333. The Recreational Department, (602) 941-7284, has current lists of events in addition to:

Indian Men's and Women's Basketball Tournaments
Held January through March.

**Southwest All-Indian
Women's Softball Tournament**
Held in Mid-August.

Southwestern Indian Pottery. Courtesy of Gila River Indian Arts & Craft Center.

**Red Mountain Classic All-Indian
Men's Softball Tournament**
Held in August.

All Indian Southwest Baseball Tournament
Held in late August.

Recreational Opportunities:

Salt River Recreation Area: Shoreline camping, fishing and picnic grounds. From Phoenix-Scottsdale, east on Hwy 87 to Ft. McDowell Rd. (just before the highway crosses the Verde River). Right turn onto the paved road, south 3 miles. Turnoffs to the left of the road lead to the Verde River.

Tables and barbecue pits are provided. Tribal rangers collect fees for use of the area, including hiking and fishing. Hiking on the reservation is permitted, but certain areas are restricted for cultural, religious, and archaeological reasons. For information regarding fees and restricted access areas, contact Tribal Law & Order, (602) 941-7255.

Tubing: The Salt River flows into the Verde just above the low Granite Reef Dam. This is the tribe's popular "tubing" river. Many "floaters" start their journey below Saguaro Lake several miles to the north, and float down into the reservation to Blue Point Bridge.

Cypress Golf Course
(602) 946-5155
Two 9-hole courses – a long par 38 and a short par 30. Driving range, putting green, snack bar, fully equipped pro-shop, riding or pull carts available. Open 7 days a week; green fees are reasonable.

ARCHAEOLOGICAL & HISTORIC SITES:

Contact tribal museum or community relations staff for information.

BUSINESSES & INDUSTRIES:

Native Hands
8806 East McDowell
Scottsdale, AZ 85256
(602) 423-1660
American Indian restaurant provides authentic, regional Native American foods along with regular American fare. Adjoining arts and crafts shop specializes in authentic Native American art.

San Carlos Apache Reservation

TRIBAL PROFILE:

The San Carlos Apache Tribe occupies a reservation of more than 1.8 million acres lying to the south and east of the Fort Apache Reservation; the two reservations, established as a single reservation in 1871, were partitioned in 1897. San Carlos tribal enrollment is about 12,600. Tribal government is under a constitution approved in 1954 and is led by an 11-member tribal council. Most of the tribe lives in the town of San Carlos or in one of the small communities along US 70. Tribal economic development projects range from timber and cattle operations to promoting hunting and fishing for tourists.

Apache Crown Dancer. Courtesy of John Running.

LOCATION:

In the mountains of southeastern Arizona, due east of Phoenix. US 60 and US 70 cross the reservation and intersect at Globe, at the western edge.

ADDRESS:

San Carlos Apache Tribe
P.O. Box O
San Carlos, AZ 85550
(602) 475-2361

SPECIAL EVENTS:

Girls' Rites and Spirit Dances
Contact the tribal office for details about those festivals open to the public. Held summer weekends.

Tribal Fair
Includes traditional dancing; held Veteran's Day weekend.

Recreational Opportunities:

Recreation and Wildlife Department
Hwy 70 and Moonbase Rd.
Peridot, AZ
(602) 475-2343
Fishing, hunting and camping opportunities abound on the San Carlos Reservation. The reservation has about 200 small ponds, or tanks, that hold trout or catfish. Permits from the tribe are required; call, write or stop by to obtain maps, regulations and permits.

Talkalai Lake: Newest of 3 recreational lakes built by the Apache in recent years. Excellent fishing, only electric motors allowed; ramadas with picnic tables on shoreline. On the San Carlos River, northeast of the community of San Carlos. Ask for directions to this remote scenic area.

Point of Pines Lake: Stocked with rainbow trout, features a small campground; access roads are unpaved but well graded; best fishing early and late in the year.

Seneca Lake Recreational Park: 25-acre lake nearly surrounded by cattails so that a boat is helpful for fishing. Camping and picnic facilities and a small store with fishing permits available. Just off US 60, about 30 miles north east of Globe.

San Carlos Lake: Formed by the construction of Coolidge Dam on the Gila River in 1920. Water amounts vary considerably, depending on a variety of climatic conditions; well stocked and offering ideal growing conditions for fish. Mostly bass, crappie, catfish and bluegill. Fishing permit required. Open year round; off US 70, about 20 miles east of Globe.

Hunting: Because San Carlos Indian Reservation is large and undeveloped, it provides excellent hunting. The big game list includes deer, elk, javelina, bear and lion; limited numbers of permits are issued. Access to most areas requires 4-wheel drive vehicle. Hunters need to be well equipped and self-sufficient.

Small game permits cover quail, waterfowl and squirrels. Seasons as established by Arizona Game and Fish Department.

Businesses & Industries:

Bylas General Store
Native arts and crafts, groceries, dry goods. Open weekdays 8:00 a.m.-5:00 p.m.; Saturdays 9:00 a.m.-5:00 p.m.

San Carlos Cafe
Main Street
San Carlos, AZ
(602) 475-9909
Featuring Indian specialties as well as standard menu items. Open weekdays, 8:00 a.m.- 5:00 p.m.

San Carlos General Store
Between Globe and Scraton
(602) 475-2848
Tribally operated; native arts and crafts, groceries, dry goods. Open weekdays 8:00 a.m.-5:00 p.m.; Saturdays 9:00 a.m.-5:00 p.m.

Tribal Farm
Raising crops, horses, 2 cattle herds, 1 of which is registered Herefords. In San Carlos and Bylas; Call Tribal Planning to arrange a tour.

Dripping Springs Tree Farm
(602) 475-2732
Call for tours and information.

San Juan Southern Paiute Reservation

Tribal Profile:

The San Juan Southern Paiute Indians have lived in northern Arizona and southern Utah for hundreds of years. The greatest concentration of Paiute Indians is in Nevada. The San Juan Southern Paiute Tribe was recognized by the U.S. government in 1989; there are about 190 tribal members.

Location:

Northern Arizona, at Hidden Springs; 1 mile east of US 89, 8 miles north of the junction with US 160, near Tuba City.

ADDRESS:

San Juan Southern Paiute Tribe
P.O. Box 2656
Tuba City, AZ 86045
(602) 283-4583, -4587

SPECIAL EVENTS:

San Juan Southern Paiute Pow Wow
Hidden Springs, AZ
(602) 283-4583
Outdoor event; dancers from far and near come traditionally dressed. Events begin Friday night with Dancers' Campout; Saturday SJSP princess is crowned. Held 2nd weekend of June.

TRIBAL ORGANIZATIONS:

San Juan Southern Paiute Yingup Weavers Assn.
P.O. Box 1336
Tuba City, AZ 86045
(602) 283-4109
Association formed to preserve and develop tribal art of basketry. Recognized for excellence by National Endowment for the Arts.

ACCOMMODATIONS:

Open land for camping. There are no hotels or motels; nearest towns are Tuba City, 21 miles east on US 160, or Greymountain, 35 miles south on US 89 toward Flagstaff.

Exquisite basketry is only one of the handcrafts produced by Arizona Indian tribes. Courtesy of Arizona Office of Tourism.

Tohono O'odham Reservation

TRIBAL PROFILE:

The Tohono O'odham Reservation, with tribal membership estimated at 19,700, totals almost 2.8 million acres, headquartered at Sells. It combines the Papago, San Xavier and Gila Bend Reservations, which recently joined together to enable a representative tribal government based upon 11 districts. Minerals, including copper, gravel, building stone and clay, are found on the reservation, and leases granted by the tribe are a primary source of tribal income. The Tohono O'odham Reservation is in the desert, with hot days and cool nights and a growing season of 300 days, making it particularly attractive for visits during the winter months.

LOCATION:

Hwy 86 runs through the reservation from Tucson to the east and Ajo to the west. The reservation is bounded on the south by Mexico and extends northward approximately 90 miles, almost to Casa Grande National Monument.

ADDRESS:

Tohono O'odham Nation
P.O. Box 837
Sells, AZ 85634
(602) 383-2221

San Xavier del Bac Mission on Tohono O'odham Reservation. Courtesy of R.P. Anderson.

CULTURAL INSTITUTIONS:

Mission San Xavier del Bac: "White Dove of the Desert" was founded in 1700. The present building was begun in 1783; regarded as one of the finest examples of mission architecture in the Southwest. Open to the public except Sundays. Still in use as a Catholic church.

SPECIAL EVENTS:

San Xavier Fiesta
San Xavier Mission Grounds
(602) 294-2624
Evening festival. Main event is torch-light procession of Tohono O'odham and Yaqui tribal members, late in the evening. Children's dance groups begin performing about 6:00 p.m.; food booths featuring traditional Indian foods open earlier. Mission is about 10 miles south of Tucson on San Xavier Road, off I-19. Held the Friday after Easter.

All-Indian Papago Tribal Fair and Rodeo
Biggest event on the reservation, the fair includes a pow wow, Miss Papago contest, rodeo, arts and craft sales and food booths. Held on a weekend in late November.

Celebration of Christmas Season
San Xavier Mission Grounds
Held 1st week of December.

RECREATIONAL OPPORTUNITIES:

Papago Bingo
Benson Hwy, Tucson
(602) 294-9951
In the Santa Vera Mission area; open 24 hours daily, 7 days a week.

Camping: There are several areas where visitors can camp on the Tohono O'odham Reservation. Camping permits are required; obtained from the district office in which the camping area is located.

Chukut Kuk District	(602) 383-2221, ext. 493
Gu Vo District	(602) 362-2268
Gu Achi District	(602) 383-2404
Hickiwan District	(602) 362-2363
Komelik District	(602) 361-2372
Pisinemo District	(602) 383-2442
San Lucy District	(602) 682-2913
San Xavier District	(602) 294-5727
Schuk Toak District	Call Tribal Office.
Sells District	(602) 383-2281

Archaeological & Historic Sites:

Ventana Cave: Open to the public free of charge, but the district office must be notified. Near village of Gu Achi, Hickiwan District, in the Santa Rosa Valley, off Hwy 15 between Quijotoa and Casa Grande.

Children's Shrine
Gu Achi District

Forteleza Ruins: Monument to Hohokam people, believed to be first ancestors of the Tohono O'odham. Outside Casa Grande.

Businesses & Industries:

Arts and Crafts Sales
San Xavier Plaza
(602) 6006
Santa Vera Mission area of Tucson; different tribal artists offer their wares. Open daily.

Papago Egg Farm
North Komelik District
(602) 361-2372
Contact office for directions and to arrange tour.

Papago Farms
Pisinemo District
(602) 836-4743
Major crops are cotton, beans and other vegetables. Tours on request; contact district office for arrangements and directions.

Tonto Apache Reservation

Tribal Profile:

The Tonto Apache Reservation was authorized by an Act of 1972, setting aside 85 acres for this small band of Apache tribal members. The tribe, which has an enrollment of approximately 100, is governed under a constitution approved in 1980. The reservation is in southeastern Arizona near Payson in the heart of Tonto National Forest. The tribe has no tourist enterprises at present.

Tonto Apache Tribal Council
Tonto Reservation #30
Payson, AZ 85541
(602) 471-5000

Yavapai-Prescott Reservation

Tribal Profile:

The Yavapai-Prescott Reservation was established in 1935; it presently totals almost 1,400 acres, in Prescott, and is home for about 120 resident tribal members. Tribal enrollment is approximately 1,400; the tribe is governed by an elected board of directors. The tribe is actively involved in economic development programs, including partial ownership of the Sheraton Resort on the reservation.

Location:

Prescott, northwest of Phoenix; accessible via US 89.

Address:

Yavapai-Prescott Indian Tribe
530 E. Meritt
Prescott, AZ 86301
(602) 445-8790

Special Events:

Yavapai-Prescott All-Indian Pow Wow
Pow wow, competition dancing, food booths and princess pageant. Small admission fee for those over 18. Held 3rd weekend in June; Saturday and Sunday, 11:00 a.m. to midnight.

Sheraton Hotel & Conference Resort, Prescott, AZ., partially owned by the Yavapai-Prescott Indian community. Courtesy of Sheraton Hotel-Prescott.

Recreational Opportunities:

Yavapai Bingo
1505 E. Hwy 69
Prescott, AZ 86301
(602) 445-0286

Accommodations:

Sheraton Hotel and Resort
1500 Hwy 69
Prescott, AZ 86301
(602) 776-1666
Facilities include luxurious rooms with balconies, fine dining in the Thumb Butte Room, dancing in Buckey O'Neill Lounge, and a cocktail lounge with piano bar. Work of Yavapai County artists displayed throughout. Gift Shop offers jewelry, fine art, books and unique gifts. Heated swimming pool. Staff will arrange tours and events, including chartered flights over the Grand Canyon. At the junction of US 89 and 69.

Northern California

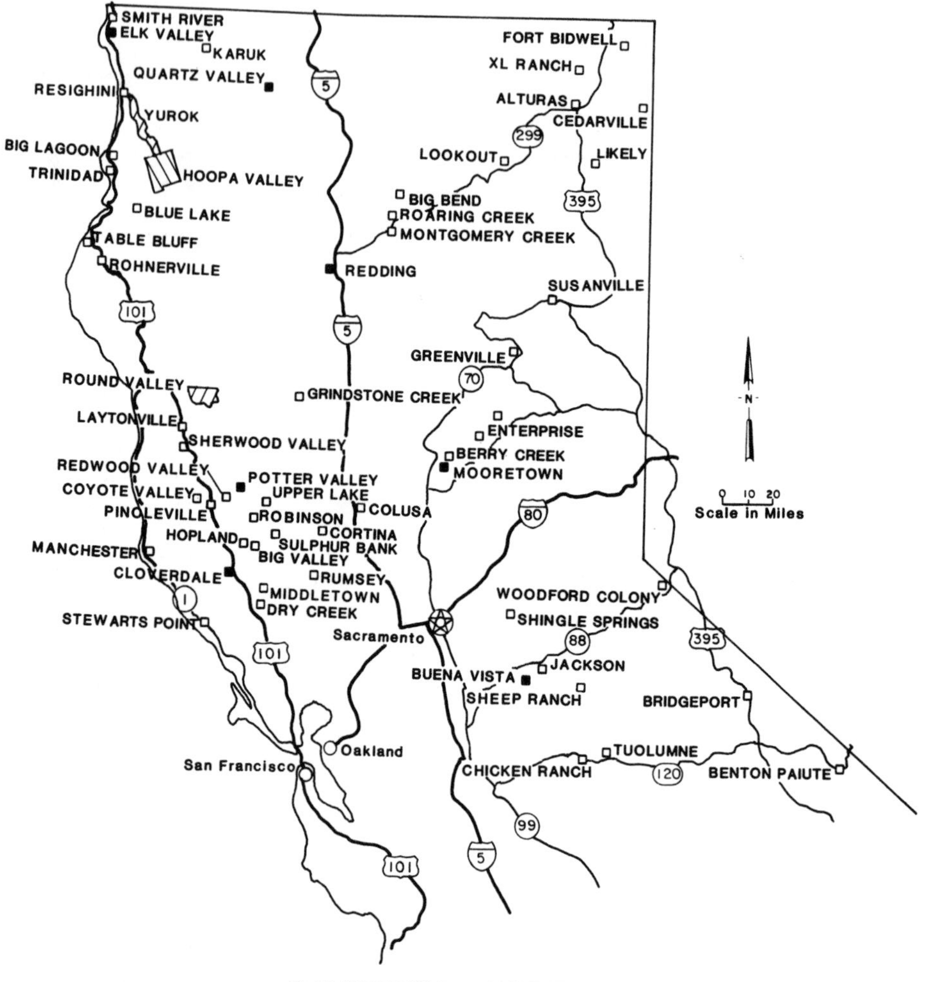

CALIFORNIA - NORTH HALF

(L) Hotel Arcata - front view from park. Courtesy of Steve Baldy/Big Lagoon Rancheria. (R) Clam beach area within 6 minutes of Hotel Arcata. Courtesy of Steve Baldy/Big Lagoon Rancheria.

Big Lagoon Rancheria

TRIBAL PROFILE:

Tucked away in scenic coastal Northern California, Big Lagoon Rancheria comprises 25 acres of land, home to 29 members of the Yurok and Tolowa tribes of Northern California. These tribes have retained many teachings of their ancestors, practice their traditions, and live off the land's resources. Current tribal economic development projects are designed to improve the tribes' self-sufficiency.

LOCATION:

On the Pacific coast 330 miles north of San Francisco via US 101, Big Lagoon Rancheria is 25 miles north of Eureka, directly off the highway.

ADDRESS:

Big Lagoon Rancheria
P.O. Box 3060
Trinidad, CA 95570
(707) 826-2079

RECREATIONAL OPPORTUNITIES:

Tribal Eco-Tourism
c/o Hotel Arcata
708 Ninth Street
Arcata, CA 95521
(800) 344-1221
(707) 826-2081

Through the eco-tours offered by the Big Lagoon Rancheria, the general public has the chance to appreciate the history of people, land, plants and forest animals from the Native American perspective. Offering 3-day and expanded 6-day eco-tours. The 6 day tour includes a jet boat journey on the Klamath River and a rafting trip on the Trinity River. A special weekend package includes a unique redwood dugout boat tour of the Big Lagoon area. Call for package information, fees, and times.

Depending upon the season, golf courses, hiking, fishing, and hunting are all within a short drive from the Hotel Arcata.

ACCOMMODATIONS:

Historic Hotel Arcata
708 Ninth Street
Arcata, CA 95521
(800) 344-1221
(707) 826-2081
Purchased by the tribe in 1990, the Hotel Arcata was built in 1915 and is a National Historic Site. The hotel features 33 rooms, including 5 suites, overlooking the Historic Plaza in the central business district of Arcata. Restaurant and lounge on the ground floor; banquet room available for private use. Amenities include beauty salon, dress shop, and jewelry and gift shop off the lobby.

Chicken Ranch Rancheria

TRIBAL PROFILE:

Surrounded by lakes and reservoirs in the foothills of the Sierras, 2.85 acre Chicken Ranch Rancheria is home to 6 members of the Me-Wuk tribe.

LOCATION:

West of Yosemite National Park and slightly northeast of Modesto in the Stanislaus National Forest, the Rancheria is off Hwy 108.

ADDRESS:

Chicken Ranch Rancheria
P.O. Box 1699
Jamestown, CA 95327
(209) 984-3057

RECREATIONAL OPPORTUNITIES:

Chicken Ranch Bingo
Hwy 108
Jamestown, CA
(800) 752-4646
High-stakes bingo establishment seating 1,500. Doors open 6:00 p.m., Thursday-Saturday; Sunday matinee 1:30 p.m. Bingo begins an hour after the doors open.

ACCOMMODATIONS:

Camping, cabins, and motels throughout the region.

Colusa Rancheria

TRIBAL PROFILE:

Colusa Rancheria is home to the Cachil Dehe Band of Wintun Indians; the band currently has 68 members. The original lands were purchased in 1907, with several subsequent acquisitions, to form the present-day 273 acre Colusa Rancheria. The Sacramento River flows through Rancheria lands in this mountainous region with moderate temperatures and rainfall.

LOCATION:

Northwest of Sacramento and west of Marysville near I-5, Colusa Rancheria is on Hwy 45. East of the Sacramento, Colusa, and Delevan National Wildlife Refuges. 4 miles north of Colusa.

ADDRESS:

Colusa Indian Community
P.O. Box 8
Colusa, CA 95932
(916) 458-8231

RECREATIONAL OPPORTUNITIES:

The Colusa Indian Community has a bingo operation. Call the tribe at (916) 458-8231 for specifics as to time, dates and cost.

Coyote Valley Rancheria

TRIBAL PROFILE:

Famous for their intricate basket patterns and designs, the Pomo Indians have long lived in this region of northern California. The original reservation of the Coyote Valley Band of Pomo Indians was purchased by the U.S. Corps of Engineers and is now under the waters of Lake Mendocino.

Today's 58-acre Coyote Valley Rancheria belongs to the 225 members of this band of Pomo Indians who work and attain higher education while maintaining cultural skills and original beliefs.

LOCATION:

North of the Napa Valley, on the shores of Lake Mendocino. Redwood Valley is north of Ukiah, off US 101 and Hwy 20.

ADDRESS:

Coyote Valley Tribal Council
P.O. Box 39
7901 Hwy 101 North
Redwood Valley, CA 95470-0039
(707) 485-8724

CULTURAL INSTITUTIONS:

Lake Mendocino Pomo Cultural Visitor's Center & Craft Gallery
Marina Drive
Ukiah, CA
(707) 485-8685
Displays of famous Pomo baskets and video presentations discussing the Pomo language, basketry, and the construction of Lake Mendocino. Craft gallery offers authentic, handmade wares created by Mendocino and Lake County Indian tribes. Open April-October, 9:00 a.m.-5:00 p.m. Wednesday-Sunday; only Saturday and Sunday the rest of the year. Special group tours can be arranged any time; call or write to the Center. On Lake Mendocino.

Fort Bidwell Reservation

TRIBAL PROFILE:

Joint resolution of Congress authorized the Secretary of the Interior to set aside Fort Bidwell Military Reserve for the use of this band of the Paiute Indians in 1879. The reservation was enlarged in 1917, and acreage currently stands at 3,334. Most of the 163 tribal members live on sloped and sage-covered lands where ranching, farming, and forestry are important occupations. Some individuals produce arts and crafts as a home industry.

LOCATION:

In the far northeast corner of northern California, situated in the heart of the Warner Mountains and Modoc National Forest, near numerous lakes. Due east of Yreka, the Fort Bidwell Reservation is near US 395, on Hwy 447.

ADDRESS:

Fort Bidwell Indian Tribe
P.O. Box 129
Fort Bidwell, CA 96112
(916) 279-6310, -2233

CULTURAL INSTITUTIONS:

Beading Group
(916) 279-6310
Will make beaded items such as jewelry and moccasins to order. Write to or call the tribal office.

SPECIAL EVENTS:

Fort Bidwell Elders Pow Wow
Fort Bidwell, CA
Dancers come from many areas of the Western U.S. to participate. A host drum is set up and other drummers are welcome to join in. Held in April. Fee.

RECREATIONAL OPPORTUNITIES:

Space to pitch tepees and RV electricity hook-ups offered during the pow wow. Check with the tribal office.

ARCHAEOLOGICAL & HISTORIC SITES:

People's Church & Cemetery
Fort Bidwell Reservation
Check with the tribal office for directions to the site.

TRIBAL ORGANIZATIONS:

Fort Bidwell Cattleman's Association
Fort Bidwell, CA

ACCOMMODATIONS:

The town of Fort Bidwell has a hotel and restaurant.

Hoopa Valley Reservation

Tribal Profile:

The Hoopa Valley Reservation border follows a portion of the beautiful coastal range of Northern California, the Trinity River, and the Salmon Trinity Alps Wilderness. The Hupa live on this reservation of 87,000 acres created in 1876, with a current membership of 4,000. Actively involved in maintaining their culture, the Hupa hold cultural dances, such as the White Deerskin Dance, and various celebrations throughout the year and have established a cooperative to encourage traditional arts of basket weaving and beadwork.

Location:

Northeast of Eureka near the Northern California coast. From US 101 at Arcata, take Hwy 299 east to Hwy 96 north. Or exit I-5 at Redding and take Hwy 299 west to Hwy 96.

Address:

Hoopa Valley Tribe
P.O. Box 1348
Hoopa, CA 95546
(916) 625-4211

Cultural Institutions:

Hupa Tribal Museum
P.O. Box 1348
Hoopa, CA 95546
(916) 625-4110
Displays of Hupa dance regalia and basketry.

Special Events:

All-Indian Invitational Men's Basketball Tournament
Hoopa High School
(916) 625-4239
An 8-team national basketball tournament; includes a queen/princess contest, Native American dancers, and public dance. Held in mid-March. Admission fee.

Logging Show
(916) 625-4239
Features pole climbing, choker setting, jack and jill, open stock saw, and ax throwing, men's and women's, and men's double bucking. Admission charged. Held in early May.

Whitewater Boat Race
(916) 625-4239
Whitewater hydro-plane boat race covering approximately 60 miles, with the boats reaching speeds of up to 70 miles per hour. 15 to 25 boats per race. Donations accepted. Trinity River – behind Hoopa Shopping Center. Held Mother's Day and Father's Day.

Hoopa Open Rodeo
Hoopa Rodeo Grounds
(916) 625-4239
Sanctioned by the California Pro-Rodeo Cowboy Association; draws participants from all over the U.S. Admission fee. Held in late June.

4th of July Celebration
(916) 625-4239
The Hoopa Valley Tribal Recreation Department sponsors the 4th of July Celebration, featuring a parade, softball tournament, horseshoe pitching, fireworks, dance, go-cart rides, salmon barbecue, picnic, and Native American dancers. Admission fee.

Hoopa All-Indian Rodeo
Hoopa Rodeo Grounds
(916) 625-4239
Along with the rodeo events, concessions, arts and crafts, community dance, Native American dancers, and a queen contest are part of the festivities. Admission fee; held in mid-August.

Hupa Sovereign Days
(916) 625-4211
Celebrating the passage of the Settlement Act and the signing of the 1864 treaty. No admission charge. Held in mid-August.

Annual Janice McCovey Memorial Women's Softball Tourney
Pookie's Park
A true double elimination women's softball tournament that draws participants from the Hoopa area. Trophies for 1st through 4th place teams, and individual awards. Free to the public, charge for entry in tourney. Held in early August.

Masten, Brown, Vigil, LeMieux Memorial Softball Tournament
(916) 625-4239
An all-day men's 16 team slow pitch softball tournament draws teams from California. Held in August.

Hoopa Hillclimb
P.O. Box 1090
Willow Creek, CA 95573
(916) 629-2640
For this regional auto sport event, The 2-lane road up Bald Hill is closed to traffic, and participants race against the clock from the bottom to the top of the hill. No admission fee; there is a participant fee. Held in August.

American Indian Day
Hoopa Elementary School
(916) 625-4223
This bi-annual Indian pow wow and festival features arts, dances, Indian cards, and food. Every 2nd year the local dances are observed, notably the White Skin and Jump Dances, and festivities are not held at the school. Free. Held the 4th Friday in September.

ARCHAEOLOGICAL & HISTORIC SITES:

Vista Point: Hoopa Reservation – Off Hwy 96.

TRIBAL ORGANIZATIONS:

Hoopa Rodeo Association
Hoopa, CA 95546
(916) 625-4712

Hoopa Recreation Committee
P.O. Box 274
Hoopa, CA 95546
(916) 625-4275, -4239

ACCOMMODATIONS:

Tsewaldin Inn
P.O. Box 219, Highway 96
Hoopa, CA 95546
(916) 625-4294
Motel and restaurant.

Karuk Reservation

TRIBAL PROFILE:

The Karuk Reservation totals about 243 acres with the Klamath River flowing through it. Secluded in lovely mountains where fish and game abound, the Karuk Tribe of California numbers 1,500 tribal members.

LOCATION:

Near the Oregon border in Klamath National Forest; exit I-5 10 miles north of Yreka and travel west on Hwy 96.

ADDRESS:

Karuk Tribe of California
P.O. Box 1016
Happy Camp, CA 96039
(916) 493-5305

RECREATIONAL OPPORTUNITIES:

Karuk-Beartooth Wilderness School
P.O. Box 352
Happy Camp, CA 96039
(916) 493-5304
A unique opportunity, the wilderness school offers trips on the Klamath River, plus wilderness skills workshops: for example, basket weaving and edible and medicinal plants. The school is 3 miles above the Klamath River, with a view of the Marble Mountains, and guests stay in tepees on the 68 acre site. Camping available. Open Memorial Day through Labor Day.

ACCOMMODATIONS:

Mountain View Ranch
P.O. Box 389
Orleans, CA 95556
(916) 627-3354
Camping, RV hookups, and lodging available, as well as river guide service.

Sandy Bar Lodge
Box 295
Orleans, CA 95556
(916) 627-3379
Units and cabins.

Forest Lodge
P.O. Box 1535
Happy Camp, CA 96039
(916) 493-5424
Right on Hwy 96 in town.

Mountain vista. Courtesy of Dianna Muraski.

Quartz Valley Reservation

TRIBAL PROFILE:

Federal recognition of the Quartz Valley Indians was restored on December 15, 1983, as a result of the class action suit **Tillie Hardwick vs. United States of America**. Tribal affiliations are with the Shasta and Upper Klamath, and the governing body at this time is the General Community Council. Tribal lands held in trust for individuals amount to approximately 24 acres.

LOCATION:

In the heart of wilderness country, among mountain ranges, national forest and recreation areas, Etna is on the Scott River, south of Yreka near the Oregon/California border, west of I-5 on scenic Hwy 3.

ADDRESS:

Quartz Valley Indian Community
P.O. Box 737
Etna, CA 96027
(916) 467-5409, -3307

BUSINESSES & INDUSTRIES:

Quartz Valley Tribal Gift Shop
516 North Hwy 3
Etna, CA 96027
(916) 467-5409
Indian arts and crafts such as blankets, graphics, and jewelry by local and regional artists.

ACCOMMODATIONS:

Marble Mtn. View Motel
Fort Jones, CA
(916) 468-2394

Resighini Rancheria

Tribal Profile:

Land purchased by the federal government in 1938 for this band of the Yurok Tribe is the home of 74 Coast Indian Community members. The Resighini Rancheria covers 228 acres close to the Pacific Ocean. The tribe plans to expand agricultural endeavors and to open a sand and gravel business to be more self-supporting.

Location:

Northern California, near Redwood National Park, the Pacific Ocean and the Klamath River. On US 101 24 miles south of Crescent City.

Address:

Coast Indian Community of the Resighini Rancheria
P.O. Box 529
Klamath, CA 95548
(707) 482-2431

Recreational Opportunities:

Ch-ere Campground/RV
Resighini Rancheria
(707) 482-2545
Camping and RV services; fishing allowed. Open from May to October, check with tribal office for use in other months. Fee.

Accommodations:

Motels nearby in Klamath and Crescent City.

Robinson Rancheria

Tribal Profile:

Beautiful Clear Lake and Mendocino National Forest provide the setting for Robinson Rancheria. The 211 resident members of the Pomo Indian Tribe live on 107 acres purchased in 1987. The original reservation was established in the 1930s, and portions of it are still privately owned by individual members of the tribe.

Location:

The Rancheria is 2 hours north of San Francisco and 1 hour from the wine country of Napa Valley. Between US 101 and I-5 via Hwy 20.

Address:

Robinson Rancheria of Pomo Indians
1545 E. Hwy 20
P.O. Box 1119
Nice, CA 95464
(707) 275-0527

Special Events:

Indian Cultural Day
Native American dancers come from throughout Lake County and a dinner is served. Held in September.

Robinson Rancheria Annual Track Meet
Contestants from ages 5 to 18 are welcome to participate in this inter-tribal meet; prizes awarded to all. Held in September.

Recreational Opportunities:

Kabatin Two Indian Bingo
Robinson Rancheria
(707) 275-3140
Just off Hwy 20 on Robinson Rancheria. Open Thursday through Saturday 5:00-11:00 p.m.; Sunday, 12:00-5:30 p.m.

Accommodations:

There are many places to stay in this resort area. Lakeport, 4 miles south, and Lucerne, 6 miles east, are closest to the Rancheria.

Restrictions and/or Special Considerations:

No alcohol or drugs allowed on Robinson Rancheria.

Round Valley Reservation

Tribal Profile:

Executive order created Round Valley Reservation in 1870. The six major tribal bands – Yuki, Pit River, Pomo, Concow, Wailaki, and Nomlachi – and several other Indian groups were all settled on the lands, and membership today stands at 2,615. Forestry is a source of tribal income on the 30,537 acre reservation.

Location:

North of San Francisco off US 101, Covelo is 62 miles north of Ukiah and east of US 101. Round Valley Reservation can be reached by travelling Hwy 162, which follows the Eel River.

Address:

Covelo Indian Community
P.O. Box 448
Covelo, CA 95428
(707) 983-6126

Special Events:

California Indian Days
Hidden Oaks Recreational Park
A combined baseball tournament and pow wow, featuring arts and crafts, hand games, and a parade. Held the last weekend in September.

Accommodations:

Hotels and motels in Covelo.

Rumsey Rancheria

Tribal Profile:

On the verge of termination and with three residents in the 1970s, Rumsey Indian Rancheria now boasts 50 tribal members and 185 acres. The original land purchase was made for the Wintun tribe in 1907. Agriculture is the main source of income.

Location:

Northwest of Sacramento; Cache Creek and scenic Hwy 16 pass Rumsey Indian Rancheria, 1 hour from Napa Valley wine country and Clear Lake. From I-505, Hwy 16 north to Brooks.

Address:

Wintun Tribe - Rumsey Rancheria
P.O. Box 18
Brooks, CA 95606
(916) 796-3400

Special Events:

Almond Festival
(916) 787-3433
A valley-wide affair celebrating the agricultural season. Arts and crafts, wine tasting, barbecue, and a classic car show. Held the last Sunday in February.

Recreational Opportunities:

Cash Creek Indian Bingo & Casino
14455 State Hwy 16
Brooks, CA 95606
(800) 452-8181
Open Monday, Wednesday, and Friday evenings, and Sunday and Saturday starting at 1:30.

Cache Canyon Campground: In Rumsey, 25 miles north of Rumsey Rancheria.

Accommodations:

Hotels in Woodland, CA, 30 miles east of the Rancheria.

Napa Valley vineyard. Photo by Nanci Kerby. Courtesy of California Office of Tourism.

Sherwood Valley Rancheria

TRIBAL PROFILE:

The Sherwood Valley Rancheria was purchased in 1909 for California Indians with no designation regarding which tribes would live there, and additional lands were added in 1916. The gross acreage is 350, and the reservation is now the home of 155 Pomo Indians.

LOCATION:

Ukiah is on US 101 north of San Francisco and the Napa Valley wine country; south of Lake Mendocino and the junction of US 101 and scenic Hwy 20.

ADDRESS:

Sherwood Valley Rancheria
2141 S. State St.
Ukiah, CA 95482
(707) 468-1337

CULTURAL INSTITUTIONS:

Sherwood Valley Arts & Crafts Store
2197 South State Street
Ukiah, CA 95482
(707) 468-1337
Selling beading supplies, handmade arts and crafts, American Indian jewelry, cards, and calendars. Open Monday-Friday, 8:00 a.m.-5:00 p.m.

Big Lagoon Rancheria tour area. Courtesy of Steve Baldy/Big Lagoon Rancheria.

Trinidad Rancheria

TRIBAL PROFILE:

Trinidad Rancheria was established in 1917 by the Secretary of the Interior on lands purchased for the Cher-Ae Heights Indian Community in 1906. The 55-acre Rancheria is owned by the 128 Yurok, Miwok and Tolowa Indians who live on its rugged bluffs overlooking Trinidad Harbor and the Pacific Ocean.

LOCATION:

Tucked between the Pacific Ocean and the Coast Ranges of Northern California, Trinidad Rancheria is just south of Redwood National Park. This land of high coastal bluffs, redwoods, and rocky shoreline is near US 101, about 25 miles north of Eureka.

ADDRESS:

Cher-Ae Heights Indian Community
P.O. Drawer 630
Trinidad, CA 95570
(707) 677-0211

RECREATIONAL OPPORTUNITIES:

Cher-Ae Heights Bingo
Trinidad Rancheria
(707) 677-3611
High stakes Indian bingo. Open Thursday & Friday 5:30 p.m., Saturday & Sunday 11:00 a.m.

BUSINESSES & INDUSTRIES:

Ab-Originals
P.O. Drawer 850
Trinidad, CA 95570
(707) 677-3738
Fashioning necklaces, earrings, hair pieces, belts and other accessories from traditional Indian materials such as shells, quills, feathers, and glass beads, but utilizing mainly semi-precious stones. 1 mile south of US 101 on the Rancheria. No set hours; call before stopping in.

ACCOMMODATIONS:

The closest lodgings are in historic Arcata, 6 miles south.

Tuolumne Rancheria

Tribal Profile:

The Tuolumne Band of the Me-Wuk Indians resides on the 336 acre Tuolumne Indian Rancheria, established in 1910. The rancheria is organized under the Indian Reorganization Act of 1936 and is governed by a four-member community council. This band of the Me-Wuk numbers 350, and it has maintained its cultural dances and traditions.

Location:

In the western foothills of the Sierra Nevada Mountains near Yosemite National Park, approximately 120 miles southeast of Sacramento; due east of Stockton, about a 3 hour drive from San Francisco. Tuolumne is off Hwy 120 on Hwy 108, just east of Hwy 49.

Address:

Tuolumne Band of Me-Wuk Indians
P.O. Box 699
19595 Mi Wu Street
Tuolumne, CA 95379
(209) 928-3475

Special Events:

Acorn Festival
An annual event celebrating the traditional Me-Wuk Indian heritage; includes traditional foods and Me-Wuk dances, arts and crafts, and displays of objects of cultural significance. Held the 2nd weekend of September.

Recreational Opportunities:

Private campsite with facilities. Contact the Tribal Office in advance for camping.

Archaeological & Historic Sites:

Shadow of the Mi-Wok Trail
Summit Ranger Station
Stanislaus National Forest
Pinecrest, CA
(209) 965-3434

Tribal Organizations:

Central Sierra Me-Wuk Cultural and Historic Preservation Committee
P.O. Box 699
Tuolumne, CA 95379
(209) 928-3475

Other Northern California Reservations

Please contact the following reservations or rancherias directly for tourism information.

Benton Paiute Reservation
Star Route 4, Box 56-A
Benton, CA 93512
(619) 933-2321

Berry Creek Rancheria
1779 Mitchell Avenue
Oroville, CA 95966
(916) 534-3859

***Big Bend Rancheria**
P.O. Drawer 1570
Burney, CA 96013
(916) 335-5421

Big Valley Reservation
P.O. Box 153
Finley, CA 95453

Blue Lake Rancheria
P.O. Box 248
Blue Lake, CA 95525
(707) 668-5101

Bridgeport Indian Colony
P.O. Box 37
Bridgeport, CA 93517
(619) 932-7083

Buena Vista Rancheria
4650 Coalmine Road
Ione, CA 95640

Cedarville Rancheria
P.O. Box 126
Cedarville, CA 96104
(916) 279-2270

Cloverdale Rancheria
285 Santana Drivea
Cloverdale, CA 95424

Cortina Rancheria
P.O. Box 7470
Citrus Heights, CA 95621
(916) 726-7118

Dry Creek Rancheria
P.O. Box 607
Geyserville, CA 95441
(707) 431-8232

Elk Valley Rancheria
P.O. Box 1042
Crescent City, CA 95531
(707) 464-4680

Enterprise Rancheria
Oroville, CA

Greenville Rancheria
1304 E St., Suite 106
Redding, CA 96001
(916) 241-3941

Grindstone Rancheria
P.O. Box 63
Elk Creek, CA 95939
(916) 968-5116

Hopland Rancheria
P.O. Box 610
Hopland, CA 95449
(707) 744-1647

Inaja-Cosmit Reservation
715 B Street, #5
Ramona, CA 92065

Jackson Rancheria
1600 Bingo Way
Jackson, CA 95642
(209) 223-3931

Laytonville Rancheria
P.O. Box 48
Laytonville, CA 95454

***Likely Rancheria**
P.O. Drawer 1570
Burney, CA 96013
(916) 335-5421

***Lookout Rancheria**
P.O. Drawer 1570
Burney, CA 96013
(916) 335-5421

Manchester-Pt. Arena Rancheria
P.O. Box 623
Point Arena, CA 95468
(707) 882-2788

Middletown Rancheria
P.O. Box 292
Middletown, CA 95461

***Montgomery Creek Rancheria**
P.O. Drawer 1570
Burney, CA 96013
(916) 335-5421

Mooretown Rancheria
P.O. Box 1842
Oroville, CA 95965
(916) 533-3625

Pinoleville Rancheria
367 North State Street, Suite 204
Ukiah, CA 95482
(707) 463-1454

Pit River Tribe of California
P.O. Drawer 1570
Burney, CA 96013
(916) 335-5421

Potter Valley Rancheria
2191 South State Street
Ukiah, CA 95482
(707) 468-7494 or 7495

Redding Rancheria
2000 Rancheria Road
Redding, CA 96001-5528
(916) 241-1871

Redwood Valley Rancheria
P.O. Box 499
Redwood Valley, CA 95470
(707) 485-0361

Rohnerville Rancheria
P.O. Box 108
Eureka, CA 95502-0108
(707) 442-6403

Sheep Ranch Rancheria
Sheep Ranch, CA

Shingle Springs Rancheria
P.O. Box 1340
Shingle Springs, CA 95682
(916) 676-8010

Smith River Rancheria
P.O. Box 239
Smith River, CA 95567
(707) 487-9255

Stewarts Point Reservation
P.O. Box 54
Stewarts Point, CA 95480

Sulphur Bank Rancheria (Elem Colony)
P.O. Box 618
Clearlake, CA 95423

Susanville Rancheria
P.O. Drawer 1570
Susanville, CA 96130
(916) 257-6264

Table Bluff Rancheria
P.O. Box 519
Loleta, CA 95551
(707) 733-5055

Upper Lake Rancheria
P.O. Box 245272
Sacramento, CA 95820
(916) 371-5637

***XL Ranch**
P.O. Drawer 1570
Burney, CA 96013
(916) 335-5421

*The Pit River Tribal Constitution approved by the Assistant Secretary on December 3, 1987, recognized jurisdiction over the following land bases: XL Ranch, Montgomery Creek Rancheria, Roaring Creek Rancheria, Big Bend Rancheria, Burney Tract, Lookout Rancheria, Likely Rancheria, and other lands.

Southern California

CALIFORNIA - SOUTH HALF

Palm Tree Grove. Courtesy of California State Office of Tourism.

Agua Caliente Reservation

TRIBAL PROFILE:

The desert resort of Palm Springs is situated on the Agua Caliente Reservation, in the desert at the base of Mt. San Jacinto National Wilderness. The reservation of approximately 23,173 acres was established under an Act of Congress in 1896 and belongs to the Agua Caliente Band of Cahuilla Indians, whose tribal membership stands at 244. Located in a moderate climate, the tribe lives on its ancestral homeland and continues to retain language, songs, and traditional foods and cooking.

LOCATION:

Palm Springs is 12 miles south of I-10 on Hwy 111.

ADDRESS:

Agua Caliente Tribe
960 E. Tahquitz Canyon Way, Suite 106,
Palm Springs, CA 92262
(619) 325-5673

CULTURAL INSTITUTIONS:

Agua Caliente Cultural Museum
Under construction; scheduled to open in 1993.

SPECIAL EVENTS:

Agua Caliente Heritage Fiesta
Andreas Ranch - Indian Canyons
Festival with games, food; Indian, Hispanic, and Western entertainers; arts and crafts. Organized as a family event; offers many activities for children – organized games, nature walks, hay rides, and pony rides. At the end of S. Palm Canyon Dr. in Palm Springs. Admission charged. Held during daylight hours in late April.

RECREATIONAL OPPORTUNITIES:

Desert Adventures
68-733 Perez Rd.
Cathedral City, CA 92234
(619) 324-3378
Experienced nature guides introduce travelers to the history of the Agua Caliente Band of Cahuilla Indians. The visitor will see traces of ancient

settlements, including rock art, house pits, irrigation ditches and reservoirs, trails, and food processing areas. Tours leave from Palm Canyon Trading Post daily. Guides will take private parties on little-known trails and back roads when arrangements are made in advance. Fees charged.

Smoke Tree Stables
2500 Toledo Avenue
Palm Springs, CA 92264
(619) 327-1372
South of Palm Springs near the Indian Canyons.

ARCHAEOLOGICAL & HISTORIC SITES:

Agua Caliente Indian Canyons: Listed in the National Register of Historic Places, Palm, Andres, Murray, and Tahquitz Canyons were home to the Agua Caliente Cahuilla Indians. Horse and hiking trails lead to canyons of startling beauty and contrast that offer glimpses of wild mountain ponies, mountain sheep and some endangered species of birds. Andreas Canyon reveals Cahuilla rock art and remains of mortars and metates. Palm Canyon Trading Post is found in Palm Canyon. Tahquitz Canyon has magnificent waterfalls and pools. South Palm Springs.

ACCOMMODATIONS:

Spa Hotel & Mineral Springs
100 N. Indian Canyon
Palm Springs, CA 92262
(619) 325-1461

Barona Reservation

TRIBAL PROFILE:

The 420 member Barona Band of Mission Indians occupies 5,180 acres of land near San Diego, on Barona Indian Reservation. The Barona lands were set aside by Executive Orders in 1875 and 1883; with a semi-arid climate, the tribal economy relies mainly on cattle raising and dry farming. This area offers many opportunities for recreational activities.

LOCATION:

15 miles east of San Diego off I-8; from El Cajon north on Hwy 67 to Lakeside.

ADDRESS:

Barona Band of Mission Indians
1095 Barona Road
Lakeside, CA 92040
(619) 443-6612

CULTURAL INSTITUTIONS:

Barona Reservation Mission
1055 Barona Road
Lakeside, CA
(619) 443-3412
This Roman Catholic Church was built 57 years ago and is owned by the tribe.

Barona Indian Mission Sign at entrance.
Courtesy of Verona M. Worthman.

SPECIAL EVENTS:

Barona Barbecue
Barona Reservation Mission
1054 Barona Road
Lakeside, CA 92040
Traditional style, deep pit barbecue with the meat marinated and cooked on hot coals underground. Various foods, traditional and non-traditional; game and crafts booths; live band; Indian dancing, pow wow style; and local singing, Kumeyaay bird songs. 5 miles north of Lakeside. Held the 1st Sunday in August.

Barona Indian Mission front view. Courtesy of Verona M. Worthman.

Pacific Coast Indian Club Annual Pow Wow
(619) 697-0250
Sponsored by the Pacific Coast Indian Club and held at the Barona Reservation softball fields on Labor Day weekend in September.

RECREATIONAL OPPORTUNITIES:

Barona Bingo
1000 Barona Road
Lakeside, CA 92040
(619) 443-8133

ACCOMMODATIONS:

RV facilities, campsites, and motels are available in El Cajon, which is 20 to 25 miles from the reservation. Camping is permitted on the reservation during the pow wow.

Cabazon Reservation

TRIBAL PROFILE:

Created by Executive Order in 1876, the Cabazon Indian Reservation, about 1,500 acres in the Southern California desert, is home to 25 members of the Cabazon Band of Mission Indians. This small band of Indians is held together by its traditional culture. A thriving bingo and casino complex is part of tribal economy, and the Indian Housing Development is preparing to open a 1,200 unit complex.

LOCATION:

In the desert near Palm Springs, Joshua Tree National Monument, and the Salton Sea. Directly off I-10, Indio Exit. Take Auto Center Dr., north, and head east on Indio Springs Drive.

ADDRESS:

Cabazon Band of Mission Indians
84-245 Indio Springs Drive
Indio, CA 92201-3405
(619) 342-2593

RECREATIONAL OPPORTUNITIES:

Indio Bingo Palace & Casino
84-245 Indio Springs Drive
Indio, CA 92201
(619) 342-5000, ext. 3041 or
(800) 827-2946
24-hour, 7-day a week poker/pan card casino, with off-track betting (horse racing) and high stakes bingo, including Million Dollar MegaBingo.

BUSINESSES & INDUSTRIES:

Colmac Energy
Cabazon Band of Mission Indians Reservation
(619) 342-2593
A bio-mass powerplant. Call for tour availability.

ACCOMMODATIONS:

Big America Rodeway Inn
84096 Indio Springs Rd.
Indio, CA
(619) 342-6344
1/4 mile from the reservation, the inn gives special rates to Cabazon Reservation visitors.

Chemehuevi Reservation

TRIBAL PROFILE:

The reservation consists of 30,654 acres. West of the Colorado River Valley, the area is mountainous, with the Whipple Mountains forming the southern border of the reservation and the Chemehuevi Mountains on the west. The population is about 500; tribal income is derived from business licenses, permits and residential leases. The reservation enjoys a dry, sunny climate with rainfall averaging between 5 and 10 inches annually.

LOCATION:

Southeastern California, with a 25-mile shoreline along the Colorado River and Lake Havasu, on the border with Arizona. Access is via Hwy 95 from I-40. Needles provides the closest public transportation services, also available in Lake Havasu City, AZ, directly across the River.

ADDRESS:

Chemehuevi Indian Tribe
P.O. Box 1976
Chemehuevi Valley, CA 92363
(619) 858-4531

RECREATIONAL OPPORTUNITIES:

Water sports, hiking, camping hunting and fishing.

Havasu Landing Resort
(619) 858-4600
For campground reservations, call (619) 858-4593.

Colorado River Reservation

See Arizona

Country scene near Fort Independence Reservation. Courtesy of Dianna Muraski.

Fort Independence Paiute Reservation

TRIBAL PROFILE:

The eastern Sierra Nevadas shelter Fort Independence Reservation, a 356-acre reservation established by Executive Orders of 1915 and 1916. This small group of Western Paiutes numbers 123; agriculture is a source of income.

LOCATION:

Due east of Fresno in the eastern foothills of the Sierra Nevadas. US 395 bisects the reservation from north to south. Fort Independence is 3 miles north of Independence and 43 miles south of Bishop.

ADDRESS:

Fort Independence Paiute Indian Tribe
P.O. Box 67
131 N. Hwy 395
Fort Independence, CA 93526
(619) 878-2126

RECREATIONAL OPPORTUNITIES:

Fort Independence Campground
(619) 878-2126
Offering pull-throughs, shade trees, 30-amp electrical, quality well water, dump station, and showers. Open all year. Fee.

Kings Canyon and Sequoia National Parks are quite near.

ARCHAEOLOGICAL & HISTORIC SITES:

Fort Independence Monument: Caves soldiers used during the Indian uprisings. 3 miles north of Independence off Schabell Lane.

Check with the tribe for information about other areas of archaeological interest around the reservation.

ACCOMMODATIONS:

Winnedumah Hotel
211 N. Edwards
Independence, CA
(619) 878-2040
Historic inn with restaurant and lounge.

Fort Mojave Reservation

TRIBAL PROFILE:

The Fort Mojave Reservation spans the Colorado River and is comprised of 23,669 acres in Arizona, 12,633 acres in California and 5,582 acres in Nevada. The reservation population is about 700, engaged in farming and tourist businesses. A gambling casino and resort are in the planning stages, as well as a master-planned community named Aha Macav. The tribe expects to complete a total of six resorts.

LOCATION:

Between Lakes Mead and Havasu, and Lake Havasu National Wildlife Refuge, on the southern California/Nevada border, 125 miles south of Las Vegas, Nevada. Headquartered in Needles, Fort Mojave is reached via I-40 and US 95.

ADDRESS:

Fort Mojave Indian Tribe
500 Merriman Avenue
Needles, CA 92363
(619) 326-4591

SPECIAL EVENTS:

Fort Mojave Indian Days Celebration
Tribal Gym & Park
(619) 326-4810
Festivities include Miss Mojave Pageant, parade, band concert, tribal dances performed by the Mojave tribe and other tribes, games for all ages, arts and crafts show, food booths and barbecue, Relay Spirit Run, and raffles. Held Thursday through Saturday in mid-October. Free admission.

RECREATIONAL OPPORTUNITIES:

Campgrounds: Dotting the riverbanks. Mostly primitive; some provide portable toilets. Contact Tribal Police (602) 768-4521 to obtain a permit.

This area is perfect for all types of water sports.

BUSINESSES & INDUSTRIES:

Avi Kwa Ame Farm
(602)768-3232
A 3,000 acre farm cultivating mainly cotton and alfalfa.

C-Plus
In Mojave Valley, AZ. Gas, convenience market, and smoke shop south of Riviera on AZ Hwy 95.

ACCOMMODATIONS:

Hotels and motels in Bullhead City, Needles, and Lake Havasu City.

Fort Yuma Reservation

See Arizona

La Jolla Reservation

TRIBAL PROFILE:

Tribal affiliation of the La Jolla Band of Mission Indians is with the Luiseno Tribe. Living on the 8,541 acre La Jolla Reservation established by executive order in 1875 and 1876, 509 tribal members are still very involved in all aspects of their culture. The reservation is situated in fertile northern San Diego County, and farming, along with a recreation enterprise, is the mainstay of the economy.

LOCATION:

At the base of Mt. Palomar in the Cleveland National Forest; La Jolla River flows through the reservation. Accessed from I-15 or Hwy 78; crossed by Hwy 76.

ADDRESS:

La Jolla Band of Mission Indians
Star Route 158
Valley Center, CA 97082
(619) 742-3771

RECREATIONAL OPPORTUNITIES:

Amago Raceway
P.O. Box 238
Valley Center, CA 92082
(619) 742-3833, -4342
Bring your own go-cart and take a spin on the track. Fee. Go-cart racing clubs come and compete throughout the year. Open 9:00 a.m.-5:00 p.m., 7 days a week, except when races are in progress. A snack bar is open during races.

La Jolla Indian Reservation Campground
Star Route Box 158
Valley Center, CA
(619) 742-1297, -3771
On the banks of the San Luis Rey River in an area that is largely wilderness, this is one of few San Diego County campgrounds next to a natural stream. Offers 800 sites for camping and RVs, flush toilets, showers, drinking water, and catfish angling in the well-stocked creek. Inner tubing is a very popular summer activity. Trading post sells firewood, fishing tackle and supplies. State fishing license required. No dogs or motorbikes allowed. Approximately 7.5 miles east of Pauma Valley on Hwy 76. Open March - October; fees.

Sengme Oaks Water Park
Star Route Box 158, Hwy 76
Valley Center, CA
(619) 742-1921
2 giant slides and two 500-foot speed slides offer a day filled with watery delights. Amenities include showers, lockers, changing rooms, sun decks, and a snack bar. Group rates offered. Near the campground. Open 10:00 a.m.-6:00 p.m., May - September.

ACCOMMODATIONS:

A resort at Lake Henshaw offers cabins and a restaurant. The nearest motels are in Escondido.

Los Coyotes Reservation

TRIBAL PROFILE:

The Los Coyotes Reservation was set apart in 1889, but not officially established until 1900. The Los Coyotes Band of Mission Indians has a tribal affiliation with the Cahuilla. Today the band has 212 members, and about half live on the 25,049 acre reservation. The group has kept many traditions, such as language, songs, games, foods, and arts and crafts.

LOCATION:

Near San Diego, between the Cleveland National Forest and the Anza-Borrego Desert State Park, the Los Coyotes Reservation is also close to a variety of hot springs dotted throughout the region. From I-8, take scenic Hwy 79 north to Warner Springs. Hwys 78, 76, and 79 all exit east off I-15 to reach Warner Springs.

Typical mountain view near Los Coyotes. Courtesy of Verona M. Worthman.

ADDRESS:

Los Coyotes Band of Mission Indians
P.O. Box 249
Warner Springs, CA 92086
(619) 782-3269

RECREATIONAL OPPORTUNITIES:

Los Coyotes Campground
(619) 782-3269
Campsites. Also trailhead for jeep trips. Fee for camping and per vehicle for trail use.

ARCHAEOLOGICAL & HISTORIC SITES:

Eagle Rock: Geologic formation viewed off the south side of Camino San Ignacio near the entrance to the reservation.

ACCOMMODATIONS:

Julian Hotel
2032 Main St.
Julian, CA
(619) 765-0201
Hotel in nearby Historic Julian.

Pala Reservation

TRIBAL PROFILE:

The Pala Band of Mission Indians has been settled on its 11,892 acre reservation since 1903, but reservation was set aside in 1875. The tribe has 585 members, most of whom reside on tribal land. Tribal income derives from ranching, a sand and gravel business, and tourmaline mines.

LOCATION:

In a lovely valley filled with groves in north San Diego County, the Pala Reservation is built around the famous Pala Mission. East of I-15 on Hwy 76.

ADDRESS:

Pala Band of Mission Indians
P.O. Box 43
Pala, CA 92059
(619) 742-3784

CULTURAL INSTITUTIONS:

Cupa Cultural Center
Pala Indian Reservation
(619) 742-1590

Special Events:

Cupa Days
Cupa Cultural Center
An occasion featuring peon (Indian hand games), arts and crafts, and dancers. Held the 1st weekend in May. No admission charged.

Corpus Christi Fiesta
Pala Mission
(619) 742-3317
Held as a fund raiser to benefit the mission school, the Fiesta offers a procession and high mass, game and food booths, music and dancing. Held the 1st Sunday in June. No admission fee.

Children's Festival
Pala Mission
(619) 742-3317
Mission School benefit begins with a religious procession honoring St. Francis. Afterwards, arts and crafts, food, games, and dancing go throughout the day. Held 1st Sunday in October.

Recreational Opportunities:

Acorn Park: Campsites and RV facilities. Fishing. Fee charged.

Archaeological & Historic Sites:

Mission San Antonio de Pala: Spanish California mission built in 1816, fine example of Mission architecture. A Mission school was established here in 1958. Some unique attractions are the old cemetery, gardens, and shrines. Museum displays Indian artifacts and relics from the Pala Mission and Mission period of California. For further information contact: Mission San Antonio de Pala, Pala Indian Reservation, (619) 742-3317.

Businesses & Industries:

Gems of Pala
(619) 742-1356
Gem store.

Pala Fire Dept.
Pala Indian Reservation
(619) 742-1632

Pala Store
Convenience store and gas station.

Picayune Rancheria

Tribal Profile:

One of the many California tribes restored to federal recognition under the class action suit **Tillie Hardwick v. United States** on December 22, 1983, the Chuckchansi live on the 28.76 acre Picayune Rancheria. Re-established after a 20 year hiatus, the tribe opened its headquarters in October 1987. Formal tribal government, led by a seven-member council, works to address social, community, and economic issues. Property aquisitions creating a 78 acre landbase are planned; the acreage has already been selected. Chuckchansi baskets are highly prized by collectors.

Location:

East of US 99 in the Central Valley, via Hwy 41, 31 miles north of Fresno at Coarsegold. Abundant opportunities for recreation in this ski and watersports region.

Address:

Picayune Rancheria
P.O. Box 1480
352 Hwy 41
Coarsegold, CA 93614
(209) 683-6633

Special Events:

Annual PowWow
Pow wow offering local dance groups, arts and crafts, and an Indian Princess pageant. Held in the fall.

Recreational Opportunities:

Various campsites near the reservation; petroglyphs are also nearby.

Accommodations:

Motels in Oakhurst, 7 miles from Coarsegold.

California oaks in the Valley. Courtesy of Verona M. Worthman.

Rincon Reservation

Tribal Profile:

Executive Order in 1875 established a reservation for a band of the San Luiseno tribe living by the La Jolla River. Situated in a mainly agricultural region, the 4,275 acre Rincon Reservation is the home of 457 tribal members. A cultural group has been formed to enhance the tribe's knowledge of its history and culture.

Location:

San Diego County holds 18 Indian reservations, with Rincon Reservation situated in the northern sector. East of Oceanside and west of Lake Henshaw, Rincon Reservation is reached via Rte. S6 accessed from scenic Hwys 76 or 78.

Address:

Rincon Band of Mission Indians
P.O. Box 68
Valley Center, CA 92082
(619) 749-1051

Cultural Institutions:

San Luiseno Band of Mission Indians Museum
#1 West Tribal Rd.
Valley Center, CA
(619) 749-1051
Pottery, sculpture, and photographs of traditional clothing, baskets, and ceremonies. Library focuses on American Indian news and culture. Hours 8:30 a.m.-4:30 p.m., Monday-Friday.

Santa Rosa Rancheria

TRIBAL PROFILE:

The Santa Rosa Rancheria is a 170 acre reservation with a resident population of about 360 members of the Tachi, Tache and Yokut bands. This rancheria was established in 1921 by U.S. District Court Decree and additional lands were purchased in 1938.

LOCATION:

Santa Rosa Rancheria lies in the San Joaquin Valley just outside Lemoore, east of Visalia, about half way between Fresno and Bakersfield. Easily accessible from I-5 or Hwy 99 on Hwy 198 via Alkali Drive. There is a private airfield at Lemoore.

ADDRESS:

Santa Rosa Indian Community
16835 Alkali Drive
Lemoore, CA 93245
(209) 924-1278

SPECIAL EVENTS:

March 1 Spiritual Gathering
Roundhouse Sweat Ceremonies, combining sweats and all night dance last day of February with sweat and dinner on March 1. A religious event, with an average attendance of 200; call to verify the exact location. Food and drinks available. No photography during ceremony.

RECREATIONAL OPPORTUNITIES:

Tribal Bingo Parlor
17225 Jersey Avenue
Lemoore, CA 93245
(209) 924-7751

Call for scheduling information.

TRIBAL ORGANIZATIONS:

Community Dance Group: Young people 8 to 16 years old; performs in schools and at pow wows.

ACCOMMODATIONS:

Lodgings in Lemoore.

RESTRICTIONS AND/OR SPECIAL CONSIDERATIONS:

No photography during ceremonies.

Santa Ynez Reservation

TRIBAL PROFILE:

The Santa Ynez Reservation was established in 1901; it encompasses just under 127 acres and has a population of about 200 members of the Chumash Tribe. It is nestled in the coastal mountains, not far from the Chumash Painted Cave State Historical Park and Nojoqui Falls.

LOCATION:

Approximately 30 miles north of Santa Barbara, leave US 101 at Buellton, and travel east on Hwy 246, or travel through the Santa Ynez mountains north from Santa Barbara on Hwy 154.

ADDRESS:

Santa Ynez Band of Mission Indians
P.O. Box 517
Santa Ynez, CA 93460
(805) 688-7997

RECREATIONAL OPPORTUNITIES:

Santa Ynez Campground: 24 spaces with electrical and water hookup. On Hwy 246. Fee.

Santa Ysabel Reservation

Tribal Profile:

The reservation was established by Executive Order of 1875 and covers 15,500 acres in the southwestern part of California where the land is flat, with a warm, dry climate. The arid climate has hindered economic development, but not the enthusiasm of the 300 tribal residents, members of the Santa Ysabel Band of Mission Indians.

Location:

Northeast of San Diego, east of Escondido via Hwy 78, and north of the town of Santa Ysabel. West of the Anza-Borrego Desert State Park.

Address:

Santa Ysabel Band of Mission Indians
P.O. Box 130
Santa Ysabel, CA 92070
(619) 765-0845

Cultural Institutions:

Elch-Qua-Nun (Land of the People) Community Library
Behind Tribal Headquarters
(619) 765-0845
Collection includes considerable information about many Indian tribes.

Special Events:

Santa Ysabel Pow Wow
(619) 765-0845
The pow wow draws visitors nationally. Arts and crafts are available, and the festivities include Indian peon games. Held in August.

Archaeological & Historic Sites:

Santa Ysabel Indian Mission: An historic landmark with a museum adjacent to the church and an old cemetery nearby. Open year round from sunrise to sunset. For further information contact: Santa Ysabel Indian Mission, (619) 765-0810.

Accommodations:

La Jolla Campground at the La Jolla Reservation, 20 minutes west on Hwy 76. Lodgings available in Julian.

Soboba Reservation

Tribal Profile:

The Soboba Reservation is east of the San Bernardino National Forest in Southern California, across the forest to the southwest from Palm Springs. Soboba lands were set apart by Executive Order of 1883, but not formally established until 1913. Luiseno tribal members operate a sand and gravel business and a citrus farming project on their 5,915 acre reservation.

Location:

North of Hwy 74, 7 miles from Hemet.

Address:

Soboba Band of Mission Indians
P.O. Box 487
San Jacinto, CA 92383
(714) 654-2765

Special Events:

Soboba Grand Prix
A motorcycle race that draws a regional audience. Contact the Tribal Office for details.

The 68,000 square foot Sycuan Gaming Center offering all five forms of legalized gambling. Six miles east of El Cajon, CA. Courtesy of Sycuan Gaming Center.

Sycuan Reservation

Tribal Profile:

Sycuan Reservation covers rolling hills amid oaks, cottonwoods, willows, chaparral, boulders, cactus, and wild flowers. A stream bed flows through this restful 640 acre reservation, which is home to roughly 120 tribal members. The Sycuan Indians are a band of the Kumeyaay Tribe, one of the first to inhabit California. The reservation was established by Executive Order in 1875. The Sycuan Band of Mission Indians continues to observe some ancestral ways while moving into non-traditional forms of financial security with the opening of its gaming center.

Location:

In the coastal mountains of San Diego County, 6 miles east of El Cajon City limits. Exit I-8 at Jamacha Road, south, to Washington Avenue. East on Washington to Dehesa Rd.

Address:

Sycuan Band of Mission Indians
5459 Dehesa Road
El Cajon, CA 92019
(619) 445-2613, -2614

Special Events:

Sycuan Pow Wow
Sycuan Reservation Softball Field
Drums from tribes throughout the West, dancers, food, arts and crafts are all part of the action. Camping available during the pow wow, with bathrooms and running water. Held in mid-September.

Recreational Opportunities:

Sycuan Gaming Center
5469 Dehesa Road
El Cajon, CA 92019
(619) 445-6002
Diversions encompass poker casino, bingo hall, keno, satellite wagering (horse racing), turf club & restaurant. Open 24 hours a day, 365 days a year.

Accommodations:

Nearby lodging in both El Cajon and Alpine.

Restrictions and/or Special Considerations:

Sycuan Reservation lands are closed to the public, except for in the areas indicated above.

Tule River Reservation

TRIBAL PROFILE:

The Tule River Reservation was established by Executive Order in 1873; it is home to almost 600 members of the Tule River Tribe of Yokut Indians. Nestled in the Sierra Nevada Mountains, the reservation encompasses 55,350 acres with timber, a river and a small valley. The Tule River Reservation is almost surrounded by the Sequoia National Forest, and public campgrounds and ski areas are nearby.

LOCATION:

East and north of Bakersfield, at the western edge of the Sierra Nevadas. Porterville, at the intersection of CA Highways 190, east-west, and 65, north-south. The reservation is about 21 miles east of Porterville; take CA 190 to Reservation Road.

ADDRESS:

Tule River Tribe
P.O. Box 589
Porterville, CA 93257
(209) 781-4271

CULTURAL INSTITUTIONS:

Tule River Silversmiths Guild
310 Indian Reservation Road
Porterville, CA 93257
(209) 784-6137

SPECIAL EVENTS:

Celebration - Porterville Pow Wow
Porterville Fairgrounds
(209) 784-4509
More than 500 Indian dancers compete for over $8,000 in contest money. A 2-day pow wow featuring contests of inter-tribal and specialty dancing. More than 75 Indian arts vendors participate; the cultural area features Indian artists demonstrating basketry, beadwork, soapstone carving and Navajo weaving. Held last weekend of September; Saturday 10:00 a.m. to 11:00 p.m., Sunday 10:00 a.m. to 6:00 p.m.

Tule River. Courtesy of Dianna Muraski.

ARCHAEOLOGICAL & HISTORIC SITES:

Painted Rocks: 7 miles from the reservation entrance; for more information contact the Tule River Tribal Council: (209) 781-4271

TRIBAL ORGANIZATIONS:

Native American Heritage Council
Route 7, Box 251
Porterville, CA 93257
(209) 784-4509

Viejas Reservation

TRIBAL PROFILE:

Established by Executive Order of December 27, 1875, the 1,609 acre Viejas Reservation is home to a portion of the Capitan Grande Band of Mission Indians. Viejas, Barona, and non-reservation groups each own 1/3 of the 15,753 acre Capitan Grande Reservation, as well as their own. Although the native language is rarely spoken, the tribe preserves much of its traditional culture. The Viejas people have contributed much in the fields of fire ecology, irrigation, and highway transport systems. Situated in temperate Southern California surrounded by the Cleveland National Forest, the reservation and its environs are ideal for travel, particularly in the cold season.

LOCATION:

In the foothills 35 miles east of San Diego, north of I-8 and Alpine.

ADDRESS:

Viejas Band of Mission Indians
P.O. Box 908
Alpine, CA 92001
(619) 445-3810

RECREATIONAL OPPORTUNITIES:

Viejas Casino & Turf Club
5000 Willows Rd.
Alpine, CA 91903
(619)445-5400
Off-track horse race betting and poker. Open 24 hours, Wednesday through Sunday.

Mar-Ta-Awa Park
#25 Browns Road
Alpine, CA 91901
(619) 445-3275
RV park with full services at monthly, weekly, and daily rates; camping in both primitive and developed sites; grocery; laundromat; pool and jacuzzi; Gift shop carries beautiful basketry, beadwork, textiles and clothing. Exit I-8 onto Willows Road, head north. Open all year.

Other Southern California Reservations

Please contact the following reservations or rancherias directly for tourism information.

Augustine Reservation
Thermal, CA
Big Pine Reservation
P.O. Box 700
Big Pine, CA 93513
(610) 938-2003

Big Sandy Reservation
P.O. Box 337
7302 Rancheria Lane
Auberry, CA 93602
(209) 855-4003

Bishop Reservation
P.O. Box 548
Bishop, CA 93584
(619) 873-3514

Cahuilla Reservation
P.O. Box 391760
Anza, CA 92539
(714) 763-5549

Campo Reservation
1779 Campo Truck Trail
Campo, CA 91906
(619) 478-9046

Cold Springs Rancheria (Sycamore Valley)
P.O. Box 209
Tollhouse, CA 93667
(209) 855-2326

Cuyapaipe Reservation
4390 La Posta Truck Trail
Pine Valley, CA 92062

Jamul Indian Village
461 Las Brisas
Escondido, CA 92027
(619) 480-9888

La Posta Reservation
1064 Barona Road
Lakeside, CA 92040
(619) 561-2924

Lone Pine Reservation
101 S. Main
Lone Pine, CA 93545
(619) 876-5414

Manzanita Reservation
P.O. Box 1302
Boulevard, CA 92005
(619) 478-5028

Mesa Grande Reservation
P.O. Box 270
Santa Ysabel, CA 92070
(619) 782-3835

North Fork Rancheria
P.O. Box 120
North Fork, CA 93643

Pauma & Yuima Reservation
P.O. Box 86
Pauma Valley, CA 92061
(619) 742-1289

Pechanga Reservation
P.O. Box 1477
Temecula, CA 92390
(714) 676-2768

Ramona Reservation
P.O. Box 26
Anza, CA 92306

Rincon Reservation
P.O. Box 68
Valley Center, CA 92082
(619) 749-1051

San Manual Reservation
5438 N. Victoria Avenue
Highland, CA 92346
(714) 862-8509

San Pasqual Reservation
P.O. Box 365
Valley Center, CA 92082
(619) 749-3200

Santa Rosa Reservation
325 N. Western Avenue
Hemet, CA 92343
(619) 741-5211

Table Mountain Rancheria
P.O. Box 243
Friant, CA 93626
(209) 822-2125

Timba-Sha Shoshone (Death Valley)
P.O. Box 206
Death Valley, CA 92328
(619) 786-2374

Torres-Martinez Reservation
66-725 Martinez Road
Thermal, CA 92274
(619) 397-0300

Twenty-Nine Palms Reservation
c/o Glen Calac
1150 E. Palm Canyon Drive, #75
Palm Springs, CA 92262
(619) 322-7488

Colorado

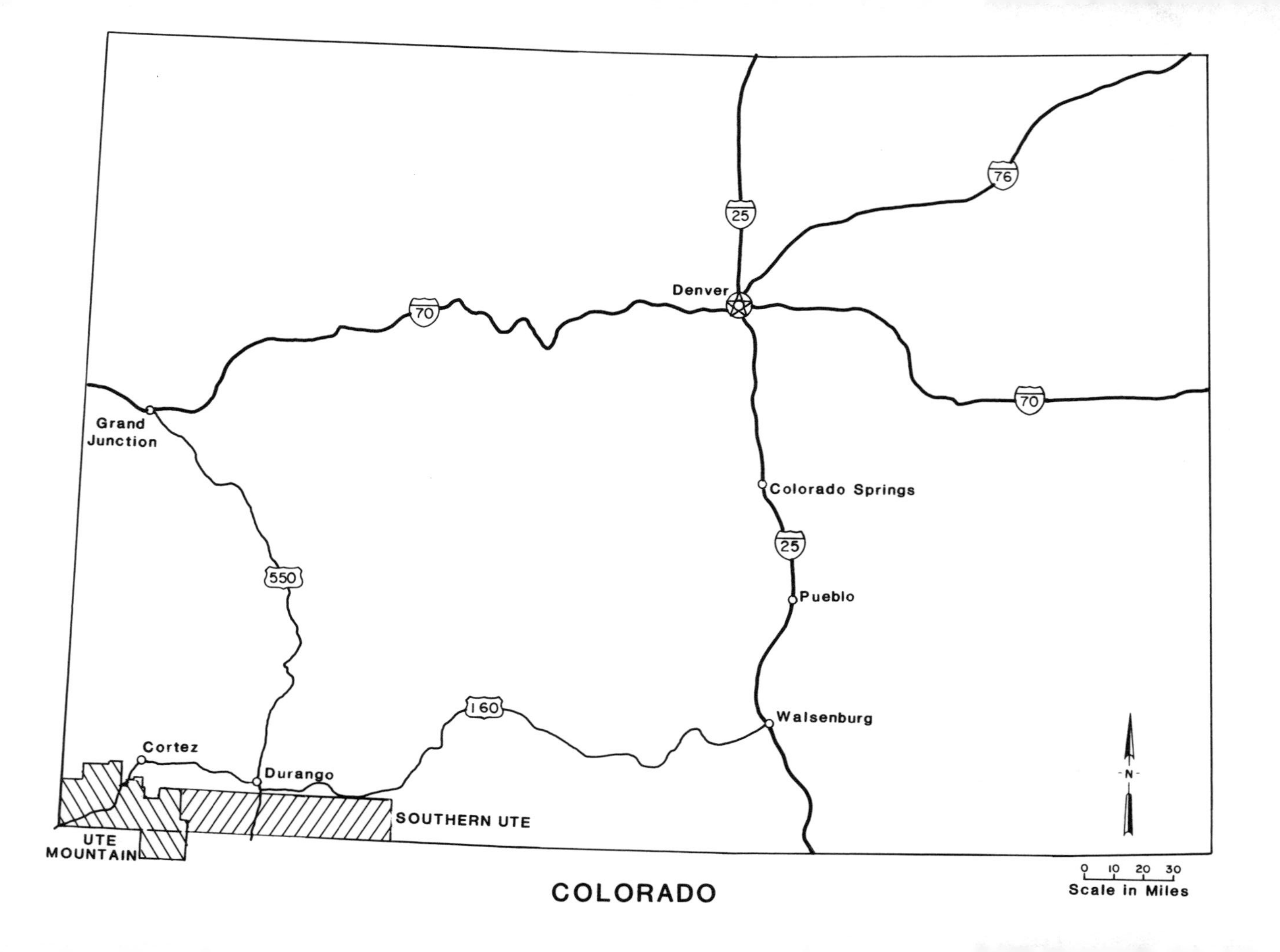
25
76
Denver
70
Grand Junction
70
Colorado Springs
25
550
Pueblo
160
Walsenburg
Cortez
Durango
SOUTHERN UTE
UTE MOUNTAIN
N
0 10 20 30
Scale in Miles

COLORADO

(L) Welcome sign upon entering the Southern Ute Reservation. Courtesy of Southern Ute Tribe. (R) Ice Fishing on the So. Ute Reservation. Photo by Chris Ribera. Courtesy of the Southern Ute Tribe.

Southern Ute Reservation

TRIBAL PROFILE:

Established in 1868 and located in the southwestern corner of Colorado, the Southern Ute Indian Reservation covers approximately 307,100 acres. The reservation features timbered ranges in the east and flat mesas to the west, and is crossed by 7 rivers. With a present membership of just over 1,200, the tribe is developing its oil, gas, sand and gravel deposits. Tribal businesses include a public radio station, custom farm services, convention center, water treatment plant and big game hunting opportunities. Ski resorts and well known tourist attractions such as Mesa Verde National Park are nearby.

LOCATION:

Tribal headquarters is in Ignacio, 24 miles southeast of Durango, reached via Hwy 172, south from US 160, 8 miles from La Plata County Airport.

ADDRESS:

Southern Ute Tribe
P.O. Box 737
Ignacio, CO 81137
(303) 563-4525

Southern Ute Tribal Enterprises
P.O. Box 550
Ignacio, CO 81137
(800) 876-7017

CULTURAL INSTITUTIONS:

Southern Ute Cultural Center & Gallery
P.O. Box 737
Ignacio, CO 81137
(303) 563-4531
The only Ute-funded and operated Indian museum in Colorado, the Cultural Center features a multimedia production shown daily, depicting the early history of the Utes. Displays include examples of the beautiful bead and leather work for which the Utes are famous.

Sky Ute Gallery adjoins the Cultural Center and features the finest in traditional and modern American Indian arts and crafts. Owned and operated by members of the Southern Ute Tribe.

SPECIAL EVENTS:

Ute Heritage Dancers and BBQ
Sky Ute Lodge
(800) 876-7017; (303) 563-4531
Tour of the Cultural Center, Western-style barbecue and a performance by the Southern Ute Heritage Dancers. Fee; special rate for senior citizens. Held Wednesday evenings, June through September.

Southern Ute Bear Dance
(800) 772-1236, ext. 300
Traditional dance and feast celebrating the emergence of the bear from hibernation. Held Memorial Day weekend, in late May.

Young dancer at the Southern Ute Cultural Museum. A Dale W. Anderson Photo, 1990. Courtesy of Aztec Media Workshop.

Sky Ute Stampede Rodeo
Sky Ute Downs
(303) 563-4502
Call for full schedule of events. Held 1st weekend of June.

Southern Ute Sun Dance
(800) 772-1236, ext. 300
Traditional religious dance. No photography or recording allowed; check with the tribe for other restrictions. Held 2nd weekend in July.

Southern Ute Fair/Pow Wow
(800) 772-1236, ext 213
Activities include parade, run/walk races, games, food, dances, a pow wow, and arts and crafts sales and displays. Held 2nd weekend in September.

When attending the Bear Dance, Sun Dance, or Tribal Fair and accommodations are desired, the visitor is advised to make reservations well in advance.

Recreational Opportunities:

Lake Capote
Lake Capote, P.O. Box 737
Ignacio, CO 81137
(303) 731-5256 during season
(800) 772-1236 year round.
State fishing license not needed; tribal fishing permit required. Camping, including 15 RV sites with hookups. At the junction of US 160 and Hwy 151. Regular season April to November. Open year round.

Navajo Lake State Park: Museum, fishing, boating and day camping. 22 miles south of US 160 and Lake Capote on Hwy 151.

Sky Ute Bingo
P.O. Box 550
Ignacio, CO 81137
(303) 563-9583
High stakes bingo each Friday night, 7:00 p.m.

Archaeological & Historic Sites:

Ute Memorial Park: Monuments to past chieftains, chairmen and veterans. At Tribal Headquarters.

Chimney Rock Ruins: The U.S. Forestry Service maintains this archaeological site. Seen by tour only; visitors should be at the gate by 9 a.m. 35 miles east of Ignacio, 4 miles south of US 160 and Lake Capote on Hwy 151. Donation requested. Open May to September. For further information: U.S. Forestry Service, (303) 264-2268.

Accommodations:

Sky Ute Lodge
P.O. Box 550
Ignacio, CO 81137
(800) 876-7017 or (303) 563-4531
36-room lodge with restaurant, lounge and swimming pool. Transportation available to and from La Plata County Airport.

Ute Mountain Reservation

TRIBAL PROFILE:

The Ute Mountain Reservation covers 597,288 acres of alloted and deeded lands, primarily in Colorado, but extending into New Mexico and Utah. The reservation is home to about 1,200 people, mostly members of the Ute Mountain Ute Tribe. The tribe derives income from various mineral deposits, largely gas and oil, that are found on the reservation. Mesa Verde National Park is surrounded on three sides by the Ute Mountain Reservation.

LOCATION:

Southwestern Colorado, in the Four Corners area, 15 miles south of Cortez, on the Navajo Trail; US 160/666 runs through the reservation from north to south.

ADDRESS:

Ute Mountain Ute Tribe
P.O. Box 52
Towaoc, CO 81334
(303) 565-3751

CULTURAL INSTITUTIONS:

Towaoc Library
Towaoc, CO 81334
(303) 565-3751
Collection includes tribal archives; contact the tribe for permission to consult these records.

SPECIAL EVENTS:

Ute Mountain Bear Dance
General Delivery - Echo Department
Towaoc, CO 81134
(303) 565-3751
A 5-day celebration of spring, with dancing, singing and traditional ceremonies; a feast is included on the final day. Free; average attendance is 1,000. Held the 1st week of June, Thursday to Monday.

RECREATIONAL OPPORTUNITIES:

Ute Mountain Bingo
P.O. Box 52
Towaoc, CO 81334
(303) 565-8549
Contact for days and times.

Ute woman in traditional dress. Photo by Jeff Andrew, courtesy of Colorado Tourism Board.

ARCHAEOLOGICAL & HISTORIC SITES:

Ute Mountain Tribal Park: Approximately 125,000 acres of the Ute Mountain Reservation, the Tribal Park has been set aside by the tribe to preserve the prehistoric culture of the Anasazi. It is operated primarily as a primitive area in order to protect its cultural and environmental resources. Guided tours are scheduled daily, leaving the Ute Mountain Pottery Plant in Towaoc, 15 miles south of Cortez, on US 160/666. Various day hikes and backpacking trips are available to explore more primitive areas. Call for full details and reservations: Ute Mountain Tribal Park, Towaoc, CO, (303) 565-3751, ext. 282, or 565-8548.

"Warrior From Capote Lake" by Orlando Jor, Ute Mtn. Ute Artist. A Dale W. Anderson Photo, 1990. Courtesy of Aztec Media Workshop.

BUSINESSES & INDUSTRIES:

Ute Mountain Pottery
US 666
Towaoc, CO 81334
(303) 565-8548
Small groups are welcome to tour at any time; large groups should call for an appointment. 15 miles south of Cortez.

ACCOMMODATIONS:

In Cortez, 15 miles north of Towaoc.

RESTRICTIONS AND/OR SPECIAL CONSIDERATIONS:

The various ruins and artifacts are irreplaceable. Obtain permission before exploring off-highway. Use care when exploring; remove nothing.

Dry desert climate and long distances require particular attention to food and fuel supplies when setting out into undeveloped areas.

Connecticut

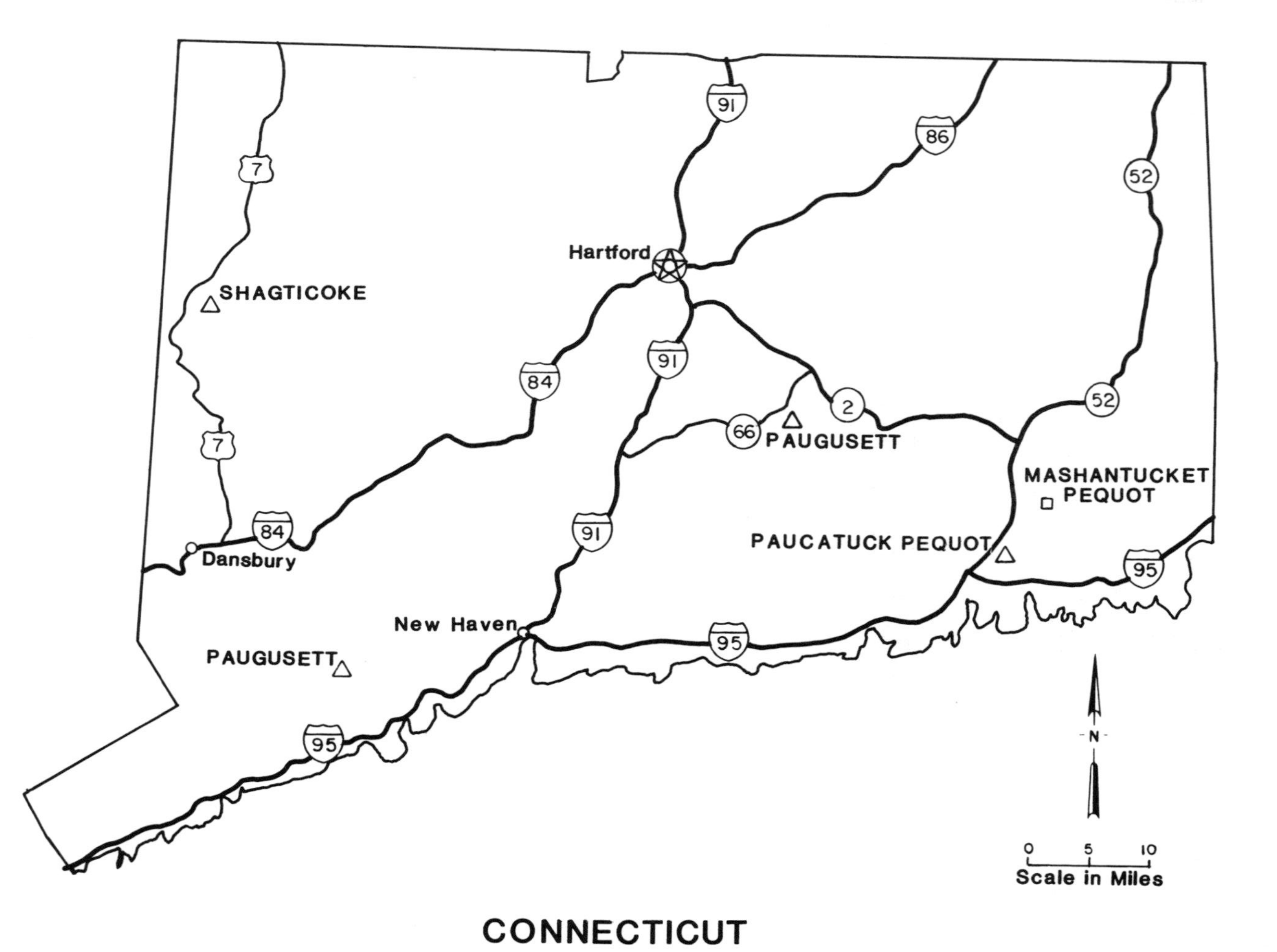

CONNECTICUT

Architectural drawing of Foxwoods High Stakes Bingo & Casino: L to R - Casino, Atrium and Valet Parking, Bingo. Courtesy of Foxwoods Bingo & Casino.

Mashantucket Pequot Reservation

TRIBAL PROFILE:

After the massacre of 1637, the survivors of the Mashantucket Tribe were finally settled on a portion of ancestral lands in 1667. Federal recognition occurred in 1983, halting further appropriations of the original allotment; the lands consist of 214 acres. Tribal membership totals 250, with 165 living on the reservation. The Mashantucket strive to provide services, jobs, and housing; to improve self-sufficiency; and to revive Mashantucket culture and tradition.

LOCATION:

North of Mystic and I-95, near the Rhode Island border and the coast. Hwy 214 passes through the reservation.

ADDRESS:

Mashantucket Pequot Tribe
P.O. Box 160
Indiantown Rd.
Ledyard, CT 06339
(203) 536-2681

CULTURAL INSTITUTIONS:

Mashantucket Pequot Research Library
Indiantown Rd.
Ledyard, CT 06339
(203) 536-2681

RECREATIONAL OPPORTUNITIES:

Foxwoods High Stakes Bingo & Casino
Rt. 2, Box 410
Ledyard, CT 06339
(800) PLAY BIG or (203) 885-3000
Provides seating for 2,400 in the bingo game room, fully equipped with concessions, no-smoking areas, wheelchair access, and plenty of parking. Casino offers more than 100 gaming tables for patrons to try their luck at poker, blackjack, roulette, dice, the Big 6 Money Wheel, baccarat, and specialty games.

Three restaurants are part of this extraordinary complex, along with entertainment lounges and a gift shop, all set under a dramatic glass-roofed atrium. Atrium space includes an exhibit "Mashantucket Pequot: A Proud Tradition" to answer visitors' questions about the tribe.

Foxwoods Bingo & Casino complex contains a deli, restaurants, and bars:

Expresso's Deli
Pequot Grill
Festival Buffet
Al Dente
Atrium Bar
Sports Bar

ACCOMMODATIONS:

Numerous lodgings along the I-95 corridor, within 20 miles of the reservation.

Paucatuck Eastern Pequot Reservation

TRIBAL PROFILE:

The Paucatuck Eastern Pequot Tribe inhabits just under 225 acres on Long and Bush Ponds. Tribal membership stands at 140, with a handful living on the reservation. The trading post is the main source of income for the tribe at this time, and most of the members live and work off the reservation. The tribe is working to improve its economic base and bring more members back to tribal lands, one project being a housing grant to create more housing, as well as jobs.

LOCATION:

Southeastern Connecticut; attractive coastal region near Long Island Sound. Just north of I-95 on Hwy 117.

ADDRESS:

Paucatuck Eastern Pequot Tribe
935 Lantern Hill Rd.
Ledyard, CT 06339
(203) 572-9899

SPECIAL EVENTS:

Pequot Harvest Moon Pow Wow
North Stonington, CT
(203) 572-9899
Arts and crafts, Native American foods, dancing and drumming in North Stonington; sponsored by Conn. River Pow Wow Society. Held Columbus Day weekend. Off Hwy 95 at Exit 92.

RECREATIONAL OPPORTUNITIES:

Fishing and camping are plentiful around Long Pond and Bush Pond.

BUSINESSES & INDUSTRIES:

Leaping Deer Trading Post
Paucatuck Pequot Indian Reservation
Lantern Hill Rd.
(203) 572-7770
Selling bait and tackle. Open during fishing season.

Paugussett Golden Hill Reservation

TRIBAL PROFILE:

The Paugussett Golden Hill Tribe has two reservations, one-quarter acre of land near Nichols in the Bridgeport area, and 107 acres in Colchester. The tribe is state-recognized and was historically part of the Wappinger Confederacy. A small tribe that has been scattered about the state, Golden Hill has no tourism at this time. Nichols is north of Bridgeport and the Merritt Parkway at the junction of Shelton Road and Hwy 108.

Paugussett Golden Hill Tribe
427 Shelton Road
Nichols, CT 06111

Schaghticoke Reservation

TRIBAL PROFILE:

The Schaghticoke is a state-recognized tribe in the process of reorganization. According to the state, the tribe has about 278 acres on the Housatonic River in western Connecticut south of Kent, just off US 7.

Schaghticoke Tribe
626 Washington Road
Woodbury, CT 06798

Florida

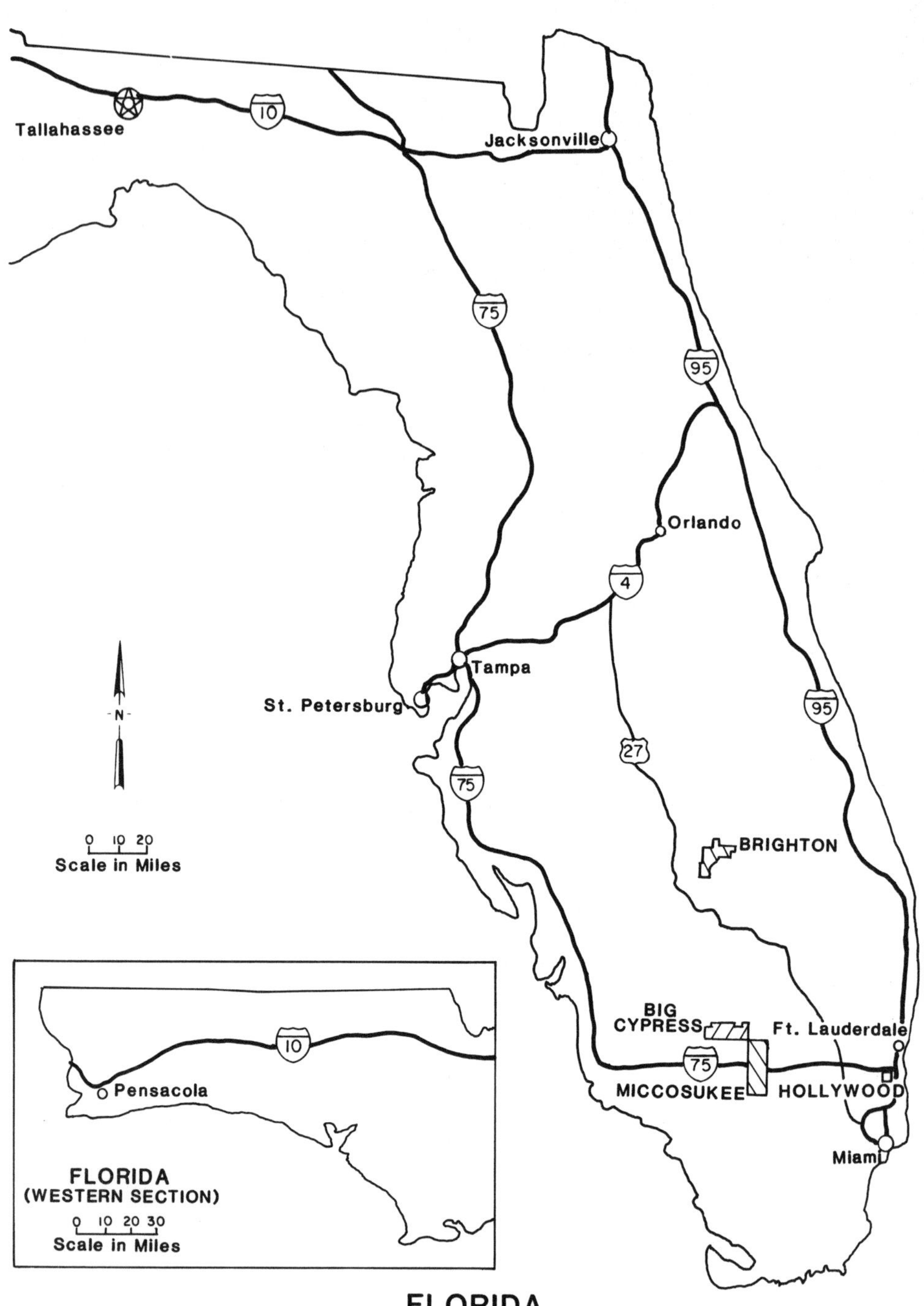
Tallahassee
10
Jacksonville
75
95
Orlando
4
Tampa
St. Petersburg
N
95
27
75
0 10 20
Scale in Miles
BRIGHTON
BIG
CYPRESS
Ft. Lauderdale
10
Pensacola
75
MICCOSUKEE
HOLLYWOOD
Miami
FLORIDA
(WESTERN SECTION)
0 10 20 30
Scale in Miles

FLORIDA

Traditional Chickee. Courtesy of Andexler Photography/Ft. Lauderdale, FL.

Miccosukee Reservation

TRIBAL PROFILE:

Federally recognized in 1962, the Miccosukee Tribe of Indians of Florida works actively to promote the well-being of its members and to preserve its cultural heritage. The Miccosukees are closely related to the Seminoles and historically were part of the Creek Confederacy. The 375 tribal members who live in Florida are descended from the few who escaped removal to Oklahoma in the 19th century. The tribe has established schools, businesses and adult education programs that enable its members to participate in contemporary American life without sacrificing their cultural heritage.

LOCATION:

South central Florida, in the Everglades. 25 miles west of Miami on the Tamiami Trail (US 41).

ADDRESS:

Miccosukee Tribe of Indians of Florida
P.O. Box 440021
Tamiami Station
Miami, FL 33144
(305) 223-8380

For more detailed directions and information on the activities and institutions listed below, call the tribal office.

CULTURAL INSTITUTIONS:

Miccosukee Culture Center and Indian Village
(305) 223-8380
(305) 223-8388 (weekends)
A living museum. Traditional-style village with craft demonstrations: woodworking, cooking, sewing. Features include amphitheater, historic displays, alligator wrestling exhibitions, and airboat tour. Tribal guides or self-guided tours. Gift shop with tribal crafts and work from other tribes.

Miccosukee Information Center
(305) 223-8388 (weekends)
Across US 41 from the Culture Center, provides information about activities in the area.

SPECIAL EVENTS:

Florida Annual Indian Arts Festival
Miccosukee Culture Center and Indian Village
More than 40 tribes gather to dance, sing, exhibit new works and perform at the Village. Held December 26 to January 2.

Annual Everglades Music and Craft Festival
Miccosukee Culture Center and Indian Village
International music: rock, reggae, blues. Held 4th weekend in July.

RECREATIONAL OPPORTUNITIES:

Airboat Rides
Piloted by skilled tribal members, 15 and 30 minute tours into the Everglades; unusual birds and animals are frequently seen. Longer tour stops at an island camp still occupied by the family who built it more than 100 years ago. Continuously every day.

BUSINESSES & INDUSTRIES:

Miccosukee Restaurant
Next door to Information Center; serves both traditional dishes and a standard menu.

ACCOMMODATIONS:

Everglades Tower Inn
(305) 559-7779
1 block from the Village.

Seminole Tribe of Florida

• Big Cypress Reservation • Brighton Reservation • Dania Reservation
• Hollywood Reservation • Immokalee Reservation

TRIBAL PROFILE:

The Seminole Tribe of Florida occupies five reservations; Big Cypress, Brighton and Dania are federal reservations, while Hollywood and Immokalee are chartered by the State of Florida. In 1953 the Seminoles organized themselves formally under the provisions of the Indian Reorganization Act of 1934. Having thus achieved the right to self-determination, they continue to be as self-sufficient as possible, fostering their own way of life to preserve their culture and traditional lifestyles.

LOCATION:

The Everglades in south-central Florida; Big Cypress is north of I-75 and accessed from the north, via Rte. 833. Brighton is northwest of Lake Okeechobee.

ADDRESS:

Seminole Tribe of Florida
3240 North 64th Avenue
Hollywood, FL 33024
(305) 584-0400

CULTURAL INSTITUTIONS:

Ah-Tha-Thi-Ki Museum
3240 North 64th Avenue
Hollywood, FL 33024
(305) 964-4882
New project, begun in 1989 to preserve and interpret the culture, language and customs of the Seminole by safeguarding timeless traditions Elders have carried into the modern world. Site includes water and land trails, and 7 buildings that combine diverse exhibit and meeting areas with resources for study, storage and conservation of the museum's collections. Attractions include a village, burial site, nature trails, pond and dock, hunting camp, canoe and airboat exhibits. Facilities include meeting rooms, theater, dining rooms and kitchen. Enter from Rte. 833.

RECREATIONAL OPPORTUNITIES:

Seminole Indian Bingo
Near the Seminole Native Village on Big Cypress. Call the tribe at (305) 584-0400 for specifics as to time, dates and cost.

Alligator Wrestler. Bill Held Photo/Hialeah, FL.

Taking pictures from jeep - Lake and village in background. Courtesy of Lee Tiger & Associates/Miami, FL. Right, deer on Billy Swamp Safari. Courtesy of Andexler Photography/Ft. Lauderdale, FL.

Billie's Swamp Safari Park and Everglades Camping Village
Everglades Wildlife Preserve
(813) 983-6101
Featuring guided wildlife safari tours in jeeps and swamp buggies through Everglades Wildlife Preserve, operated by the Seminole Tribe. Special photo safaris available. Guided bus/jeep tours include a meal and last about 5 hours or include overnight lodging in screened "chickee" structures. Evening and night packages include folkloric music shows and Indian theme dinners. RV and camp sites available. About 65 miles west of Fort Lauderdale 18 miles north of Alligator Alley Expressway (I-75) via Snake Road. Reservations can be made through Lee Tiger and Associates in Miami, (305) 257-3737.

Native Village
3551 N. State Road 7
Hollywood, FL 33021
(305) 961-4519
Reconstruction of a traditional Seminole village, presenting artisans working on traditional arts and crafts, wildlife and Everglades scenery, alligator wrestling, and snake shows. Gift shop offers hand crafted items and accepts custom orders. Special rates for large groups, for which advance reservations are needed.

Lee Tiger's World Famous Everglades Tour
Conway Tours
Miami, FL 33316
(305) 525-8100
Day-long tours leaving Miami's hotels; including an airboat ride, lunch, a tour of the Hollywood Seminole Reservation and a visit to the Native Village. Reservations can be handled by hotel bellmen or the front desk, as well as by calling Conway Tours.

Idaho

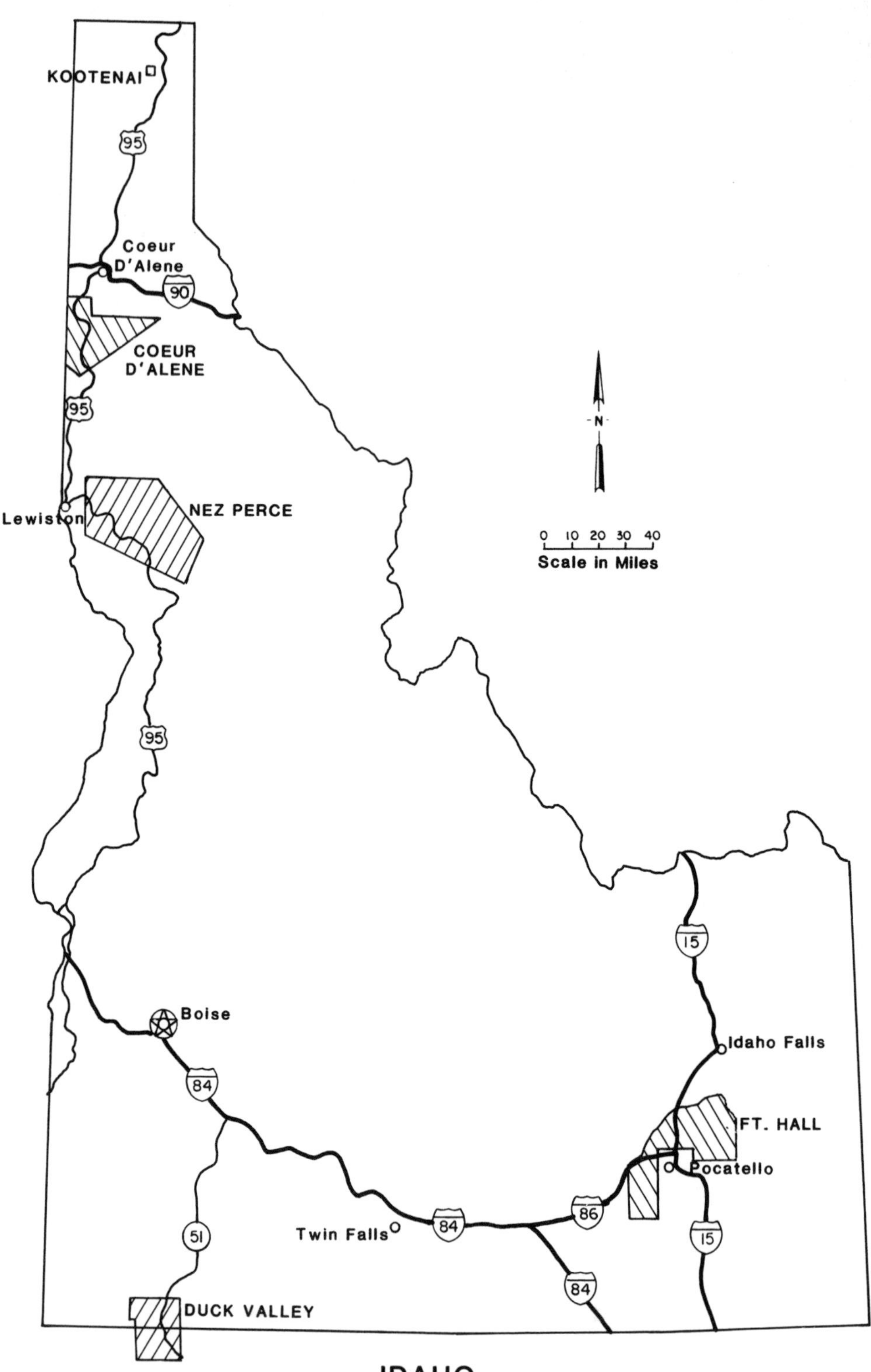

KOOTENAI
95
Coeur
D'Alene
90
COEUR
D'ALENE
95
Lewiston
NEZ PERCE
N
0 10 20 30 40
Scale in Miles
95
15
Boise
Idaho Falls
84
FT. HALL
Pocatello
86
Twin Falls
84
51
15
84
DUCK VALLEY

IDAHO

Coeur D'Alene Reservation

TRIBAL PROFILE:

The Coeur D'Alene Reservation, created by Treaty in 1858, covers about 69,300 acres in northwestern Idaho. The Coeur D'Alene Tribe was one of the 25 semi-nomadic Plateau Indian Tribes and was particularly well known for its basketry. The tribe is organized under a constitution approved in 1949, providing for a seven-member tribal council to administer business activities.

ADDRESS

Coeur D'Alene Tribal Council
Plummer, Id 83851-9704
(208) 274-3101

Duck Valley Reservation

See Nevada

Fort Hall Reservation

TRIBAL PROFILE:

The Shoshone and Bannock Indians were assigned to the Fort Hall Reservation by treaty in 1868. Originally 1.8 million acres, reservation lands have dwindled to their present 544,000. The 3,378 enrolled members elect seven council members to sit on the Fort Hall Business Council, which was formed to establish organization, promote Shoshone-Bannock welfare, conserve and develop lands and resources, and exercise self-government. Major revenues accrue from land leases, phosphate mining and a variety of tribal enterprises.

LOCATION:

Southeastern Idaho; the 2 segments of the Fort Hall Reservation lie north and west of Pocatello. Easy access from I-86 and I-15. The Snake River forms the western boundary of the reservation.

ADDRESS:

Shoshone-Bannock Tribes
Fort Hall Indian Reservation
P.O. Box 306
Fort Hall, ID 83203
(208) 238-3802

CULTURAL INSTITUTIONS:

Shoshone-Bannock Tribal Museum
Fort Hall, ID
(208) 237-9791
Holdings include contemporary and historic exhibits; small collection, rich in culture. Hours: 10:00 a.m.-7:00 p.m.

The museum manager provides school tours of the reservation April-May and to the public June-fall, excluding Sundays. Some tour packages: tour & buffalo stew dinner; tour, dinner, and dance presentation by Shoshone-Bannock dancers. Reservations recommended.

SPECIAL EVENTS:

Fort Bridger Treaty Day
Fort Hall, ID
(208) 238-3802
Commemoration of the treaty between the Shoshone-Bannock and the U.S.; racing activities, dancing. Held throughout the reservation in early July. Admission fee.

Shoshone-Bannock Annual Indian Festival & Rodeo
Fort Hall, ID
(208) 238-3888
This 5-day traditional celebration of culture and sports draws 25,000 guests. Pow wow and festival with rodeos, softball tourneys, music, Indian handgames, intertribal dancing, beauty pageants, 5-K and 12-K races, and parades. Teams from all over come to compete in the exciting Indian Relay. August 6-9. General admission fee.

RECREATIONAL OPPORTUNITIES:

Shoshone-Bannock Bingo
P.O. Box 868
Fort Hall, ID 83203
(208) 237-8774
Contact the bingo office for times and days of operation. Near the trading post complex; take I-15, Exit 80 and drive 1/4-west on Simplot Rd.

Camping: Tepee encampment is available on the festival grounds.

ARCHAEOLOGICAL & HISTORIC SITES:

Old Fort Hall Monument, The Oregon Trail, & Fort Hall Bottoms: Fort Hall Bottoms holds evidence of Shoshone-Bannock occupations 3,000 years ago. In order to view these historic sites, a trespass permit must be requested from the Fort Hall Business Council 1 to 2 months in advance.

BUSINESSES & INDUSTRIES:

Fort Hall Trading Post Complex
Fort Hall, ID 83203
(208) 237-8433
Arts and crafts stores specializing in gorgeous beadwork and buckskin goods, as well as the Oregon Trail Restaurant, post office, credit union, gas station, supermarket, and deli.

Dressed for Festival. Courtesy of John Running.

Oregon Trail Restaurant
Fort Hall
(208) 237-0472
Off I-15, Exit 80.

Clothes Horse
Trading Post Complex
(208) 237-8433.
Features western wear and a large display of contemporary arts and crafts of the Shoshone-Bannocks; handmade, one of a kind items mainly in beadwork and leatherwork. Arts and crafts catalogue available.

ACCOMMODATIONS:

Closest hotel/motel lodgings are in Blackfoot or Pocatello.

Kootenai Reservation

Tribal Profile:

The Kootenai Indian Reservation is approximately 300 acres and serves as headquarters for the Kootenai Tribe of Idaho, with an enrollment of about 100. One of the many Plateau Tribes that traditionally fished and hunted the area now divided into Washington, Oregon and Idaho, the Kootenai are widely known for their outstanding basketry techniques and horsemanship.

Location:

Northernmost tip of the Idaho panhandle, about 30 miles south of the U.S./Canadian border. Just off US 95, 10 miles from Bonners Ferry. This is a region filled with numerous recreational opportunities, summer and winter.

Address:

Kootenai Tribe of Idaho
County Road 38A
P.O. Box 1269
Bonners Ferry, ID 83805
(208) 267-3519

Special Event:

Kootenai Tribe of Idaho Pow Wow
Three-day pow wow that includes war dance and stick game tourneys. Held 2nd week of June.

Accommodations:

Best Western Kootenai River Inn
Springs Restaurant
Eagle Springs Gift Shop
Kootenai River Plaza
Bonners Ferry, ID 83805
(208) 267-8511

Nez Perce Reservation

Tribal Profile:

Lewis and Clark met the Nez Perce Indians when they traveled through the Northwest. The Nez Perce signed their first treaty with the U.S. in 1855. The Nez Perce Reservation's present size was established by treaty in 1877; it covers approximately 87,500 acres and is home to the Nez Perce Tribe of Idaho. Tribal enrollment is about 3,000, and 1,800 members live on the reservation, working for the B.I.A. or Indian Health Service, the tribe, in the timber industry or fisheries. The tribe operates under a constitution that was approved in 1958, allowing for a nine-member tribal executive committee. The Nez Perce are well-known for breeding the famous Appaloosa horses.

Location:

Northwestern Idaho, near the Washington-Oregon border, just east of Lewiston; US 95 runs through the reservation from north to south. US 12, the Lewis and Clark Highway, also crosses the reservation.

Address:

Nez Perce Tribe of Idaho
P.O. Box 305
Lapwai, ID 83540
(208) 843-2253

Special Events:

For detailed directions and information on the activities listed below, call the Recreation Department at (208) 843-2253.

Mat-Al-Ym'a Pow Wow and Root Feast
Kamiah, ID
Thanksgiving festival to offer thanks to the Great Spirit for the roots that once formed such an important part of the Nez Perce diet. Traditional dancing. Generally the 3rd weekend of May; depends on seasonal development of the roots.

Chief Joseph and Warriors Memorial Pow Wow
Lapwai, ID
Honors the famed Nez Perce chief and his warriors. Held 3rd week in June.

Top, White Bird Battlefield. Courtesy of Nez Perce National Historic Park.

Left, Ladies riding Appaloosas. Courtesy of Chief Joseph Foundation.

Looking Glass Pow Wow
Kamiah, ID
Looking Glass was another famed Nez Perce leader who lost his life in the Nez Perce War of 1877. Dancing and singing honor him. Held 3rd or 4th week in September.

ARCHAEOLOGICAL & HISTORIC SITES:

Nez Perce National Historic Park:
24 sites located on the Nez Perce Reservation and surrounding north central Idaho that tell the story of the Nez Perce Tribe; touring all of them is a trip of about 400 miles. Operated by the National Park Service under an agreement with the Tribe. On the reservation are Park Headquarters and Visitor Center and several historic sites at Spalding; also Lenore Archeological Site, inhabited by the Nez Perce and their ancestors for about 10,000 years; Canoe Camp, where Lewis and Clark built dugout canoes; and Clearwater Battlefield, where General O.O. Howard was unable to defeat the Nez Perce in 1877. For further information contact: Nez Perce National Historic Park, P.O. Box 93, Spalding, ID 83551, (208) 843-2261.

TRIBAL ORGANIZATIONS:

Nez Perce Appaloosa Horse Club
P.O. Box 88
Spalding, ID 83551
Formed to care for 15 Appaloosas donated to the tribe by a breeder in New Mexico. The intent is to reunite the tribe with the breed of horses they developed centuries ago.

BUSINESSES & INDUSTRIES:

Donalds Valley Foods
Sells native crafts as well as groceries.

The Nez Perce Express
2 convenience stores; in Kamiah and at the reservation border near Lewiston.

ACCOMMODATIONS:

Lodging available in Lewiston.

Iowa

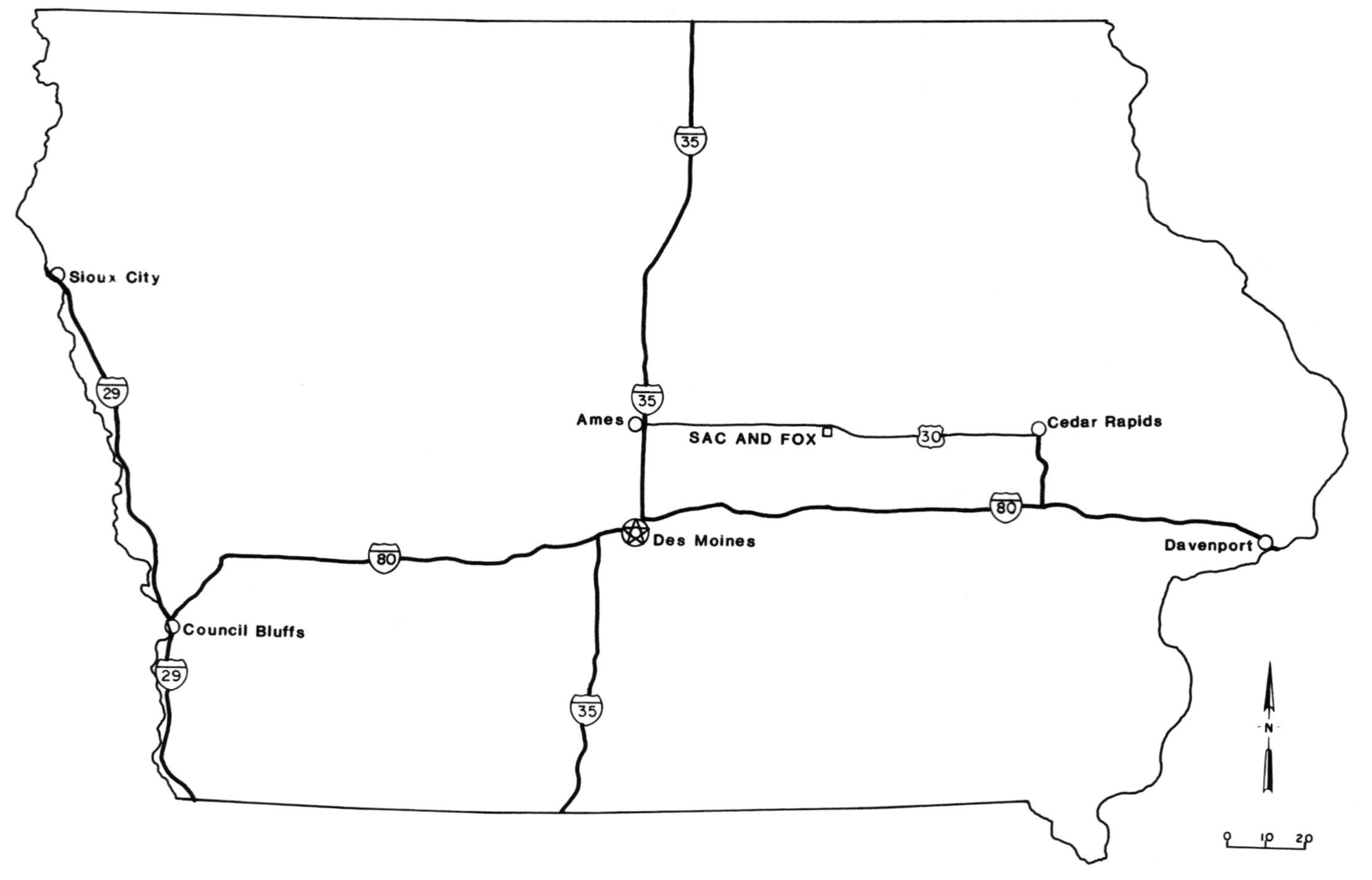
Sioux City
29
35
Ames
35
SAC AND FOX
30
Cedar Rapids
80
Des Moines
Davenport
80
Council Bluffs
29
35
N
0 10 20
IOWA

Sac & Fox Settlement (Reservation)

TRIBAL PROFILE:

The Sac and Fox Tribes, also known as Mesquakie and Osakiwug, were woodland tribes who united in the late 1700s; both are now situated in Iowa, Kansas, and Oklahoma. The first purchase of land, an 80 acre tract, was made in 1856, and with additional acreage it was placed in trust by the U.S. government in 1896. Today all 3,485 acres are owned in common by the 1,026 member tribe, which is governed by a seven member council under a constitution adopted in 1937. Farm leases and gaming provide the main source of revenues; the tribe has also formed an enterprise corporation to plan, direct and organize development on tribal lands. Arts and crafts pursued today include ribbonwork, silverwork, weaving, and the Sac and Fox are well known for their beautiful beadwork.

LOCATION:

East central Iowa between Marshalltown and Cedar Rapids; on a county road near the junction of US 30 and US 63. The Iowa River bisects the reservation.

ADDRESS:

Sac & Fox Tribe
Sac & Fox Tribal Office
Rte. 2, Box 56C
Tama, IA 52339
(515) 484-4678, -5358

SPECIAL EVENTS:

Mesquakie Annual Celebration
Bureau of Indian Affairs Bldg.
Sac & Fox Settlement
Traditional pow wow activities and arts and crafts sales. 2nd weekend in August, running Thursday-Sunday.

RECREATIONAL OPPORTUNITIES:

Mesquakie Bingo
Sac & Fox Settlement
Tama, IA
(515) 484-2108
Doors open 5:00 p.m. Monday, Thursday, and Friday; Saturday, 4:00 p.m.; Sunday at noon.

Fishing & Hunting: Check with the tribal office regarding fishing, hunting, and camping on or around the Iowa River.

ACCOMMODATIONS:

Budget Inn Motel
Hwy 30
Toledo, IA
515-484-2305

Foley's Motel
Hwy 30, east
Tama, IA
(515) 484-3148

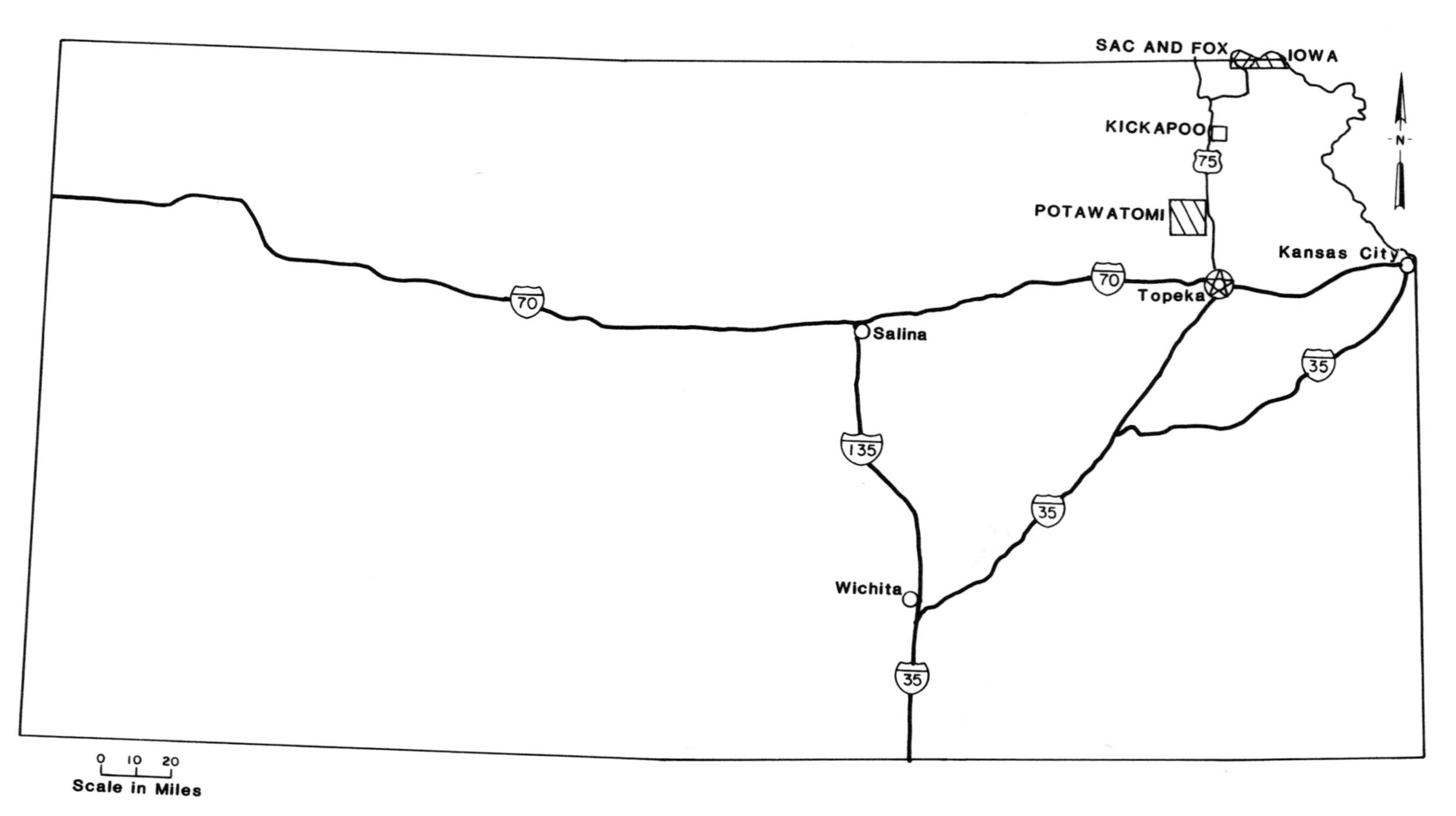
SAC AND FOX
IOWA
KICKAPOO
75
POTAWATOMI
N
Kansas City
Topeka
70
70
Salina
135
35
35
Wichita
35
0 10 20
Scale in Miles

KANSAS

Iowa Reservation

Tribal Profile:

The Iowa Reservation was originally established by Treaty of 1836 and has a total land area today of 1,378 acres. Approximately half of the tribally owned land is assigned to individuals in the 1,500 member Iowa Tribe. In 1937 the tribe adopted a constitution and bylaws creating an executive committee to administer in all areas of governmental responsibility. Income derives mainly from agriculture.

Iowa Tribal Bingo Hall. Courtesy of Iowa Tribe of Kansas & Nebraska.

Location:

The Kansas/Nebraska border splits the reservation, which is flanked on the east by the Missouri River and on the west by the Sac and Fox Reservation. White Cloud is on Rte. 7, about 70 miles northeast of Topeka and 40 miles northwest of St. Joseph, MO.

Address:

Iowa Tribe of Kansas & Nebraska
P.O. Box 58A
Rural Rte. #1
White Cloud, KS 66094
(913) 595-3258

Cultural Institutions:

The tribe is in the process of establishing an historical museum.

Special Events:

Chief White Cloud Annual Rodeo
A IPRA and URA approved event. Held in June.

All Encampment Pow Wow
An inter-tribal event featuring open competition and prizes. Held in September.

Recreational Opportunities:

Iowa Tribal Bingo
(913) 595-6640
Offering prizes ranging from $300-500, as well as a $500 door prize on week-end evenings. Open Thursday through Saturday starting at 6:30 p.m.; Sunday doors open at 12:30 p.m. Restaurant on premises, open every day.

Fishing & Hunting: With the Missouri River as its eastern boundary, the reservation offers an abundance of fishing and hunting. Possibilities for game include turkey, whitetail deer, rabbits, quail, and pheasants. Contact the Tribal Office for permission to hunt and fish and for fee schedules.

Businesses & Industries:

Flaky Mills
(913) 595-3201
A grain processing plant making corn flakes. Contact the plant manager to arrange tours.

Ioway Nation Grain Co.
Craig, MO
Grain elevator.

The Grandview Oil Co.
White Cloud, KS
Filling station and tire shop.

Kickapoo Reservation

Tribal Profile:

The Kickapoo Tribe of Kansas numbers 1,500 members with 450 reservation residents. The Kickapoo originally were settled on a reservation in Missouri but petitioned for new lands in Kansas, settling there in 1832. The original Kansas allotment was 678,000 acres; in 1854 reservation lands were reduced and allotted in 1862, today covering 5,000 acres. Tribal government, organized under the I.R.A., is led by seven elected council members; Kickapoo government is the largest employer on the reservation, along with the BIA School.

Location:

Situated 50 miles north of Topeka, the Kickapoo Reservation is on US 75. The Delaware River flows through the heart of the Reservation.

Address:

Kickapoo of Kansas Tribal Council
Rte. 1, Box 157A
Horton, KS 66439
(913) 486-2131

Special Events:

Annual Youth Pow Wow
Kickapoo Pow Wow Grounds
In honor of American Indian Day. Held in September.

Recreational Opportunities:

Casino: Under development.

Fishing and Hunting: Bird and deer hunting, as well as fishing and camping, around the Delaware River. Contact the tribal office for details regarding permits.

Businesses & Industries:

The tribe maintains an 80-head buffalo herd on KS Hwy 20; buffalo meat is available for purchase.

Buffalo Cafe
(913) 486-3562

Kickapoo Trading Post
(913) 486-2907
Offering traditional arts and crafts.

Potawatomi Reservation

Tribal Profile:

The Prairie Band of the Potawatomi lives on the 11- square mile Potawatomi Reservation established by Treaty in 1864; almost 20,000 acres are held in trust. The Tribe almost 4,000 enrolled members, 610 of whom live on the reservation. The main sources of income on the reservation are the bingo operation and tribal administration, and many residents are employed in Topeka. Tribal income derives also from land lease revenues.

Location:

Due north of Topeka and I-70 in northeastern Kansas, the reservation is west of US 75, just outside of Mayetta.

Address:

Potawatomi Tribe
Rte. 2, Box 50A
Mayetta, KS 66509
(913) 966-2255

Special Events:

Annual Pow Wow
Held Thanksgiving weekend.

Recreational Opportunities:

Potawatomi Bingo
Mayetta, KS
(913) 966-2375
Offering bingo Thursday through Sunday all year round. Call for specific times.

A buffalo herd. Photo by Chris Ribera. Courtesy of the Southern Ute Tribe.

Businesses & Industries:

The tribe keeps a small buffalo herd near tribal headquarters.

Tribal Organizations:

Potawatomi Activity Club
This cultural organization sponsors pow wows.

Sac and Fox Reservation

Tribal Profile:

Established under treaty in 1861, the reservation is home to the Sac and Fox Tribes, joined together by political alliance in the early 1700s. Tribal enrollment stands at approximately 300, with a small percentage living on tribal lands. Agriculture forms the main portion of their economic base.

Location:

Near the Missouri River, Reserve is 3 miles south of the Nebraska/Kansas state line off US 73. Sac and Fox territory stretches across the border into Nebraska; the western boundary adjoins the Iowa Nation of Kansas and Nebraska Reservation.

Address:

Sac & Fox Tribe of Missouri
Rte. 1, Box 60
Reserve, KS 66434
(913) 742-7471

Cultural Institutions:

Iowa Sac and Fox Mission Museum
Highland, KS
(913) 442-3304
Collection includes artifacts from the Sac and Fox Tribes and the Iowa Tribe. Run by the State of Kansas.

Businesses & Industries:

Sac & Fox Tradin' Post
Rte. 1, Box 60
Reserve, KS 66434
(913) 742-7472
Gas station and smokeshop. Next door to the tribal office.

Accommodations:

Camping and motels around Hiawatha, KS.

Louisiana

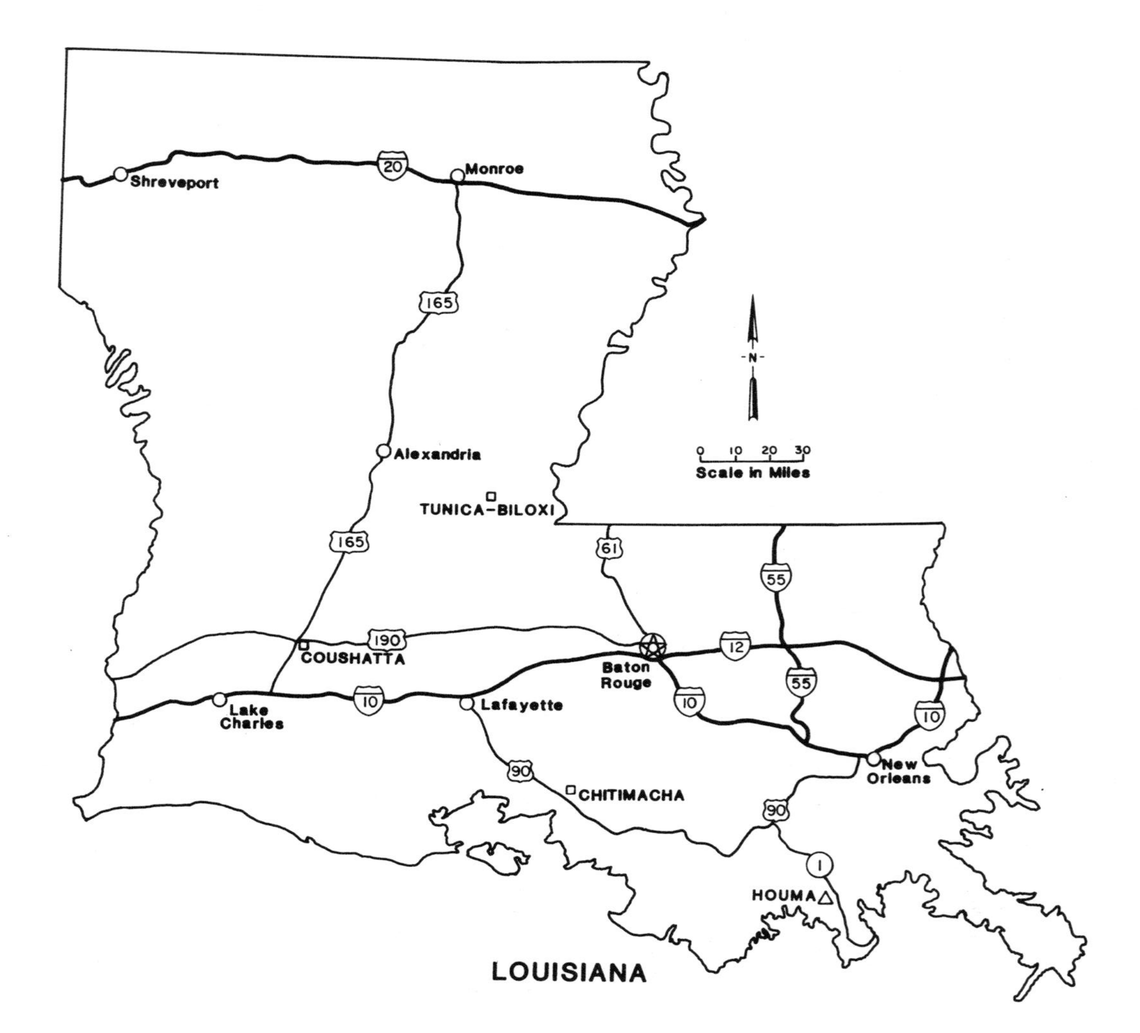

Shreveport
20
Monroe
165
Alexandria
TUNICA-BILOXI
165
N
0 10 20 30
Scale in Miles
61
55
190
COUSHATTA
12
Baton Rouge
55
10
Lake Charles
Lafayette
10
10
New Orleans
90
CHITIMACHA
90
1
HOUMA
LOUISIANA

Chitimacha Reservation

Tribal Profile:

Recognized by both federal and state governments, the Chitimacha Tribe resides on a 283 acre reservation in south-central Louisiana that has been held in trust by the federal government since 1935. Membership of the Chitimacha Tribe stands at 640, with 350 living on the reservation. Income for Chitimacha people stems mainly from tribal employment , commercial fishing and work in oil fields. The tribe is known for its fine cane baskets.

Location:

Southern Louisiana. Charenton is on Hwy 326, southeast of Lafayette off US 90. The reservation is just west of Grand Lake.

Address:

Chitimacha Tribe
P.O. Box 661
Charenton, LA 70523
(318) 923-7215

Cultural Institutions:

Visitors Center
Tribal Office Complex
(318) 923-7215

Chitimacha Unit of Jean Lafitte National Historic Park
(318) 923-4830
Includes a museum with video on history of tribe, as well as a gift shop selling Chitimacha baskets, pottery. Open weekdays 8:00 a.m.-4:30 p.m.; weekends 9:00 a.m.-5:00 p.m.

Recreational Opportunities:

Chitimacha Bayouland Bingo Hall
(318) 923-7284 or (800) 284-4386
Open Wednesday and Saturday; every day for tours. Call ahead to arrange large group tours.

Camping: Roadside tables, picnic areas, and a playground next to the Visitors Center. Contact museum at Jean Lafitte Historic Park for camping information.

Fishing: Plentiful opportunities on Grand Lake and other nearby waterways.

Businesses & Industries:

Trading Post
(318) 923-7487

Chitimacha Craft Shop
318) 923-7547

Crafts by Nix
(318) 923-4222
Selling crafts including beadwork and jewelry; Indian story teller.

Dee Dee's Gift Shop
(318) 923-7998

L & L Crafts & Collectibles
(318) 923-7526

Chitimacha Charenton Fire Dept.
(318) 923-4326

Chitimacha Seafood
(318) 923-7218
Processing plant selling crawfish and crabs, when in season. Contact plant owner in advance to arrange for tour.

Accommodations:

Lodgings available in Franklin, 10 miles east.

(L) Social dances at Coushatta Pow Wow. (R) Full regalia for pow wow. Photos courtesy of Coushatta Tribe of Louisiana.

Coushatta Reservation

TRIBAL PROFILE:

The Coushatta Reservation opened to the public in 1991 for the first time in 200 years. About 570 tribal members live on the 233-acre state reservation. Widely known for pine needle basketry, the Coushatta strive to preserve their traditions and customs. The tribe's goal to is to be self-sufficient by the year 2000. To meet that mandate, the tribe plans to purchase 250 acres for a casino complex with bingo rooms, restaurants, and other amenities. A convenience store, gift shop, restaurant and custom clothing shop were recently opened.

LOCATION:

Southwestern Louisiana, southeast of Lake Charles, in the heart of Cajun country. North of I-10, near junction of US 190 and Hwy 26, 3 miles north of Elton.

ADDRESS:

Coushatta Tribe of Louisiana
P.O. Box 818
Elton, LA 70532
(318) 584-2261

CULTURAL INSTITUTIONS:

Coushatta Tribe Visitors Center & Museum
Coushatta Reservation
(318) 584-2261
Tribal history and culture exhibits. Tribal dances, foods, and crafts demonstrations; check for scheduling. Gift shop offers crafts and other handmade goods. Open Monday-Saturday 9:00 a.m.-5:00 p.m. Admission fee.

SPECIAL EVENTS:

Coushatta Pow Wow
Coushatta Reservation
Dance contest, and booths offering Native American art, crafts and foods. Call Public Relations (318-584-2249) for details and location. Held last weekend in September.

BUSINESSES & INDUSTRIES:

Bayou Indian Enterprise
P.O. Box 668
Elton, LA 70532
(318) 584-2653
Arts, crafts, and collectibles from local artisans as well as other tribes; working to promote Coushatta and other Indian tribal crafts. In downtown Elton. Hours: 9:00 a.m.-5:00 p.m., Monday-Saturday.

Coushatta Convenience Store
(318) 584-2260

Coushatta Custom Clothing
T-shirts, caps, sweatshirts, custom-design dresses and T-shirt dresses. Between the Health Dept. and the Visitors Center.

Pineywood Restaurant
(318) 584-2247
Indian fry bread and tacos, Cajun-style cooking.

ACCOMMODATIONS:

Lodgings nearest the reservation are in Jennings.

Houma Reservation

Tribal Profile:

The Houma Nation spreads over five parishes in southeast Louisiana. The largest community is in Dulac. The Nation has revived traditional Houma crafts, songs and dances.

Location:

Tribal headquarters in Golden Meadow is on Hwy 1, south of New Orleans and a few miles from the Gulf of Mexico, numerous bays, inlets, and wildlife refuges. Dulac is on Rte. 57, next to Lake Boudreaux and directly west of Golden Meadow.

Address:

Houma Nation
Star Rte. Box 95-A
Golden Meadow, LA 70357
(504) 475-6640

Cultural Institutions:

Indian Crafts Cooperative
Dulac, LA

Special Events:

Contact the main office (504-475-6640) for information on events occurring in the individual parishes.

Annual Festival
Houma Air Base
Features a pow wow and crafts. Held Labor Day weekend.

Recreational Opportunities:

In the heart of bayou country, the reservation offers excellent fishing; contact the main office for details.

Accommodations:

Lodgings are available in the town of Houma.

Tunica-Biloxi Reservation

Tribal Profile:

The Tunica-Biloxi Indian Tribe is descended from the Mound People and actively works to retain its cultural heritage and crafts. The tribe achieved federal recognition in 1981; its members live on the 134 acre Tunica-Biloxi Reservation. The Tunica-Biloxi government is led by a seven-member council elected by the enrolled members, a total of about 440 individuals.

Location:

East-central Louisiana; Marksville is southeast of Alexandria, 25 miles west of the Mississippi River. Hwy 1 passes north-south through town, east of I-49. The reservation is 1/4 mile south of Marksville.

Address:

Tunica-Biloxi Tribe
P.O. Box 331
Marksville, LA 71351
(318) 253-9767

Cultural Institutions:

Tunica-Biloxi Regional Indian Center & Museum
(318) 253-8174
Houses a spectacular collection of Indian and European artifacts from the Colonial period returned to the tribe under the Indian Graves and Repatriation Act. The museum is built like a mound in the traditional style and holds a tribal library and learning center in addition to the museum. Offers visitors walking and bus tours, as well as instruction in traditional crafts such as basket weaving. Just off Hwy 1 across from the Tribal Center. Open 8:00 a.m. to 4:30 p.m., Tuesday through Saturday.

Special Events:

Corn Festival
Major occasion for the tribe; held in July.

Accommodations:

Lodgings nearby in Marksville.

Maine

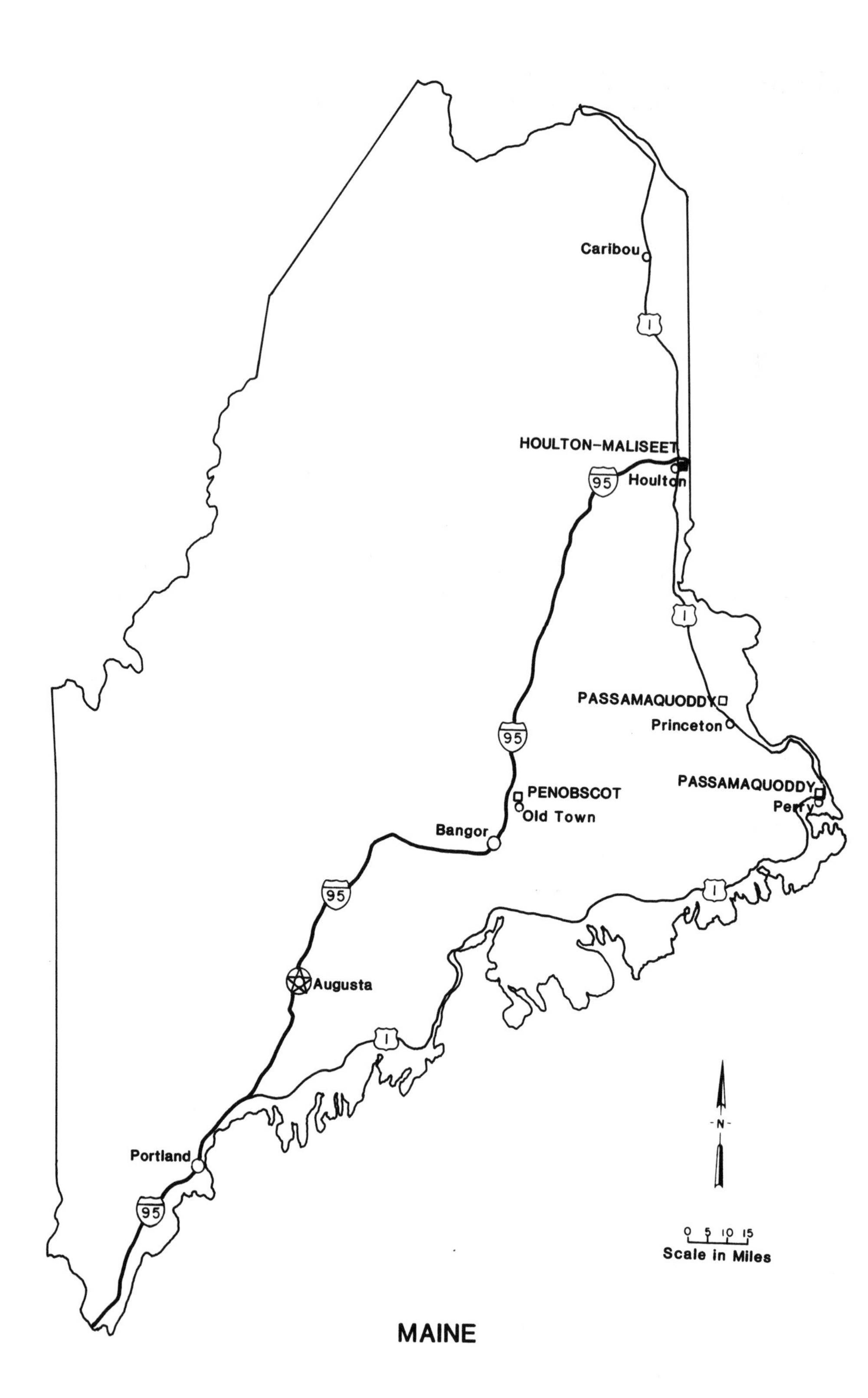

Caribou
HOULTON-MALISEET
Houlton
PASSAMAQUODDY
Princeton
PASSAMAQUODDY
Perry
PENOBSCOT
Old Town
Bangor
Augusta
Portland
95
1
N
0 5 10 15
Scale in Miles

MAINE

Houlton Band of Maliseet

Tribal Profile:

Located in northeastern Maine, the Houlton Band of Maliseet Indians is divided between the United States and Canada. Council headquarters is in Houlton, at the intersection of I-95 and US 1.

Address:

Houlton Band of Maliseet Council
P.O. Box 748-Bell Rd.
Houlton, ME 04730
(207) 532-4273

Cultural Institutions:

Passamaquoddy-Maliseet Bilingual Program
Box 295
Perry, ME 04667
(207) 853-4045
Developing text books in Passamaquoddy and English, teaching culture and history. Publications for sale.

Businesses & Industries:

Several tribal members create traditional ash basketry; please contact the tribal office for names and addresses.

Indian Township Reservation

Tribal Profile:

Indian Township Reservation covers 23,000 acres and is home to approximately 350 members of this band of the Passamaquoddy Tribe. The reservation has evolved into two communities, one at Princeton and the other at Peter Dana Point, with Calais serving as an economic center. A landmark decision in 1980, the Maine Indian Settlement Act, resolved an eight-year legal dispute involving the Passamaquoddy Tribe, the Penobscot Nation, and the United States. This Act compensated the two Indian groups for the loss of 12 million acres of land. The monies awarded have greatly enhanced the economic welfare of the Passamaquoddy.

Location:

Eastern Maine, near the New Brunswick border. Princeton is on US Hwy 1. Reservation is about 6 miles north of town.

Address:

Passamaquoddy Tribe
P.O. Box 301
Princeton, ME 04667
(207) 796-2301

Cultural Institutions:

Wabanaki Museum & Resource Center
Pleasant Point, ME 04668
(207) 853-4001
See Pleasant Point Reservation for details.

Special Events:

Indian Days
This Indian festival offers arts and crafts sales and sporting events. Held 4th of July weekend or 1st weekend in July.

Recreational Opportunities:

Indian Township Recreational Center
Rte. 1
Indian Township
Princeton, ME
(207) 796-2664
Amenities include 10-lane bowling alley, indoor swimming pool, sauna, jacuzzi, fitness center, and weight room.

Camping: Tribe owns a campground known to the Passamaquoddy as the "Pit." Contact the tribal office for location and details.

Businesses & Industries:

Longacre Enterprises, Inc.
P.O. Box 196
Old Eastport Rd.
Perry, ME 04667
(207) 853-2762
Offering traditional splint and sweet grass baskets. Open seasonally, by appointment.

Accommodations:

Minku Lodge
Indian Township
Princeton, ME
(207) 796-2701
Restaurant and cabins. Open year round.

Micmac Tribe

Tribal Profile:

Recently recognized by the federal government, the Micmac Tribe resides in portions of Maine and Canada; it is a large Northeastern tribe with over 12,000 members. There are sizable communities of Maine Micmac Indians in Houlton and Presque Isle.

Location:

Northeastern Maine; I-95 ends at the Canadian border, extending 1 mile beyond Houlton and US 1, which continues north through Presque Isle.

Address:

Aroostook Micmac Council, Inc.
P.O. Box 772
Presque Isle, ME 04769
(207) 764-1972

Businesses & Industries:

Basket Bank
Aroostook Micmac Council, Inc.
521-D Main St.
Presque Isle, ME 04769
(207) 764-7667
Selling many sizes and styles of baskets. Open 8:00 a.m.-4:00 p.m. Monday-Friday, year round. Special and mail order accepted.

Pleasant Point Reservation

Tribal Profile:

Pleasant Point Reservation was created by the Commonwealth of Massachusetts for the Passamaquoddy Tribe, and treaty obligations were assumed by the state of Maine in 1820. Situated in the eastern-most county in the U.S., the Passamaquoddy Tribe at Pleasant Point lives on approximately 100 acres in a region abundant with both freshwater and saltwater life and products. The tribe's main source of revenue is through timber sales. With the assistance of a writing system developed by MIT, the Passamaquoddy people now can write their language in a 17 character alphabet, and many books, tapes and dictionaries exist to help preserve the language and culture for future generations.

Location:

On US 1 on the rugged coast due east of Bangor, Pleasant Point Reservation is just outside the town of Perry, near the border with New Brunswick, Canada.

Address:

Passamaquoddy Tribe
Pleasant Point Tribal Government
P.O. Box 343
Perry, ME 04667
(207) 853-2551

CULTURAL INSTITUTIONS:

Wabanaki Museum & Resource Center
P.O. Box 295
Perry, ME 04667
(207) 853-4001
The museum collection includes Indian artifacts from the region, including old baskets, tools for basket making and a 17-foot birch-bark canoe; historical photographs; and mannequins modelled after reservation residents, created by the Augusta State Historical Museum. Open Monday-Friday 8:00 a.m.-4:00 p.m. Tours of the museum are given if reservations are made in advance.

SPECIAL EVENTS:

Sipayik Ceremonial Day
Community Building
Perry, ME
People come from throughout the state to participate in this Indian pow wow and sporting event. Activities include a pageant, walkathon, 5-mile run, 3-mile run, 1-mile family fun run, archery and horseshoe pitching contests, arts and crafts, traditional Indian meal, and a social with sacred fire, drumming and chanting. Chemical free; donation requested. Held 2nd weekend of August, beginning Saturday at 11:00 a.m.

BUSINESSES & INDUSTRIES:

Sipayik Super Saver
Route 190
Perry, ME
Grocery store.

ACCOMMODATIONS:

Bed & breakfast inn, motels, and camping all in nearby Eastport.

Penobscot Reservation

TRIBAL PROFILE:

Penobscot Nation Reservation lands total 4,446 acres, covering 146 islands in the Penobscot River, and were part of the Nation's original domain. Indian Island, the location of tribal headquarters, is the only island occupied year-round on a consistent basis. One of many tribes that never negotiated with the federal government, the Penobscot Nation established treaties with various colonial administrations and was acknowledged by Maine upon its statehood in 1820. Traditionally semi-nomadic, the Penobscot were adept at hunting, fishing, trapping, and canoeing. Many skills associated with the processing and use of animal products became highly developed, along with expertise in pipe carving, quill and bead work. Some traditional arts continue today.

LOCATION:

Indian Island is in the middle of Penobscot River across from Old Town in east-central Maine. 16 miles north of Bangor on US 2; off I-95, east on Hwy 43.

ADDRESS:

Penobscot Nation
Community Building
6 River Road
Indian Island, ME 04468
(207) 827-7776

CULTURAL INSTITUTIONS:

Indian Island Museum: Closed pending funding for operations. Contact the tribal office for status.

RECREATIONAL OPPORTUNITIES:

Penobscot Indian Bingo
6 River Road
Indian Island Community Building
(207) 827-7750 or (800) 255-1293
Games include Bonanza and Super Jackpot Coverall, door prizes, and up to $1,200 instantly with pull tabs. Sometimes held in the Sockalexis Arena, 4 miles off I-95, Exit 52. Saturday and Sunday; doors open at 9:00 a.m., games begin at noon. Accepts MC/Visa.

ARCHAEOLOGICAL & HISTORIC SITES:

St. Ann's Roman Catholic Church: Built around 1827, St. Ann's is the 3rd church on this site; possibly the 2nd oldest existing catholic church in New England. On the island, 1/8-mile from the church, is the oldest Catholic cemetery in New England with some pre-historic grave sites. Near the foot of the bridge from Old Town to the island. For further information contact: St. Ann's Roman Catholic Church, Indian Island, ME 04468, (207) 827-2172.

BUSINESSES & INDUSTRIES:

Chief Poolaw Tepee Trading Post
88 Main Street
Old Town, ME 04468
(207) 827-8674
Offering Penobscot sweet grass baskets, moccasins, beadwork, and wood carvings, along with crafts by other tribes. Send a stamped, self-addressed envelope for mail order information. Open Monday-Saturday 10:00 a.m.-5:00 p.m.; Sunday, 10:00 a.m.-3:00 p.m.

Indian Island Take-Out
Indian Island, ME
(207) 827-6801
Fast food restaurant.

Waponahki Arts
Indian Island
P.O. Box 453
Old Town, ME 04468
(207) 827-3447
Traditional Penobscot arts and crafts. Mail orders accepted. Hours vary; call ahead.

Olamon Industries
(207) 827-7776
Manufacturing audio cassettes. Tours by arrangement.

Some individuals sell arts and crafts out of their homes.

ACCOMMODATIONS:

Maine is renowned for its tourism opportunities; many hotels, motels, and bed and breakfasts are available throughout the region.

Massachusetts

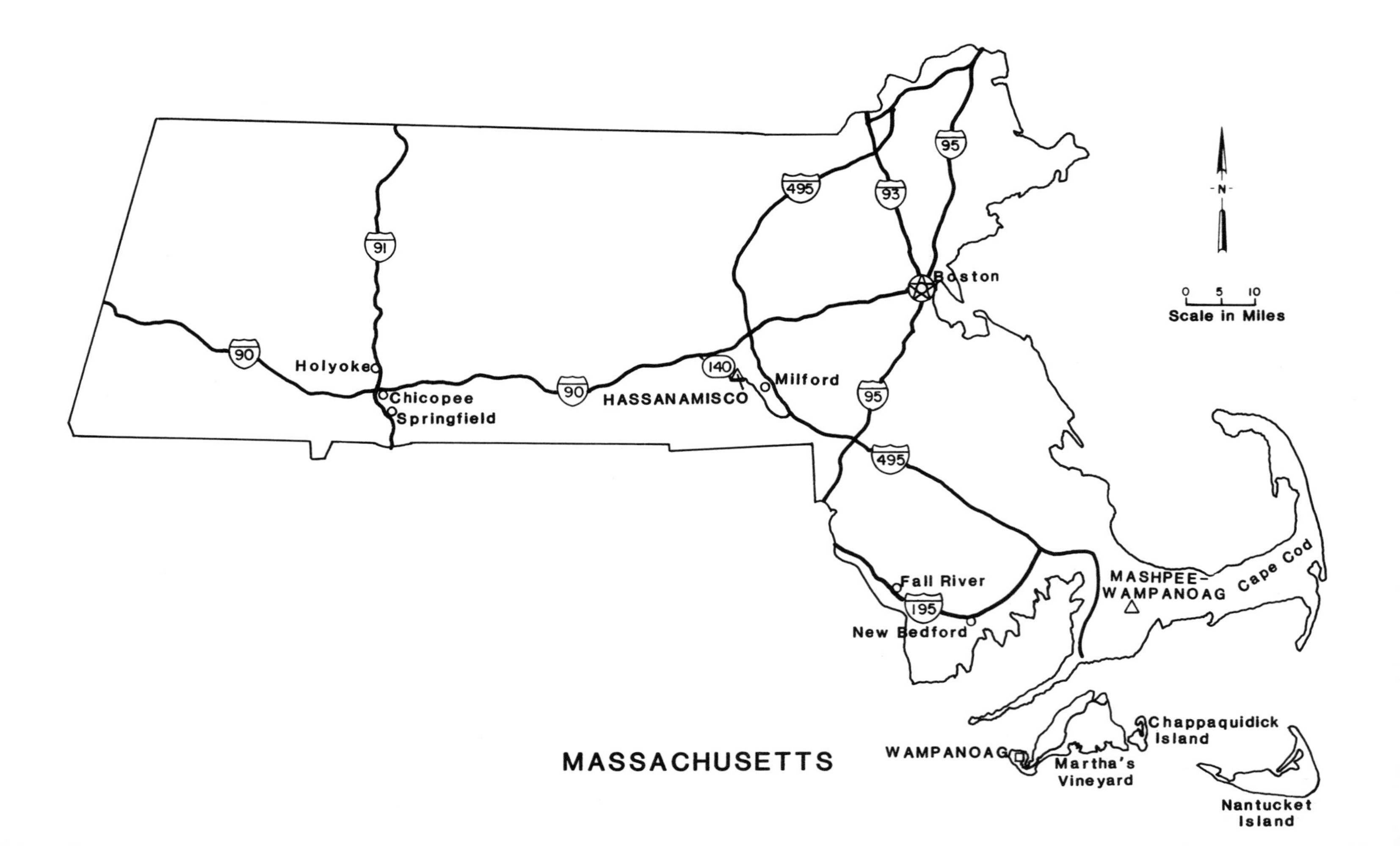
MASSACHUSETTS
Boston
Holyoke
Chicopee
Springfield
Milford
HASSANAMISCO
Fall River
New Bedford
MASHPEE-
WAMPANOAG
Cape Cod
WAMPANOAG
Martha's
Vineyard
Chappaquidick
Island
Nantucket
Island
N
0 5 10
Scale in Miles
90
91
140
495
93
95
195

Hassanamisco Reservation

TRIBAL PROFILE:

The Hassanamisco-Nipmuc Tribe lives on a 12 acre state reservation in this rural area of Massachusetts. The reservation was created before 1728 by negotiation between the tribe and the Massachusetts Bay Colony. In 1848 the State of Massachusetts set aside the land for the current reservation. This small tribe is governed by a chairman and board of directors, although the sachem is still the traditional leader.

LOCATION:

South-central Massachusetts, south of I-90 and about 8 miles southeast of Worcester; Grafton is on Hwy 140.

ADDRESS:

Nipmuc Tribal Council
Hassanamisco Indian Reservation
Grafton, MA 01518
(508) 839-7394 or 753-5034

CULTURAL INSTITUTIONS:

Longhouse Museum: Displays of Nipmuc Nation artifacts and a library. By appointment only. In Grafton, MA.

Old Longhouse: Traditional structure housing life-size mannequins and authentic regalia. Due to re-open in the near future; contact the tribal office.

SPECIAL EVENTS:

Annual Fair
Grafton, MA
Activities include a ceremonial show and Indian name giving, storytelling, traditional dance contest, face painting, and more. Notable basketry and weaving, along with other arts and crafts. Native American and American-style foods for sale. Gates open 11:00 a.m., ceremonial show starts 2:00 p.m.; admission price varies. No drugs or alcohol allowed. Held last Sunday in July.

Mashpee-Wampanoag Reservation

TRIBAL PROFILE:

The Mashpee-Wampanoag Tribe is situated in the central portion of Cape Cod, and has continued throughout much of this region for hundreds of years. Two well-known ancestors are Massasoit and King Philip. The tribe owns 55 acres of land outside Mashpee, although none of its 1,100 enrolled members live on the property. Most of this band of the Wampanoag Tribe lives in the town of Mashpee and its environs; it is a state recognized tribe.

LOCATION:

Central Cape Cod, surrounded by numerous bays, ponds, and state parks. Mashpee is easily accessible from scenic US 6. Take Exit 2 onto Hwy 130; northeast of Woods Hole, which is on the southernmost tip of the Cape, due west of Hyannis.

ADDRESS:

Mashpee-Wampanoag Indian Tribe
P.O. Box 1048
Mashpee, MA 02649
(508) 477-0208

CULTURAL INSTITUTIONS:

Mashpee-Wampanoag Museum
Rte. 30
Mashpee, MA
(508) 477-1350
Collection focuses on the Mashpee-Wampanoag Indians. Open Tuesday-Saturday 10:00 a.m.-2:00 p.m.

Mashpee Archives Building
Mashpee, MA
(508) 539-1400
Open Thursdays only.

Special Events:

Mashpee Indian Pow Wow
Mashpee, MA
Held 1st weekend in July.

Once-A-Month Social
Mashpee, MA
This potluck occasion is open to the public. Held October-March.

Recreational Opportunities:

Cape Cod is well known as a recreational district rich in water sports and beach activities.

Archaeological & Historic Sites:

Mashpee Tribal Meetinghouse
Hwy 28
Mashpee, MA
An old Indian meeting house, in a region important to the Wampanoag. Contact the tribal office for permission to visit.

Wampanoag Tribe of Gay Head (Aquinnah)

Tribal Profile:

This band of the Wampanoag Tribe has lived on the island now known as Martha's Vineyard for many centuries. Long functioning as a non-profit corporation chartered by the Commonwealth of Massachusetts, the Wampanoag Tribe of Gay Head, Aquinnah, received federal recognition in 1987. That August, Presidential Act P.L. 100-95 returned approximately 485 acres of private and common lands from the town of Gay Head to the 600 member tribe. The tribe actively pursues major projects to develop their economic potential and self-sufficiency. Although the tribe has no enterprises at this time, it has been preparing the infrastructure necessary to promote that development in the future. Some projects include affordable housing, a tribal museum and fine arts/cultural center, a shopping complex, and a resort complex.

Location:

Trust lands are on a spit on the southwestern end of Martha's Vineyard. The 93 square-mile island is off the coast of Massachusetts, south of the mainland of Cape Cod.

Address:

Wampanoag Tribal Council of Gay Head (Aquinnah)
RFD 137, State Rd.
Gay Head, MA 02535
(508) 645-9265, -3401

Special Events:

Indian Days
Gay Head, MA
Social gathering featuring performances of the Noepe Cliff Singers & Drummers, a group of school children. Held in early August.

Cranberry Day
Wild Cranberry Bogs
A tribal holiday for over 100 years. Families picnic and pick cranberries at this traditional site. Held 2nd Tuesday in October.

Recreational Opportunities:

Visits to the Wild Cranberry Bogs, Herring Creek, and Gay Head Cliffs should not be missed. Gay Head beaches are some of the finest on the East Coast.

Businesses & Industries:

Among Wampanoag members, there are perhaps over 15 entrepreneurs operating businesses. In the Gay Head Cliff area, tribal members own a large restaurant, 4 fast food shops, and 3 gift shops.

Michigan

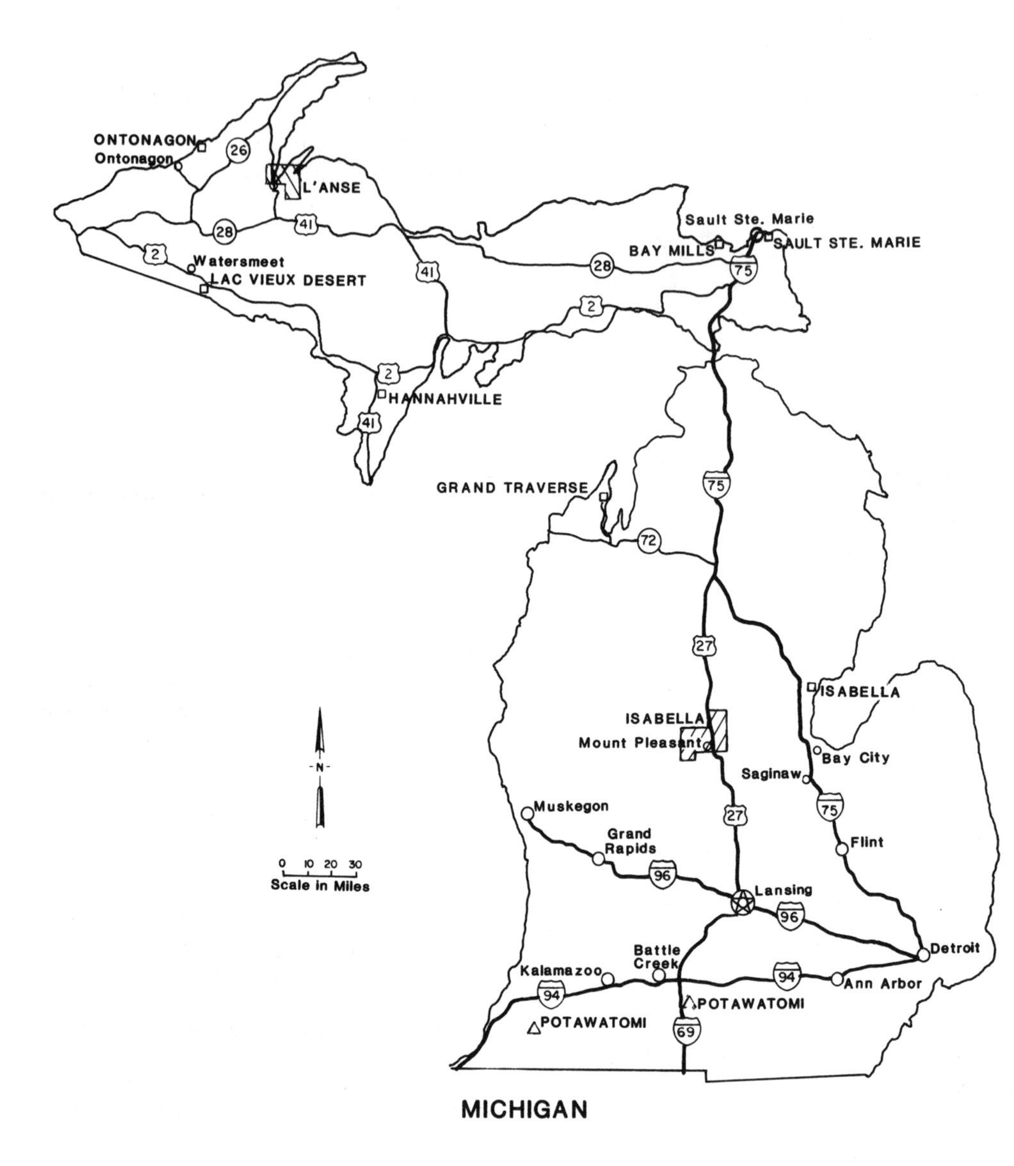
ONTONAGON
Ontonagon
26
L'ANSE
28
41
2
Watersmeet
LAC VIEUX DESERT
41
Sault Ste. Marie
BAY MILLS
SAULT STE. MARIE
28
75
2
2
HANNAHVILLE
41
GRAND TRAVERSE
75
72
27
ISABELLA
ISABELLA
Mount Pleasant
Bay City
Saginaw
75
N
Muskegon
27
Grand Rapids
Flint
0 10 20 30
Scale in Miles
96
Lansing
96
Detroit
Battle Creek
Kalamazoo
94
94
Ann Arbor
94
POTAWATOMI
POTAWATOMI
69

MICHIGAN

Bay Mills Reservation

TRIBAL PROFILE:

The original land for the Bay Mills Reservation was purchased by the Methodist Mission Society for the tribe under treaties signed in 1855. The reservation was established by the Act of June 19, 1860, with a total area of 2,189 acres. The band of Chippewa Indians that lives here is governed by a five-member council elected by enrolled members. Tribal population stands at 915.

LOCATION:

On Whitefish Bay on the Michigan Peninsula, due west of Sault Ste. Marie near the Canadian border. Accessed from I-75 via Hwy 28 to Hwy 221.

ADDRESS:

Sault Ste. Marie Band of Chippewa Indians
Rte. 1
Brimley, MI 49715
(906) 248-3241

RECREATIONAL OPPORTUNITIES:

Bay Mills Reservation has a bingo operation. Call the tribe at (906) 248-3241 for specifics as to time, dates and cost.

Grand Traverse Reservation

TRIBAL PROFILE:

This reservation of 375 acres was established by proclamation of the Secretary of the Interior in 1984. The population is about 1,350 members of the Ottawa and Chippewa tribes, centered at the Peshawbestown Indian Village; total tribal membership is 1,811.

LOCATION:

Northwestern Michigan on Grand Traverse Bay, Lake Michigan, sharing a point of land with Sleeping Bear Dunes National Lakeshore. Peshawbestown is 4 miles north of Suttons Bay on Scenic Hwy 22.

ADDRESS:

Grand Traverse Band Economic Development Authority
Rte. 1, Box 157-A
Suttons Bay, MI 49682
(616) 271-6477

SPECIAL EVENTS:

Peshawbestown Pow-Wow
(616) 271-3538
Features traditional dance and song, traders, singers and drums keeping alive the songs and history of the tribe. Directional information posted in Peshawbestown. Small admission fee. Held last weekend of August.

RECREATIONAL OPPORTUNITIES:

Leelanau Sands Casino
(616) 271-4104
Open Monday through Friday, 6:00 p.m. to 2:00 a.m; Saturday noon to 2:00 a.m.; Sunday, noon to 9:00 p.m. 20 miles south of Traverse City.

Grand Traverse Band Super Bingo Palace
(616) 271-6852
Open Wednesday through Friday at 5:00 p.m.; Saturday at 4:00 p.m.; Sunday at noon. Near the Casino.

The Leelanau Sands Casino, Peshawbestown, MI. Courtesy of Grand Traverse Band of Ottawa & Chippewa Indians, Economic Development Authority.

BUSINESSES & INDUSTRIES:

Tribal businesses are mostly open year round; tours are available upon request. Contact the Economic Development Authority: (616) 271-6477.

Grand Traverse Band Craft Store
(616) 271-3318
Open during the warm season, offering crafts from tribal artisans.

ACCOMMODATIONS:

Grand Traverse Band Motel
(616) 271-6330

52 units. Offers continental breakfast, discount coupons for casino. On Hwy 22, north of Traverse City.

Hannahville Reservation

TRIBAL PROFILE:

The 4,025 acres that comprise the Hannahville Indian Community are held in trust or individually owned by this band of the Wisconsin Potawatomi. The reservation was created by Act of June 30, 1913, and is administered by a 12-member council. Hannahville Community members number over 300.

LOCATION:

Near the Wisconsin border, on the Michigan Peninsula, near the junction of US 41 and US 2.

ADDRESS:

Hannahville Community of Michigan
Hannahville Rte. 1, Road N14911
Wilson, MI 49896
(906)-466-2342

RECREATIONAL OPPORTUNITIES:

Hannahville Community has a bingo operation. Call the tribe at (906)466-2342 for specifics as to time, dates and cost.

Huron Potawatomi Reservation

TRIBAL PROFILE:

Today the Huron Potawatomi, a tribe most closely associated with the Chippewa and Ottawa, has over 50 members living on the state-recognized Huron Potawatomi Reservation. Descendants of a band led by Chief Mo-ga-jo, this group of Potawatomi refused to relocate to Kansas in the early 1800s. As a result, President James K. Polk conveyed 40 acres of land to the Governor of Michigan to be held in trust; another 80 acres were given by a private party.

ADDRESS:

Huron Potawatomi Inc.
2221 1 ½ Mile Road
Fulton, MI 49052
(616) 455-5400

Isabella Reservation

TRIBAL PROFILE:

The Isabella Reservation was established by treaty in 1864 and is home of the Saginaw Chippewa Indian Tribe of Michigan. Of the initial allotment of land, about 1,405 acres remain in the reservation. Just over 70 acres of the Isabella Reservation, known as the Saganing District, are near Saginaw Bay, north of Bay City, and serve primarily residential purposes. The tribal enrollment is about 1,700, governed by a 12-member tribal council.

LOCATION:

Central Michigan near Mt. Pleasant, along US 27, a major north-south corridor; Hwy 20 crosses reservation east-west.

ADDRESS:

Saginaw Chippewa Tribe
7070 East Broadway
Mt. Pleasant, MI 48858
(517) 772-5700

SPECIAL EVENTS:

Little Elks Retreat Pow-Wow
Saginaw Chippewa Campground
Includes traditional dances and dance competition, traders, food and refreshments. Examples of Woodland crafts including ash baskets, quillwork, beadwork, ribbon shirts, pottery and sculptures are available for sale. Admission is charged. Held 1st weekend of August.

RECREATIONAL OPPORTUNITIES:

Saginaw Chippewa Bingo
Mt. Pleasant, MI
(800) 338-9092
High stakes bingo games, drawing participants from a wide area. Open year round Wednesday through Sunday, 6:00-11:00 p.m., at the Tribal Center.

Saginaw Chippewa Card Room
A7498 E. Broadway
Mt. Pleasant, MI
(517) 772-0827 or
(800) 338-9092 (in-state)
Broad spectrum of Vegas-style games, including blackjack and poker. Wednesday through Saturday 5:00 p.m.-midnight and Sunday, noon-7:00 p.m., year round. Admission is charged.

Saginaw Chippewa Campground
Semi-wooded area just south of the Tribal Center in Mt. Pleasant. 64 sites, 45 with full hook-ups. Amenities include swimming pool and picnic area.

Left, young dancer at one of many Michigan Indian pow wows. Right, waiting for a contest to start. Photos courtesy of Michigan Travel Bureau.

Lac Vieux Desert Reservation

TRIBAL PROFILE:

Located in Ottawa National Forest, Lac Vieux Desert Indian Reservation, almost 28 acres in size, was established by P.L. 100-420 in 1988, in a mountainous area where outdoor sports abound. The resident band of Lake Superior Chippewa, numbering about 170, is actively involved in economic development projects, including an arts and crafts store, a casino, and bingo parlor. Its government is led by a nine-member council under an interim constitution approved in 1986.

LOCATION:

At the western end of the Michigan Peninsula, near the Wisconsin border, at Watersmeet. North-south access via US 45; east-west access via US 2.

ADDRESS:

Lac Vieux Desert Band of
Lake Superior Chippewa
P.O. Box 446
Watersmeet, MI 49969
(906) 358-4577

SPECIAL EVENTS:

Annual Lac Vieux Pow Wow
Old Reservation
Traditional pow wow, features grand entry, arts and crafts sales and food concessions. Admission is free. Held last weekend of August.

Recreational Opportunities:

Lac Vieux Desert Bingo
Choate Road
Watersmeet, MI
(906) 358-4577
Regular and special bingo games 5 days a week; call for times.

Lac Vieux Desert Casino
Choate Road
Watersmeet, MI
(906) 358-4226, -4227
Las Vegas style games including poker, blackjack, craps and slot machines. Next door to bingo hall.

Archaeological & Historic Sites:

Lac Vieux Desert Old Reservation
Site for pow wows, festivals, and camping; 8 miles south of Watersmeet.

Businesses & Industries:

Lac Vieux Desert Arts & Crafts Store
Watersmeet, MI
Features handmade items. Open 7:00 a.m. to 3:30 p.m. Monday through Friday. At Tribal Headquarters and Bingo Center.

Accommodations:

Gateway Hotel & Lodge
Land O'Lakes, WI
(715) 547-3321
About 5 miles south of the reservation.

L'Anse Reservation

Tribal Profile:

L'Anse Reservation was established by treaty between the Chippewa and the federal government in 1854; it was created for three tribes, the Keweenaw, Ontonagon and Lac Vieux Desert. Tribal lands cover 15,253 acres, with a population of 785 members of the L'Anse and Ontonagon Bands of Chippewa. An additional 120 acres was the home of the Ontonagon Band at the time the reservation was created; at the present time no one lives on this parcel. The tribe owns a construction company, and several tribal enterprises such as a ski and resort complex are contemplated.

Location:

On Keweenaw Bay on the northwestern Michigan Peninsula, north of the Wisconsin border on US 141.

Address:

Keweenaw Bay Indian Community
Keweenaw Bay Tribal Center
Rte. 1, Box 45
Baraga, MI 49908
(906) 353-6623

Recreational Opportunities:

Big Bucks Bingo
MI Hwy 38 & Bear Town Rd.
Baraga, MI
(906) 353-7002
Open Tuesday and Thursday, 5:00 p.m.; early bird game begins 5:15 p.m., regular games 6:45 p.m.

Bowling Lanes and Lounge
MI Hwy 38 & Bear Town Rd.
Baraga, MI
(906) 353-6414, -9904
Next to Big Bucks Casino.

Accommodations:

Ojibwa Resort Motel
Rte. 1, Box 284A
Baraga, MI 49908
(906) 353-7611
Amenities include an indoor pool, whirlpool, sauna, and a full-service restaurant. Next to Big Bucks Bingo.

Potawatomi Reservation

Potawatomi Indian Nation, Inc.
The Pokagon Band
53237 Town Hall Road
Dowagiak, MI 49047
(616) 782-6323
A state-recognized band.

Sault Ste. Marie Chippewa Reservation

Tribal Profile:

The Sault Ste. Marie Reservation was established by proclamation of the Secretary of the Interior in 1974, and the tribe approved its constitution in 1975. A 13-member board of directors governs the reservation. While approximately 400 acres are held in trust for the tribe, its service area encompasses the seven counties of the Michigan Peninsula. The tribal population in the service area is almost 9,000, and there are approximately 15,800 enrolled members of the Sault Ste. Marie Tribe of Chippewa Indians. Tribal enterprises include a full-service janitorial and cleaning service that specializes in smoke damage cleaning and sells cleaning supplies.

Location:

Sugar Island, east of Sault Ste. Marie, at the extreme eastern end of the Michigan Peninsula, near the Canadian border. I-75 ends at Sault Ste. Marie.

Address:

Sault Ste. Marie Tribe
206 Greenough Street
Sault Ste. Marie, MI 49783
(906) 635-6071

Recreational Opportunities:

Vegas Kewadin
Shunk Road
Sault Ste. Marie, MI
(906) 632-0530

An 800-seat casino offering blackjack, craps, roulette, $25,000 keno and an assortment of slot machines. Open 24 hours per day, 7 days a week.

Kewadin Shores
St. Ignace, MI
(906) 643-7071
Las Vegas style gaming.

Accommodations:

Kewadin Inn
3411 I-75 Business Spur
Sault Ste. Marie, MI
(906) 635-5274
Features 46 units, offers casino packages with room rental.

Minnesota

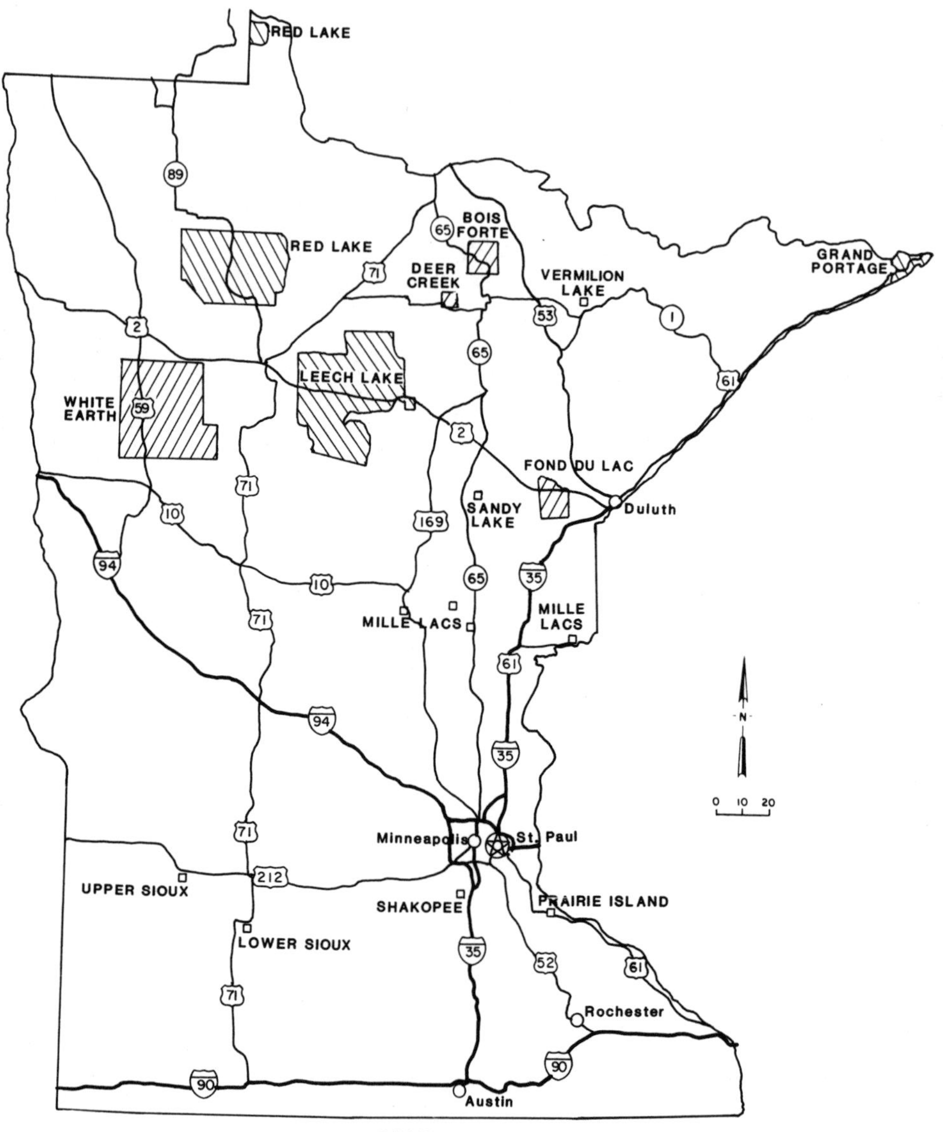
RED LAKE
89
BOIS FORTE
65
RED LAKE
71
DEER CREEK
VERMILION LAKE
GRAND PORTAGE
2
53
1
65
LEECH LAKE
WHITE EARTH
59
61
2
FOND DU LAC
71
10
Duluth
SANDY LAKE
169
94
10
65
35
MILLE LACS
71
MILLE LACS
61
N
94
35
0 10 20
71
Minneapolis
St. Paul
UPPER SIOUX
212
SHAKOPEE
PRAIRIE ISLAND
LOWER SIOUX
35
52
61
71
Rochester
90
90
Austin

MINNESOTA

Ojibwe rice harvest. Courtesy of John Running.

Bois Forte (Nett Lake) Reservation

Tribal Profile:

The Bois Forte (Nett Lake) Reservation was established by treaty in 1866 and Executive Order in 1881. It is home for the Vermilion Lake and Bois Forte Bands of Lake Superior Chippewa Indians. The reservation boundaries encompass 110,000 acres of which more than 45,000 acres are in trust, more than half is owned by non-Indians; tribal enrollment is about 2,000. The eastern sector of the reservation is on Lake Vermilion. Bois Forte's five-member business committee oversees reservation government, and the tribe participates in the Minnesota Chippewa Tribe of Minnesota, headquartered in Cass Lake. Tribal enterprises include a wild rice processing plant and a sewing and manufacturing enterprise.

Location:

Northern Minnesota, about a 50-mile drive south from International Falls and the Canadian border. Access to Nett Lake on Rte. 23 via US 53. Casino is in Tower, about 50 miles southeast of Nett Lake on Hwy 169.

Address:

Bois Forte Band of Chippewa
P.O. Box 16
Nett Lake, MN 55772
(218) 757-3261

Special Events:

The Bois Forte Band holds no competition pow wows, only social dances. Pow wows are scheduled seasonally; call tribal offices for precise dates and directions.

Mid-Winter Pow Wow
Celebration of the renewal of life, marking the advance to a new year. Feasts sponsored by the community for dancers, singers and visitors. Free admission. Held in February.

Sah-Gi-Bah-Gah Days
Celebration of the recession of the ice and of the prosperity received from the lake. Traditional social event; dancing and singing. Held late May or early June.

Vermilion Spring Pow Wow
Celebrates the opening of the lakes; feast includes walleye and other traditional foods. On the shore of Lake Vermilion, eastern sector of reservation.

Bois Forte Softball Tournament
Sponsored by local softball team which is joined by teams from all over northern Minnesota, including other Indian reservations. Held in June.

Mii-Gwech-Mi-No-Min Days
Celebration of annual wild rice harvest from Nett Lake. World-renowned fresh and hand-parched wild rice is for sale. Held in the 1st half of October.

RECREATIONAL OPPORTUNITIES:

Bois Forte Guide Services
(218) 757-3261
Bois Forte Reservation is internationally known as a duck hunter's paradise. Accommodations are rustic and ducks are plentiful, attracted by pure water and abundant wild rice crops. Call the tribal office for information about guides and hunting season.

Fortune Bay Bingo Casino
County Road 77
Tower, MN 55790
(218) 753-6400 or (800) 992-7529
In addition to bingo, casino offers blackjack, roulette, poker machines and video machine gambling. Features a fine restaurant and lounge. On the eastern portion of the reservation by Lake Vermilion. Call for hours.

TRIBAL ORGANIZATIONS:

Anishinaabe Mikana
(218) 757-3295
"The Ojibwa Road," a committee of local residents who work to ensure the continuance of communities' Ojibwa culture, arts and language. Contact through Bois Forte Social Services (218) 757-3295.

Deer Creek Reservation

See Leech Lake Reservation

Fond du Lac Reservation

TRIBAL PROFILE:

The Fond du Lac Indian Reservation was established by treaty in 1854 and presently incorporates trust acreage totalling almost 22,200 acres. The Fond du Lac Lake Superior Band of Chippewa Indians has about 2,915 enrolled members, almost 1,500 of whom live on the reservation. The tribe is governed under a constitution approved and ratified in 1934. The Fond du Lac Band participates in the Minnesota Chippewa Tribal Council headquartered in Cass Lake.

LOCATION:

East-central Minnesota, about 15 miles west of Duluth. Off I-35 on Hwy 33.

ADDRESS:

Fond du Lac Chippewa
105 University Road
Cloquet, MN 55720
(218) 879-4593

SPECIAL EVENTS:

Fond du Lac Pow Wow
Fond Du Lac Reservation
Traditional dancing, arts and crafts. Held in July.

RECREATIONAL OPPORTUNITIES:

Fond du Lac Big Bucks Bingo & Casino
Big Lake Road
Cloquet, MN
(218) 879-4691
Features bingo and video slots; call for hours and most current gaming information.

Grand Portage Reservation

Tribal Profile:

The Grand Portage Indian Reservation occupies almost 47,000 acres and is home to about 230 of the 790 members of the Grand Portage Lake Superior Band of Chippewa Indians. Established by treaty in 1854, the reservation is governed by a five-member business committee under a constitution ratified in 1937. The Band participates in the Minnesota Chippewa Tribal Council headquartered in Cass Lake. Tribal enterprises include a fishery and a timber business.

Location:

A triangle at the northeastern tip of Minnesota, bordered by Canada on the north, Lake Superior on the south and east, and Grand Portage State Forest on the west. Access is via US 61, following the shore of Lake Superior northeast from Duluth, about 150 miles.

Address:

Grand Portage Tribal Office
P.O. Box 428
Grand Portage, MN 55605
(218) 475-2277 -2279

Cultural Institutions:

Community Arts Center
Grand Portage, MN

Special Events:

Summer Rendezvous Days
Grand Portage, MN
Traditional singing and dancing commemorating fur trading rendezvous held here for many years. Festival includes traditional foods such as moose stew and wild rice soup, and arts and crafts sales. Held 2nd weekend of August.

Recreational Opportunities:

Grand Portage Casino
Grand Portage, MN
(218) 475-2401
US: (800) 232-1384
Canada: (800) 534-1384
Casino is at the Grand Portage Lodge; games played include blackjack, video slots, pull tabs and bingo.

Grand Portage Marina
Boat rentals and launching facilities.

Grand Portage-Isle Royale Ferry
Passenger ferry running between Grand Portage and Isle Royale National Park; operates summer only.

Cross Country Skiing: Tribe maintains almost 75 miles of cross country ski trails for public use.

Archaeological & Historic Sites:

Grand Portage National Monument
(218) 728-1237
Good visitor facilities; features partially reconstructed trading post and stockade. At Crawford House, Ojibwa women demonstrate beadwork and other crafts.

Businesses & Industries:

Grand Portage Trading Post
(218) 475-2282

Accommodations:

Grand Portage Lodge and Conference Center
Hwy 61
Grand Portage, MN
(218) 475-2401
Modern lodge featuring indoor pool, tennis, game room and lawn games. Restaurant decorated with Ojibwa art work, specializing in Indian foods and Lake Superior fish.

Minnesota lakes produce some large fish. Photo by Amoose. Courtesy of Great Lakes Indian Fish & Wildlife Commission.

Leech Lake Reservation

TRIBAL PROFILE:

Part of the Chippewa Tribe was settled on the Leech Lake Reservation in the mid-1800s; the reservation was established by Treaty of February 22, 1855, with two subsequent treaties and executive orders. The Mississippi and Pillager Bands of Chippewa Indians have in trust 28,725 acres of land in Cass, Itasca, Hubbard, and Beltrami Counties. The Leech Lake Reservation incorporates the Deer Creek and Sandy Lake Reservations. Many of the 6,619 tribal members live on the reservation and are involved in such tribal enterprises as the construction company, fisheries, solid waste removal, and an incubator center. Leech Lake is headquarters for the Minnesota Chippewa Tribal Council.

LOCATION:

In the heart of Chippewa National Forest in north-central Minnesota. Scenic US 2 passes east-west midway through the reservation, between Leech and Winnibigoshish Lakes. Due east of Grand Rapids.

ADDRESS:

Minnesota Chippewa Tribe
Leech Lake Reservation Business Committee
Rte. 3, Box 100
Cass Lake, MN 56633
(218) 335-8200

SPECIAL EVENTS:

Leech Lake Reservation holds annual pow wows throughout the year. Contact the tribal office for specific dates and other details.

RECREATIONAL OPPORTUNITIES:

Leech Lake Bingo & Palace Casino
Cass, MN
(218) 335-6787 or (800) 228-6676
Offering video slots, bingo, blackjack, and pull tabs. Check for scheduling.

Hunting and Fishing: A land of lovely lakes and beautiful scenery, Leech Lake is a popular hunting, fishing, and camping area. Contact the tribal office for further information regarding location, season, and availability of activities.

BUSINESSES & INDUSTRIES:

Che-Wa-Kah-E-Gon Restaurant
Hwy 2
Cass Lake, MN
(218) 335-2589
Restaurant complex also features gift shop, groceries, bait shop, bulk fuel oil, and gas.

Lower Sioux Reservation

TRIBAL PROFILE:

Established on June 29, 1888, Lower Sioux Reservation is headquarters for over 500 enrolled members of the Minnesota Mdewakanton Dakota. Although land has been assigned to individuals for homesites, the tribe owns all 1,743 acres that comprise the reservation. The tribe is organized under the Indian Reorganization Act, and a constitution and bylaws were approved in 1936. Members ratified the corporate charter in 1937. Agriculture is the main source of tribal income.

LOCATION:

Southwest of Minneapolis, adjoining the Minnesota River amid state parks. Off Hwy 19, south of Morton. Access from I-90 is via US 71.

ADDRESS:

Minnesota Mdewakanton Sioux
Community Center
Rural Rte. 1, Box 308
Morton, MN 56270
(507) 697-6185

RECREATIONAL OPPORTUNITIES:

Jackpot Junction
Morton, MN 56270
(507) 644-300 or
(800) LETTER-X
Games include video slots, bingo, blackjack, pull tabs, Keno, and lottery tickets. On US 71 east of Redwood Falls.

ARCHAEOLOGICAL & HISTORIC SITES:

Redwood Ferry: Site of battle between the Dakota and U.S. troops.

Mille Lacs Reservation

TRIBAL PROFILE:

The Mille Lacs Indian Reservation was established by treaty in 1855, but much of the original acreage has been lost; present trust lands are about 4,030 acres. There are 2,381 enrolled members of the tribe, governed under a constitution approved and ratified in 1934. Mille Lacs tribal government is led by a five-member council; the chair and secretary represent the Mille Lacs band on the Minnesota Chippewa Tribal Council.

LOCATION:

East-central Minnesota; the Mille Lacs Reservation is in 4 portions with tourist opportunities available at 2 of them, 1 on the west side of Mille Lacs Lake, 1 1/2 hours north of Minneapolis/St. Paul via US 169. The other is about half way between Minneapolis and Duluth, east of I-35 and Hinckley, reached via Hwy 48.

ADDRESS:

Mille Lacs Band of Ojibwa
HCR 67 Box 194
Onamia, MN 56359
(612) 532-4181

CULTURAL INSTITUTIONS:

Mille Lacs Museum
HCR 67, Box 95
Onamia, MN 56359
(612) 532-3632
Fine collection of Ojibwa and Dakota artifacts, including clothing, food, medicine, hunting and other exhibits. 12 miles north of Onamia on the shore of Mille Lacs Lake.

SPECIAL EVENTS:

Grand Celebration
Grand Casino Hinckley
Hinckley, MN
(612) 532-4181
Festivities feature contest pow wow, senior and junior categories; Tri-Star Champion competition; Moccasin Game, 3-man team tournament; and a boxing exhibition. $50,000 in prize money. Admission fee. Held last weekend of May.

Annual Traditional Pow Wow
Mille Lacs Pow Wow Ground
A traditional pow wow. Dancers and drums are compensated. Feast daily. Held last weekend of August, Friday through Sunday.

RECREATIONAL OPPORTUNITIES:

Grand Casino Mille Lacs
(612) 449-9206 or (800) 626-LUCK
Features video slots and blackjack. US 169, 8 miles south of Garrison, west side of Mille Lacs Lake.

Grand Casino Hinckley
Hinckley, MN
(612) 449-9206
I-35E, East of Hinckley exit, half way between Minneapolis and Duluth.

Hunting and Fishing: Opportunities abound for watercraft, hunting, fishing, and ricing throughout the reservation. Contact the tribal office for details.

Good fishing on Minnesota reservations. Photo by Amoose. Courtesy of Great Lakes Indian Fish & Wildlife Commission.

Sandy Lake Reservation

See Leech Lake Reservation

Shakopee Reservation

TRIBAL PROFILE:

Reserved by Acts of 1888, 1889, and 1890 for the Shakopee Mdewakanton Sioux, tribal lands cover 825 acres in Scott County. The tribe organized under the Indian Reorganization Act (IRA) with a constitution approved in 1969 that established a three-member council. The Shakopee Reservation is home to 286 Indians; tribal membership stands at around 150. Shakopee refers to a series of chiefs leading this portion of the Sioux throughout their history.

LOCATION:

Southwest of the Minneapolis suburbs off US 169, Prior Lake is on Hwy 13 at its junction with Rte. 27.

Canoeing on one of Minnesota's many waterways. Photo by Amoose. Courtesy of Great Lakes Indian Fish & Wildlife Commission.

ADDRESS:

Shakopee Mdewakanton Sioux Community
2330 Sioux Trail N.W.
Prior Lake, MN 55372
(612) 445-8900

RECREATIONAL OPPORTUNITIES:

Little Six Casino
Prior Lake, MN
(218) 445-9000 or (800) LITTLE 6
Offering video slots, bingo, blackjack, and pull tabs.

Prairie Island Reservation

TRIBAL PROFILE:

The Prairie Island Sioux Reservation was established in 1889; it encompasses about 600 acres and is home to a small number of Minnesota Mdewakanton Sioux; estimated tribal enrollment is about 400. The tribe's primary business activity is the operation of its casino and bingo hall.

LOCATION:

Southeast of St. Paul, by the Mississippi River on US 61 near Red Wing.

ADDRESS:

Prairie Island Sioux Community
5750 Sturgeon Lake Road
Welch, MN 55089
(612) 385-2554

RECREATIONAL OPPORTUNITIES:

Treasure Island Casino Bingo
5734 Sturgeon Lake Road
Welch, MN 55089
(612) 385-2574
Casino offers blackjack tables, poker, keno and slot machines. Facility also features bingo hall, gift shop, restaurant and banquet facilities. Open daily except Christmas.

ACCOMMODATIONS:

Motels in Red Wing or Hastings.

Grand Entry flag bearers. Photo by Amoose. Courtesy of Great Lakes Indian Fish & Wildlife Commission.

Red Lake Reservation

Tribal Profile:

Through a series of treaties beginning in 1863, the Red Lake Band of the Chippewa was positioned on the 805,722 acre Red Lake Reservation. Property allotted to the band is in three parts, with the main portion where tribal communities are located, surrounding Upper and Lower Red Lakes. Another portion covers a point of land attached to Manitoba, Canada, directly north, and the third is east of Red Lake in the heart of Pine Island State Forest. Tribal lands are home to a large portion of the 7,600 enrolled members, many of whom are involved in forestry and construction. Tribal enterprises include a sawmill, construction, fisheries, and commercial rice production; the tribe is also involved in wildlife and waterfowl management.

Location:

Near the Canadian border in north-central Minnesota, scenic Hwy 89 crosses the reservation north-south. US 2 is 22 miles south of Red Lake.

Address:

Red Lake Band of Chippewa Indians
Red Lake Tribal Council
P.O. Box 550
Red Lake, MN 56671
(218) 679-3341

Special Events:

Red Lake Nation Contest Pow Wow
Held 4th of July weekend.

Tribal Fair & Pow Wow
Held in late August.

Annual Ponemah Labor Day Pow Wow
Held Labor Day Weekend.

Recreational Opportunities:

Red Lake Bingo Palace
Red Lake, MN
(218) 679-3941
Also has a game room. Call for scheduling and times.

Lake of the Woods Casino
Warroad, MN
(218) 386-3381
Features 150 video slot machines and 4 blackjack tables. Concession offers pop and snacks. Near Canadian border at Warroad.

Lake of the Woods Resort
Warroad, MN
(218) 386-1124
Lovely lake front setting, with a sandy beach and 3 large docks. 40-room motel, with full-service,

year-round restaurant that seats 95. Bait and tackle shop offers gas service, fish cleaning, boat and motor rentals and public restrooms.

Excellent hunting and fishing throughout the region. Contact the tribal office for details.

Red Lake Fishery Association
Redby, MN 56670
(218) 679-3513
Cooperative with 400 member-owners. Established in 1917 in one of the oldest commercial freshwater fisheries in the United States; most common species caught are walleye, northern pike and yellow perch.

ARCHAEOLOGICAL & HISTORIC SITES:

St. Mary's Mission: Started by the Benedictines in 1858 as an Indian mission. At Red Lake; for information, call (218) 679-3614.

BUSINESSES & INDUSTRIES:

Chippewa Indian Craft and Gift Shop
Goodridge, MN 56725
(218) 378-4210, -4322

Chippewa Trading Post
Red Lake, MN
(218) 679-3888
Facilities include laundromat, grocery, video, hardware, automotive parts, and gas station.

Another trading post is under construction in Ponemah.

Red Lake Forest Products Company
Redby, MN 56671
(218) 679-3346
New, modern saw mill complex with dry kiln and planing equipment, producing lumber and related forest products.

Upper Sioux Indian Community

TRIBAL PROFILE:

The original Sioux reservation created in the early 1800s spanned the Minnesota River and extended ten miles in each direction to Big Stone Lake and what is now St. Paul. The present Upper Sioux Reservation was established by Proclamation of the Secretary of the Interior on October 6, 1938, for this group of Mdewakanton, Sisseton, and Santee Sioux. The Upper Sioux Community is governed by the Upper Sioux Board of Trustees, a five-member council, under a constitution approved in 1974. The Indian Community covers 745 acres, headquarters for 350 tribal members.

LOCATION:

On the Minnesota River in southwestern Minnesota west of Minneapolis. Granite Falls is at the junction of scenic US 59, Hwy 23, and US 212.

ADDRESS:

Upper Sioux Community of Minnesota
P.O. Box 147
Granite Falls, MN 56241
(612) 564-2360, -2550

RECREATIONAL OPPORTUNITIES:

Firefly Creek Casino
Hwy 67 East
Granite Falls, MN
(612) 564-2547
(800) 232-1439
Opened in 1990, this facility offers a blend of Native American culture and history with exciting casino action. Live blackjack, video keno and poker, progressives and other traditional line games for video slot machines and pull tabs. Features a restaurant offering Indian specialties and a gift shop stocked with Native American crafts and casino souvenirs. 5 minutes southeast of Granite Falls on Hwy 67 East. Open daily; Monday through Thursday from 10:00 a.m. to 2:00 a.m., and 24 hours Friday through Sunday.

ACCOMMODATIONS:

Motels, campgrounds and RV facilities are nearby.

Vermilion Lake

See Bois Forte Reservation

White Earth Reservation

Tribal Profile:

Established by treaty in 1867, the White Earth Reservation covers almost 59,500 acres and has a tribal enrollment of about 20,000. The largest portion of tribal income derives from forestry, but the tribe's economic development projects include fisheries, a garment company and gaming establishments, in addition to a saw mill and building supplies.

Location:

Northwestern Minnesota, between US 10 and US 2. US 59 bisects the White Earth Reservation from north to south. Nearby cities are Detroit Lakes and Bemidji.

Address:

White Earth Tribal Council
Highway 224
P.O. Box 418
White Earth, MN 56591
(218) 983-3285

Special Events:

Annual White Earth Celebration
White Earth Pow Wow Grounds
(218) 983-3285, ext. 206
Celebrated to honor the signing of the White Earth Treaty on June 14, 1867. This event offers traditional pow wow activities, including dancers, drummers and singers. Indian arts and crafts are sold. Held in June, on the weekend closest to the 14th, from Friday evening to Sunday midnight.

Recreational Opportunities:

Golden Eagle Bingo
Tribal Headquarters
White Earth, MN
(218) 935-2244 (office) or 983-3285
Contact manager for days and hours.

A second bingo parlor will be part of a hotel and casino complex in Mahnomen, when completed.

Dancers ready for pow wow. Photo by Amoose. Courtesy of Great Lakes Indian Fish & Wildlife Commission.

Shooting Star Casino
Mahnomen, MN
(218) 935-2244
Open 24 hours.

Tribal Campground: At Pow Wow Grounds in White Earth, behind tribal headquarters.

Archaeological & Historic Sites:

St. Benedicts Mission: Presently unused; 2 miles south of White Earth on White Earth Lake; before visiting, contact tribal headquarters.

Accommodations:

Various lodgings are available in Detroit Lakes and Mahnomen.

Mississippi

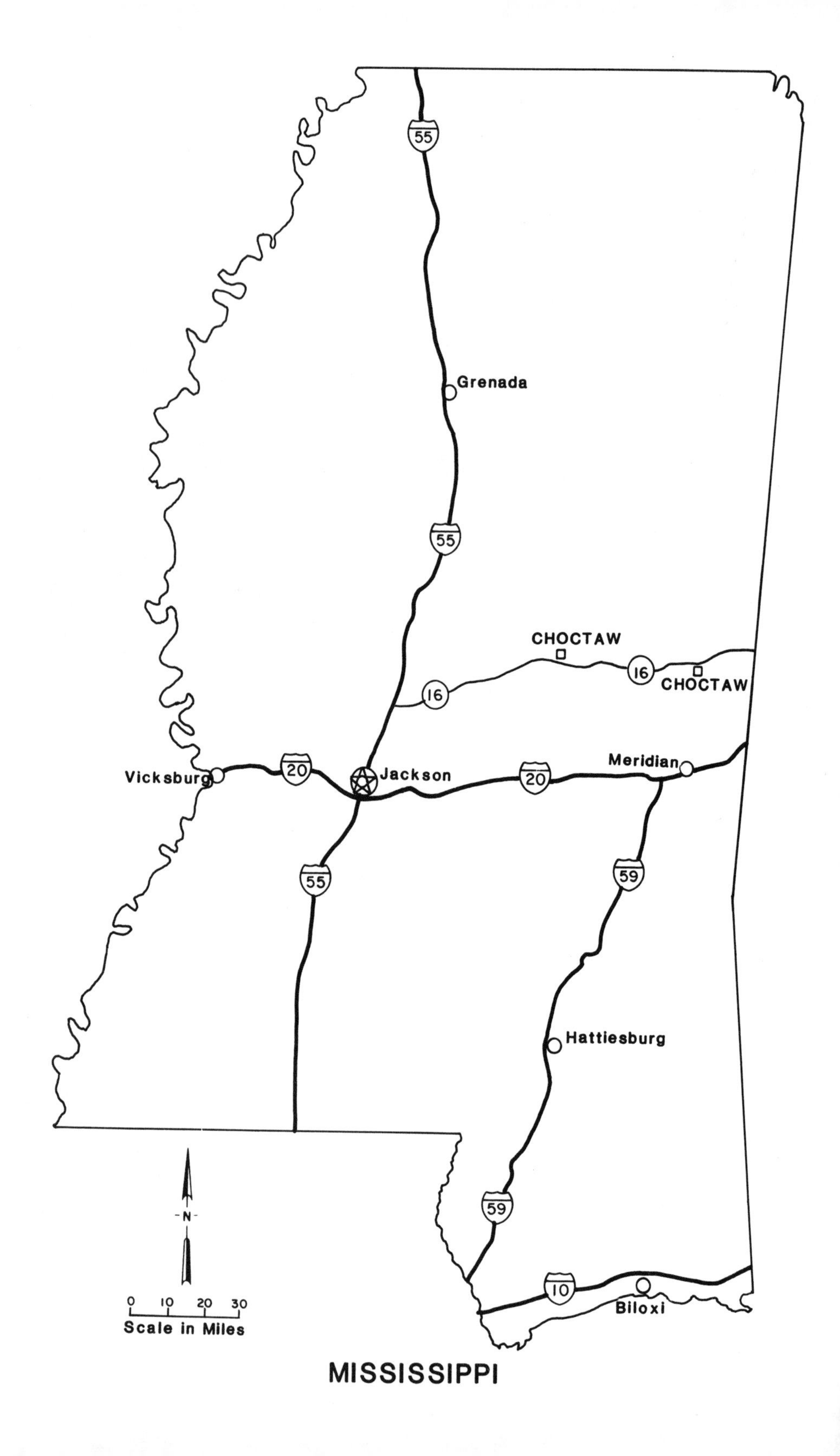
55
Grenada
55
CHOCTAW
16
16
CHOCTAW
Vicksburg
20
Jackson
20
Meridian
55
59
Hattiesburg
N
59
0 10 20 30
Scale in Miles
10
Biloxi
MISSISSIPPI

Choctaw Reservation

Choctaw Stealing Partners Dance. Courtesy of Kelsey/MBCI Communications.

TRIBAL PROFILE:

The Mississippi Band of Choctaw Indians, a small portion of the original tribe, has lived in Mississippi since around A.D. 800. It is generally agreed the tribe descends from the Mound Builders and built the Nanih Waiya, or Mother Mound, found near Preston. Now living on a 21,000 acre reservation in east central Mississippi, the band numbers 5,000. Although they are primarily farmers, the Choctaw incorporate arts in their economy, making beautiful woven baskets, appliqued clothing, dolls, and wood carvings. Many jobs are provided by the six manufacturing plants on the reservation.

LOCATION:

In east-central Mississippi, near Philadelphia. About 30 miles north of I-20 via Hwy 15. West on Hwy 16, which passes through the reservation.

ADDRESS:

Mississippi Band of Choctaw Indians
P. O. Box 6010-Choctaw Branch
Philadelphia, MS 39350
(601) 565-5251

CULTURAL INSTITUTIONS:

Choctaw Museum of the Southern Indian
P. O. Box 6010-Choctaw Branch
Philadelphia, MS 39350
(601) 656-5251, ext. 317
Open weekdays 8:00 a.m. - 4:30 p.m. Closed weekends.

SPECIAL EVENTS:

Choctaw Indian Fair
An annual Indian festival and flea market offering sporting events, arts and crafts, art exhibits, Indian musical entertainment, and a pageant. Held the 2nd week in July, Wednesday through Saturday.

ARCHAEOLOGICAL & HISTORIC SITES:

Nanih Waiya Mound
Preston, MS
Although no longer part of Choctaw lands, this mound was built by tribal ancestors and is an important part of its history. Located between Noxapater and Preston off Hwy 491. Currently a state-owned park without funding.

BUSINESSES & INDUSTRIES:

All the following businesses give tours when arrangements are made in advance. Call the Office of Economic Development (601) 656-5251.

Zula Chitto, Choctaw basketmaker. Courtesy of Kelsey/MBCI Communications.

Chahta Enterprise
Pearl River, DeKalb, and Conehatta, MS
3 plants making wiring harnesses for automobile dashboards.

Choctaw Electronics Enterprise
A joint venture with Oxford Speaker Company building automotive speakers.

Choctaw Greetings Enterprise
Hand-finish cards for American Greetings.

Choctaw Manufacturing Enterprise
Redwater, MS
Circuit board manufacturing for Westinghouse Electric Corp., Navistar International, and Xerox Corp.

TRIBAL ORGANIZATIONS:

Choctaw Heritage Council
P. O. Box 6010-Choctaw Branch
Philadelphia, MS 39350
(601) 656-5251, ext. 317

ACCOMMODATIONS:

In nearby Philadelphia: inn, motel and campground with RV facilities.

Montana

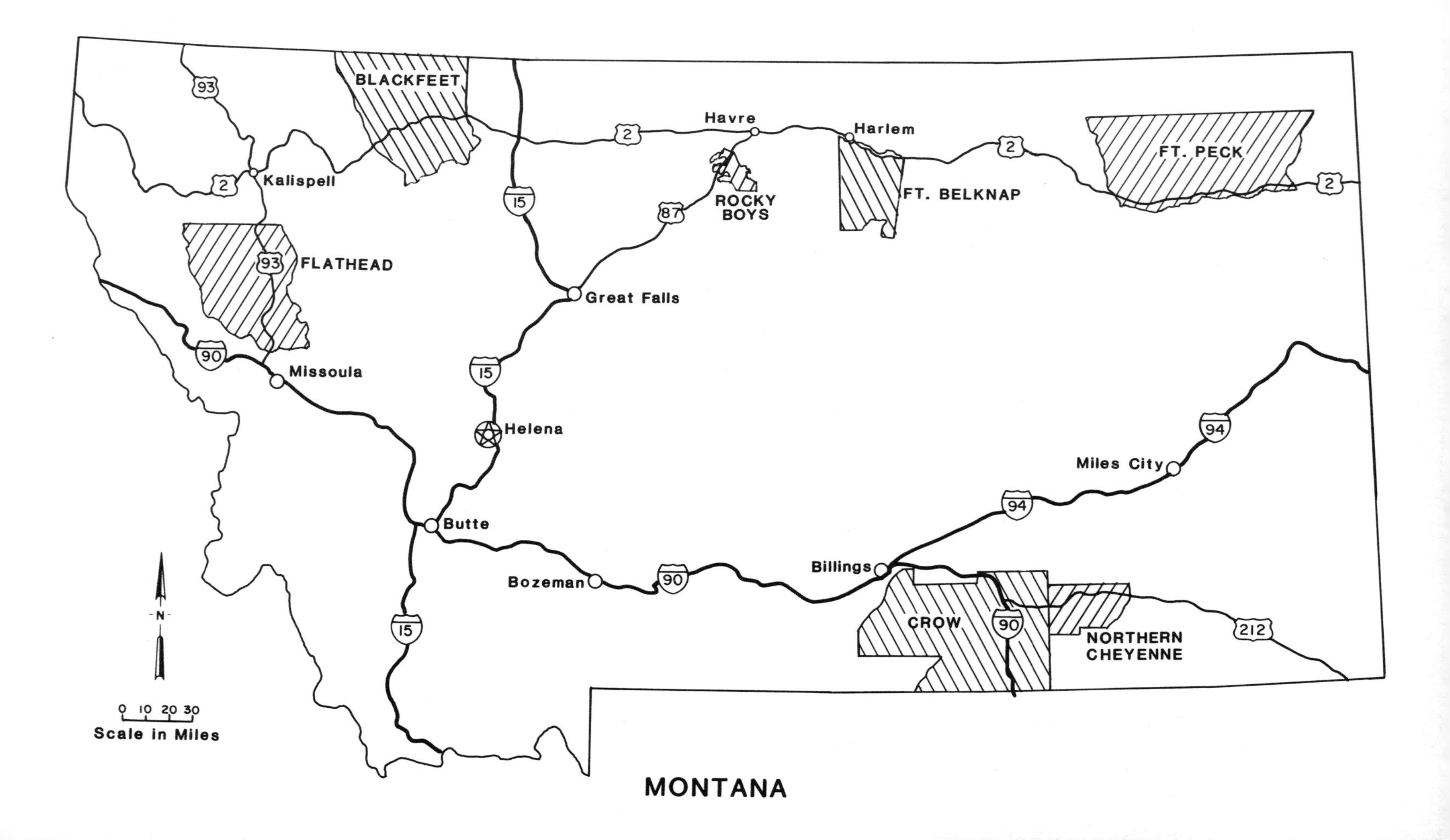
BLACKFEET
Havre
Harlem
FT. PECK
Kalispell
ROCKY
BOYS
FT. BELKNAP
FLATHEAD
Great Falls
Missoula
Helena
Miles City
Butte
Billings
Bozeman
CROW
NORTHERN
CHEYENNE
N
0 10 20 30
Scale in Miles
93
2
15
87
90
94
212

MONTANA

Mountains in Glacier National Park. Courtesy of the Council of Energy Resource Tribes, Photo Files.

Blackfeet Reservation

TRIBAL PROFILE:

The Blackfeet Tribe of Montana lives on a reservation of about 1.6 million acres that extends from the Rocky Mountains to the rolling plains. Tribal enrollment is about 14,000, with half living on the reservation. The reservation is governed by an elected nine-member Tribal Business Council. Browning is the seat of tribal government.

LOCATION:

Northwestern Montana, bordered on the north by Canada and on the west by Glacier National Park. US 2 crosses the reservation east to west; US 89 angles across it from north to southeast. Cut Bank, on the east edge of the reservation, is about 20 miles from I-15.

ADDRESS:

Blackfeet Nation
P.O. Box 850
Browning, MT 59417
(406) 338-7276

CULTURAL INSTITUTIONS:

Museum of the Plains Indian
US 89
Browning, MT
(406) 338-2230
Founded in 1941, museum exhibits creative achievements of North American artists. Permanent exhibit presents diversity of artifacts of Northern Plains tribal peoples; 2 galleries house changing exhibits. Gift shop. West of town on US 89. Open year round; special summer hours. Free admission.

Next to the museum is "**In the Footsteps of the Blackfeet**," a reconstruction of an authentic 1850 era Blackfeet encampment. Tribal members in full traditional dress perform traditional songs and dances and interpret tribal history and culture. Arts and crafts and traditional foods are for sale.

Blackfeet Community College
P.O. Box 819
Browning, MT
(406) 338-5441

SPECIAL EVENTS:

North American Indian Days
Blackfeet Tribal Fairgrounds
(406) 338-7276
Tepees are pitched on the pow wow grounds for 4 days of Indian dancing, games, sports events, parade, arts and crafts, rodeo and socializing. One of the largest gatherings of U.S. and Canadian tribes. Festivities begin at noon daily; free admission. Held 2nd week of July.

Mountain Lake, Blackfeet Reservation. Courtesy of the Council of Energy Resource Tribes, Photo Files.

RECREATIONAL OPPORTUNITIES:

Blackfeet Tribal Fish, Wildlife and Parks Department
P.O. Box 850
Browning, MT 59417
(406) 338-7521, ext. 223
Fishing Blackfeet tribal lands is not for everyone; lakes are often difficult to find, few have developed facilities, and roads deteriorate when it rains. However, the rewards for the fisherman willing to explore are great: rainbow trout of 4 to 6 pounds are frequently caught, 12 pounds, common, and rainbows up to 30 pounds occasionally caught. Fishing license from the Blackfeet Tribe is required; boating requires a permit. Camping is allowed only in designated areas. There are several tribal outfitters who are well informed about where fishing is particularly good at any time. Contact Tribal Fish, Wildlife and Parks Department for current information, maps and list of outfitters.

Duck Lake Campground
(406) 338-5042
Fishing, campsites, boat dock. Reservations suggested. Minutes from Glacier National Park.

Chewing Blackbones KOA Campground
(406) 732-4452
Marina, hot showers, laundromat, coffee shop, picnic facilities, children's play area. 120 developed RV sites providing utilities; numerous tent sites. On St. Mary Lake.

Red Eagle Campground
(406) 226-5512
Fishing, camping, picnicking and water skiing in summer, ice fishing in winter. Laundry facilities and camp store. Near the town of East Glacier Park on Two Medicine Lake.

St. Mary's KOA Campground
(406) 732-4422
Provides over 200 campsites; laundromat, store and miniature golf. 1/4 mile from town of St. Mary.

Blackfeet Community Bingo
Browning, MT
(406) 338-5751

ARCHAEOLOGICAL & HISTORIC SITES:

Blackfeet Historic Site Tour
P.O. Box 238
Heart Butte, MT 59448
(406) 338-2058
Offers half and full-day tours that begin at Museum of the Plains Indian in Browning and provide the visitor with spectacular views and an opportunity to see and hear about a variety of sites important to the Blackfeet Tribe, including buffalo jumps, Old Agency, trading posts, tepee ring, Blackfeet Indian Ranch, Two Medicine River. The full-day tour travels further north and includes St. Mary Lake and River, Duck Lake, and Alty's Mining Camp. Full-day tour extends into Canada to visit Head-Smashed-In Buffalo Jump, one of the largest, oldest and best preserved bison jump sites in North America, declared a World Heritage Site by UNESCO.

Businesses & Industries:

Morning Star Outfitters
(406) 338-2785

High Plains Outfitters
(406) 338-7413.

Blackfeet Writing Company
Tours by appointment, or walk in. At the Blackfeet Planning Department.

Crow Reservation

Tribal Profile:

The Crow initially lived in the forests of the Northeast but began moving westward in the early part of the 19th century, absorbing Plains Indian culture as it moved. The Crow Reservation was established by a treaty in 1851 and reduced to its present size of about 2.5 million acres by 1888. The Crow Tribe, with an enrollment of approximately 8,700, is governed by a tribal council composed of all adult members, who elect the tribal executive committee. Tribal income derives from surface leases, coal, oil and gas royalties and bonuses.

Location:

Southeastern Montana, crossed from north to south by I-90. Extends from the Wyoming border northward for about 50 miles. Billings is less than 10 miles from the northwestern boundary of the reservation.

Address:

Crow Tribe of Indians
Box 159
Crow Agency, MT 59022
(406) 638-2601

Special Events:

Crow Fair Pow Wow, Rodeo and Race Meet
Crow Fair Grounds
Crow Agency, MT
(406) 638-2601, ext. 112
First held in 1904; parade daily at 10:00 a.m., rodeo and race meet at 1:00 p.m.; pow wow dancing competition nightly; grand entry at 1:00 and 7:00 p.m. Arts and crafts and art exhibit; food booths also featured. Admission fee for rodeo. Held Thursday-Sunday, 3rd week of August.

The Crow also hold feast days, tribal ceremonies (particularly Sun Dances) and tribal competitions (hand games and arrow games). Contact tribal headquarters for particulars.

Yellowtail Dam and switchyard area. Courtesy of Hardin Photo Service, Hardin, MT.

Left, Kitty Bell Deernose, Curator at Custer Battlefield. Right, Custer Battlefield and Visitors Center. Both photos courtesy of Hardin Photo Service, Hardin, MT.

RECREATIONAL OPPORTUNITIES:

Bighorn Canyon Reservoir
The Crow Reservation is bisected by the Bighorn River and surrounds much of the Bighorn National Recreation Area; offering a wide variety of outdoor recreational opportunities including boating, fishing and camping.

ARCHAEOLOGICAL & HISTORIC SITES:

Yellowtail Dam
Fort Smith, MT
(406) 666-2412
525 feet high and spanning 1,480 feet, this variable-thickness, arch-type dam backs up the waters of the Bighorn River for 71 miles, forming Bighorn Lake.

Plenty Coups Memorial Museum
Pryor, MT
(406) 252-1289
Home and burial site of this well known Crow chief. Crow Indian artifacts. Picnic area. Open 9:00 a.m.-5:00 p.m.; closed Wednesday and Thursday.

Little Bighorn National Monument
Crow Agency, MT
(406) 638-2621
Commemorates the famous battle in June 1876 in which the Sioux and Cheyenne Nations soundly defeated U.S. General George Custer and the 7th Cavalry. Museum and Visitors Center. Site of battle preserved; markers describe action.

ACCOMMODATIONS:

Hotels, motels, RV and camping sites available in and near Hardin, 12 miles north of Crow Agency.

Flathead Reservation

TRIBAL PROFILE:

This dramatic country has been the source of life for Native American peoples for centuries. In 1855, the Hellgate Treaty created the Flathead Reservation, now over 1.2 million acres, that is home for the Salish, Kootenai and Pend d'Oreilles people. Estimated tribal enrollment is about 6,700, of which half live on the reservation, working to perpetuate their culture, preserve natural resources and provide economic well-being for this and future generations. Timber, small agriculture and tribal government are the primary employers on the reservation.

LOCATION:

The high ranges and fertile valleys of northwestern Montana; north of I-90, between Missoula and Kalispell. US 93 crosses the reservation from north to south. Flathead Lake is the largest natural fresh water lake in the West.

ADDRESS:

Confederated Salish & Kootenai Tribes
P.O. Box 278
Pablo, MT 59855
(406) 675-2700 or (800) 634-0690

Flathead Lake, flanked by rugged mountains. Courtesy of C.S.K.T. Wildland Recreation Program.

Cultural Institutions:

Sqelix'u Aqlcmaknik Culture Center
(406) 675-0160
"The Peoples" center for preservation of Salish, Kootenai and Pend d'Oreille lifestyles. Scheduled to be in full operation in 1993. Check with the tribal offices for the status and to arrange to see the material archived for the museum.

Agnes Vanderburg Cultural Camp
Salish Culture Committee
(406) 745-4572
Under direction of Salish Culture Committee and other tribal elders, camp teaches language, crafts, customs and lore of Salish and Pend d'Oreilles peoples. Named for the full-blooded Salish tribal member who founded it. Classes are free. West of US 93, south of Ravalli. Held summer months.

Special Events:

Arlee 4th of July Celebration
Arlee, MT
Hosted by the Salish and Pend d'Oreille Tribes, this festival includes ritual dancing, dance competition, drumming competition, song, traditional gaming, teen dance, softball tournament, rodeo, parade and food. Alcohol strictly prohibited. Held 4th of July weekend.

Standing Arrow Pow Wow
Elmo Pow Wow Grounds
Elmo, MT
Hosted by the Ksanka Band of the Kootenai Nation and drawing a crowd of 5,000, this colorful celebration features ritual dancing, song, competitions, softball tournament and food. Alcohol strictly prohibited. Pow Wow Ground is on the west shore of Flathead Lake. No admission fee. 24 hours a day, Thursday through Sunday, 3rd weekend of July.

Recreational Opportunities:

Tribal Fish and Game Office
Pablo, MT
(406) 675-2700, ext. 356
The Flathead Reservation abounds in outdoor recreation opportunities. The tribe has prepared a flyer that details them with a map to provide access information. Tribal recreation permit and appropriate stamps are required for fishing, hunting, camping and other activities on the reservation. Guided tours are available. There are no usage fees charged by the Flathead Nation. A sampling of possibilities follows:

Camas Hot Springs Spa: Therapeutic mineral mud and artesian mineral water baths; open year round. Off Hwy 28, west side of reservation.

Mission Mountain Tribal Wilderness Area: Access to numerous high-country lakes and peaks for fishing, hunting, observing wildlife. 9 trails enter the wilderness from the west; some periodic closure for grizzly bear protection. Mountainous area east of Hwy 93.

Blue Bay Tribal Park: Tent and trailer camping along the eastern shore of Flathead Lake with picnicking, boat launch, fishing and restroom facilities. Entrance fee. Alcohol strictly prohibited.

Top, still water in rugged wilderness. Bottom, big horn sheep on the Flathead Reservation. Photographed by Dale Becker. Both photos courtesy of C.S.K.T. Wildland Recreation Program.

Jocko River Fishing Access: Excellent catch and release trout fishing; obtain permit at tribal headquarters and check for current restrictions.

North Fork of the Jocko Campground: View eagles, deer and other wildlife; camping and picnicking.

McDonald Lake Campground: Beautiful lake below the towering Mission Range. Camping, fishing, picnicking, wildlife viewing and boat launch facilities (15 hp motor limit).

ARCHAEOLOGICAL & HISTORIC SITES:

Undeveloped, with restricted access; contact tribal office.

Wildlife Refuges: Within the boundaries of the Flathead Reservation are several national wildlife refuges including the National Bison Range and Ninepipe National Wildlife Refuge, a natural system of ponds and wetlands that attracts hundreds of thousands of waterfowl, great blue heron, eagles and other birds.

ACCOMMODATIONS:

Kwataqnuk Resort
Polson, MT
(406) 883-6363
(800) 882-6363 for reservations
New resort facility at Flathead Bay. Freaturing 112 guest rooms, restaurants, lounge, casino, convention center , banquet hall, gift shops, gallery and a wide variety of recreational facilities. Scheduled for completion in summer 1992.

RESTRICTIONS AND/OR SPECIAL CONSIDERATIONS:

Some primitive areas are restricted to tribal members only. Contact Tribal Office for information.

Fort Belknap Reservation

TRIBAL PROFILE:

The Fort Belknap Indian Reservation, established by an Act of Congress in 1888, is home to two tribes, the Assiniboine and Gros Ventre, with a combined tribal enrollment of about 4,250. The reservation is approximately 652,523 acres, extending from the Milk River south to the Little Rocky Mountains. The two tribes are equally represented on the Fort Belknap Community Council, the governing body of the reservation. Tribal economic development projects have resulted in health and recreation facilities and a variety of tourist attractions. The community is planning bed & breakfast inns.

LOCATION:

North-central Montana; US 2 runs east-west just inside the northern border of the reservation, with US 66 crossing the reservation from north to south. The Gros Ventre call the Little Rocky Mountains "The Island Mountains" because they lie isolated like an island in an ocean of plains. Rising from 3,000 to 5,000 feet within a few miles, they make a majestic and surprising site in the middle of the prairie.

ADDRESS:

Fort Belknap Community Council
R.R. 1, Box 66
Fort Belknap Agency
Harlem, MT 59526
(406) 353-2205

CULTURAL INSTITUTIONS:

Fort Belknap Community College
Fort Belknap Agency
(406) 353-2607

Fort Belknap Tourism Office
RR 1, Hwy 2 & 66
Harlem, MT 59526
(406) 353-2527
Information and rest area directly across from the Tribal Kwik Stop. Staff provide tours of the Mission areas, Snake Butte area, ancient tepee ring areas and the tribal Buffalo Pasture. Also provides information regarding fees and permits required.

SPECIAL EVENTS:

Fort Belknap hosts several festivals and pow wows that draw visitors and participants from throughout the world. Tribal Tourism Office has complete information for the following:

Prairie and mountains meet in central Montana. Courtesy of Harvey King, Harlem, MT.

Fort Belknap Mid-Winter Fair
Builders Building
Fort Belknap Agency
Native American art and handicraft is highlighted at the fair, along with traditional feasts, giveaways, and pow wow. Held the 1st week of February.

Hays Community Pow Wow
Mission Canyon
Held 3rd weekend of July.

Milk River Indian Days
Fort Belknap Pow Wow Grounds
Annual celebration and pow wow featuring grand entries, contest dancing, giveaways and special family feeds or dinners. Held 4th weekend of July.

Cole's Memorial Roping
Cole's Arena - Hwy 66
Wild Horse Butte
Indian Rodeo, honoring deceased members of the Cole Family. Held 2nd week of September.

Rodeos: Several are held annually on the reservation. Rodeo information is provided by the Tribal Tourism Office.

Recreational Opportunities:

The reservation features many scenic areas with fishing, horseback riding and camping. Wild game is abundant, enabling the visitor to observe buffalo, deer, antelope, upland game, and one of the largest prairie dog colonies in the U.S. The area offers lakes, rivers, dams, mountains, caves, historic sites, and numerous scenic canyon areas. The necessary tribal hunting and fishing licenses can be purchased from the Tribal Land Services Department located in the tribal administration building.

Snake Butte
Natural spring with fishing and camping. Reservoir is stocked with trout and bass. Rock from Snake Butte was used to construct the Fort Peck Dam. Snake Butte is traditionally a place to seek spiritual visions. 7 miles from the Fort Belknap Kwik Stop.

Mission Canyon
Near Hays
Best known site on the Fort Belknap Indian Reservation. Offers camping and picnic areas. The Natural Bridge, Wilson Park, Devil's Kitchen, Needle Eye, and Kid Curry's Hideout are a few of the attractions.

Browns Canyon and Mouse Canyon
Scenic canyons near Lodge Pole.

Horse Capture Park
US 2
Fort Belknap Agency
Picnic area, RV hookups and disposal site. Across the road is a pen of buffalo and buffalo calves for viewing and photography.

Fort Belknap Recreational Complex
Features a roller skating rink, weight room, swimming pool, gymnasium, sauna, shower and bathroom facilities. Contact Tourism Office.

Fort Belknap Bingo Enterprises
Builders Building
Fort Belknap Agency
(406) 353-2965; (800) 343-6107 in-state
Megabingo played during evening sessions. Hours 9:00 a.m. to midnight, Wednesday and Friday. Saturday, 5:00 p.m. to midnight; Monday, Tuesday and Thursday, 9:00 a.m. to 5:00 p.m.; closed Sunday. Directly behind Indian Health Service Hospital.

ARCHAEOLOGICAL & HISTORIC SITES:

Saint Paul's Mission Church
Hayes, MT
Established in 1887; provides educational services for grades K-8.

Saint Thomas Parish Church
Lodge Pole, MT
Established in 1898. Built of rock quarried from the nearby mountains.

Sacred Heart Church: Built in 1931; on US 2 about 7 miles east of the Agency.

BUSINESSES & INDUSTRIES:

Fort Belknap Ventures
Fort Belknap Tourist Info. Center
Jct. US 2 & Hwy 66
(406) 353-2205, ext. 403
Features hand-crafted Native American art. Open Monday - Friday, 9:00 a.m. to 5:00 p.m.

Rugged, wind-sculptured pine. Courtesy of Harvey King, Harlem, MT.

ACCOMMODATIONS:

Fort Belknap Tepee Village
(406) 353-2527
At Tourism Office. Offers the opportunity to spend the night in an authentic Indian tepee.

Fort Belknap Kwik Stop
Across From Tourist Info. Center
(406) 353-4964
Food, gas, delicatessen; winter hours, 7:00 a.m. to 11:00 p.m.; summer, until midnight.

Fort Peck Reservation

TRIBAL PROFILE:

The Fort Peck Indian Reservation was established by an Act of Congress in 1888, in the homeland of the Assiniboine Tribe. When members of the Sioux Tribe sought refuge from the U.S. Cavalry there, the Fort Peck agency was directed to treat them as residents, and it has been so ever since. The reservation consists of almost 2.1 million acres in the fertile Missouri River Basin. The tribes' current enrollment is about 6,800 members. Fort Peck Reservation has a well organized economic development committee that, among other enterprises, has overseen the creation and growth of a prosperous industrial park in Poplar, providing a viable source of jobs and income for the tribes and their members.

Location:

Northeastern Montana, 40 miles from North Dakota and 50 miles from the Canadian border. Southern border of reservation is the Missouri River; US 2 runs along the southern edge, near the river. Hwy 13 crosses the reservation from north to south.

Address:

Fort Peck Assiniboine and Sioux Tribes
P.O. Box 1027
Poplar, MT 59255
(406) 768-5155

Cultural Institutions:

Fort Peck Assiniboine and Sioux Culture Center & Museum
P.O. Box 1027
Poplar, MT 59255
(406) 768-5155
Open seasonally, May through September.

Fort Peck Tribal Archives
312 Boulevard
Poplar, MT 59255
(406) 768-5141
Open to the public 8:00 a.m.-4:30 p.m., Monday-Friday.

Traditional Indian Village
(406) 653-1804
Visitors can view modern reconstruction of a traditional Indian village; rental of tepees for lodging is planned. 5 miles SE of Wolf Point. Open summer months.

Fort Peck Community College
Poplar, MT 59225
(406) 768-5155

NAES College
P.O. Box 1027
Poplar, MT
(406) 768-2360

Special Events:

All of the festivals listed below are organized by community groups, but full information can be gotten at tribal headquarters: (406) 768-5155.

Red Bottom Celebration
Frazer, MT
Indian pow wow. Held mid-June.

Badlands Celebration
Brockton, MT
Indian pow wow. Held on a weekend in late June.

Fort Kipp Celebration
Fort Kipp, MT
Indian pow wow. Held over July 4th holiday.

Iron Ring Celebration
Poplar, MT
Indian pow wow. Held 3rd weekend of July.

Wadopana Celebration
Wolf Point, MT
Indian pow wow. Held late July, early August.

Oil Discovery Celebration
Poplar, MT
Indian pow wow celebrating the discovery of oil on the reservation. Held late August, Friday through Sunday.

Recreational Opportunities:

Wolf Point Community Organization's Casino & Bingo Hall
Hwy 13 East
Wolf Point, MT
(406) 653-3476
High stakes bingo. Weekends, year round. Friday and Saturday, at 7 p.m.; Sunday at 2:30.

Smaller bingos are held during the week in other communities on the reservation.

Archaeological & Historic Sites:

Sacred Sites, Old Forts and Fossil Beds
Several places of interest are located on the reservation. For directions and permission to visit, contact Fort Peck Tribal Water Resource Office, (406) 768-5155.

Businesses & Industries:

Senior Citizens Arts and Crafts Shop
700 Block of A Street
Poplar, MT
(406) 768-3673, -3866
Features hand-crafted quilts, beadwork, traditional Native American foods, herbal medicines. Open Monday - Friday, occasionally on weekends, especially during pow wows.

Fort Peck Assiniboine & Sioux Tribal Museum. Courtesy of Wotanin Wowapi News, Poplar, MT.

A & S Tribal Industries
Industrial Park
P.O. Box 308
Poplar, MT 59255
(406) 768-5151
One of the largest employers in Montana, a variety of enterprises, including metal fabrication and sewing processes, operate here. Call to arrange a tour; available at any time.

West Electronics
Industrial Park
P.O. Box 577
Poplar, MT 59255
(406) 768-5511
Tribally owned; quality manufacturer of sophisticated electronic products and systems designed to the specification of governmental and commercial customers.

Wotanin Wowapi
Tribal Headquarters
P.O. Box 1027
Poplar, MT 59255
(406) 768-5155
Weekly newspaper published by the tribes, covering reservation, state and national news. In existence over 23 years, it is one of oldest tribal newspapers in the U.S.

Northern Cheyenne Reservation

Tribal Profile:

The Northern Cheyenne Reservation is comprised of 444,525 acres; the tribe has about 6,400 enrolled members, approximately 5,500 of whom live on the reservation. The tribe is organized under a constitution adopted in 1936. Terrain of the reservation varies from low grass-covered hills to high, steep hills and narrow valleys, in altitudes from 3,000 to 5,000 feet. The Northern Cheyenne economy is based primarily on ranching and farming activities, but about 90,000 acres of forest land are commercially managed. The tribe maintains elk and buffalo herds.

Location:

Southeastern Montana, bordered on the east by the Tongue River and on the west by the Crow Reservation; approximately 110 miles southeast of Billings and 75 miles north of Sheridan, Wyoming. US 212 crosses the reservation from east to west.

Address:

Northern Cheyenne Tribe
P.O. Box 128
Lame Deer, MT 59043
(406) 477-6284, -8338

Cultural Institutions:

Northern Cheyenne Tribal Museum
Lame Deer, MT
(406) 477-6284
Presents the history and culture of the Cheyenne Indians. Craft Center at the museum offers beadwork and other crafts. Open Monday-Friday, 8:00 a.m.-5:00 p.m. There are camping and picnic facilities on the grounds.

Dull Knife Memorial College
Lame Deer, MT
(406) 477-6215

Special Events:

Call Tribal Headquarters at (406) 477-6284 for specifics on the celebrations listed below, as well as dances and pow wows that take place at other times during the year.

New Year's Day Pow Wow
Busby, MT

Memorial Day Pow Wow and Rodeo
Lame Deer, MT

4th of July Celebration
Lame Deer, MT
Pow wow featuring contest dancing, giveaways, specials, honor dances, princess pageant, arts and crafts booths, sometimes horse races. 4 miles south of Lame Deer on Hwy 39. Free admission. Held in July.

Pow Wow
Birney, MT
Held in mid-August.

Labor Day Pow Wow
Ashland, MT

Veteran's Day Pow Wow
Busby, MT

Recreational Opportunities:

Northern Cheyenne Bingo
Lame Deer, MT 59043
(406) 477-6677
Open for playing the poker machines noon-2:00 a.m., 7 days a week. Bingo is played on a varying schedule; call for most current information.

Camping: Call the Environmental Affairs Office at tribal headquarters for details about camping on the reservation.

Crazy Head Springs Recreation Area
Swimming, camping, picnic tables, and fireplaces. Just south of Morning Star and Ice Wells Campgrounds.

Ice Wells Campground
Amenities include campsites, picnic tables and fireplaces. Between Lame Deer and Ashland, between Morningstar View Rd. and Greenleaf Fishing Pond. A tribal buffalo herd is pastured nearby.

Morning Star View Campground
Campsites, picnic tables and fireplaces. Next to Craft Center in Lame Deer.

Archaeological & Historic Sites:

St. Labre Indian School
Ashland, MT 59004
(406) 784-2200
Established in 1884 by the Catholic Church. Features visitors center, Plains Indian Museum and Little Coyote Gallery.

Businesses & Industries:

Cheyano Designs
P.O. Box 838
Lame Deer, MT 59043
(406) 477-6401
Manufactures designer clothing.

Karen Locher Big Hair
#2 Little Coyote Drive
Lame Deer, MT
(406) 477-8294
Sells beadwork, moccasins, jewelry, belts, wallhangings, paintings, traditional Indian flutes, ribbon shirts and shawls, and various crafts. Monday-Friday 9:00 a.m.-5:00 p.m.; special orders accepted.

Northern Cheyenne Industries
Lame Deer, MT 59043
(406) 477-6690
Manufactures tepees, other articles.

Accommodations:

Colstrip and Ashland offer nearest lodgings; about 20 miles north and east of reservation, respectively.

Rocky Boy's Reservation

Tribal Profile:

Rocky Boy's Reservation, 50,035 acres, was established in 1916 on part of the Fort Assiniboine Military Reserve to provide a home for Chippewa and Cree tribes. The present reservation population is about 2,700, governed by the Tribal Business Committee. To provide jobs and income, the tribe is actively pursuing development of its natural resources: timber, natural gas, coal, gold, silver, copper, iron, lead and zinc.

Location:

Less than 40 miles from the Canadian border, 100 miles northeast of Great Falls in north-central Montana; US 87 runs north-south at the west border of the reservation, connecting to the north with US 2.

Address:

The Chippewa Cree Business Committee
Box 544 Rocky Boy Route
Box Elder, MT 59521
(406) 395-4421

Cultural Institutions:

Stone Child College
Rocky Boy Agency
(406) 395-4269

Special Events:

Rocky Boy's Annual Pow Wow
Rocky Boy Agency
(406) 395-4421
Organized by a community-based pow wow committee, this event includes Indian contest dancing with as much as $50,000 in prize money, arts and crafts booths, food concessions, handgames, poker games, Indian relay runs and sobriety walks. Free admission. Held 1st weekend of August, beginning Thursday.

Recreational Opportunities:

4 C's Casino/Cafe
(406) 395-4850
Offers poker machines, keno, bingo, card and handgames. Cafe serves basic American menu. 1/2 mile north of Agency.

Businesses & Industries:

Rocky Boy Manufacturing
Havre, MT
(406) 265-1247

Fuel and Groceries
Agency Junction
(406) 395-4606

Friede's Highway Market
Box Elder, MT
(406) 352-4591

Agency Laundromat
Agency Grounds
(406) 395-4421

Nebraska

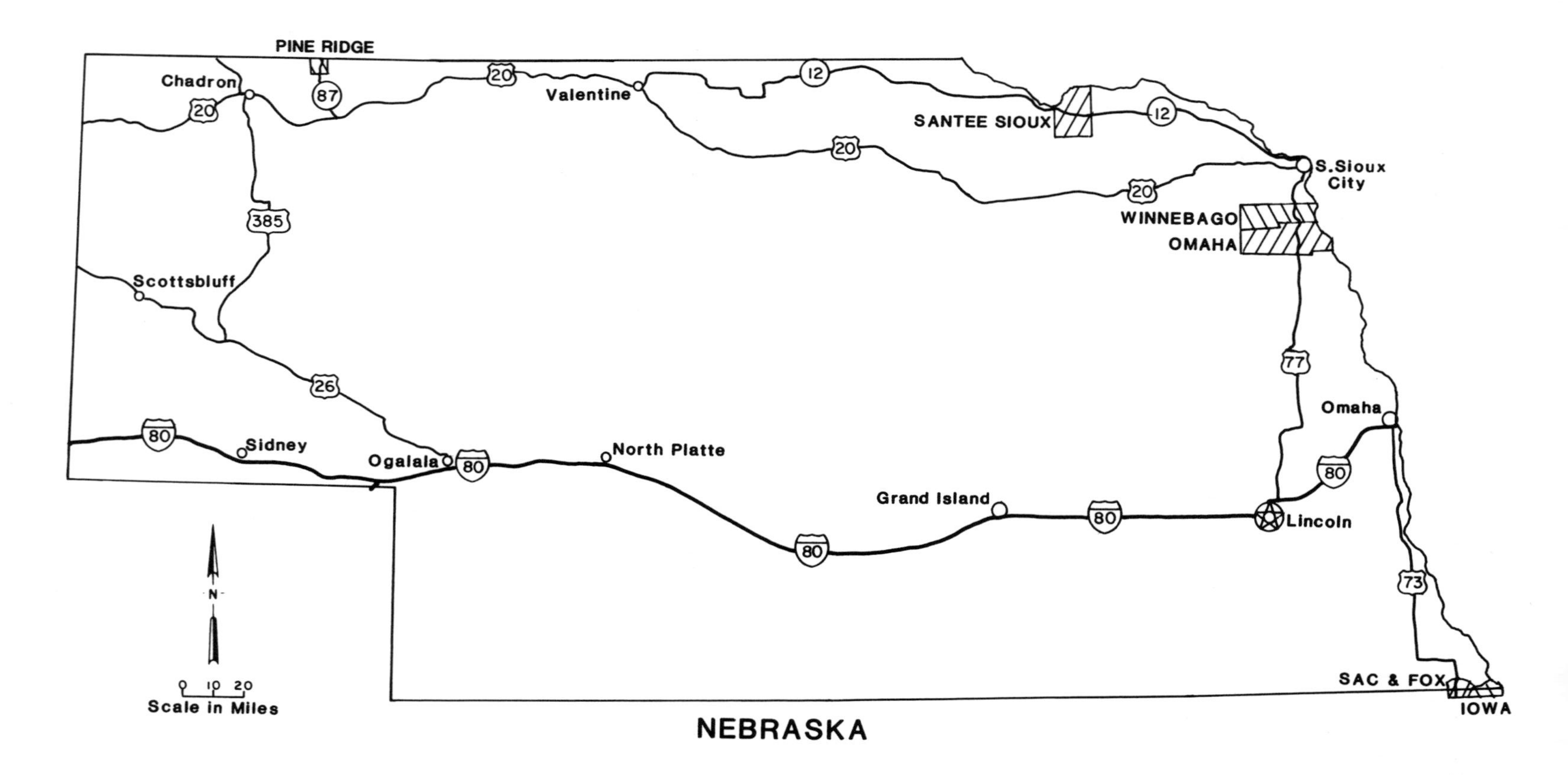
PINE RIDGE
Chadron
Valentine
SANTEE SIOUX
S.Sioux City
WINNEBAGO
OMAHA
Scottsbluff
Sidney
Ogalala
North Platte
Grand Island
Omaha
Lincoln
SAC & FOX
IOWA
N
0 10 20
Scale in Miles
20
87
12
385
26
80
77
73

NEBRASKA

Omaha Reservation

TRIBAL PROFILE:

The Omaha Tribe of Nebraska was established on the Omaha Reservation in 1854; reservation land in trust totals almost 27,000 acres today. About 1,860 members of the tribe live on the reservation, and tribal enrollment is approximately 4,000. The Omaha Tribe is governed by a seven-member council under a constitution approved and ratified in 1936. The reservation is in eastern Nebraska, immediately south of the Winnebago Reservation, on the western bank of the Missouri River. Macy is on US 75.

ADDRESS:

Omaha Tribe of Nebraska
P.O. Box 368
Macy, NE 68039
(402) 837-5391

Pine Ridge Reservation

See South Dakota

Ponca Tribe of Nebraska

TRIBAL PROFILE:

The Ponca Tribe of Nebraska received federal recognition in October 1991. The tribe has no land base at this time.

ADDRESS:

Ponca Tribe of Nebraska
Lake Andes, SD 57356
(605) 384-3651

Sac and Fox Reservation

See Iowa

Santee Sioux Reservation

TRIBAL PROFILE:

The Santee Sioux Tribe of Nebraska was established on this reservation in 1863. The present tribal enrollment is approximately 2,200, and about 500 members live on the reservation, where approximately 10,000 acres are held in trust. Tribal government is under a constitution approved in 1936; it is led by a 12-member tribal council. The reservation is in northeastern Nebraska; its northern boundary is the Missouri River where Lewis and Clark Lake is formed by the Gavins Point Dam.

ADDRESS:

Santee Sioux Tribe
Rte. 2
Niobrara, NE 68760
(402) 857-3302

Winnebago Reservation

TRIBAL PROFILE:

The Winnebago Reservation was established in Nebraska by treaties in 1865 and 1874. It encompasses almost 27,540 acres in Thurston County, and about 1,200 of the Winnebago Tribe's 2,000 members live there. Tribal government is under a constitution adopted in 1936 and led by a nine-member council. The Winnebago have joined with the Omaha and Santee Sioux to form the Nebraska Indian Inter-Tribal Development Corporation to manage government sponsored programs for the benefit of tribal members.

LOCATION:

Northeastern Nebraska; reservation borders the Missouri River and Iowa on the east; the Omaha Reservation lies to the south. Winnebago is at the junction of US 75 and US 77. About 60 miles north of Omaha and 20 miles south of Sioux City, Iowa.

ADDRESS:

Winnebago Tribe of Nebraska
Hwy 75, P.O. Box 687
Winnebago, NE 68071
(402) 878-2272

SPECIAL EVENTS:

Annual Homecoming Celebration
Veteran's Memorial Park
Winnebago, NE 68071
(402) 878-2272, ext. 24
For over 120 years this festival has taken place to celebrate the return of Chief Little Priest and Company A 34th Nebraska Volunteers in 1865. Pow wow featuring grand entries at 1:00 and 7:00 p.m. Small admission fee. Held Thursday through Sunday, last full weekend of July.

RECREATIONAL OPPORTUNITIES:

Winne Vegas Casino
Sloan, IA
(712) 428-3305
Offering Las Vegas-style games, open 24 hours a day. 3 miles west of Sloan, Iowa.

Missouri River Fishing: There are several fishing sites on the reservation; catfish are the most common catch. Permission from tribal headquarters and a reservation fishing permit are required.

Camping: sites available at Veteran's Memorial Park near Winnebago; no RV hookups.

BUSINESSES & INDUSTRIES:

Leedom Leather Crafts
Winnebago, NE 68701
(402) 878-2254
Part-time business offering crafts of various tribal artisans; features leatherwork, beadwork, ribbonwork and quilting.

Winnebago Indian News
Winnebago Tribal Offices
Winnebago NE
(402) 878-2272
Published biweekly, featuring news of the Winnebago Reservation and the Omaha Reservation.

Nevada

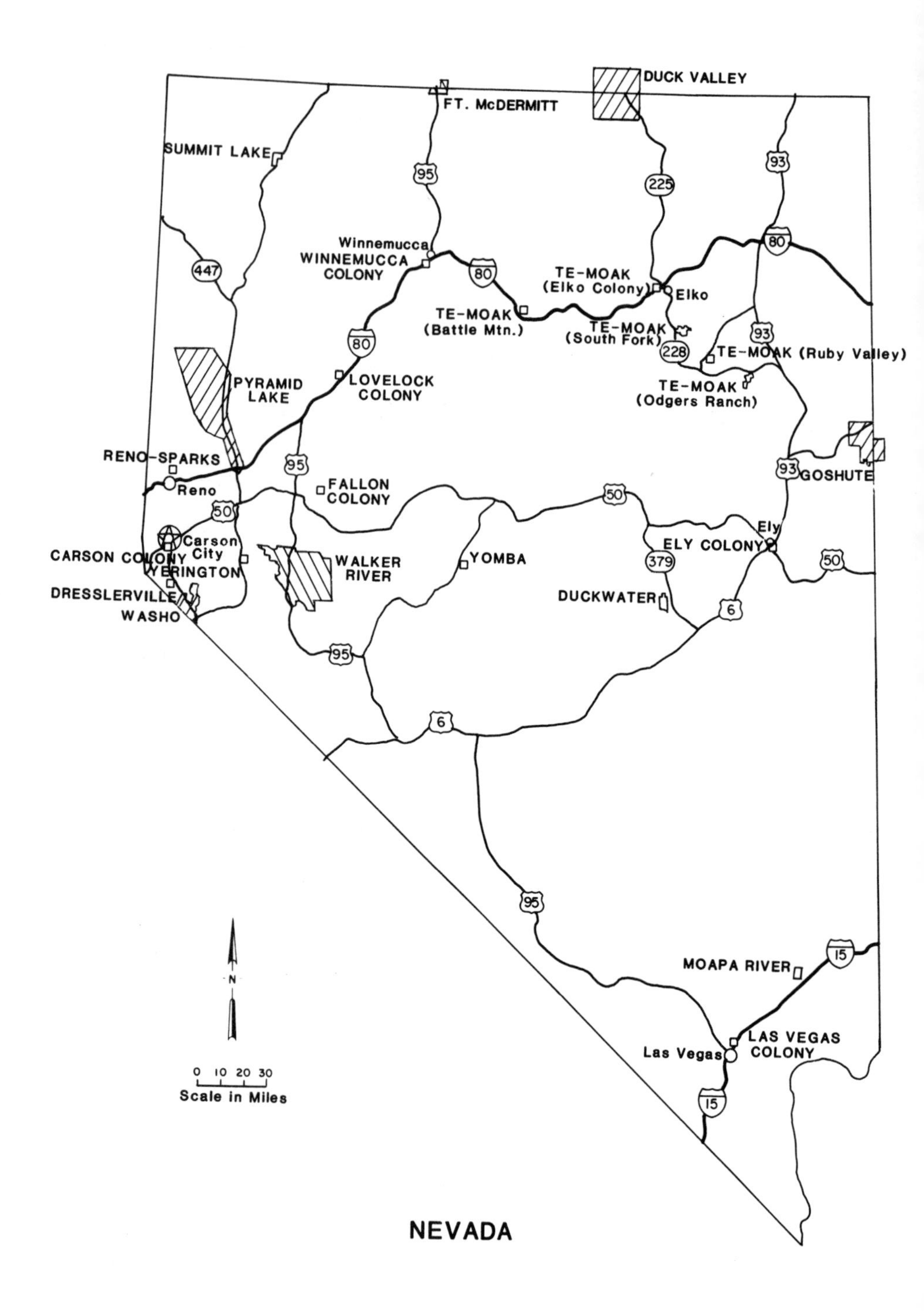
DUCK VALLEY
FT. McDERMITT
SUMMIT LAKE
95
225
93
447
Winnemucca
WINNEMUCCA
COLONY
80
TE-MOAK
(Elko Colony)
Elko
TE-MOAK
(Battle Mtn.)
TE-MOAK
(South Fork)
228
TE-MOAK (Ruby Valley)
TE-MOAK
(Odgers Ranch)
PYRAMID
LAKE
LOVELOCK
COLONY
RENO-SPARKS
Reno
FALLON
COLONY
GOSHUTE
50
Carson
City
CARSON COLONY
YERINGTON
DRESSLERVILLE
WASHO
WALKER
RIVER
YOMBA
Ely
ELY COLONY
379
DUCKWATER
6
MOAPA RIVER
15
LAS VEGAS
COLONY
Las Vegas
N
0 10 20 30
Scale in Miles

NEVADA

Carson Indian Colony

TRIBAL PROFILE:

Carson Indian Colony is part of Washoe Tribe lands; the main office for the Washoe Tribe is in Gardnerville. Land owned by the Carson Colony stands at 156 acres, purchased by the tribe in 1917; it is the home of about 1,200 enrolled members of the Carson Colony.

LOCATION:

Carson City, the capital of the State of Nevada, is in extreme west-central Nevada on US 395, east of Lake Tahoe. Tribal headquarters at Gardnerville is due south of Carson City.

ADDRESS:

Carson Indian Colony
Carson City, NV 89703
(702) 883-1446

Carson Indian Community Council
2900 S. Curry St.
Carson City, NV 89703
(702) 883-6431

Washoe Tribe
919 Hwy 395 South
Gardnerville, NV 89410
(702) 265-4191

SPECIAL EVENTS:

July 4th Pow Wow
Fuji Park
Carson City, NV
Indian festival and social pow wow; includes an arts and crafts fair.

La Ka Le'l Be Pow Wow
Fuji Park
Carson City, NV
Highlight of the year. Held in late October.

BUSINESSES & INDUSTRIES:

Washoe Tribe Smoke Shop
Carson City, NV
(702) 885-9550
Cigarettes and Indian arts and crafts.

Duck Valley Reservation

TRIBAL PROFILE:

Established by treaty on October 1, 1863, the Duck Valley Reservation originally had defined boundaries of lands in Utah, Nevada, California, Oregon, and Idaho. The treaty empowered the president to establish reservations and conferred an annuity to be paid for 20 years. While the reservation was created for the Western Shoshone, a band of the Paiute Tribe settled here in 1886. The two bands were combined and organized under the Indian Reorganization Act in 1938. Today, tribally owned lands cover 289,819 acres, split by the Nevada/Idaho border. Shoshone-Paiute membership stands at over 1,700, and tribal enterprises, farming, and grazing provide income for the tribe.

LOCATION:

Spanning the border of eastern Nevada and western Idaho near the Independence Mountains, in an area dotted with rivers and forests. North of I-80 at Elko, Owyhee is on Hwy 225.

ADDRESS:

Duck Valley Shoshone Paiute Tribes
P.O. Box 219
Owyhee, NV 89832
(702) 757-3161, -3211

SPECIAL EVENTS:

Annual 4th of July Rodeo
Owyhee, NV
Handgames and pow wow. Held July 4th week.

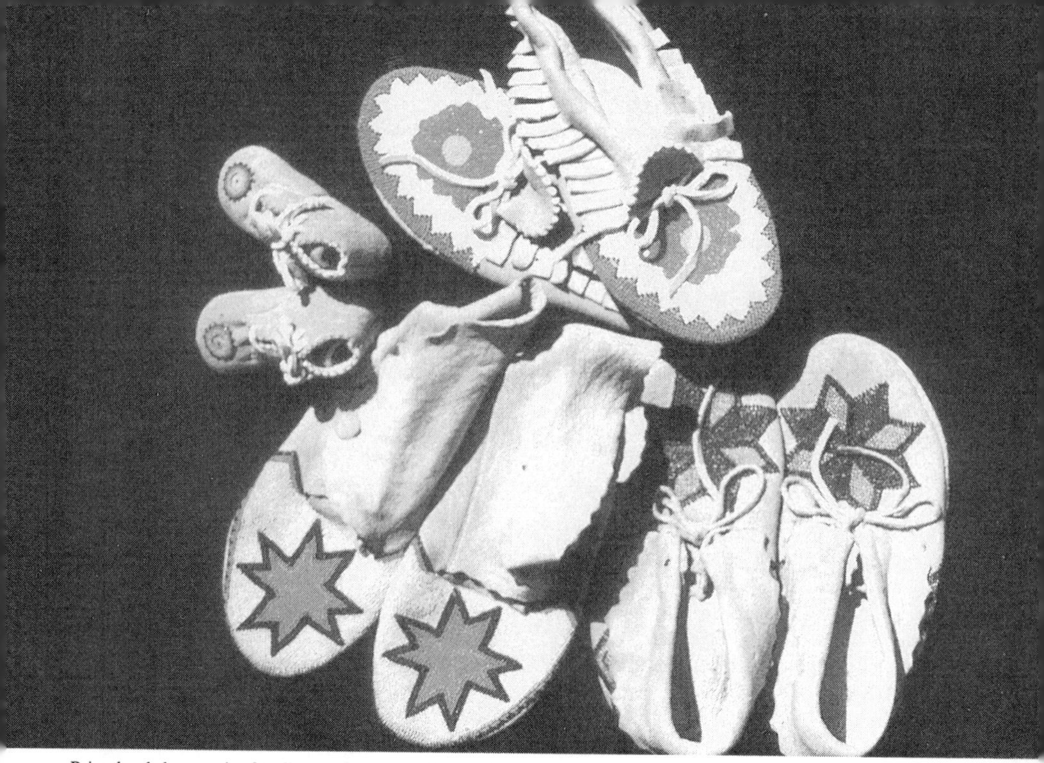

Paiute beaded moccasins for all ages. Courtesy of Nevada Commission on Tourism.

Indian Day Pow Wow
Owyhee, NV
The date of this occasion varies; check with the tribal office beforehand. Held in September.

Veteran's Day Pow Wow
Owyhee, NV
Held Veteran's Day weekend.

RECREATIONAL OPPORTUNITIES:

Mountain View Reservoir
Sheep Creek Reservoir
Two terrific areas for camping and trout fishing.

Owyhee River
Popular for rafting and fishing.

BUSINESSES & INDUSTRIES:

Rec Hall Cafe
Owyhee, NV
(702) 757-9955

ACCOMMODATIONS:

Feather Lodge
Owyhee, NV
(702) 757-3080
10 unit motel.

Duckwater Shoshone Reservation

TRIBAL PROFILE:

The Duckwater Shoshone Reservation is just under 3,800 acres of land set aside for the Shoshone Tribe in 1940, on former tribal land which had been homesteaded by non-Indians during the 1870s. Tribal membership is about 290; government is by a tribal council under the constitution ratified in 1940.

LOCATION:

Valley lands near Humboldt National Forest, southwest of Ely in eastern Nevada; from US 6, travel north on Rte. 379 to reach Duckwater.

ADDRESS:

Duckwater Shoshone Tribe
P.O. Box 140068
Duckwater, NV 89314
(702) 863-0227

SPECIAL EVENTS:

Duckwater All-Indian Rodeo
Ely, NV
Rodeo sanctioned by Western States Indian Rodeo Association and Rocky Mountain Rodeo Association. Ely is about 75 miles northeast of the reservation. Small admission fee. Held in June or July.

ACCOMMODATIONS:

Motels and RV sites in and around Ely.

Ely Indian Colony

TRIBAL PROFILE:

Ely Colony was established by an Act in 1930 that authorized a small land purchase for certain tribal groups without reservations . The Act provided rights to land privileges and government services and allowed for appropriation of monies for the purchase of 10 acres for Ely Colony. It now occupies land that this band of the Shoshone Tribe had used as a camp. Many here still speak the Shoshone language, and some traditional crafts are practiced. Tribal enterprises include a smoke shop, laundromat and day care center.

ADDRESS:

Ely Indian Colony
16 Shoshone Circle
Ely, NV 89301
(702) 289-3013

Fallon Colony & Reservation

TRIBAL PROFILE:

The Fallon Colony and Reservation, covering some 5,540 acres, are home to bands of the Shoshone and Paiute Tribes. Agriculture and tribal enterprises form the economic foundation for the 810 members. The main goal of the tribes is to bring families home by providing affordable housing and expanding job opportunities. Watch for expansion of tourism opportunities; the tribes are in transition.

LOCATION:

Western Nevada. Directly south of Carson Sink and Fallon National Wildlife Refuge, Fallon Reservation is east of Sparks, 6 miles west of Stillwater. On Rte. 116, off US 50.

ADDRESS:

Fallon Paiute-Shoshone Tribe
8955 Mission Rd.
Fallon, NV 89406
(702) 423-6075

SPECIAL EVENTS:

Fallon All-Indian Stampede & Pow Wow
Fallon Fairgrounds
Fallon, NV
(702) 423-2544
Family-organized event featuring rodeo and dancing. Held on a weekend in mid-July.

RECREATIONAL OPPORTUNITIES:

Pheasant Club
(702) 423-4676
Commercial hunting club open for pheasant hunting following the state season, from October 1 to March 31. Planning to open a trap shoot, skeet shoot, rifle ranges, sporting clay range, fishing accommodations and club house in fall 1992.

Left, Nevada Paiute Indian basket. Right, Nevada Indian jewelry. Courtesy of Nevada Commission on Tourism.

BUSINESSES & INDUSTRIES:

Fortunate Eagle's Round House Gallery
7133 Stillwater Rd.
Fallon, NV 89406
(702) 423-6663
Selling creations of stone, wood and metal; paintings and beadwork; as well as crafts by others. Educational facility also; owner conducts guided tours of gallery/museum and studio to expand public awareness of American Indians. Hours vary. Special orders accepted.

Nifty Thrifty
991 Rio Vista
(702) 423-4225
Thrift shop.

Fallon Smoke Shop & Indian Gift Center
987 Rio Vista
Fallon, NV
(702) 423-6663
Convenience store and snack bar, also selling wide variety of arts and crafts, tobacco, liquor and beer.

Fort McDermitt Reservation

TRIBAL PROFILE:

The Fort McDermitt Indian Reservation straddles the Nevada/Oregon state line, which divides its 24,650 acres into two roughly equal portions. Lands of an abandoned military post were allotted to the Shoshone and Paiute tribes in 1892; present tribal membership is just under 700. Government is by an eight-member tribal council under a constitution approved in 1936.

LOCATION:

Northern Nevada and southern Oregon; north of I-80 via US 95 at Winnemucca. The reservation borders national forest lands.

ADDRESS:

Fort McDermitt Paiute-Shoshone Tribe
P.O. Box 457
McDermitt, NV 89421
(702) 532-8259

SPECIAL EVENTS:

Red Mountain Days
Fort McDermitt
Pow wow and rodeo that includes queen/princess contest and Father's Day barbecue, as well as arts and crafts sales and performance of Indian music. Admission is free. Held 3rd weekend of June.

Las Vegas Colony & Reservation

TRIBAL PROFILE:

In 1911, 12 acres were deeded by a private party to a band of Paiute Indians, today known as the Las Vegas Colony. Now that acreage is in downtown Las Vegas. At one time, Paiute territory extended over much of Nevada, and the tribe was semi-nomadic, following the food supply. The Las Vegas Colony is governed by a three-member colony council; the colony has purchased land for a reservation outside the city.

Pow wow dancer. Courtesy of Nevada Commission on Tourism.

LOCATION:

Tribal offices are in downtown Las Vegas.

ADDRESS:

Las Vegas Paiute Tribe
No. 1 Paiute Dr.
Las Vegas, NV 89106
(702) 386-3926

SPECIAL EVENTS:

Las Vegas Paiute Snow Mtn. Pow Wow
Las Vegas Colony Reservation
A 3-day festival. Held in May or June; check with the Tribal Office for specific dates and directions.

Lovelock Colony & Reservation

TRIBAL PROFILE:

The Lovelock Paiute Tribe has an enrolled membership of 93, and reservation population is 230. Following several treaties in the late 1800s, the Lovelock band was allotted land by the Secretary of the Interior in 1907. Today 20 acres are held in trust, all of it used for residential purposes. Governed by a five-member tribal council, the Colony adopted a constitution and bylaws in 1968. It is a member of the Inter-Tribal Council of Nevada.

Lovelock Paiute Tribe
Lovelock Colony Council
P.O. Box 878
Lovelock, NV 89419
(702) 273-7861

Moapa River Reservation

Tribal Profile:

The Moapa River Reservation, just north of Lake Mead National Recreation Area and the Muddy Mountains, was created in 1873 on property in southeastern Nevada designated for use of Indians in the region. Today the 250-member Moapa Band of the Paiute Tribe lives on a 1,174 acre reservation. A six-member Moapa Business Council governs under a constitution and bylaws adopted in 1942. The tribe has formed a farming cooperative, and agriculture is the base of its economy.

Address:

Moapa Band of Paiute Indians
P.O. Box 56
Moapa, NV 89025
(702) 865-2787

Pyramid Lake Reservation

Tribal Profile:

Pyramid Lake Reservation was created by Executive Order of March 23, 1874, for Paiutes and other Indians residing in the area. This region is part of traditional Paiute homeland, and reservation lands encircle beautiful Pyramid Lake, long important to the tribe's culture and tradition. The reservation covers 475,085 acres and is home to over 1,589 residents; tribal membership is 1,798.

Location:

Northeast of Reno and Sparks, Rtes. 445 and 447 run along the west and east sides of the reservation, connecting with I-80.

Address:

Pyramid Lake Paiute Tribe
P.O. Box 256
Nixon, NV 89424
(702) 574-0140

Special Events:

Fishing Contest & Pyramid Lake Triathlon
Pyramid Lake
Held in August.

Pyramid Lake Pow Wow & Indian Rodeo
Rodeo Grounds
Nixon, NV
Held Nevada Day, last weekend in October.

Federation of Fly Fishers Derby
Nixon, NV
Held in November.

Recreational Opportunities:

Pyramid Lake: Long integral to Paiute life, the lake is home to the endangered cui-ui fish and is one of the most spectacular high desert lakes in the U.S. Look for petroglyphs in the area surrounding the Lake. Offers camping, fishing, hiking, boating, and picnicking on 70 miles of sandy beach. Day use fee. Obtain fishing license and permit from tribe.

I-80 Campground: Facilities include 7 campsites and 21 RV sites, electrical and water, pay showers, restrooms. Daily, weekly, and monthly rates. Next to Smoke Shop.

Tribal Organizations:

Cattleman's Association: 40 individual tribal members working cattle ranches.

Businesses & Industries:

I-80 Smoke Shop & Market
Wadsworth, NV
(702) 575-2181
Convenience store, arts and crafts, gas, diesel, recreation permits. Open 5:30 a.m.-11:00 p.m.

Accommodations:

Sparks offers nearest lodgings.

Top, Pyramid Lake. Bottom, Tufa formations at Pyramid Lake. Courtesy of Nevada Commission on Tourism.

Reno-Sparks Colony

Tribal Profile:

The Reno-Sparks Indian Colony is comprised of 28 acres in Reno and an additional 1,920 acres in nearby Hungry Valley. Colony members are from the Washoe and Paiute Tribes and total about 740; the colony is part of Washoe Tribe lands. The Reno-Sparks Colony also participates in Nevada Urban Indians, Inc., a multi-tribe organization that owns a shopping mall and craft store. The Washoe in particular were renowned artisans; best known was Dat-so-la-lee, a willow-basket maker whose creations are highly valued by collectors.

Location:

Western Nevada, near the California border. I-80 crosses the reservation east-west.

Address:

Reno-Sparks Colony
98 Colony Road
Reno, NV 89502
(702) 329-2936

Special Events:

Barbecue & Pow Wow
Held in late June.

Numaga Indian Days Celebration
Festival includes competition pow wow, arts and crafts, and musical entertainment. Free admission. 3 days; held Labor Day weekend.

Christmas Sale
Held 2nd weekend in December.

Red Star New Year's Pow Wow
Festivities begin 7:00 p.m., ending midnight, New Year's Eve.

Businesses & Industries:

Earth Window
Nevada Urban Indians, Inc.
401 W. 2nd St.
Reno, NV 89503
(702) 786-5999
Sells unique and highly collectable Great Basin Indian arts and crafts from the Shoshone, Paiute and Washoe. In the Reno-Tahoe Visitors Center. Open Tuesday-Friday, 9:30 a.m.-5:30 p.m., Saturday until 5:00 p.m.

Indian Colony Mall
2001 E. 2nd Ave.
Reno, NV
Indoor shopping complex with discount cigarette shop, arts and crafts shops, book store, jewelry stores, and beauty salon.

Native Nevadan
1575 Crane Way
Sparks, NV
Monthly magazine published by Sierra Press.

Sierra Press
1575 Crane Way
Sparks, NV
(702) 329-2936
Printing magazines, tabloids, and newspapers for 5 years. Tours by arrangement.

Summit Lake Reservation

Tribal Profile:

The Paiute Tribe has long lived throughout much of what is now called Nevada. The Summit Lake Reservation was created on the old Camp McGarry Military Reserve in 1913, and tribally owned lands cover 10, 506 acres in Humboldt County at Summit Lake. Presently the reservation population is 16; tribal membership is 112, and these numbers continue to increase slowly. Fishing revenues, land leases and grazing permits form the economic base for this band of the Paiute Tribe.

Summit Lake Paiute Tribe
P.O. Box 1958
Winnemucca, NV 89445
(702) 623-5151

Te Moak Reservation

TRIBAL PROFILE:

Operating under a constitution and bylaws approved in 1982 to establish the Te-Moak Western Shoshone Council, the Western Shoshone Tribe has four separate colonies: Battle Mountain, Elko, South Fork, and Wells. Each colony participates in the Council, which has total jurisdiction over all tribal lands, although the colonies retain sovereignty over all other affairs. The main office for the Western Shoshone Tribe is in Elko.

Te Moak Tribe of Western Shoshone
525 Sunset St.
Elko, NV 89801
(702) 738-9251

Battle Mountain Colony
035 Mtn. View Dr. #138-13
Battle Mountain, NV 89820
(702) 635-2004
Established on June 18, 1917, by Executive Order, Battle Mountain Colony covers 680 acres. The Shoshone settled at this site claim to be direct descendants of Chief Te-Moak, grandson of the Chief Te-Moak who signed the 1863 treaty resolving a conflict between the Indians and the U.S. military. There are 514 enrolled members.

Elko Band Colony
P.O. Box 748
Elko, NV 89801
(702) 738-8889
Elko Colony was created by Executive Order in 1918, reserving for the Shoshone 160 acres on two separate parcels. Colony lands stand today at 195 acres and tribal enrollment at 1,143. Economic development projects include a smoke shop and commercial leases.

South Fork Band Colony
Box B-15
Lee, NV 89829
(702) 744-4273
South Fork Band Colony lands cover 15,156 acres. The first land purchases were effected in 1938 and 1939, with later additions; the reservation was created by Executive Order in 1941. South Fork belongs to the Inter-Tribal Council of Nevada as part of efforts to improve reservation resources for its 239 tribal members.

Wells Band Colony
P.O. Box 809
Wells, NV 89835
(702) 752-3045
Over 2,000 registered members live on Wells Colony lands, approximately 160 acres. On March 25, 1918, lands were reserved for the Shoshone and Paiute Indians living near Elko. Both Wells and Elko Colony lands are situated on the 160 acre allotment. Development enterprises include a smoke shop and cut and sew operations.

Walker River Reservation

TRIBAL PROFILE:

The Walker River Indian Reservation, comprising 324,000 acres, is home to members of the Paiute Tribe. About 830 members out of a total tribal enrollment of 1,555 live on the reservation. Government is by a seven-member council under a constitution adopted in 1937. The Walker River tribal economy is based on agricultural enterprises, including livestock and the leasing and operating of heavy construction equipment, as well as small commercial enterprises.

LOCATION:

On the Walker River in western Nevada, east of Lake Tahoe and Carson City and north of Walker Lake. US 95 crosses the reservation north-south.

ADDRESS:

Walker River Paiute Tribe
P.O. Box 220
Schurz, NV 89427
(702) 773-2306

Walker Lake on the Walker River Reservation. Courtesy of Nevada Commission on Tourism.

SPECIAL EVENTS:

Annual Pinenut Festival
Family event featuring Pinenut Blessing, games, All-Indian rodeo, handgame tourney, horseshoe tourney, Indian car parade, and Miss Indian Walker River and Li'l Miss Pinenut Festival pageants, as well as arts and crafts and Indian music. Admission is free. Held 3rd weekend in September.

RECREATIONAL OPPORTUNITIES:

Hunting, trapping, fishing, and hiking are permitted on reservation lands; secure a license from the tribal office. RV park near Black Mountain Truck Stop.

BUSINESSES & INDUSTRIES:

Four Season's Market & Smoke Shop
South Hwy 95
Schurz, NV
(702) 773-2588
Offering arts and crafts, gas, groceries, cigarettes.

Black Mountain Truck Stop
Schurz Hwy/US Alt 95
Schurz, NV
(702) 773-2306
24-hour stop with full-service restaurant, showers, cultural center, smoke shop, and RV park.

Winter Moon Trading Company
P.O. Box 189
Schurz, NV 89427
(702) 773-2510
Beaded and silver jewelry, horsehair baskets, pottery, and arrowheads. Open 10:00 a.m.-5:00 p.m., Wednesday-Sunday. Mail order accepted.

Washoe Tribe of Nevada & California

• Carson Colony • Dresslerville Colony • Reno-Sparks Colony
• Stewart Colony • Woodsford Colony

TRIBAL PROFILE:

Retaining much of its language and culture, the Washoe Tribe lives primarily in five colonies near Reno: Carson, Dresslerville, Reno-Sparks, Stewart, and Woodsford Colonies. The main office for the Washoe Tribe is in Gardnerville. Total trust acreage for the tribe is 1,071, with a tribal membership of 812. Colony lands, tribally owned or allotted, number as follows: Carson, 156 acres; Dresslerville, 40 acres; Stewart, 2,877 acres; Washoe Ranches, 795 acres; and Woodsford, 80 acres. Smoke shops, a farm, and a trailer park are some of the economic development projects the tribe has undertaken. Agriculture, campgrounds, and businesses constitute the major sources of tribal income.

ADDRESS:

Washoe Tribe of Nevada & California
919 Hwy 395 South
Gardnerville, NV 89410
(702) 265-4191

Yerington Colony & Reservation

TRIBAL PROFILE:

Land purchased for the Yerington Paiute Reservation in 1936 and 1941 totals 1,156 acres. Yerington Colony lands cover 9,456 acres and were acquired for non-reservation Indians in 1917. The Yerington Paiute Tribe numbers 659; it is a member of the Inter-Tribal Council of Nevada, formed by the state's tribes to promote the economic development of their reservations.

LOCATION:

Southeast of Carson City; Tribal administration offices are on Hwy 95A, 8 miles north of Yerington.

ADDRESS:

Yerington Paiute Tribe
171 Campbell Lane
Yerington, NV 89447
(702) 463-3301 or 883-3895

ARCHAEOLOGICAL & HISTORIC SITES:

Wovoka Historical Marker: Erected by the Paiute people to honor the famous prophet Wovoka, remembered by many as the founding father of the Ghost Dance religion. At Campbell Ranch. For further information contact: Yerington Colony Elder Center, Yerington, NV.

BUSINESSES & INDUSTRIES:

Arrowhead Market
Yerington Paiute Reservation
(702) 463-4866
Mini-mart and gas station.

Dairy Queen
198 Goldfield
Yerington, NV
(702) 463-4040

Yerington Paiute Smoke Shop
601 W. Bridge Street
Yerington, NV
(702) 463-3670

ACCOMMODATIONS:

Motels in downtown Yerington.

Yomba Shoshone Reservation

TRIBAL PROFILE:

The Yomba Shoshone reside in the Shoshone Mountains; tribal lands follow Rock River, covering some 4,682 acres in the heart of Toiyabe National Forest. Several old ranches comprise the reservation, and it is checkered with non-Indian ranches. Yomba Reservation is home to a band of the Western Shoshone, who have long lived throughout Idaho, Utah, Nevada, and California. The six-member Yomba Business Council is the governing body which oversees tribal affairs.

ADDRESS:

Yomba Shoshone Tribe
Rte. 1, Box 24
Austin, NV 89310
(702) 964-2463, -2248

New Mexico

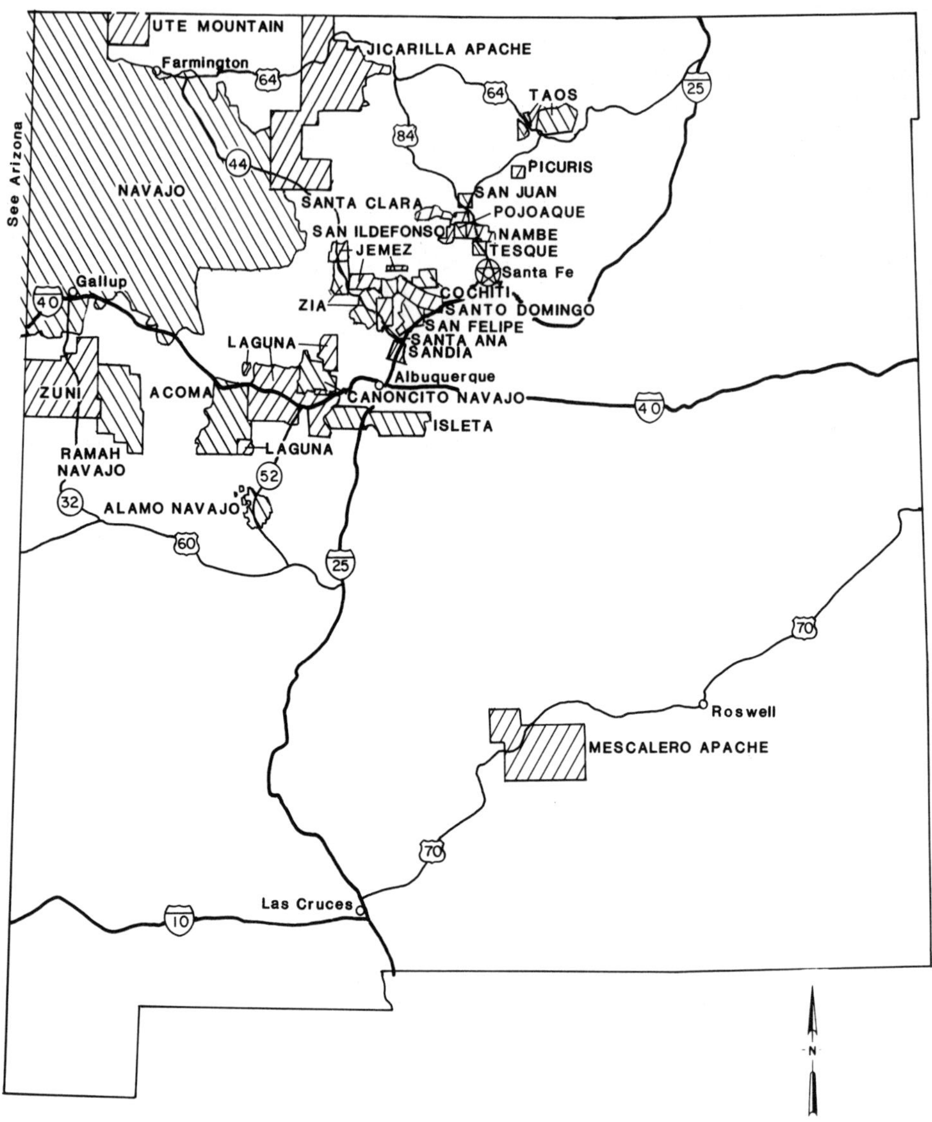
UTE MOUNTAIN
JICARILLA APACHE
Farmington
64
TAOS
25
84
PICURIS
44
NAVAJO
See Arizona
SANTA CLARA
SAN JUAN
POJOAQUE
SAN ILDEFONSO
NAMBE
JEMEZ
TESQUE
Santa Fe
Gallup
40
ZIA
COCHITI
SANTO DOMINGO
SAN FELIPE
LAGUNA
SANTA ANA
SANDIA
Albuquerque
ZUNI
ACOMA
CANONCITO NAVAJO
40
ISLETA
RAMAH NAVAJO
LAGUNA
52
32
ALAMO NAVAJO
60
25
70
Roswell
MESCALERO APACHE
70
Las Cruces
10
N
0 10 20
Scale in Miles

NEW MEXICO

"Sky City" – Acoma Pueblo. Courtesy of Acoma Pueblo Visitors Center.

Acoma Pueblo

TRIBAL PROFILE:

Originally referred to as the "Sky City" because it sits on a 350-foot high mesa, the Pueblo of Acoma has been continuously inhabited for at least 1,000 years. Nearby farming villages have become permanent home for many of the 4,350 Acoma Indians residing on this 249,947 acre reservation. The Spanish made the original land grant to the Pueblo of Acoma on September 20, 1689; it was confirmed by a patent issued by President Hayes on November 19, 1877. Famous for their pottery, the Acoma also pursue ranching, farming and developing natural resources such as coal, oil, natural gas and uranium.

LOCATION:

Close to I-40. About 65 miles west of Albuquerque, near Grants, the Acoma Pueblo mesa offers dramatic views of the surrounding valley. The Visitor Center is on Rte. 38.

ADDRESS:

Pueblo de Acoma
P.O. Box 309
Acomita, NM 87034
(505) 552-6604

CULTURAL INSTITUTIONS:

Acoma Tourist Visitor Center
P.O. Box 309
Acomita, NM 87034
(505) 252-1139 or (800) 747-0181
Houses a museum, native food and crafts shops, and tour and tourist information. Recently completed permanent museum exhibit entitled "One Thousand Years of Clay: Pottery, Environment and History".

SPECIAL EVENTS:

Governor's Feast
Pueblo of Acoma, NM
Held in February.

Easter Celebration
Acomita and McCartys, NM
Held in March/April, depending upon the date for Easter.

Santa Maria Feast
McCartys, NM
Held 1st Sunday in May.

Rooster Pulls
Pueblo of Acoma, NM
Held on traditional feast days: San Juan's Day, June 24; Sts. Peter & Paul's Day, June 29; and Santiago's Day, July 29. There are no scheduled times; the pulls happen when everyone is ready.

Fiesta Day
Acomita, NM
A celebration of San Lorenzo's Day. Held August 10.

Harvest Dance & Annual Feast of San Estevan
Pueblo of Acoma, NM
A harvest and social dance honoring St. Stephen, patron saint of the Acoma Pueblo. Activities include a saint procession, Indian music, arts and crafts sales. Held September 2.

Christmas Festivals
San Estevan del Rey Mission
Held December 25-28.

RECREATIONAL OPPORTUNITIES:

Acoma Bingo
near Acomita, NM
(505) 552-6604; Sundays -6608
Hours: Wednesday-Friday, 6:30-10:00 p.m., Sunday, 12:30-4:00 p.m. Off I-40 at Exit 102, south; follow the bingo signs.

The tribe is in the process of developing Acomita Lake for recreation.

ARCHAEOLOGICAL & HISTORIC SITES:

Acoma Pueblo: Very old, 2nd only to Old Oraibi Village on the Hopi Reservation in Arizona for length of habitation and period of construction. Tours offered daily except for July 10-13 and the 1st and 2nd week-ends of October; contact the Visitor Center for hours, cost and to arrange tours.

Enchanted Mesa: Looms large in Acoma history and above the valley from which it rises 400 feet. Acoma legend teaches that the Mesa was inhabited by their ancestors. Hwy 23 passes by, offering a splendid view.

San Esteban del Rey Mission: Sharing the massive sandstone mesa with the Pueblo of Acoma, the mission was completed in 1640 on the site of a previous village. A National Historic Landmark. Visitors must register at the Visitor's Center for guided tours.

ACCOMMODATIONS:

Closest lodgings are in Grants, west of Acoma Pueblo.

RESTRICTIONS AND/OR SPECIAL CONSIDERATIONS:

Check in at the vistors center upon arrival. Please stay within plaza and street areas and do not climb any structures. No camera/video recorder use allowed at ceremonies or dances; no photography without a permit. No camping, hiking, or climbing rock formations in this fragile area.

Alamo Navajo Reservation

TRIBAL PROFILE:

Rather than continue the long march to the northern New Mexico/Arizona Navajo Reservation from Fort Sumner, this portion of the Navajo tribe elected to settle in west-central New Mexico. Approximately 1,100 tribal members live on the 63,109 acre Alamo Reservation and form a chapter of the Navajo Nation. Please see the section on the Navajo in the Arizona state listing for more detailed information about the Navajo Nation as a whole and particulars on what to see and do on the Alamo Navajo Reservation ***(Navajo - Eastern section).***

LOCATION:

Alamo Navajo Reservation is in a mountainous region southwest of Albuquerque. Bordered on 3 sides by national forest, this remote reservation can be reached on paved road only via Rte. 169, off US 60 at Magdalena.

ADDRESS:

Alamo Navajo Chapter
Alamo, NM 87825
(505) 854-2686

ACCOMMODATIONS:

There are locations for camping, fishing, hunting, and hiking throughout the area. Lodging available in Magdalena.

Cañoncito Navajo Reservation

TRIBAL PROFILE:

Cañoncito Reservation was settled by part of the Navajo tribe who chose to remain in this area rather than continue the long trek to the Navajo Reservation from Ft. Sumner. The 76,000-acre Cañoncito reservation is home to about 740 residents and is a chapter of the Navajo Nation. Please see the section on the Navajo in the Arizona state listing for more detailed information about the Navajo Nation as a whole and particulars – **in the Eastern section** – on what to see and do at Cañoncito.

LOCATION:

Due east of Albuquerque, north of I-40, Cañoncito Reservation lies between two portions of the Laguna Indian Reservation on a county road. Close to the Ciboleta Mountains and Indian Petroglyph State Park.

ADDRESS:

Cañoncito Navajo Chapter
Cañoncito, NM 87026
(505) 854-2686

ACCOMMODATIONS:

There are locations for camping, fishing, hunting, and hiking throughout the area.

Cochiti Pueblo

TRIBAL PROFILE:

Approximately 1,000 tribal members living at the Cochiti Pueblo continue to farm and create jewelry, pottery and storyteller figures, although many work in Albuquerque or Santa Fe. The arts of Cochiti Pueblo are widely acclaimed, particularly their storyteller figures and drums. The 50,669 acre reservation lies west of the Rio Grande River, and with the construction of Cochiti Dam, opportunities for water sports have multiplied. The land lease for development of the Town of Cochiti Lakes is a major source of tribal income.

LOCATION:

West of I-25, 25 miles south of Santa Fe, near Cochiti Dam; west of the Rio Grande River. A county road crosses the pueblo.

ADDRESS:

Pueblo of Cochiti
P.O. Box 70
Cochiti, NM 87041
(505) 867-3211 or 465-2244

SPECIAL EVENTS:

Riverman's Day
Pueblo of Cochiti
Celebration honoring Santa Cruz. Held on May 3.

Dances & Ceremonies
Pueblo Church
Celebrations praying for rain for the crops. Held throughout the summer; check with Governor's Office for details and specific dates.

San Buenaventura Feast Day
Pueblo of Cochiti
Honoring the patron saint of the Pueblo, San Buenaventura, and a most important commemoration. Held July 14.

RECREATIONAL OPPORTUNITIES:

Cochiti Lakes Golf Course
(505) 465-2239
Amenities include an 18-hole championship golf course, driving range, putting green, restaurant serving breakfast and lunch, and a games room. Tee times are booked a maximum of 7 days in advance.

Cochiti Lake Golf Course. Courtesy of Bill Winfield.

Cochiti Lakes Marina
(505) 465-2219
Canoe and outboard motorboat rentals available on a seasonal basis, usually April through October. The one paved road in the area goes directly to the marina. Advance booking recommended as the number of boats is modest.

The Lakes themselves have areas for camping, fishing, and swimming. Permits can be purchased from the US Army Corps of Engineers.

Cochiti Recreation Center
Town of Cochiti Lakes
(505) 465-2239
Facilities include tennis courts, a jr. olympic swimming pool and children's pool, bingo, volleyball, horseshoes, and a children's playground. Open year-round; the pool is open late May-September.

ARCHAEOLOGICAL & HISTORIC SITES:

San Buenaventura Mission: Built in 1628 in honor of San Buenaventura. Much of the structure has been rebuilt and remodelled; however, some original portions remain. Obtain permission to tour the church from Governor's Office.

BUSINESSES & INDUSTRIES:

Allsups Convenience Store
Cochiti Lakes Plaza
(505) 465-2352
A wide variety of the basics; also fishing tackle and ice. A laundromat next door.

Cochiti Development Corporation
(505) 465-2219
Manages the Town of Cochiti Lake.

RESTRICTIONS AND/OR SPECIAL CONSIDERATIONS:

Check with Governor's Office or community center regarding photography and visiting the Pueblo of Cochiti. No photography allowed.

Isleta Pueblo

TRIBAL PROFILE:

The largest of the Tiwa speaking pueblos, Isleta is home to 3,000. Several communities scattered along the Rio Grande constitute the Pueblo of Isleta; the river bisects the 211,000 acre reservation. Pueblo members actively pursue farming and ranching. Production of traditional polychrome pottery, black or red on white, continues, and the Pueblo's mastery of pottery and cloth techniques is widely acclaimed. Some available resources are sand and gravel, oil and gas, lead, copper, and important leases and permits to outside interests.

LOCATION:

Directly south of Albuquerque off I-25 on Rte. 47.

ADDRESS:

Pueblo of Isleta
P.O. Box 317
Isleta, NM 87022
(505) 869-3111, -6333

SPECIAL EVENTS:

San Reyes Day
Laguna Plaza
Corn Dance is performed in celebration of the coming of the 3 kings. Held the 1st or 2nd weekend in January.

Social Dances
Laguna Plaza
For 2 succeeding weekends Pueblo men and women join hands and dance to traditional songs. Held in March after water is let into the ditches at the beginning of farming season.

Palm & Easter Sunday Races
Laguna Plaza
Both youths and adults engage in foot races, with dancing held afterwards.

Governor's Feast
Isleta Pueblo
Dances and a feast follow a mass celebrating Saint Augustine, patron saint of the Pueblo. Held 3rd or 4th week of June.

Saint Augustine Day
Isleta Pueblo.
Honoring the Pueblo's patron saint, the festival begins with a mass and saint's procession, succeeded by dances, a small carnival, food, arts and crafts, and musical entertainment. Held on August 28.

Saint Augustine's Feast Day
Isleta Pueblo
The most important celebration of the year, paying tribute to this venerated saint. An evening mass, procession, vigil and dances take place on the eve of the celebration. The morning begins with another mass and procession. Dances go on throughout the afternoon, and a feast, small carnival, arts and crafts sales and music round out the day. Held September 14.

Christmas Dances
Saint Augustine Church
(505) 869-3398
Dancing continues for 4 consecutive days, concluding with Innocents Possessive Day, an occasion when children who are dancing for the first time are celebrated with small gifts and goods thrown into the air for the performers and the public to catch.

RECREATIONAL OPPORTUNITIES:

Isleta Bingo Palace
11000 Broadway SE
Albuquerque, NM 87105
(505) 869-2614 (800) 843-5156
Luxurious, modern bingo center offering large jackpots, pull tabs, group tour and fund raising opportunities, a complete snack bar, and free bus transportation from many areas. Open 7 nights a week; hours vary.

Isleta Lakes
(505) 893-3111
Camping, picnicking, and fishing. Purchase permits at the Lakes.

ARCHAEOLOGICAL & HISTORIC SITES:

Saint Augustine Church: Established in 1613. Constructed of adobe bricks, the walls range from 4 to 10 feet thick. Much of the interior of the church was incinerated during a pueblo revolt, but restoration began with the return of the Isleta people 20 years later. In more recent times stained glass windows have been added, illuminating paintings of the saints, some at least 200 years old. Open daily to the public.

RESTRICTIONS AND/OR SPECIAL CONSIDERATIONS

Some times during the year the Pueblo is closed to outsiders for religious rites. Only St. Augustine Church may be photographed. Religious buildings, such as kivas, are off limits to all non-Isletans and are marked by signs.

Jemez Pueblo

TRIBAL PROFILE:

The only remaining Towa speaking pueblo, Jemez Pueblo is surrounded by high desert plains in the Jemez Mountains. Legend states that the tribe has inhabited the lands bordering the Jemez River and its tributaries for centuries. The original Pueblo grant was made by the Spanish in 1689, and confirmed by both Act of Congress in 1858 and patent from President Lincoln on November 1, 1864. Today, the reservation stretches over 89,617 acres, in several parcels. The Jemez have a traditional tribal government with no written constitution.

Agriculture still has a place here, and there are some excellent chili and corn fields, although many Jemez people have found occupations in local forestry operations. The highlight of Jemez craftsmanship is the beautiful traditional polychrome pottery; the Pueblo is home to celebrated ceramicists. Pueblo artisans are also well known for their weaving, particularly of fine yucca baskets. Mineral resource development (sand and gravel, timber, and geothermal) has increased in importance since 1987.

LOCATION:

55 miles from Albuquerque; easily accessible from I-25 via Hwy 44 at Bernalillo. Jemez Pueblo is on Rte. 4.

ADDRESS:

Pueblo of Jemez
P.O. Box 78
Jemez Pueblo, NM 87024
(505) 834-7359
FAX: (505) 834-7331

CULTURAL INSTITUTIONS:

Jemez Visitor's Center
Jemez Pueblo
(505) 834-7359
Arts and crafts and tourist information, including questions regarding the Pueblo, details about the material contained in this write-up.

SPECIAL EVENTS:

Ceremonies and feast days open to the public include those taking place on August 2, November 12, December 25, and January 6. Jemez has additional ceremonies that may or may not be open to the traveller. For specific information contact Governor's Office.

RECREATIONAL OPPORTUNITIES:

Jemez Red Rocks Area: Situated in a breathtaking region just 3 miles north of Jemez Pueblo on Rte. 4.

Holy Ghost Springs: Ideal spot for camping and fishing.

Dragonfly Recreation Area: Camping and fishing available here.

Hunting and Camping: Special elk hunt offered for non-tribal people every year; only a limited number may participate; price varies. Hunting also allowed on a personal basis. Spring brings the opportunity to participate in the turkey bow hunt. Contact Governor's Office for permission to hunt, fish or camp.

Hot Springs: The Santa Fe National Forest maintains several hot springs in this region.

ARCHAEOLOGICAL & HISTORIC SITES:

Jemez State Monument: One-of-a-kind museum in visitors center focuses on Jemez People's perspective; hands-on displays. A self-guided tour takes the visitor through Guisewa (Towa for Place At The Boiling Waters) Pueblo ruins dating from A.D. 1250-1300, and a Spanish mission built in 1620s. 1,100 ft. trail takes approximately 25 minutes to walk. Open 7 days week, 8:30 a.m.-4:30 p.m., in winter; 9:00 a.m.-6:00 p.m., in summer. Information: (505) 829-3530. 14 miles north of Jemez Pueblo. Entry fee for those 16 and over.

Jicarilla Apache baskets from the Arts and Crafts Cooperative. A Dale W. Anderson Photo. Courtesy of Aztec Media Workshop.

Jicarilla Apache Reservation

TRIBAL PROFILE:

The Jicarilla Apache Tribe occupies a reservation of 870,000 acres in the mountains of northern New Mexico, established in 1887 with additions in later years. The reservation straddles the continental divide and provides a wide variety of outdoor recreation opportunities. Terrain in the southern portion of the reservation is more open, with plains, rolling hills edged with sandstone and deep mesa canyons. Tribal membership is about 2,800, governed by tribal council under a constitution ratified in 1937. Active economic development efforts by the tribe have resulted in several businesses on the reservation and a variety of business investments in other areas of the U.S.

LOCATION:

Northwest New Mexico; crossed east-west by US 64 and Rte. 44; north-south by Rte. 537. Bordered on the north by the Southern Ute Reservation in Colorado. Paved, 5,200-foot, all-weather airstrip in Dulce.

ADDRESS:

Jicarilla Apache Tribe
P.O. Box 507
Dulce, NM 87528
(505) 759-3242

CULTURAL INSTITUTIONS:

Jicarilla Apache Arts & Crafts Shop and Museum
Dulce, NM
(505) 759-3242, ext. 274
Jicarilla Tribe is famous for their basketry; Jicarilla literally means "little basket." At the museum, tribal craftsmen demonstrate basket weaving using traditional techniques. Gift shop offers these baskets, individually designed beadwork and paintings by reservation artists. Weekdays and Saturday, 8:00 a.m. to 5:00 p.m.

SPECIAL EVENTS:

Little Beaver Round Up
Jicarilla Rodeo Grounds
Dulce, NM
(505) 759-3242, ext. 275
Festival includes parade, 3-day open and all-Indian rodeo, Indian dances, carnival, cross-country pony express race, and crownings of Little Beaver, Rodeo Queen, attendants and princess. Many area tribes participate. Held 3rd weekend of July.

Stone Lake Fiesta
Fiesta Grounds
Stone Lake, NM
Ceremonial relay races between the Red and White Clans. Amateur rodeo and traditional Indian dances. Tribal Clans gather to camp. Open to the public, but mainly a family reunion. About 18 miles south of Dulce. Free admission. Held mid-September.

Clockwise , from right: Trophy elk hunting. Courtesy of Byran Vigil. Stone Lake, looking east. A Dale W. Anderson Photo. Courtesy of Aztec Media Workshop. Jicarilla Inn at Dulce, New Mexico. A Dale W. Anderson Photo. Courtesy of Aztec Media Workshop.

RECREATIONAL OPPORTUNITIES:

Department of Game and Fish
P.O. Box 546
Dulce, NM 87528
(505) 759-3255
With carefully managed hunting areas and 7 fishing lakes, the Jicarilla Reservation offers excellent hunting and fishing opportunities. Trophy quality deer and elk abound; guides are required for all hunts. Permits on a first-come basis. Fees vary according to services requested.

Dulce, Enbom, Hayden, Horse, La Jara, Mundo and Stone Lakes and the Navajo River are stocked annually with rainbow, cutthroat and brown trout. Camping is permitted at reservation lakes; tables, grills and shelters available. Ice fishing in winter. Limited boating permitted. Tribal fishing permit required; state fishing license not necessary.

The reservation's abundant lakes and ponds provide excellent waterfowl hunting, especially at Stinking Lake (no fishing here). Fine spring bear and turkey hunting; guides required for bear hunts.

Horse Lake Mesa Game Park
Game Park Manager
P.O. Box 313
Dulce, NM 87528
(505) 759-3442
Area set aside by the tribe for elk hunting; black bear and predatory animal hunts also available. Exceptional big game habitat, in elevations ranging from 7,500 to 8,500 feet, on the western slope of the Rocky Mountains. Offers superb hunting conditions and record-quality game animals. Guide required to hunt in the park; fees charged.

ARCHAEOLOGICAL & HISTORIC SITES:

Scattered throughout the Jicarilla Apache Reservation are ruins, spectacular natural formations, lookout towers and historic places such as the Jicarilla Apache Historic District at the old agency site. Contact or stop by the tribal office in Dulce for a detailed map of the reservation.

ACCOMMODATIONS:

Best Western Jicarilla Inn
P.O. Box 233
Dulce, NM 87528
(505) 759-3663; (800) 528-1234
Offers the finest in accommodations with luxurious rooms, elegant decor and open-air atmosphere. Facilities include Hill Crest Restaurant featuring regional and American specialties, Timber Lake Lounge, and Gojiiya Conference Center. Apache Mesa Gallery and Gift Shop displays original traditional and contemporary arts and craft of Jicarilla artisans. Package tours for the nearby Cumbres and Toltec narrow gauge railroad available.

Laguna Pueblo

Old Laguna Pueblo, looking west. Courtesy of Gary Robinson, Santa Fe.

TRIBAL PROFILE:

The Pueblo of Laguna was settled some time before the late 1600s by an Indian people called the Keres. The Pueblo consists of six small villages mostly located along the Rio San Jose Valley. Tribal trust lands total 528,684 acres in three locations, with the two smaller segments sitting southwest and northwest of the main reservation.

The Laguna continue to hold on to their language, traditional lifestyle and religion, although some non-Indian religions are also active on the reservation. The Laguna Pueblo Reservation is rich in natural resources and those, along with recreation and tribal enterprise, contribute greatly to tribal income.

LOCATION:

Due west of Albuquerque in west-central New Mexico, the Laguna Reservation is sandwiched between the Acoma Pueblo on the west and the Isleta Pueblo on the east. Laguna Pueblo stands out against a background of mesas and mountains just off I-40.

ADDRESS:

Pueblo of Laguna
P.O. Box 194
Laguna, NM 87026
(505) 243-7616, 552-6654, -6655

Laguna Pueblo Mission Church. Photo by Mark Nohl. Courtesy of New Mexico Magazine.

Special Events:

The following fiestas and dances are held throughout the Laguna Reservation; their locations are indicated under the name of the occasion. Unless otherwise noted, performers dance the Harvest Dance and other dances, with activities beginning mid-morning and continuing until sunset. Questions about social and religious ceremonies should be directed to the Governor of the Pueblo.

St. Joseph's Feast Day
Old Laguna Village
The original Feast Day. Held in mid-March.

Feast Days
All 6 Villages
Also called Grab Day as the people with names of patron saints throw small wares or baked goods from the rooftops of their homes. Feast Days named: St. John's (June 24), San Pedro's (June 29), St. James (Santiago), and St. Lawrence (August 15).

St. Ann's Feast Day
All 6 Villages
Held July 26.

The Assumption of Our Blessed Mother's Feast Day
Mesita Village, NM
Held August 15.

The Nativity of the Blessed Virgin Mary's Feast Day
Encinal Village, NM
Held September 8.

St. Joseph's Feast Day
Old Laguna Village, NM
All of Laguna Pueblo turns out to celebrate this day with a fair that draws people from throughout the state. Held September 19.

St. Elizabeth's Feast Day
Paguate Village, NM
Held September 25.

St. Margaret's Feast Day
Paraje Village, NM
Held October 17.

Christmas Eve Mass
All 6 Villages
After a midnight mass, dancers dramatize the Harvest, Arrow, Deer and other dances. The Harvest dance continues for 3 days, until December 28.

Archaeological & Historic Sites:

St. Joseph's Mission: Built by the Laguna Pueblo people in 1699 and recently restored. In Old Laguna. Open weekdays 9:00 a.m.-3:00 p.m. For information contact: St. Joseph's Mission, (505) 552-9330.

Businesses & Industries:

Casa Blanca Market Plaza
(505) 552-9030
Supermarket; Laguna Pueblo people sell their arts and crafts, such as Indian belts, pottery, jewelry, baskets, and paintings. Off I-40, Exit 108.

Laguna Industries, Inc.
#1 Mesita Industrial Parkway
P.O. Box B
Laguna, NM 87026
(505) 552-6041
Manufacturing sheet metal components, metal fabrication and finishing, electrical cables and harnesses, electrical mechanical assembly, and other products for use by the US Army in their communication shelters. Schedule tours in advance. Off I-40.

Restrictions and/or Special Considerations:

Photographs, sketches, or tape recordings of ceremonies are strictly forbidden. Contact the Governor of the Pueblo for permission. Check with the individual villages regarding photography of their communities.

Mescalero Apache Reservation

Tribal Profile:

The 460,678 acre Mescalero Apache Reservation was established in 1852; it is currently home to about 3,000 members of the Mescalero Apache Tribe. The tribal economy is based upon timber, cattle, tourism and outdoor recreation. The varied terrain provides beautiful scenery and a wide variety of recreational opportunities summer and winter.

Location:

In the mountains of south-central New Mexico, west of Roswell, just northeast of Alamogordo. US 70 runs through the reservation.

Address:

Mescalero Apache Tribe
P.O. Box 176
Mescalero, NM 88340
(505) 671-4494

Cultural Institutions:

Mescalero Tribal Cultural Center & Museum
Mescalero, NM 88340
(505) 671-4494, ext. 254

Special Events:

July Ceremonials
Mescalero Feast Grounds
(505) 671-4494
Four days and nights of dancing, eating and paying tribute to the young maidens participating in the puberty rites. Includes rodeo, food booths, arts and crafts and a parade on the 4th of July. Held in early July.

Recreational Opportunities:

Mescalero Bingo
(505) 257-9268
High stakes bingo; 400 seat hall, 1.5 miles from the Inn of the Mountain Gods on US 70. Food concession, no alcohol on premises, must be over 18. Sessions Sunday, Wednesday, Friday and Saturday.

Ski Apache
P.O. Box 220,
Ruidoso, NM 88345
(505) 336-4589
Full service ski area with 7 chair lifts and a gondola; ski school, equipment rentals, restaurants. Lodging and lift ticket packages through Inn of the Mountain Gods. At the northern edge of the reservation. Call (505) 257-9001 for recorded report on skiing conditions.

Mescalero Apache Recreation Office
P.O. Box 176
Mescalero, NM 88340
(505) 671-4494
The tribe operates full-hookup RV parks at Eagle Creek Lake and Silver Lake. Fire danger sometimes causes closure; contact Recreation Office to obtain most current information.

Mescalero Apache Tribe Conservation Office
P.O. Box 176
Mescalero, NM 88340
(505) 671-4427
Contact this office for details about hunting seasons and guided hunts, fishing opportunities, fees and regulations. The Mescalero Tribe operates the following locations for fishing and camping.

Ruidoso Recreational Area: Camping, fishing and picnicking facilities; fee. Open early May to early September.

Silver Springs: Camping, fishing and picnicking facilities; fee. Open April through October.

Eagle Creek: Camping, fishing and picnicking facilities; fee. Open early May to early September.

Lake Mescalero: Open year round; camping and picnicking are not permitted. Fee for fishing, slightly higher April through October.

Archaeological & Historic Sites:

Three Rivers Pictographs: US 54, at Three Rivers.

Heading for the top – Ski Apache gondola. Courtesy of Ski Apache Resort.

Inn of the Mountain Gods. Courtesy of Inn of the Mountain Gods.

BUSINESSES & INDUSTRIES:

Mescalero Apache Tribal Store
Mescalero, NM
Groceries, dry goods and gas.

Mescalero Tribal Lounge & Package Store
Mescalero, NM

ACCOMMODATIONS:

Inn of the Mountain Gods Resort
P.O. Box 269
Mescalero, NM 88340
(800) 545-9011 or (505) 257-5141
Five-star resort offering lodging, restaurants, lounges, conference facilities, video games, golf course, bicycling, boating and fishing, stables, tennis courts and a skeet and trap range. Tennis and golf packages available. Big game hunts on the reservation organized through the inn; different packages offered seasonally: turkey - spring; bear - summer; elk - fall.

Nambe Pueblo

TRIBAL PROFILE:

The Pueblo of Nambe has been home to the tribe since A.D. 1300, although today fewer than 24 pre-colonial buildings remain. The Pueblo is registered as a national historic landmark. Approximately 400 people live on 19,075 acres of striking terrain, encompassing waterfalls, mountains and lakes. Members of the Eight Northern Indian Pueblos Council, the Nambe strive to maintain and preserve the culture and social fabric of Pueblo life by expanding human services and establishing economic enterprises. They are revitalizing traditional rituals and arts and crafts; micaceous pottery in particular is seeing a comeback, as are weaving and beadwork. At this time, most adults work in nearby Espanola or Los Alamos.

LOCATION:

25 miles north of Santa Fe in a beautiful area surrounded by national forest in the Sangre de Cristo Mountain Range. East off US 285/84 on Rte. 503.

ADDRESS:

Pueblo of Nambe
Rte. #1, Box 117 BB
Santa Fe, NM 87501
(505) 455-7692

Special Events:

There are times when the Pueblo is not open to the public; check prior to stopping in. Various dances take place in January and March. Check with the tribal office for names, dates, and times.

Nambe Falls Celebration
Nambe, NM
Held July 4.

St. Francis Feast Day
Nambe, NM
Various dances performed. Held early October.

Recreational Opportunities:

Nambe Falls: A marvelous spot for fishing, picnicking, and hiking in the mountains above the Pueblo. Hours: 6:00 a.m.-9:00 p.m. in summer; 7:00 a.m.-7:00 p.m. in winter. Closed November to March. Fees.

Businesses & Industries:

Cloud Eagle Studios Gallery
Rte. 1, Box 117-H
Santa Fe, NM 87501
(505) 455-2662 or (800) 288-4824
Native American fine art sculptures designed in stone, bronze, and mixed-media. Other arts and crafts on site. On Nambe Waterfalls Hwy. Hours: Monday-Friday 9:00 a.m.-5:00 p.m.; other times by appointment.

Creations in Clay by Lonnie
Rte. 1, Box 121-C
Santa Fe, NM 87501
(505) 455- 2871
Creations handmade from micaceous clay gathered and prepared by the artist. On Nambe Pueblo; call for appointment.

Roderick and Lela Kaskalla
Rte. 1, Box 120-F
Santa Fe, NM 87501
(505) 455-3578
Traditional and contemporary channel inlay a specialty. Upper Village of Nambe; appointment only.

Nambe Smoke Shop
Junction of Hwy 503 & Nambe 101
(505) 455-3688
Discount cigarettes.

Native American Heirlooms
Rte. 1, Box 114-M
Santa Fe, NM 87501
(505) 455-3429
Unique Nambe pottery fashioned by traditional methods. West of Nambe Plaza on Hwy 19. Closed on holidays; by appointment only.

Pottery by Robert Vigil
Rte.1, Box 119-C
Santa Fe, NM 87501
(505) 455-2212
Traditional and contemporary pottery, carved micaceous a specialty. On Nambe Pueblo, near the old Day School. Open Tuesday-Saturday 10:00 a.m.-4:00 p.m.

Restrictions and/or Special Considerations:

When attending dances, please watch and listen in silence. Certain areas of the pueblo, such as cemeteries and kivas, are sacred and off-limits and sometimes are marked by signs. Stay off of adobe structures; they are old and will crumble.

Fees charged for sketching or photography. Contact Governor's Office (505) 455-2036 for details.

Navajo Reservation

See Arizona

Storyteller nativity scene. Photo by Mark Nohl. Courtesy of New Mexico Economic & Tourism Dept.

Picuris (San Lorenzo) Pueblo

TRIBAL PROFILE:

History is long on Picuris Pueblo, with occupation in the area dating as early as A.D. 900. Today, Picuris houses 200 on 14,947 acres. High in the Sangre de Cristo Mountains, this remote pueblo belongs to the Eight Northern Indian Pueblos Council and works hard to maintain and preserve its tribal culture and to improve economic conditions. Economic development projects include expanding the visitors center, entering into a partnership to build the Santa Fe Hotel, and developing timber, range land, and agricultural enterprise.

LOCATION:

Listed on road maps as San Lorenzo, Picuris Pueblo is between Taos and Santa Fe, on Rte. 75, which intersects both scenic Rte. 68 and Rte. 76.

ADDRESS:

Picuris Pueblo
P.O. Box 127
Penasco, NM 87553
(505) 587-2519

CULTURAL INSTITUTIONS:

Picuris Pueblo Museum
Picuris Pueblo
Displays pottery, beadwork, weaving and other fine locally produced masterpieces. A gift shop selling Indian arts and crafts and cigarettes is also part of the facility.

SPECIAL EVENTS:

There are times when the pueblo is not open to the public; check prior to stopping in. Various dances take place in January and March. Check with the tribal office for names, dates, and times.

High Country Arts and Crafts Festival
Held 1st weekend in July.

Sunset Dance
Held in early August.

San Lorenzo Feast Day
Features various dances and pole climbing.

Sundown Torchlight Procession of the Virgin
Held December 24.

Matachine Dance
Held December 25.

RECREATIONAL OPPORTUNITIES:

Pu-Na Lake and Tu-Ha Lake: Regularly stocked fishing ponds and picnic areas, camping sites, and ruin tours all offered. Pu-Na Lake has grills and shelters. Fees. Fishing permits required, available at the Museum, Governor's Office or from the Tribal Game and Fish Warden.

ARCHAEOLOGICAL & HISTORIC SITES:

Ruins: 700-year-old kivas and storage rooms, excavated in the 1960s.

BUSINESSES & INDUSTRIES:

Hidden Valley Shop and Restaurant
(505) 587-2957
Convenience store and smoke shop selling fishing equipment and licenses, and arts and crafts. The restaurant prepares native Picuris and American-style dishes. Restaurant open 7 days a week, 10:30 a.m.-7:00 p.m. daily; breakfast served Sundays only, 9:00 a.m.-noon.

Picuris Enterprises
Pueblo of Picuris
P.O. Box 487
Penasco, NM 87533
(505) 587-2957

ACCOMMODATIONS:

Hotel Santa Fe
Paseo de Peralta at Cerillos
Santa Fe, NM 87501
(505) 982-1200; (800) 825-9876
A suite hotel with 131 rooms, including 91 one and two bedroom suites. Santa Fe's only Native American-owned hotel, owned by Picuris Pueblo in partnership with private business.

RESTRICTIONS AND/OR SPECIAL CONSIDERATIONS:

When attending dances, please be silent. Fees for sketching and photography; contact Picuris Enterprises.

Pojoaque Pueblo

TRIBAL PROFILE:

Since 1934, 11,601 acres of aboriginal Pojoaque lands have been restored, and reoccupied, to the tribe by order of the Pueblo Lands Court and federal court. Little remains of the original pueblo, abandoned before 1900 following a severe smallpox epidemic. From a membership of about 11 in 1932, pueblo population has grown to 132 today. Tribal members strive to revive and sustain their cultural heritage and identity, working closely with nearby pueblos to re-acquaint themselves with their native language, arts, and ceremonials. Living in a master-planned community, the pueblo operates an official state tourist center and a thriving shopping center. Pojoaque is a member of the Eight Northern Indian Pueblos Council, which at present oversees 54 programs aimed at health, education, welfare, and economic improvement.

LOCATION:

The average elevation in this region of north-central New Mexico is 7,000 feet, with moderate temperatures year round that make it ideal for summer and winter activities. Pojoaque is on US 84/285, 15 miles north of Santa Fe.

ADDRESS:

Pueblo of Pojoaque
Governor's Office
Rte. 11, Box 71
Santa Fe, NM 87501
(505) 455-2278

Left, Pojoaque Pueblo Tourist Center off Hwy 84. Right, interior view of Pojoaque gift shop. Photos by Jim Pierce. Courtesy of CERT-TSC Pojoaque Project.

CULTURAL INSTITUTIONS:

Poeh Cultural Center Museum
(505) 455-3590 or -2278
Scheduled to open in 1993, the collection will feature a living museum, dances, and artist demonstrations. The facilities will include a Tewa resource center for the Northern Pueblos, offering classes, conferences and other activities with the Tewa perspective.

SPECIAL EVENTS:

Various dances and ceremonials take place in January, March, and on Easter. Check with Governor's Office for names, dates, and times.

Pueblo Plaza Fiesta
Held the 1st week in August.

Guadalupe Feast Day
Various dances performed. Held December 12.

RECREATIONAL OPPORTUNITIES:

Pojoaque Pueblo Tourist Center & RV Park
P.O. Box 3687
Santa Fe, NM 87501
(505) 455-3460
Carries handcrafted jewelry, pottery, rugs, kachinas and other native hand crafts, and disseminates pueblo and state tourist information. RV spaces with hookup available.

BUSINESSES & INDUSTRIES:

George Rivera - Sculptor
Rte. 11, Box 71-#2
Santa Fe, NM 87501
(505) 455-3590
Artist specializing in clay and stone sculptures dealing with pueblo themes, including dancers and kachinas. On Pojoaque Pueblo.

Pottery by the Talachy's
P.O. Box 3504
Pojoaque, NM 87501
(505) 455-2386
Specializing in beautiful stone-polished, red and polychrome pottery. On Pojoaque Pueblo.

Pueblo Plaza Supermarket
Pojoaque Shopping Center;
Fresh produce, meat, liquor, bakery and deli. Open daily all year, 8:00 a.m.-6:00 p.m.

V & S Variety Store
Rte. 11, Box 21
Santa Fe, NM 87501
(505) 455-7111, -3561
A general store in the Pueblo Plaza Shopping Center. Open daily, hours vary.

Butterfly Springs Mobile Home Park
Rte. 11, Box 21F
Santa Fe, NM 87501
(505) 455-2071
Behind the Pueblo Plaza Shopping Center, this 202-space mobile home park incorporates many modern features.

ACCOMMODATIONS:

Hotel Santa Fe
Paseo de Peralta at Cerillos
Santa Fe, NM 87501
(505) 982-1200; (800) 825-9876
A suite hotel with 131 rooms, including 91 one and two bedroom suites. Santa Fe's only Native American-owned hotel.

RESTRICTIONS AND/OR SPECIAL CONSIDERATIONS:

Contact Governor's Office for specifics on Pojoaque restrictions.

Ramah Navajo Reservation

TRIBAL PROFILE:

A part of the Navajo Nation, the Ramah Chapter Reservation is about 40 miles south of the main Navajo lands. In a region of complex land ownership, 1476,000 acres are considered tribally owned, home to about 2,117 members. The Ramah Navajo tribe is one of 109 Chapters of the Navajo Nation. Please see the section on the Navajo under the Arizona listing for more detailed information about the Navajo Nation as a whole and particulars – in the **Eastern Section** – on what to see at Ramah.

LOCATION:

Accessible from I-40 at Grants; bordered on the west by the Zuni Reservation, Ramah Navajo lands are west of Albuquerque on Rte. 53. South of Cibola National Forest and west of the Ice Caves.

ADDRESS:

Ramah Navajo Chapter
Rte. 2, Box 13
Ramah, NM 87321
(505) 775-3310, -3389

ACCOMMODATIONS:

There are locations for camping, fishing, hunting, and hiking throughout the area. Lodging available in Ramah.

Sandia Pueblo

TRIBAL PROFILE:

The Pueblo of Sandia reservation covers approximately 23,000 acres and is inhabited by 368 tribal members. The Pueblo of Sandia considers itself a traditionally structured tribe, led by a governor and council. The Sandia, or Nafiat, have lived in the region since at least A.D. 1300. Farming and ranching have long been important to the tribe, with new endeavors such as a sod farm, an industrial park, and natural resource development gaining increasing value. Sandia Pueblo is communal in nature, and the native language and religion dominate much of society; however, it is progressive in its economic programs.

LOCATION:

Sandia Pueblo is 13 miles north of Albuquerque and 2 miles south of Bernalillo; off I-25.

ADDRESS:

Pueblo of Sandia
Box 6008
Bernalillo, NM 87004
(505) 867-3317

CULTURAL INSTITUTIONS:

Governor's Office: Houses a small display of historical photographs relating to the Sandia.

SPECIAL EVENTS:

Many dances take place throughout the year; the dates change on a yearly basis. Contact Governor's Office for details and dates.

King's Day
Feast of Epiphany and Governor's Day; activities include dances and feasting. Held on January 6.

Feast of St. Anthony
A major occasion honoring the patron saint of the Pueblo. Held on June 13.

RECREATIONAL OPPORTUNITIES:

Sandia Bingo
P.O. Box 10188
Albuquerque, NM 87184
(505) 897-2173
Jackpot, Megabingo, Bonanza, and Pick 78, available Thurs-Sun, 12:30-3:00 p.m., and every night beginning at 7:00 p.m. The Vegas Room is open 24 hrs. with video pull tabs and video bingo. Open all year. At the intersection of Tramway and I-25.

Sandia Trails
(505) 898-6970
Horse rentals on an hourly basis. Must stay on trails; guides available. Open year-round; fees vary.

Sandia Lakes Recreation Area: Includes 2 fishing lakes stocked with trout; picnic areas with grills, tables, shelters, small playground; and a nature trail. Shore fishing only; state fishing permit required. For information call (505) 897-3971. Open all year.

ARCHAEOLOGICAL & HISTORIC SITES:

Sandia Village: Still occupying its original site; reconstruction began around 1760 after the Pueblo Revolt period, and building continues today in this contemporary/old community.

BUSINESSES & INDUSTRIES:

Bien Mur Indian Market
(505) 821-5400
Selling rugs, jewelry, kachinas, pottery, moccasins, blankets and a large variety of other crafts and goods.

Los Amigos Roundup
(505) 898-8173
Arranges catering for large groups.

RESTRICTIONS AND/OR SPECIAL CONSIDERATIONS:

No photography, sketching, alcohol, firearms or fireworks. When visiting the reservation, please check in with Governor's Office.

San Felipe Pueblo

TRIBAL PROFILE:

The Pueblo of San Felipe is on the west bank of the Rio Grande; it was founded in the early 1700s, although Pueblo stories date back many years earlier. Reservation lands range over 48,858 acres, well-suited for agriculture and natural resource development. Farming and ranching still provide a livelihood for some Pueblo members, including a 172-acre tribal farm producing alfalfa. San Felipe's reputation for superior craftsmanship is on the rise, particularly for handmade turquoise, heishi and silver jewelry, and the pueblo often sponsors and hosts arts and crafts shows. Outside visitors are not encouraged except during scheduled events.

LOCATION:

Directly north of Albuquerque, east of I-25, situated mid-way between Santa Fe and Albuquerque. San Felipe Pueblo exit is marked.

ADDRESS:

Pueblo of San Felipe
P.O. Box 308
San Felipe Pueblo, NM 87001
(505) 867-3381

SPECIAL EVENTS:

Dances occur throughout the year with varying dates. Check with Governor's Office for details.

Three Kings' Day
Buffalo, Elk, Deer, and Eagle Dances presented commemorating the Epiphany. Held January 6.

Candelaria Day Celebration
Buffalo Dances take place. Held February 2.

Green Corn Dance
Feast Day of San Felipe in which hundreds of pueblo residents dressed in traditional costume dance and sing throughout the day in a huge bowl worn 3 feet lower than the plaza by generations of feet executing the time-honored steps of the dances. Held May 1.

San Pedro Feast Day
Corn Dances performed. Held June 29.

San Felipe Pueblo Arts & Crafts Show
Check with Governor's Office for particulars. Held intermittently.

ACCOMMODATIONS:

Centrally located between Albuquerque and Santa Fe.

RESTRICTIONS AND/OR SPECIAL CONSIDERATIONS:

No photography or recording of events under any circumstances.

San Ildefonso Pueblo Church. Photo by Mark Nohl. Courtesy of New Mexico Economic & Tourism Dept.

San Ildefonso Pueblo

TRIBAL PROFILE:

Home of renowned painters and potters whose work is displayed in museums around the country, the 26,197 acre San Ildefonso Pueblo houses about 580 residents, many immersed in arts and crafts, while others work in Los Alamos or Santa Fe. The Pueblo is a member of the Eight Northern Indian Pueblos Council. Presently some tribal income derives from cattle ranching and agriculture, aided by the Rio Grande River flowing through Pueblo lands.

LOCATION:

Northwest of Santa Fe in the heart of Santa Fe National Forest and in the shadow of Black Mesa, which stands between San Ildefonso and the Pueblo of Santa Clara. From US 84/285, west on Rte. 501.

ADDRESS:

Pueblo of San Ildefonso
Governor's Office
Rte. 5, Box 315-A
Santa Fe, NM 87501
(505) 455-2273

CULTURAL INSTITUTIONS:

Visitor and Information Center
Rte. 5, Box 315-A
Santa Fe, NM 87501
(505) 455-3459, -2273
Gift shop carries Indian pottery, ribbon shirts, Pueblo embroidery and more. Offers Pueblo brochures and visitor information; entry fees charged to view the pueblo. Open daily 8:00 a.m.-5:00 p.m. during the summer season; closed weekends in the winter.

San Ildefonso Pueblo Museum
Governor's Office
Exhibits of local arts, embroidery, pottery-making process, Pueblo history, and photographs. Open 8:00 a.m.-4:00 p.m.

Emerging from the kiva. Photo by Mark Nohl. Courtesy of New Mexico Economic & Tourism Dept.

San Ildefonso Feast Day drummers. Photo by Mark Nohl. Courtesy of New Mexico Economic & Tourism Dept.

Special Events:

San Ildefonso celebrates many special occasions and dances throughout the year, retaining powerful ties to their Tewa ancestry. Various dances and ceremonials take place in January, March, and on Easter. Many of these dances have been performed by the pueblos for hundreds of years. Check with the Visitor Center for names, dates, and times.

Vespers and Evening Buffalo & Animal Dances
San Ildefonso Pueblo Plaza
Held in late January.

San Ildefonso Feast Day
Comanche and Animal Dances take place. Held January 23.

St. Anthony's Feast Day
Performers recreate the Comanche Dance. Held in mid-June.

Annual Northern Pueblo Artist & Craftsman Show
Hundreds of people come from all over the U.S. to participate in this event where beautifully executed pottery, fine jewelry, hand-woven clothing, sculptures in stone and metal, and hand-painted Kachinas, all created by tradition methods, are shown and sold. Show includes demonstrations of pottery, weaving, and jewelry crafting. More than 600 artists display their work. No admission is charged, but there is a parking fee. Held the 3rd Saturday and Sunday in July, from 8:00 a.m.-6:00 p.m.

Corn Dances
Held in late August or early September.

Matachine Dance
Indian dancers present the Matachine Dance and other dances. Held December 25.

Recreational Opportunities:

San Ildefonso Lake: 4.5 acre lake well stocked with rainbow trout and catfish from the Mescalero National Fishing Hatchery. Purchase permits at the lake or from the tribal office. Open April to October, 6:00 a.m.-sundown.

Archaeological & Historic Sites:

San Ildefonso Pueblo: Listed as a historic district on the National Register of Historic Places.

San Ildefonso Pueblo Church: Fully restored church, built in the 1700s and still in use today. Can be viewed only from the outside. Near the center of the pueblo.

BUSINESSES & INDUSTRIES:

The now-traditional technique of black-on-black pottery was developed by Maria and Julian Martinez at San Ildefonso in the 1920s. Many pottery studios throughout the village are open to the public. Hours vary. Some artisans open their homes to prospective buyers.

Aguilar Arts
Rte. 5, Box 318-C
Santa Fe, NM 87501
(505) 455-3530
Specializing in red and black pottery. Next to the Visitor Center; enter off the Pueblo Plaza. Open year round.

Popovi Da Studio of Indian Arts
RFD 5, Box 309
Santa Fe, NM
(505) 455-3332
Offering pueblo pottery, paintings, jewelry, books, baskets, and kachinas. A museum is located within the store; opened by request. Among the displays is a permanent collection of works by Maria Martinez. Open May through October, 10:00 a.m.-5:00 p.m., Mon, Tues, Thurs and Fri. Closed all holidays and open in winter by appointment only.

Juan Tafoya Pottery
Rte. 5, Box 306-A
Santa Fe, NM 87501
(505) 455-2418
Black-on-black and red sienna pottery are the major areas of expertise.

Torres Indian Arts
Rte. 5, Box 312
Santa Fe, NM 87501
(505) 455-7547
The shop specialty is traditional black-on-black and buff-on-red pottery. Open all year.

ACCOMMODATIONS:

Hotel Santa Fe: Santa Fe's only Native American-owned hotel.

RESTRICTIONS AND/OR SPECIAL CONSIDERATIONS:

Fees charged for sketching and photography. Contact Governor's Office for specific constraints.

San Juan Pueblo

TRIBAL PROFILE:

Headquarters for the Eight Northern Indian Pueblos Council, San Juan Pueblo has joined its neighbors to address cultural, community, and economic concerns. San Juan Pueblo is at the forefront of the Pueblo arts renaissance, having created a crafts cooperative in 1968 that is still active today. San Juan's 2,133 residents live in both ancient (about 100 original, 700-year-old dwellings) and modern homes on the 12,237 acre reservation.

LOCATION:

Just east of the Rio Grande River, San Juan Pueblo stands north of Santa Fe, off Hwy 68.

ADDRESS:

Pueblo of San Juan
Governor's Office
P.O. Box 1099
Santa Fe, NM 87566
(505) 852-4400, -4213 (Tribal Office)

CULTURAL INSTITUTIONS:

O'Ke Oweenge
P.O. Box 1095
San Juan Pueblo, NM 87566
(505) 852-2372
A cooperative founded by the craftspeople of San Juan Pueblo in 1968 to foster the development of handmade Indian crafts.

Eight Northern Indian Pueblos Council
P.O. Box 969
San Juan Pueblo, NM 87566
(505) 852-4265
Headquarters building for the Council, initiated to meet the mandate for greater economic vitality. Enterprises include Pueblo North, producing and marketing Indian arts and crafts; a marketing center that encompasses learning and training centers; and a research facility.

Special Events:

Various dances and ceremonials take place in January, March, and on Easter. Many of these dances have been performed by the pueblos for hundreds of years. Check with Visitor Center for names, dates, and times.

Buffalo, Deer and Animal Dances
Held in February.

San Antonio's Feast Day
Comanche Dances take place to celebrate this saint's day. Held June 13.

Vespers and Evening Dance
The Buffalo Dance is performed. Held on June 23.

San Juan's Feast Day
The Comanche Dance is performed. Held June 24.

Harvest Dances
Held in September.

Sundown Torchlight Procession of the Virgin
Matachine Dances, religious procession and farolitos. Held December 24 and 25.

Turtle Dance
Held December 26.

Recreational Opportunities:

San Juan Pueblo Bingo
P.O. Box 1099
Santa Fe, NM 87566
(505 753-3132
Open Wednesday through Saturday night. Doors open 5:30, bingo begins at 7:00 p.m. Sunday afternoon doors open at noon, games begin 1:00 p.m. On US 285.

San Juan Tribal Lakes: Lake areas provide fishing and picnicking opportunities. Obtain permit information from tribal rangers or the tribal office, (505) 852-4213. Hours vary seasonally. South of San Juan Pueblo. Fees.

Archaeological & Historic Sites:

Pueblo of San Juan: An historic and archaeological site itself, with buildings hundreds of years old. It is important to walk in designated areas only in order to respect the privacy of those living in the Pueblo.

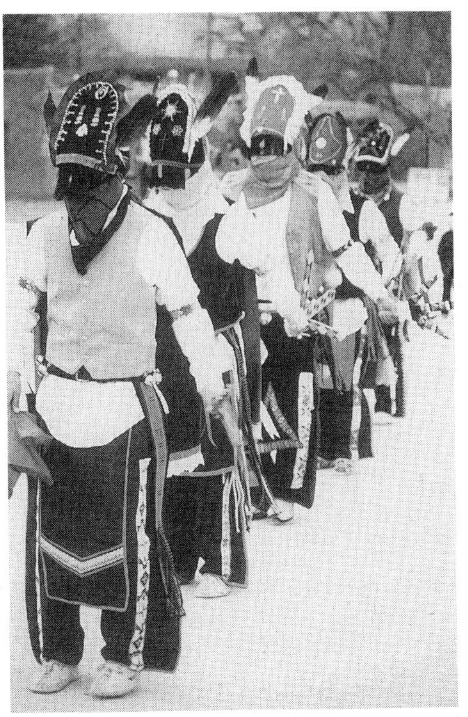

San Juan Matachine dancers. Photo by Mark Nohl. Courtesy of New Mexico Economic & Tourism Dept.

The sites of both the Village of the Mockingbird (Yunge) ruins, considered the first capitol of New Mexico, and the San Gabriel Catholic Church ruins, the oldest structure in the U.S. erected by Europeans, are indicated by a marker placed within 1 mile of the pueblo.

Businesses & Industries:

Aguino's Arts and Crafts
P.O. Box 52
San Juan Pueblo, NM 87566
(505) 667-8175, 753-9168
The focus of the arts displayed in the shop is paintings, woodcarvings, rasps, and corn dolls.

Walk-In-Beauty Fiber Arts
P. O. Box 1322
San Juan Pueblo, NM 87566
(505) 852-2734
Specializing in velvet and satin clothing in both traditional and contemporary styles. Open weekdays, 9:00 a.m.-4:00 p.m.

Tewa Indian Restaurant
Serving delectable traditional Indian foods, such as fry bread, oven bread, Indian fruit pies, Indian bread pudding, Indian tacos, and Indian teas.

Open 9:00 a.m.-2:30 p.m.; closed holidays and San Juan's Feast Day.

ACCOMMODATIONS:

Lodging nearby in Espanola. Camping opportunities in many of the surrounding pueblos.

RESTRICTIONS AND/OR SPECIAL CONSIDERATIONS:

When attending dances, please be silent. Fees for sketching and photography; contact Governor's Office for permission, and information about other constraints when visiting the Pueblo.

Santa Ana Pueblo

TRIBAL PROFILE:

The 61,375 acre Santa Ana Reservation supports 556 tribal members, many active in farming and ranching, along with farmland reclamation. Santa Ana Pueblo has entered into several long-term leases for mining, farming and homesites, among others. The mother pueblo was established in the 1700s; most people today live on farmland outside the village, returning for social and sacred activities. With the exception of feast days, the old pueblo is closed to outsiders.

Pressure from outside to develop tribal land and to be less traditional is a constant for many pueblos; Santa Ana Pueblo is working to balance both tradition and the desire for self-sufficiency. To meet that challenge, the Pueblo has started an arts and crafts cooperative association, opened a nouvelle cuisine restaurant and a 27-hole golf course, and other ventures are contemplated. Less than 10 years ago, traditional pottery was a dying art. Today, more than 20 Santa Ana members are active and gaining increasing recognition for their skills.

LOCATION:

North of Albuquerque; Rte. 44, off I-25 at Bernalillo, travels directly through Santa Ana Pueblo

ADDRESS:

Santa Ana Pueblo
P.O. Box 37
Bernalillo, NM 87004
(505) 867-3301

CULTURAL INSTITUTIONS:

Ta-Ma-Ya Cooperative Association
Santa Ana Pueblo
Star Rte., Box 37
Bernalillo, NM 87004
(505) 867-3301
Displays of pottery, Pueblo embroidery, weaving, clothing, and other Pueblo crafts. Open 10:00 a.m.-4:30 p.m., Tuesday and Thursday. On old Hwy 85, next to the tribal offices.

SPECIAL EVENTS:

Please note the old Pueblo is closed to visitors, except on the following dates: January 1 & 6, Easter, June 24 & 29, July 25 & 26, and December 25-28. Many of the celebrations and dances held on these dates are open to visitors; contact the tribal office for details.

Santa Ana Feast Day
(505) 867-3301
The major event of the year, celebrating the patron saint of the Pueblo. Held July 26.

RECREATIONAL OPPORTUNITIES:

Valle Grande Golf Course
(505) 867-9464
A 27-hole golf course with snack bar. Offering winter and summer rates; cart, both electric and pull, and club rentals available. Open 7:00 a.m.-sundown.

Coronado State Monument: Campsites and RV facilities, water, showers, toilets. Fee; open year round. For information, call (505) 867-5589.

ARCHAEOLOGICAL & HISTORIC SITES:

Old Santa Ana Pueblo: Original settlement, established around 1700. Limited access to the pueblo, as mentioned under Special Events. 13 miles west of Bernalillo.

BUSINESSES & INDUSTRIES:

Discount Smokeshop
Jemez Canyon Rd.
(505) 867-6234

Prairie Star Restaurant
Jemez Canyon Dam Rd.
(505) 867-3327
4-star restaurant with a wide variety of cuisines, along with unusual dishes such as antelope and buffalo. Off Rte. 44.

RESTRICTIONS AND/OR SPECIAL CONSIDERATIONS:

No photography during ceremonies; contact tribal office for permission at other times.

Santa Clara Pueblo

TRIBAL PROFILE:

The rights of the Santa Clara Pueblo Tribe to the reservation were guaranteed in the 1848 Treaty of Hidalgo. Santa Clara encompasses an area of approximately 45,740 acres, including timber, range land and farms. Pueblo residents number about 2,600, engaged in ranching, forestry, tourism and artistry, including beadwork, embroidery and the famous Santa Clara pottery.

LOCATION:

Scenic northern New Mexico, a hilly, forested area dotted with pueblos and historic landmarks. 28 miles north of Santa Fe via US 84; south of Espanola, on Rte. 30.

ADDRESS:

Santa Clara Pueblo
P.O. Box 580
Espanola, NM 87532
(505) 753-7326

Puye cliff dwellings. Photo by Mark Nohl. Courtesy of New Mexico Economic & Tourism Dept.

SPECIAL EVENTS:

St. Anthony's Feast Day
Comanche Dances. Held June 13.

Santa Clara Feast Day
In honor of the pueblo's patron saint, festival features a full day of traditional dances and an art exhibit. Observe restrictions regarding photography, applause, silence. Held August 12.

Other dances are performed on weekends, December to February. Call for details.

RECREATIONAL OPPORTUNITIES:

Santa Clara Canyon Recreation Area: 4 well stocked lakes along 12 miles of Santa Clara Creek, (Rte. 30). Facilities include 86 campsites, some suitable for RVs, but without hookups; and many picnic sites. Permits are required; obtained for a small fee from tribal rangers. Access to the canyon floor is limited to roads only. No swimming or wading; boats, motorcycles and motor bikes are not allowed. Open April through October.

ARCHAEOLOGICAL & HISTORIC SITES:

Puye Cliff Dwellings: Ancestral home of the Santa Clara Tribe; a National Historic Landmark in Santa Clara Canyon. Self guided as well as guided tours available. South on Hwy 30. Open year round. Fee.

BUSINESSES & INDUSTRIES:

Arts and Crafts: Santa Clara Pueblo is well known for its red and black polished and carved pottery. Visitors who knock on doors of houses displaying "pottery for sale" and "open" signs will be invited in to see art and crafts and meet the artisans.

RESTRICTIONS AND/OR SPECIAL CONSIDERATIONS:

Consideration of old pueblo ways is requested; certain areas are off limits to non-Indians. Check winter hours. Ask before taking pictures, make a donation to the family. No alcohol.

Santo Domingo Pueblo

TRIBAL PROFILE:

Santo Domingo Pueblo is the home of renowned jewelers and artisans, many of whom market their products throughout the U.S. Although it is traditionally a farming community, commercial development, leases and permits all contribute to pueblo livelihood on this 69,259 acre reservation. Santo Domingo considers itself traditionally organized, appointing a 37-member tribal council to oversee programs and govern the 3,500 member Pueblo. Ancient religious practice is central to the pueblo social structure, and the traditional language is still spoken.

Stop in at the Community Center when entering the pueblo.

LOCATION:

Between Santa Fe and Albuquerque west of I-25. Follow the frontage road to Santo Domingo Pueblo.

ADDRESS:

Pueblo of Santo Domingo
P.O. Box 99
Santo Domingo, NM 87052
(505) 465-2214

CULTURAL INSTITUTIONS:

Santo Domingo Cultural Center
(505) 465-2625
The Center houses a gift shop and museum exhibiting photographs of Santo Domingo ancestors and artifacts from jewelry and pottery production. Near Santo Domingo Village and tribal gas station.

SPECIAL EVENTS:

Dances occur throughout the year with varying dates. Check with Governor's Office or Community Center for details.

New Year's Day Celebration
Corn, Deer and Turtle Dances performed.

Three Kings' Day
Buffalo, Elk, Deer, and Eagle Dances presented commemorating the Epiphany. Held January 6.

Candelaria Day Celebration
Buffalo Dances take place. Held February 2.

Easter Weekend Celebration
Basket and Corn Dances. Held in April.

San Pedro Feast Day
Corn Dances performed. Held June 29.

Santo Domingo Pueblo Feast Day
An extensive Corn Dance, very dramatic with singers, drummers and clowns, takes place to commemorate this major Pueblo occasion. Held August 4.

Christmas Celebration
Dances held on Christmas Day.

BUSINESSES & INDUSTRIES:

Roseta's Gift Shop
Cultural Center
(505) 465-2625
Selling Santo Domingo arts and crafts.

Santo Domingo Tribal Gas Station
At I-25
(505) 465-2620

ACCOMMODATIONS:

Nearest lodgings in Santa Fe, 1/2 hour drive from Santo Domingo Pueblo.

RESTRICTIONS AND/OR SPECIAL CONSIDERATIONS:

No photography allowed. Contact Governor's Office for other constraints. At various times during the year the pueblo is closed to visitors.

Taos Pueblo

TRIBAL PROFILE:

Long an inspiration for painters and photographers, Taos Pueblo stands at the base of the 13,610 Wheeler Peak, in a beautiful region supporting farms and stock raising. The area for Taos is 95,341 acres. Like the other pueblos, the tribe's rights were confirmed by the U.S. under the Treaty of Hidalgo in 1858. Governed by the Tribal Council and administered on a day-to-day basis by the Governor, the Pueblo selects these individuals in time-honored ceremonies. The Pueblo is actively working to preserve the essence of tribal society, and toward that end Oo Oonah Art Center was established.

LOCATION:

Northernmost of the 19 New Mexico pueblos, Taos Pueblo is 2 miles north of the well-known artist community of Taos, off Hwy 68 on Rte. 240.

ADDRESS:

Taos Pueblo
P.O. Box 1846
Taos, NM 87571
(505) 758-8626

CULTURAL INSTITUTIONS:

Oo Oonah Art Center
P.O. Box 1853
Taos, NM 87571
(505) 758-1966
Art center, gallery and school for community children.

SPECIAL EVENTS:

Various dances and ceremonials take place in January, March, and on Easter. Check with Governor's Office for names, dates, and times.

New Year's Day Celebration
Turtle Dances performed.

Three Kings' Day
Buffalo or Deer Dance presented celebrating the Epiphany. Held January 6.

Feast of Santa Cruz
Foot race and Corn Dance. Held May 3.

Feast of San Antonio
Corn Dance. Held June 13.

Feast of San Juan
Corn Dance. Held June 24.

Taos Pueblo. Photo by Mark Nohl. Courtesy of New Mexico Economic & Tourism Dept.

Taos Pueblo Pow Wow
Held 2nd weekend in July.

Feast of Santa Ana and Santiago
Various dances performed. Held July 25 & 26.

San Geronimo Eve
Vespers observed at St. Jerome followed by the Sundown Dance. Held September 29.

Feast of San Geronimo
Festivities include a trade fair, clown society pole climb, early morning foot races, and social dances. Held September 30.

Sundown Torchlight Procession of the Virgin
Vespers is observed and Indian dancers present the Matachine Dances. Held December 24.

Matachine Dance
Indian dancers perform a Matachine Dance and other dances. Held December 25.

RECREATIONAL OPPORTUNITIES:

Taos Pueblo Pull Tabs
Taos Pueblo Hwy
(505) 758-4460
Bingo pull tabs for $1, $.50 and $.25. Open Monday-Saturday 11:00 a.m.-7:00 p.m., Sunday 1:00-6:00 p.m. A bingo hall is in the planning stages.

Taos Indian Horse Ranch
P.O. Box 3019
Taos, NM 87571
(505) 758-3212 or (800) 659-3210
Offering historical tours and several ride packages, such as Spiritual rides, winter sleigh rides and summer hay wagon cookouts. Camps, retreats, and trips are also offered.

ARCHAEOLOGICAL & HISTORIC SITES:

Old Taos Pueblo: The old Taos Pueblo village is highly traditional, and its residents choose to live without running water or electricity. These multi-storied dwellings are a national historic site, nominated by the World Heritage Commission in Geneva as the 15th North American site in the World Heritage Convention. Observe signs designating areas that are off-limits to visitors.

San Geronimo Mission & Cemetery: Ruins of the Mission are near the entrance to the pueblo.

BUSINESSES & INDUSTRIES:

Blue Lake Drum Shop
Taos Pueblo Plaza
(505) 758-8626
Drums and other handcrafted articles.

San Geronimo Mission. Photo by Mark Nohl. Courtesy of New Mexico Economic & Tourism Dept.

Buckskin Crafts
P.O. Box 1228
Taos, NM 87571
(505) 758-1455
Crafts handmade from deer horn and hide; for example drums, quivers, and deer horn sculptures. Just west of the church; hours 10:00 a.m.-4:30 p.m.

Buffalo Dancer
Taos Pueblo Plaza
P.O. Box C
El Prado, NM 87529
(505) 758-4707
Handmade Indian jewelry and pottery. Open 9:00 a.m.-5:30 p.m.

The Casual Indian
Taos Pueblo Plaza
P.O. Box 2022
Taos, NM 87571
(505) 776-8233
Offering pottery, Pendleton blankets and coats, jewelry, and local paintings. Open 10:00 a.m.-5:00 p.m., every day.

Maria L. Concha
Taos Pueblo Plaza
Fresh baked bread.

Indian Crafts & Gift Shop
Taos Pueblo Plaza
P.O. Box 2004
Taos, NM 87571
(505) 758-8202
A variety of handcrafted goods and Pueblo souvenirs. Open 10:00 a.m.-4:00 p.m.

Crucita's Indian Shop
Taos Pueblo Plaza
P.O. Box 1536
Taos, NM 87571
(505) 758-3376
Freshly baked Indian bread, along with pottery, jewelry, and beadwork. Open 9:00 a.m.-5:00 p.m.

Luhan's Trading Post
Taos Pueblo Plaza
P.O. Box 372
El Prado, NM 87529
(505) 758-0075
Offering jewelry, pottery, and kachina; rare/old and contemporary.

Morning Talk Gift Shop
Taos Pueblo Plaza
P.O. Box 2328
Taos, NM 87571
(505) 758-1429
Carrying a wide collection of Indian crafts; the jewelry is created and made at Taos Pueblo. Mail orders taken. Open 9:00 a.m.-4:30 p.m.

Native American Creations Guild
Taos Pueblo Road
P.O. Box 602
Taos, NM 87571
(505) 758-2786
Offering many fine examples of Indian handcrafts. Open 9:00 a.m.-5:00 p.m.

Native Arts & Crafts
Taos Pueblo Plaza
P.O. Box 2741
Taos, Nm 87571
(505) 758-9519
Silver work, beadwork, and clothing. Hours vary.

Mark A. Ortiz Studio
Taos Pueblo Plaza
P.O. Box 264
Ranchos de Taos, NM 87557
(505) 758-8781
Contemporary paintings in acrylic and oil.

Sharon "Dry Flower" Reyna
P.O. Box 3031
Taos, NM 87571
(505) 758-3790
Contemporary sculpture and pottery. Near Pueblo; open 9:00 a.m.-4:00 p.m.

Tony Reyna Indian Shops
P.O. Box 1892
Taos, NM 87571
(505) 758-3835
Authentic Indian arts and crafts in 3 shops: Taos Pueblo Road, Kachina Lodge Motel and Taos Pueblo Plaza

ACCOMMODATIONS:

Many choices for lodging in the town of Taos.

RESTRICTIONS AND/OR SPECIAL CONSIDERATIONS:

Fees for sketching/painting and photography; no photography at dances. Contact Governor's Office additional information.

Tesuque Pueblo

TRIBAL PROFILE:

Surrounded by hillsides sacred to the people, Tesuque Pueblo is the southernmost of the Eight Northern Indian Pueblos. The Pueblo itself was built near the banks of Rio Tesuque around A.D. 1250, and the tribe's rights were confirmed by treaty in 1848. Tribal lands cover 16,813 acres. Traditionally subsistence farmers, the tribe is now increasing its marketing farming, but most working members are employed in Los Alamos or Santa Fe. Many pueblo members make micaceous and non-micaceous pottery, sculptures, and paintings reflecting the richness of community life.

LOCATION:

Near Bandelier National Monument and Painted Cave, Tesuque Pueblo is just 9 miles north of Santa Fe on US 84/285.

ADDRESS:

Tesuque Pueblo
Rte. 11, Box 1
Santa Fe, NM 87501
(505) 983-2667

SPECIAL EVENTS:

Various dances and ceremonials take place in January, March, and on Easter. Check with Governor's Office for names, dates, and times.

Corn Dance
Held late May or early June.

San Diego's Feast Day
Either the Comanche or the Animal Dance is performed. Held November 12.

Matachine Dance
Indian dancers perform the Matachine Dance and other dances. Held December 25.

Tesuque Matachine dancer. Photo by Mark Nohl. Courtesy of New Mexico Economic & Tourism Dept.

RECREATIONAL OPPORTUNITIES:

Tesuque Pueblo Bingo
Rte. 11, Box 3A
Santa Fe, NM 87501
(505) 984-8414 or (800) 85BINGO (in-state)
Offering high stakes Megabingo with the opportunity to win $500,000, as well as cash prizes with bingo packages every night. Snack bar with many local favorites. Wednesday through Monday nights. Doors open at 5:00 p.m., bingo begins at 6:30 p.m.; closing time 10:20. On Hwy 84, 10 miles north of Santa Fe.

Tesuque Pueblo RV Campground
Rte. 5, Box 360-H
Santa Fe, NM 87501
(505) 455-2661, -2647 or (800) TRY RV PARK
RV hook-ups by the month, week, or day and tent sites. Amenities include a convenience store, heated swimming pool, rest rooms, showers, laundry, and security. Next to Camel Rock on US 84/285. Open year round; fees.

ARCHAEOLOGICAL & HISTORIC SITES:

Tesuque Pueblo: Excavations have uncovered evidence of inhabitation from A.D. 1250, and the pueblo is on the National Register of Historic Places. Visitors are asked to restrict sightseeing to the plaza, as houses and land surrounding it are private.

BUSINESSES & INDUSTRIES:

Duran's Pottery
Tesuque Pueblo
P.O. Box 339
Tesuque, NM 87574
(505) 983-7076
Traditional Tesuque pottery, beadwork, drums, traditional embroidery.

Joseph Tapia
Tesuque Pueblo
Rte. 11, Box 1
Santa Fe, NM 87501
(505) 983-7075
Offering traditional Indian dancer paintings in watercolor.

Teresa Tapia
Tesuque Pueblo
Rte. 11, Box 1
Santa Fe, NM 87501
(505) 983-7075
Creating Tesuque pottery, miniatures a specialty, using all-natural materials.

Tesuque Farms
Growing produce without use of pesticides.

RESTRICTIONS AND/OR SPECIAL CONSIDERATIONS:

Photography is not permitted during dances. Photo permits for taking snapshots in the pueblo may be obtained from the tribal offices. As mentioned above, restrict sightseeing to the plaza, including staying out of the surrounding hillsides, which are sacred to the tribe.

Pond with mesa backdrop. Photo by Mark Nohl. Courtesy of New Mexico Economic & Tourism Dept.

Zia Pueblo

TRIBAL PROFILE:

Situated in a land of startling contrast and intense beauty, the Pueblo of Zia occupies a 119,537 acre reservation. The pueblo has been continuously occupied since A.D. 1250, and the 700 residents continue farming, raising livestock and producing world-famous traditional pottery to sustain their economy. The tribe is also moving in new directions to augment and improve financial conditions through leasing lands, promoting film production (several movies have already been made here) and land development enterprises.

LOCATION:

Near the Jemez Mountains north of Albuquerque; west of I-25, exit at Hwy 44, which passes through Zia Pueblo lands.

ADDRESS:

Pueblo of Zia
San Ysidro, NM 87053
(505) 867-3304

CULTURAL INSTITUTIONS:

Zia Pueblo Cultural Center
San Ysidro, NM 87053
(505) 867-3304

Potters work on the center premises; some of their wares are sold. Displays include Indian dresses and Indian belts. Center houses a public library. Open 8:00 a.m.-5:00 p.m. weekdays.

SPECIAL EVENTS:

Our Lady Of Assumption Fiesta
An annual Indian festival with Corn Dance performances. Held on August 15.

RECREATIONAL OPPORTUNITIES:

Zia Lake: Open year round for catfish and trout angling. On the north side of the Jemez River, 2 1/2 miles west of the pueblo.

BUSINESSES & INDUSTRIES:

Zia Co-op
San Ysidro, NM 87053
(505) 867-3304
Grocery; hours 8:00 a.m.-8:00 p.m., 7 days a week.

ACCOMMODATIONS:

Bernalillo offers RV and tent camping and restaurants. Lodging available in nearby Cuba.

Dowa'yallane' Mountain. Photo by Mark Nohl. Courtesy of New Mexico Economic & Tourism Dept.

Zuni Pueblo

TRIBAL PROFILE:

The Zuni are widely known for their fine, handcrafted jewelry made with inlay techniques using turquoise, shell, and coral. They have perfected the art of needlepoint, a method of creating jewelry with minutely cut and polished stones set in silver. The Zuni religion is still practiced and important to the tribe. Tribal membership stands at 7,633, living on a reservation of approximately 430,000 acres.

LOCATION:

In west-central New Mexico at the Arizona border, the Pueblo of Zuni is due west of Albuquerque and directly south of Gallup on Rte. 602. Rte. 53 crosses the reservation from east to west.

ADDRESS:

Pueblo of Zuni
P.O. Box 339
Zuni, NM 87327
(505) 782-4481

CULTURAL INSTITUTIONS:

Zuni Museum
Zuni Tribal Building, Hwy 53
(505) 782-4404
Newly opened with a small collection.

SPECIAL EVENTS:

Shalako Ceremony
Zunis don larger-than-life masks to dramatize ceremonial dances in 7 or 8 newly built or remodelled houses while watchers cluster outside. Koyemshi Clowns visit the houses during this major Pueblo ceremony that lasts about a week, all together. No photography or tour groups allowed. Held in late November or early December, before the winter solstice.

Zuni Tribal Fair
Four days of festivities such as parades, rodeo, Indian dances, and a carnival. 2 miles east of the pueblo. Held Labor Day weekend.

Olla maidens. Photo by Mark Nohl. Courtesy of New Mexico Economic & Tourism Dept.

Recreational Opportunities:

Fishing & Hunting: Both Nutria Lake and the Zuni River, formed by the merging of Rio Nutria and Rio Pescado, are on reservation lands, and Cibola National Forest borders to the north, providing ample opportunity for fishing, hunting, and camping. There are 6 reservoirs stocked with rainbow and cutthroat trout, northern pike, channel catfish, and large-mouth bass. Permits for camping and fishing can be purchased in the pueblo at both gas stations, Halona Plaza, and Western Auto. Fishing on Zuni lands is strictly limited to lake fishing as the streams are home of an endangered species of fish. For information contact: Tribal Fish & Game Dept., (505) 782-5851, -5852.

Nutria Campground

Ojo Caliente Campground
Amenities include outhouses, cabanas, and picnic sites.

Businesses & Industries:

Pueblo of Zuni Arts & Crafts
P.O. Box 425
Zuni, NM 87327
(505) 782-4481, -5531
Selling Zuni turquoise, shell, coral, jet and silver jewelry; pottery, fetishes; contemporary art. At Zuni Tribal Building. Mail order; call or write for catalogue. Open daily 8:00 a.m.-4:30 p.m.; winter, Monday-Friday.

Zuni Craftsmen Cooperative Association
P.O. Box 426
Zuni, NM 87327
(505) 782-4425
This non-profit organization markets traditional arts and crafts by Zuni artists. On Rte. 53. Send a self-addressed stamped business envelope and $2 for mail order literature. Open year round 9:00 a.m.-6:00 p.m.

Zuni Archaeology
(505) 782-4814
Accepts contracts assisting enterprises seeking archaeology clearance for development projects.

Accommodations:

Nearest lodging in Gallup, about 40 miles north.

New York

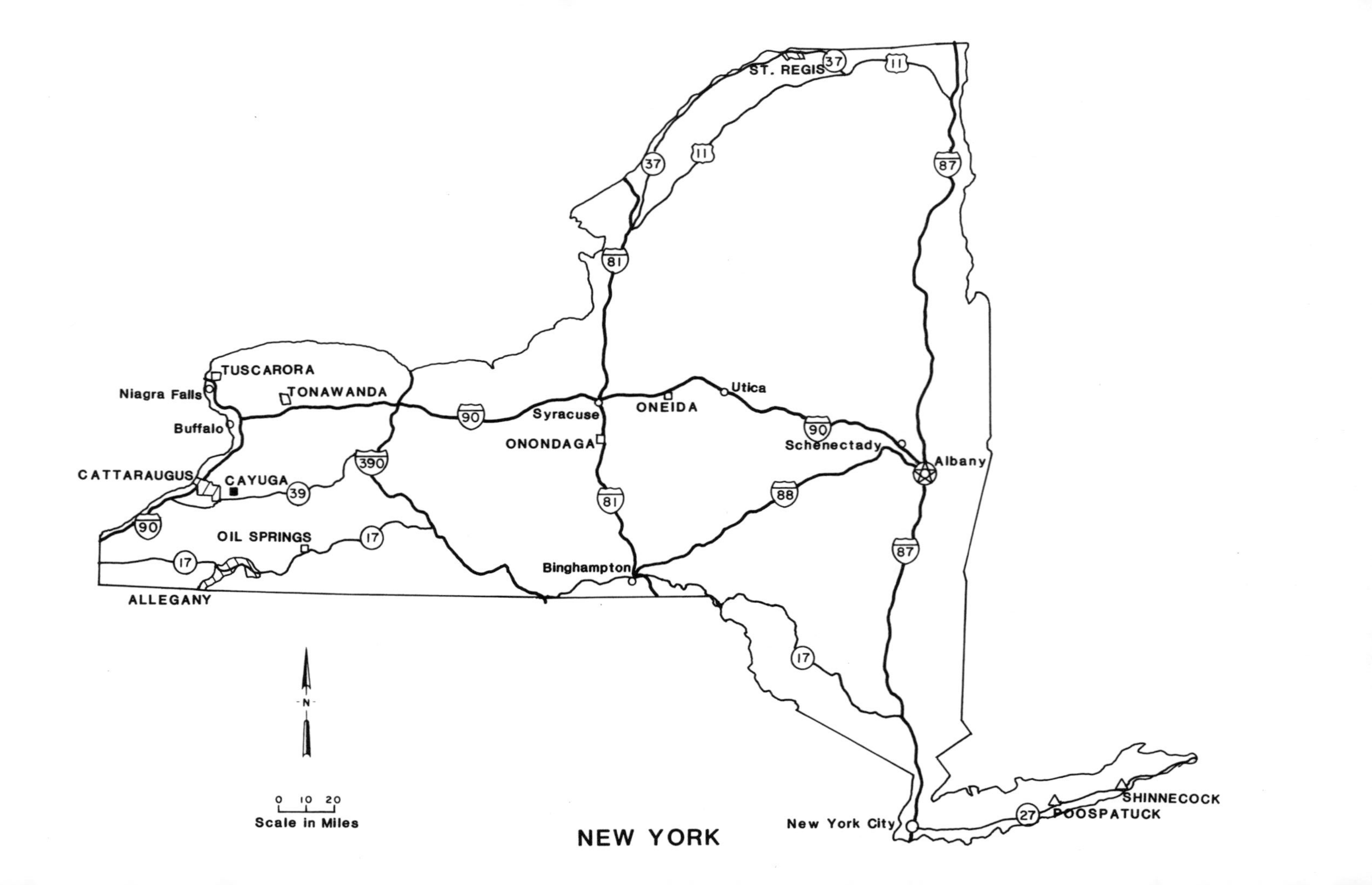
ST. REGIS
37
11
87
81
TUSCARORA
Niagra Falls
TONAWANDA
Buffalo
90
Syracuse
ONEIDA
Utica
ONONDAGA
Schenectady
Albany
CATTARAUGUS
CAYUGA
39
390
88
OIL SPRINGS
17
Binghampton
ALLEGANY
N
0 10 20
Scale in Miles
New York City
27
POOSPATUCK
SHINNECOCK

NEW YORK

Iroqouis cosmology, showing clan symbols, as depicted by Arnold Jacobs. Courtesy of Richard Hill, Santa Fe, NM.

Allegany Reservation

TRIBAL PROFILE:

Members of the Seneca Nation reside on three reservations in western New York State: Allegany, Cattaraugus, and Oil Springs; Seneca Nation headquarters is in Salamanca. Established in the Pickering Treaty of 1794, the Allegany Reservation encompasses 30,469 acres. As part of that treaty, the State of New York continues to pay the Nation annually in cloth and cash. The Seneca Nation is one of the Iroquois Nations and was a member of the Six Nations of the Iroquois League of Confederacy, a powerful Indian empire founded in the mid-16th century. Tribal enrollment, based on matrilineal lines, stands at about 5,000. The Nation strives to enhance support services, elder care, and levels of economic development and education.

LOCATION:

Southwestern New York, just east of Jamestown. Reservation lands follow the Allegheny River off Hwy 17, north of the Pennsylvania border.

Address:

Seneca Nation
Allegany Reservation
P.O. Box 231
Salamanca, NY 14081
(716) 945-1790

Cultural Institutions:

Seneca Iroquois National Museum
P.O. Box 442
Broad St. Extension
Salamanca, NY 14779
(716) 945-1738
Housing a special wampum belt exhibit, replicas of an elm-bark longhouse and a squared log cabin that were used by the Seneca in the 19th and 20th century, dioramas by well-known Seneca artist Carson Waterman, and displays of works by contemporary Iroquois artists. Guided tours available.

Gift shop carries a wide array of Iroquois wares, including baskets, wooden masks, jewelry and leather goods. Special and mail orders accepted. Open Monday-Saturday 10:00 a.m.-5:00 p.m., Sunday 12:00-5:00 p.m. year round; closed Mondays November-April.

Seneca Nation Library
Allegany Branch
P.O. Box 231
Salamanca, NY 14779
(716) 945-1795

Special Events:

Seneca Nation Indian Fair
Salamanca, NY
Held late August.

Seneca Nation Christmas Bazaar
Salamanca, NY
Held 1st Saturday in December.

Recreational Opportunities:

Seneca Bingo
790 Brad Street
Salamanca, NY
(716) 945-5130
Open 7 days a week: Monday, Tuesday, Thursday-Saturday doors open 5:30 p.m.; Wednesday doors open 9:30 p.m.; Sunday, doors open 11:30 a.m. Exit 20 off I-17.

Highbanks Campground
Salamanca, NY
(716) 354-4855
Only campground on the Allegany Reservoir. Amenities include 200 campsites, some with electricity, and 50 cabins. Docks and launch for boating, gas station. Fishing licenses available. Open year round. Off Rte. 17 at Exit 17.

Seneca Indian Reservation Group Tours
Tribal Public Relations Office
(716) 945-1738
A unique opportunity for guided travel around the Allegany Reservation. Tours can include a dinner of all Indian foods when requested. Make arrangements in advance.

Businesses & Industries:

American Indian Crafts
719 Broad St.
Salamanca, NY 14779
(716) 945-1225
Offering Seneca beadwork, masks, rattles, corn husk dolls, and crafts of other tribes. Mail order accepted. Open 9:00 a.m.-6:00 p.m. daily; closed Sundays, November-March.

Seneca Hawk
Rte. 17, exit 20
Salamanca, NY
(710) 945-2040
Gas station, restaurant and smoke shop.

Seneca Nation Mini-Mart
Rte. 17, exit 20
Salamanca, NY
(716) 945-5400
Convenience store and crafts such as headdresses and medicine wheels.

Dancers. Courtesy of Richard Hill, Santa Fe, NM.

Cattaraugus Reservation

TRIBAL PROFILE:

Cattaraugus Reservation residents are members of the Seneca Nation, which has been allotted three reservations: Allegany, Cattaraugus, and Oil Springs. Established in the Pickering Treaty of 1794, the Cattaraugus Reservation covers 21,680 acres. The Seneca Nation adopted a constitution in 1848 creating a democratic form of government. The Seneca National Tribal Council consists of 16 elected members, the seats being divided equally between the Allegany and Cattaraugus Reservations. *See the Allegany Reservation for other details regarding the Seneca Nation.*

LOCATION:

Western New York, South of Buffalo. Reservation follows the Cattaraugus River as it flows into Lake Erie. I-90, the New York State Thruway, crosses the reservation; Irving is at Exit 58.

ADDRESS:

Seneca Nation
1490 Rte. 438
Irving, NY 14081
(716) 532-4900

CULTURAL INSTITUTIONS:

Seneca Nation Library
Cattaraugus Branch
Irving, NY 14981
At reservation headquarters.

SPECIAL EVENTS:

Education Day
Saylor Community Bldg.
Children perform traditional social dances; arts and crafts from local artisans for sale. Held during spring vacation.

Seneca Fall Festival

Arts and crafts, art show. 2nd weekend in September.

RECREATIONAL OPPORTUNITIES:

Seneca Nation Bingo
Rte. 5
Irving, NY
(716) 549-4389
Presenting a wide variety of bingo, including Letter Bingo, Hammerhead, and Bow-Tie. Doors open at 6:00 p.m. Sunday-Wednesday & Friday; Thursday is late night bingo; doors open 9:30, games begin 10:30.

Seneca Sports Arena
Rte. 5, Box 207
Irving, NY
(716) 549-0888
The Seneca excel at lacrosse and are part of an Iroquois lacrosse league with teams from New York and Canada. Games take place May through September; Schedule information available at the Arena.

Hunting and fishing: Allowed on the Cattaraugus Reservation. Contact Clerk's Office at tribal headquarters for a permit and to check regulations.

BUSINESSES & INDUSTRIES:

Peter B. Jones
Box 174
Versailles, NY 14168
(716) 532-5993
Exciting and original sculptures and pottery. By appointment.

Rosein's Craft Shop
Rte. 438 & Bushroad
Gowanda, NY
(716) 532-5833
Merchandise includes turtle rattles, corn husk masks, turquoise, silver, pottery, sand paintings, blankets, and more. Open 8:00 a.m.-9:00 p.m., Monday-Friday; until 6:00 p.m. Saturday.

Ross John's Iroquois Smoke Shop
Rte. 438
Gowanda, NY 14070
(716) 532-4449

ACCOMMODATIONS:

Tepee
Rte. 438
Gowanda, NY
(716) 532-2168
Bed and breakfast.

Oil Springs Reservation

See Allegany and Cattaraugus Reservations.

Oneida Reservation

TRIBAL PROFILE:

The Oneida Nation, which means People of the Standing Stone, live on a portion of traditional lands south of Oneida Lake, their traditional home. The Oneida Nation was a member of the Iroquois Confederacy, formed in the 1500s and comprised of the Cayuga, Mohawk, Oneida, Seneca, and Tonawanda Tribes. Approximately 35 acres of the reservation remain, most of tribal lands having been sold. A large segment of the tribe emigrated to Wisconsin in the 1820s.

LOCATION:

Central New York State, between Syracuse and Utica; Oneida is just south of I-90, on Hwy 46.

ADDRESS:

Oneida Nation
P.O. Box 1 - West Rd.
Oneida, NY 13421
(315) 697-8251

RECREATIONAL OPPORTUNITIES:

Oneida Indian Bingo
Rte. 46, West Road
Oneida, NY
(315) 363-7770
Offering Jackpot, U-Pick-Em, Bonanza, and more. Players must be 18 or older. Matinees daily 12:45-4:00 p.m.; evenings 6:45-10:30 p.m. daily except Tuesday and Sunday.

BUSINESSES & INDUSTRIES:

Chrisjohn Family Arts and Crafts
RD #2, Box 315
Red Hook, NY 12571
(914) 758-8238
Oneida crafts people sell traditional and contemporary masks and wood carvings, bone jewelry, silverwork, and pipes. Special and mail order. On Indian Rd. Appointment only.

Schenandoah Trading Post
Indian Territory
Rte. 46
Oneida, NY 13421
(315) 363-1315

ACCOMMODATIONS:

Several hotels and motels in the city of Oneida.

Onondaga Reservation

TRIBAL PROFILE:

Located on a beautiful basin formed by glaciers, the Onondaga Reservation stretches over 7,300 acres, one-quarter of the land base of the Onondaga Nation at the time of the Revolutionary War. Some 600 tribal members live on the reservation, supported by annuities and individual commerce.

One of the original Six Nations of the Iroquois League, the Onondaga Nation was highly instrumental in its inception and therefore "Keepers of the Council Fires." League structure greatly impressed and influenced the architects of the American Constitution, serving as a model for government. According to tradition, the reservation serves as the capital of the Iroquois Nation, whose chief comes exclusively from the Onondaga Tribe. The Longhouse religion is central to Onondaga society; for example, only members are allowed to vote in tribal elections.

LOCATION:

Onondaga Reservation lies just south of Syracuse on the west side of I-81, Exit 16.

ADDRESS:

Onondaga Nation
Box 152
Nedrow, NY 13120
(315) 469-3738

SPECIAL EVENTS:

Green Corn Dance Festival
Annual fair activities include dances, crafts sales, traditional foods. Outstanding lacrosse teams compete. Held in mid-August.

BUSINESSES & INDUSTRIES:

Onondaga Indian Trading Post
Nedrow, NY 13120
(315) 469-4359
Iroquois corn husk dolls, turtle rattles, beadwork, and baskets. Open summers; by appointment only.

Poospatuck Reservation

TRIBAL PROFILE:

In the name of the King, the Colonial government granted this reservation to the Unkechauge Nation, who had been part of the Long Island Tribes' Montauk Confederacy. It is the smallest tribe living on the smallest reservation, 60 acres, in the state of New York. Tribal enrollment stands at about 100; the Unkechauge are governed by elected land trustees. The tribe holds an annual pow wow on Labor Day on its reservation, at the eastern end of Long Island near Fire Island National Seashore, on Moriches Bay, south of Mastic and Hwy 27.

Unkechauge Nation
Community Center
P.O. Box 86
Mastic, NY 11950
(516) 281-6464

St. Regis Mohawk Reservation

TRIBAL PROFILE:

St. Regis Mohawk Reservation crosses the U.S./Canada border, covering 23,970 acres in New York State and Ontario and Quebec Provinces. The 14,640 acre reservation at Akwesasne was settled around 1755 at the outbreak of the French and Indian War, and therefore has never been federal territory; it is now home to 7,000 Mohawk Tribe members. Tribal councils have been devised for both the U.S. and Canadian portions of the tribe; the U.S. portion is governed by three chiefs and three subchiefs, while the Canadian council consists of a chief and 11 councillors. The councils work in concert to provide jobs, better housing, health facilities, and recreation.

St. Regis Mohawk Library & Museum, off Rte 37, Hogansburg. Courtesy of St. Regis Mohawk Tribal Council.

LOCATION:

On the St. Lawrence River in north-central New York State. Hogansburg is on Rte. 37.

ADDRESS:

St. Regis Mohawk Tribe
Rte. 37
Community Bldg.
Hogansburg, NY 13655
(518) 358-2272

CULTURAL INSTITUTIONS:

Akwesasne Library/Cultural Center
Rte. 37-RR 1, Box 14-C
Hogansburg, NY 13655
(518) 358-2240

Library open Monday-Friday 8:00 a.m.-9:00 p.m., Saturday Noon-3:00 p.m. Ka ri wen ha ri (Carrying the news) newsletter published on a monthly basis.

Akwesasne Museum & Sweetgrass Gift Shop
Rte. 37
Hogansburg, NY
(518) 358-2461
Permanent collection of Mohawk and Iroquois artifacts; contemporary Mohawk and Iroquois artisans exhibits; special exhibits, demonstrations, and workshops on basket making. Offers guided tours by appointment. Carries videos, tapes and books on Native Americans. Gift shop carries baskets, beaded and silver jewelry, sweatshirts, T-shirts and more. 2 miles west of Hogansburg, on the lower level of the Cultural Center. Hours: 9:00 a.m.-5:00 p.m. Monday-Friday, noon-5:00 p.m. Saturday.

American Indian Travelling College
Cornwall Island, Canada
(613) 932-9452
Founded in the 1970s, includes a village of traditional Native American dwelling styles, museum, and resource center. All address contemporary Indians and their vital culture today, along with Mohawk history and Iroquois governance and philosophy. Resource center sells books and posters.

SPECIAL EVENTS:

Memorial Day Parade
Hogansburg
(518) 358-9976
A community event sponsored by the American Legion & Auxiliary and the Marine Corps.

Friendship Days
American Indian Travelling College
(613) 932-9452
Singing, dancing, Mohawk arts, Iroquois food, and games, often canoe races. Held 2nd weekend in July.

Akwesasne Freedom School Annual Fundraiser
Akwesasne Freedom School
Rte. 37
Hogansburg, NY
(518) 358-2073
Festivities include traditional and non-traditional foods, quilt auction, volleyball tournament, survival racing, and crafts booths. Held early August, during daylight hours Saturday and Sunday.

RECREATIONAL OPPORTUNITIES:

Billy's Bingo Hall
Hogansburg, NY
(518) 358-9993
Offering $1,000 giveaway every day, $3,200 Bonanza, quickie games, warm-up games, and a variety of packages. 2 bingo sessions per day: 2:00 & 7:30 p.m. Open 7 days a week.

Mohawk Bingo Palace
Rte. 37, north
(518) 358-2246 or
(800) 836-7470 (USA)
(800) 338-7597 (Canada)
High stakes bingo at its best; theme nights throughout the year offering cash and prizes. Games include Warm-Ups, 50/50, Bonanza, Do-It-Yourself, Jackpot, and Quickies. High stakes bingo Saturday & Sunday, low stakes bingo Wednesday-Friday, 7:00 p.m. Amenities include full service restaurant, no-smoking room, gift shop selling souvenirs and discount cigarettes. Games called in French and English.

Cedar View Golf Course
Off Rte.37-C
Rooseveltown, NY
(315) 764-9104
18-hole golf course open April-October. Proshop, restaurant, bar. 2 miles from the Canadian border.

Frogtown International Speedway
Frogtown Rd.
(518) 358-9017
Dirt oval stock-car track running 3 classes: Dirt Model 5, Semi-Pro, and Duke. Open Saturday nights, mid-May to mid-September: gates open 6:00 p.m., races start at 8:00. 1/4 mile from Rte. 37 and the Mohawk Bingo Palace, 1 mile from International Bridge.

Marina with restaurant, and a trailer court and marina are in the planning stages. Negotiations are in progress for a Tribal-State gaming compact on gaming, and St. Regis Reservation hopes to have a complex in the near future. The Mohawks have been on the cutting edge of gaming, opening the first slot machines for Indian gaming in the 1970s.

Basket by Mary Adams, at Mohawk Museum. Courtesy of Richard Hill, Santa Fe, NM.

ARCHAEOLOGICAL & HISTORIC SITES:

St. John Francis Regis Mission: On this site in 1762, the Jesuits first built a chapel which subsequently burned. Rebuilt 1791-2, it is the oldest church and mission house in the region. Open to public, offers a small tour. For further information contact: St. John Francis Regis Mission, St. Regis, Quebec, (613) 575-2066.

St. Patrick's Church: Built in 1800s. For further information contact: St. Partrick's Church, Hogansburg, NY, (518) 358-2557.

BUSINESSES & INDUSTRIES:

Bear's Den Trading Post
Rte. 37
Massena, NY
(518) 358-4229
Restaurant, gas station, and gift shop.

Dauphin Gallery
Lost Dauphin Cottage
Hogansburg, NY
(518) 358-9058
Gallery exhibits and sells works of Indian artists and hosts shows.

The Hogan
Hogansburg, NY
(518) 358-4641
Bar & restaurant.

Iroquois Bone Carvings
3560 Stony Point Rd.
Grand Island, NY 14072
(716) 773-4974
Family enterprise creating one-of-a-kind bone carvings. Also offers wares by other craftsmen. By appointment only; mail order on craft work.

Mohawk Impressions
Box 20 Mohawk Nation
Hogansburg, NY 13655
(518) 358-2467
Selling Iroquois corn-husk dolls, beadwork with quills and feathers, baskets, Mohawk paintings, and more. On Hwy 37, east of International Bridge. Open 9:00 a.m.-9:00 p.m. year round. Special and mail orders accepted.

Wild Bill's One-Stop
Hogansburg, NY
(518) 358-4465
Convenience store, gift shop and deli. Next to the Bingo Hall.

Akwesasne Notes
c/o Akwesasne Nation
Rooseveltown, NY 13683
(518) 358-9531

CKON
St. Regis, NY
(518) 358-3426

Indian Time
Mohawk Nation
P.O. Box 196
Rooseveltown, NY 13683
(518) 358-9531
Indian Time, Akwesasne Notes, and CKON radio station all housed together in the Indian Time building.

Matthew Etienne's Lacrosse Stick Factory
Rte. 344
Kanesatake (Oka)

ACCOMMODATIONS:

Bob's Motel
Rte. 37, Urban Hwy East
Massena, NY 13655
(315) 769-9197

Mary Jo Motel
Rte. 37
Ft. Covington, NY 12937
(518) 358-9971

Holiday Inn - Canada
805 Brookdale Avenue
Cornwall, Canada
(613) 933-8000 or (800) 465-4329
Across from Cornwall Island.

Shinnecock Reservation

TRIBAL PROFILE:

The Shinnecock Tribe has retained its original reservation lands since colonial government first reserved them in the name of the King. The Shinnecock, along with the Unkechauge, were part of the Montauk Confederacy and traditionally were whalers and fishermen. Shinnecock is a state reservation that covers 400 acres on Shinnecock Bay in eastern Long Island. Like the Unkechauge, the Shinnecock have elected land trustees administering tribal affairs for their over 300 enrolled members.

LOCATION:

Extreme Eastern Long Island, south of Hwy 27; reservations are protected from the Atlantic Ocean by a spit of land that creates Shinnecock Bay.

ADDRESS:

Shinnecock Tribe
Rte. 27A, Montauk Hwy
Southampton, NY 11968
(516) 283-9266

SPECIAL EVENT:

Shinnecock Labor Day Weekend Pow Wow
Festivities include Eastern Woodlands Indian foods, and arts and crafts sales, as well as traditional dance performances. Admission charged to benefit tribe and church.

Tonawanda Seneca Reservation

TRIBAL PROFILE:

In 1857, after much negotiation, the Tonawanda Tribe purchased 7,549 acres of land in Niagara, Erie, and Genessee Counties with funds realized by relinquishing lands west of the Missouri River. The lands are a portion of the original 12,000 acre reservation; about half of the approximately 850 enrolled members live on the Tonawanda Seneca Reservation. The Handsome Lake religion is still an important part of Tonawanda community.

LOCATION:

East of Buffalo in up-state New York, just north of I-90 via Hwy 63. Scenic Rte. 267 passes through the reservation connecting Basom and Akron, two service areas for the tribe.

ADDRESS:

Tonawanda Band of Seneca
7027 Meadville Rd.
Basom, NY
(716) 542-4600

CULTURAL INSTITUTIONS:

Tonawanda Indian Community House
Akron, NY 14001
(716) 542-2481
WPA arts display and library.

SPECIAL EVENTS:

Several dances and pow wows take place throughout the year at the Community House; check for dates, details.

Tonawanda Reservation Field Day
Logan Field
Councilhouse Rd.
Akron, NY
Arts and crafts sales, Iroquois food, traditional and western pow wow dancing, Seneca music, horseshoe tournament's lacrosse game, fire ball game (similar to soccer except ball is on fire). Held 1st Sunday in August.

Fishing on Lake Ontario. Courtesy of Richard Hill, Santa Fe, NM.

BUSINESSES & INDUSTRIES:

Iroquois Trading Post
Tonawanda Indian Reservation
1011 Bloomingdale Rd.
Basom, NY 14013
(716) 542-5355
Selling creations of Tonawanda artisans.

ACCOMMODATIONS:

I-90, Exit 48A at Pembroke offers nearest motels, restaurants, and service facilities.

Tuscarora beadwork. Courtesy of Richard Hill, Santa Fe, NM.

Tuscarora Nation

TRIBAL PROFILE:

The Tuscarora lived along several rivers in North Carolina when first encountered by settlers but now call upper New York State their home. In 1718, the tribe joined the Iroquois Confederacy, making it the Six Nations. Under the Treaty of 1784 the Tuscarora obtained jurisdiction over lands they occupied, a result of maintaining neutrality during the Revolutionary War. The reservation encompasses 5,700 acres, nine miles northeast of Niagara Falls. A council of chief and headmen have authority primarily over land and resources; timber sales contribute to income.

LOCATION:

Western New York, near the shores of Lake Ontario and east of Niagara River and Falls; east of I-190, Hwy 104 adjoins the northern boundary of the reservation.

ADDRESS:

Tuscarora Nation
5616 Walmore Rd.
Lewiston, NY 14092
(716) 297-4990

SPECIAL EVENTS:

Tuscarora Nation Annual Picnic & Field Day
National Grove
Mt. Hope Rd. & Walmore Rd.
Lewiston, NY
A 2 day festival held in mid-July.

Annual Free Border Crossing Celebration
Hyde Park
Niagara Falls, NY
One-day festival held in mid-July.

BUSINESSES & INDUSTRIES:

Smokin' Joe's Indian Trading Post
Tuscarora Reservation
(716) 297-0251

Tuskewe Krafts
2089 Upper Mountain Rd.
Sanborn, NY 14132
(318) 297-1821
Producing men's and women's hickory lacrosse sticks. Open weekdays 9:00 a.m.-3:00 p.m.

North Carolina

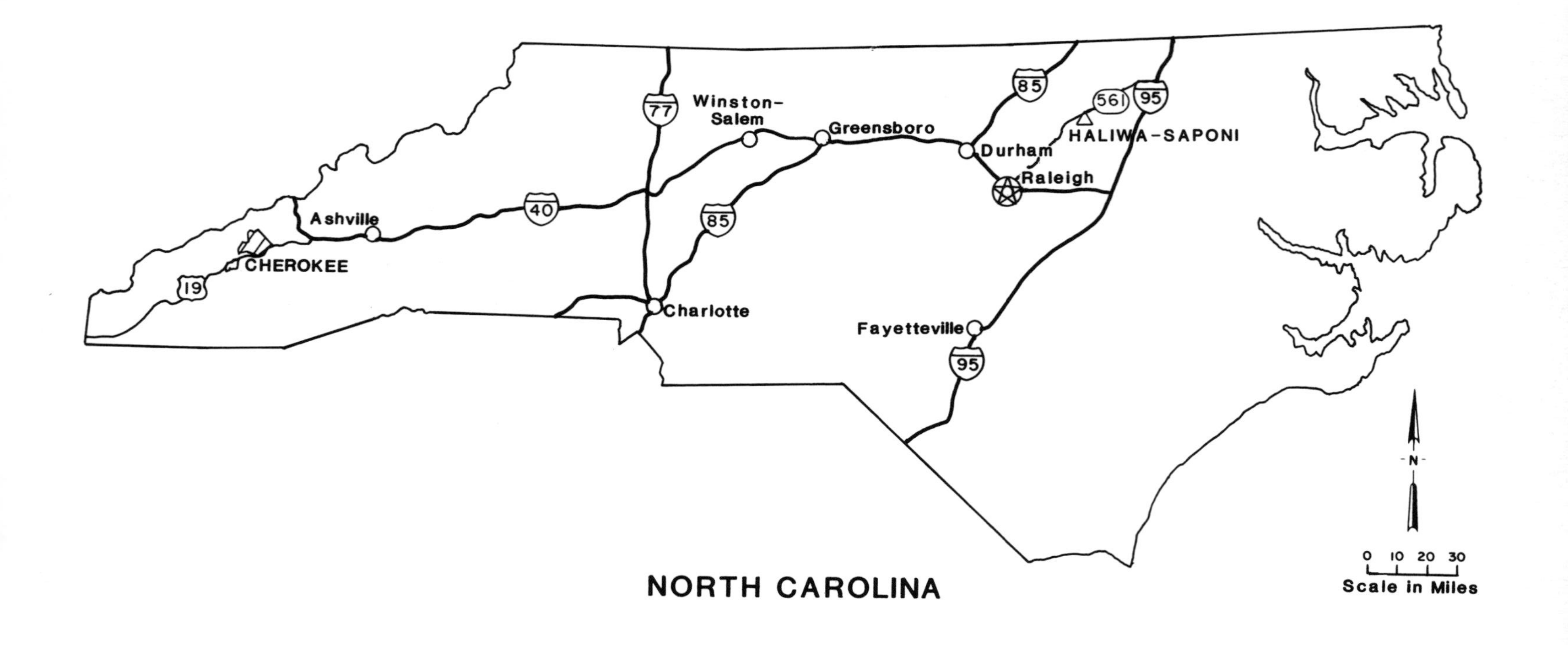

77
Winston-Salem
Greensboro
85
561
95
Durham
HALIWA-SAPONI
Raleigh
Ashville
40
85
CHEROKEE
19
Charlotte
Fayetteville
95
N
0 10 20 30
Scale in Miles
NORTH CAROLINA

Potters working at Oconaluftee Village in Cherokee. Courtesy of Cherokee Travel & Promotion.

Cherokee Reservation

TRIBAL PROFILE:

Once Cherokee territory encompassed land from the Ohio River south into portions of Georgia and Alabama. The Cherokee Indian Reservation in North Carolina comprises 56,573 acres of ancestral lands known as the Qualla Boundary, rich in scenic and historic diversity. One famous Cherokee ancestor was Sequoya, a brilliant and creative man who is best known for conceiving the Cherokee syllabary. Although the tribe's numbers are greatly reduced since those days and many Cherokee were removed to Oklahoma, the Cherokee culture in North Carolina is kept alive through legends, language, and crafts. Most of the 9,000 tribal members live in six communities on the reservation: Yellowhill, Birdtown, Painttown, Snowbird, Big Cove, and Wolftown. The Eastern Band of Cherokee began tourist enterprises in the 1940s, and today tourism is the mainstay of the tribal economy.

LOCATION:

Mountainous far western North Carolina, near the southern gateway to the Great Smoky Mountains National Park, on the Blue Ridge Parkway, southwest of Asheville. An ideal region for visitors to enjoy hiking, fishing, whitewater rafting, and the many other activities provided by people and nature.

ADDRESS:

Eastern Cherokee Tribe
P.O. Box 460
Cherokee, NC 28719
(704) 497-9195 or (800) 438-1601

CULTURAL INSTITUTIONS:

Visitors Center
P.O. Box 460
Cherokee, NC 28719
(704) 487-9195 or (800) 438-1601

Cherokee Eagle Dancer. Courtesy of Cherokee Travel & Promotion.

The removal scene from "Unto These Hills." Courtesy of Cherokee Travel & Promotion.

Museum of the Cherokee Indian
P.O. Box 1599
Cherokee, NC 28719
(704) 497-3481
Taped tours, audio-visual displays, and priceless artifacts introduce visitors to 10,000 years of Cherokee history. Gift shop on premises. Open daily 9:00 a.m. to 5:00 p.m., except Thanksgiving, Christmas, and New Year's Day. Admission fee; group discounts offered.

Qualla Arts & Crafts Mutual, Inc.
P.O. Box 310; Hwy 441
Cherokee, NC 28719
(704) 497-3103
Begun as a cooperative in 1946, today the Qualla Mutual works to keep alive the arts and crafts of the Eastern Band of the Cherokee, encouraging superior workmanship and creativity. Offering beautifully crafted pottery, beaded jewelry, wood and stone carving, baskets, and fingerweaving. Open daily.

SPECIAL EVENTS:

New events are added regularly. Contact the Visitors Center for an update on new and continuing activities.

Art Show
Museum of the Cherokee Indian
Held October 1 to 31.

Memorial Day Pow Wow
Ceremonial Grounds
Held Memorial Day weekend, late May.

July 4th Pow Wow
Ceremonial Grounds
Indian dancing; fireworks on the 4th. Held July 4th weekend.

Fall Festival
Ceremonial Grounds
Held early in October.

Unto These Hills Drama
P.O. Box 398
Cherokee, NC 28719
(704) 497-2111
A beautifully crafted outdoor drama depicting the history of the Cherokee; presented to audiences for over 40 years. Nightly except Sundays, June through August. Tickets can be reserved by phone or purchased at the box office.

Recreational Opportunities:

Cherokee Bingo
(800) 368-2464
Call for scheduling of games.

Cherokee Fun Park
Hwy 441 N
Cherokee, NC
(704) 497-5877 or (800) 438-1601
Over 4 acres, featuring a go-cart track, boats, miniature golf course, waterfall, and game room. Open April to November.

Oconaluftee Indian Village
P.O. Box 398
Cherokee, NC 28719
(704) 497-2111, -2315
A living history museum portraying Cherokee life in 1750. Services include guided tours through this accurately recreated village and demonstrations of craft work. Open mid-May to late October, 9:00 a.m. to 5:30 p.m.

Bear Land Park & Village
Hwy 441 N

Saunooke Village
Featuring many different types of bears and other exotic animals. Open daily, 9:00 a.m. to dusk, March through November; weekends in December.

Businesses & Industries:

The Cherokee Tribe and its entrepreneurial members regularly undertake new enterprises. The Visitors Center has a brochure that details the array of arts and crafts shops, restaurants, lodgings, and attractions offered on the reservation.

Saunooke Village
Hwy 441 N, Big Cove Road
A unique shopping village with many fine arts and crafts stores.

Cherokee Heritage Museum & Gallery
Saunooke Village
(704) 497-3211
Taped tours present Cherokee culture, legends and history. Also includes an Indian art gallery, gift shop, and art shows and craft demonstrations.

Bigmeat Pottery
(704) 497-9544

Medicine Man Crafts
(704) 497-2202

One Feather Trading Post
(704) 497-9045

River's Edge Gifts & Crafts
(704) 497-9548

Accommodations:

Holiday Inn
Hwy 441S
Cherokee, NC 28719
(702) 497-9181
Modern facility with 154 units, restaurants, swimming pool and other recreational facilities; shuttle to "Unto These Hills" drama.

A wide variety of camping sites, RV facilities and motels are available on and near the reservation.

Haliwa-Saponi Reservation

Tribal Profile:

The Haliwa-Saponi is a state-recognized tribe that originally inhabited much of what is now called Virginia and North Carolina. The tribe has about 3,000 enrolled members, 1,800 of whom reside in Halifax and Warren Counties. The tribe owns 45 acres and is currently pursuing federal recognition. The Haliwa-Saponi are working to meet current and future needs by expanding housing and tribal enterprise; projects include a greenhouse, nursery, and landscaping business, as well as numerous social programs such as day care, an after-school project, senior citizen nutrition sites, and outreach.

Location:

Northeastern North Carolina; Hollister is between I-85 and I-95, northeast of Raleigh-Durham and 25 miles south of the Virginia border. The reservation is 4 miles south of Hollister on Hwy 43/561.

Address:

Haliwa-Saponi Tribe
P.O. Box 99
Hollister, NC 27844
(919) 586-4017

Cultural Institutions:

Haliwa-Saponi Library
Hollister, NC
Lending library.

Haliwa-Saponi Tribal Pottery & Arts
Box 99
Hollister, NC 27844
(919) 586-4017
Offering pottery, quilts, beadwork, and stonework. On Hwy 43/561 in mobile unit. Hours: Tuesday-Thursday 6:00-9:00 p.m.; mail order accepted.

Special Events:

Haliwa-Saponi Pow Wow
Haliwa School
Hollister, NC
This event kicks off the East Coast pow wow season for almost 10,000 people, with traditional and fancy dances and storytelling, native craftspeople at work; Native American traders sell pottery, leatherwork, jewelry, beadwork and stonework. Concessions offer traditional Indian stew and fry bread, as well as hot dogs and barbecue. Held 3rd weekend in April.

Accommodations:

Nearest lodgings along I-95.

North Dakota

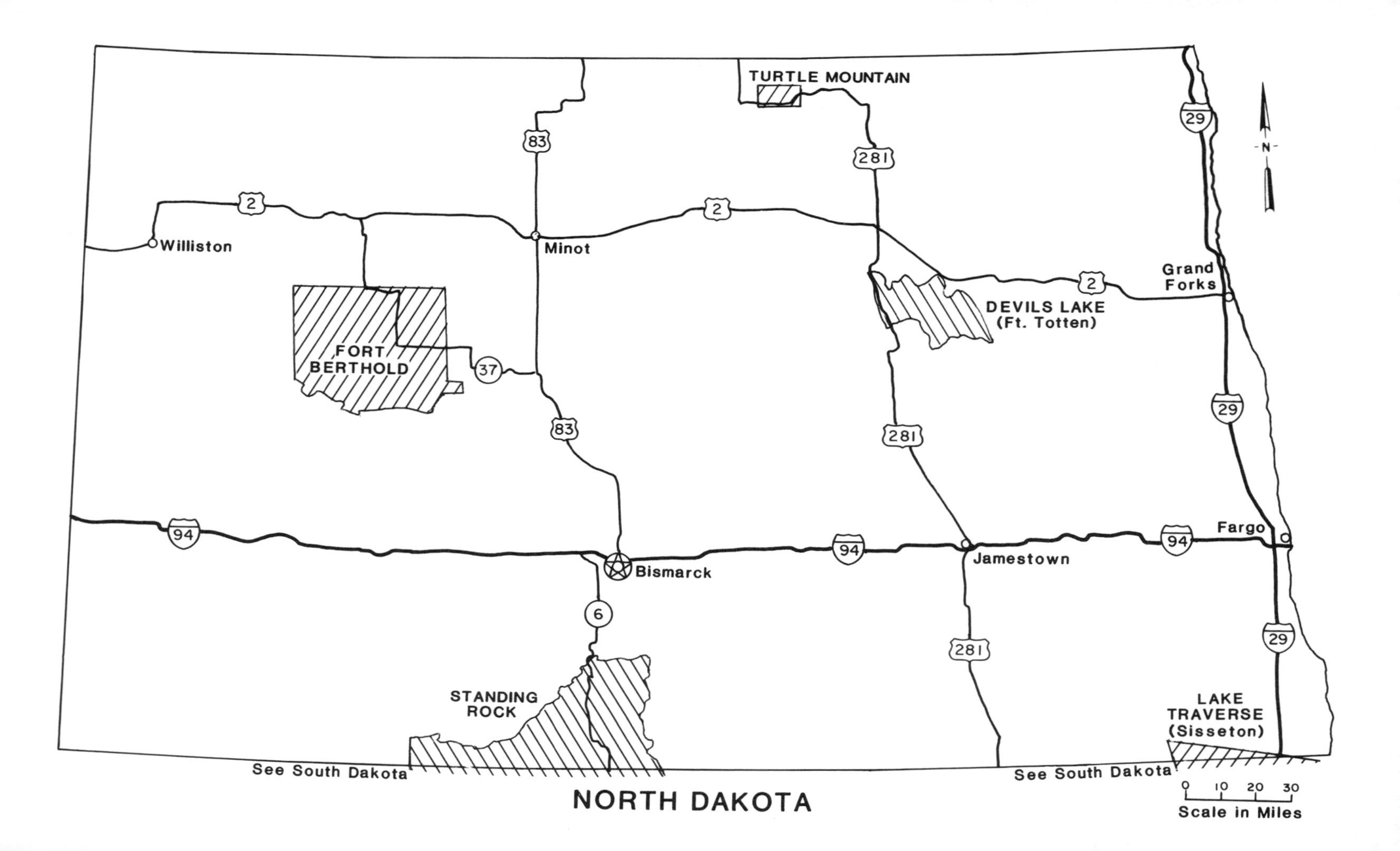

NORTH DAKOTA

Tepee encampment in the North Dakota woods. Courtesy of the Turtle Mountain Band of Chippewa Indians.

Devils Lake Sioux Reservation

TRIBAL PROFILE::

The Devils Lake Sioux Reservation was established by treaty in 1867. Today its service population is about 3,780, and trust acreage on the reservation stands at approximately 53,300 acres. Tribal government is led by a six-member tribal council under a constitution ratified in 1946 and amended since that time.

LOCATION: Northeastern North Dakota, just south of US 2 on the southern shores of Devils Lake, extending southward to the Sheyenne River.

ADDRESS:

Devils Lake Sioux Tribe
Sioux Community Center
Fort Totten, ND 58335
(701) 766-4221

SPECIAL EVENTS:

For information on activities on the reservation, call the tribal office.

RECREATIONAL OPPORTUNITIES:

Devils Lake Sioux Tribe has two bingo operations. Call the tribe for specifics as to time, dates and cost.

Fort Berthold Reservation

TRIBAL PROFILE:

The Fort Berthold Reservation was established by treaty in 1851 for the Arikara, Hidatsa and Mandan Tribes. The reservation occupies approximately 1 million acres, including Lake Sakakawea. The three tribes were formally joined as the Three Affiliated Tribes under the Indian Reorganization Act of 1934. In the 1950s, the building of Garrison Dam on the Missouri River created Lake Sakakawea, with about 600 miles of shoreline inside the reservation, dividing it into five parts that are tenuously tied together by the road system. The reservoir flooded the bottom lands that had been village sites and farming areas, and most reservation residents were relocated. The current tribal enrollment of Fort Berthold is estimated at 8,500; it is governed by the seven-member Tribal Business Council.

LOCATION:

West-central North Dakota, split by the Missouri River. Southern boundary of the reservation is almost 60 miles north of I-94; tribal headquarters is at New Town southeast of Minot on Hwy 23.

ADDRESS:

Three Affiliated Tribes
Tribal Business Office
P. O. Box 220
New Town, ND 58763
(701) 627-4781

For detailed directions and information on the activities and institutions listed below, call the tribal office.

CULTURAL INSTITUTIONS:

Four Bears Museum
Tribal Business Office

SPECIAL EVENTS:

White Shield Pow Wow
White Shield, ND
Features individual competition in Indian dancing with grand finals Sunday evening; cash prizes for top finishers. Free admission. Held 2nd weekend of July.

Mandaree Pow Wow
Mandaree, ND
Features individual competition in Indian dancing with grand finals Sunday evening; cash prizes for top finishers in each division. Free admission. Held 3rd weekend of July.

Little Shell Pow Wow
New Town, ND
Features individual competition in Indian dancing with grand finals Sunday evening; cash prizes for top finishers in each division. Free admission. Held 1st weekend of August.

Twin Buttes Pow Wow
Twin Buttes, ND
Features individual competition in Indian dancing with grand finals Sunday evening; cash prizes for top finishers in each division. Free admission. Held in August.

RECREATIONAL OPPORTUNITIES:

Four Bears Park
New Town Marina
Pouch Point

Lake Sakakawea offers excellent opportunities for water sports, particularly boating and fishing. The Affiliated Tribes own three parks that offer boat launching facilities and full service RV sites.

BUSINESSES & INDUSTRIES:

Convenience Stores: Each of the 7 districts on the reservation has at least 1 convenience store. The tribal office can provide directions.

Mandaree Electronics Corporation (MEC)
1 Community Center Road
P.O. Box 425
Mandaree, ND 58757
(701) 759-3399

Lumber Construction & Manufacturing Corporation (LCM)
Box 867
New Town, ND 58763
(701) 627-4828

ACCOMMODATIONS:

There are 4 motels on the reservation, in New Town; none is tribally owned.

Lake Traverse Reservation
and
Standing Rock Reservation

See South Dakota

Left, school tour at Anishinaubag Woodland Village. Right, totem pole guards the St. Paul's Center entrance. Photos courtesy of the Turtle Mountain Band of Chippewa Indians.

Turtle Mountain Chippewa Reservation

TRIBAL PROFILE:

The Turtle Mountain Reservation was established by Executive Order in 1882. Originally 10 million acres, the reservation now incorporates about 150,000 acres with satellite land holdings in several states. Enrolled membership of the Turtle Mountain Band of Chippewa Indians is 25,500, of whom almost 11,000 live on the reservation. Tribal government is led by a nine-member council. Turtle Mountain's heritage is lively and complex, drawn from Chippewa, Cree and French cultures; tribal members are active in business and professional fields, working to develop their community.

LOCATION:

Northern North Dakota, just south of the Canadian border. US 281 crosses the reservation from east to west.

ADDRESS:

Turtle Mountain Chippewa Tribe
Turtle Mountain Tribal Office
P.O. Box 900
Belcourt, ND 58316
(701) 477-6451

CULTURAL INSTITUTIONS:

Anishinaubag Center and St. Paul's Indian Ministries
Belcourt, ND
(701) 477-6452
In a natural setting 2 miles north of Belcourt; center includes a Plains Indian village, Mandan earth lodges, log cabins and other historic re-creations demonstrating the Native American history of the area. Also features trading post and offers canoe rental.

Turtle Mountain Chippewa Heritage Center
Belcourt, ND
Preserves and promotes the history and living traditions of the Chippewa people. Includes archives, artifacts, dioramas and art gallery. Gift shop sells quilts, jewelry, basketry and beadwork, as well as beadworking supplies.

SPECIAL EVENTS:

St Ann's Novena and Turtle Mountain Days
Belcourt, ND
Festival includes Catholic religious services and processions, historic exhibits, community seminars and ceremonies, pow wow, dancing, athletic tournaments, rodeo performances, craft demonstrations and exhibitions. Admission is charged for some events. Held 9 days in late July.

Top, domed earth homes. Right, cross and arrows monument. Courtesy of the Turtle Mountain Band of Chippewa Indians.

Annual Sun Dance
Dunseith, ND
No cameras, guns, drugs or alcohol allowed during this time of spiritual renewal and healing. Dates vary.

Turtle Mountain Pow Wow
Contest pow wow; held on Labor Day.

RECREATIONAL OPPORTUNITIES:

The Turtle Mountain Chippewa have a bingo operation. Call the tribe at (701) 477-6451 for specifics as to time, dates and cost.

BUSINESSES & INDUSTRIES:

Enterprises: There are 98 Indian-owned businesses on the Turtle Mountain Reservation, ranging from large manufacturing and data processing enterprises to numerous mom-and-pop businesses.

Bison Herd: The tribe maintains a small herd of bison just west of Belcourt on the south side of Hwy 5 in a grassy, wooded park.

Oklahoma

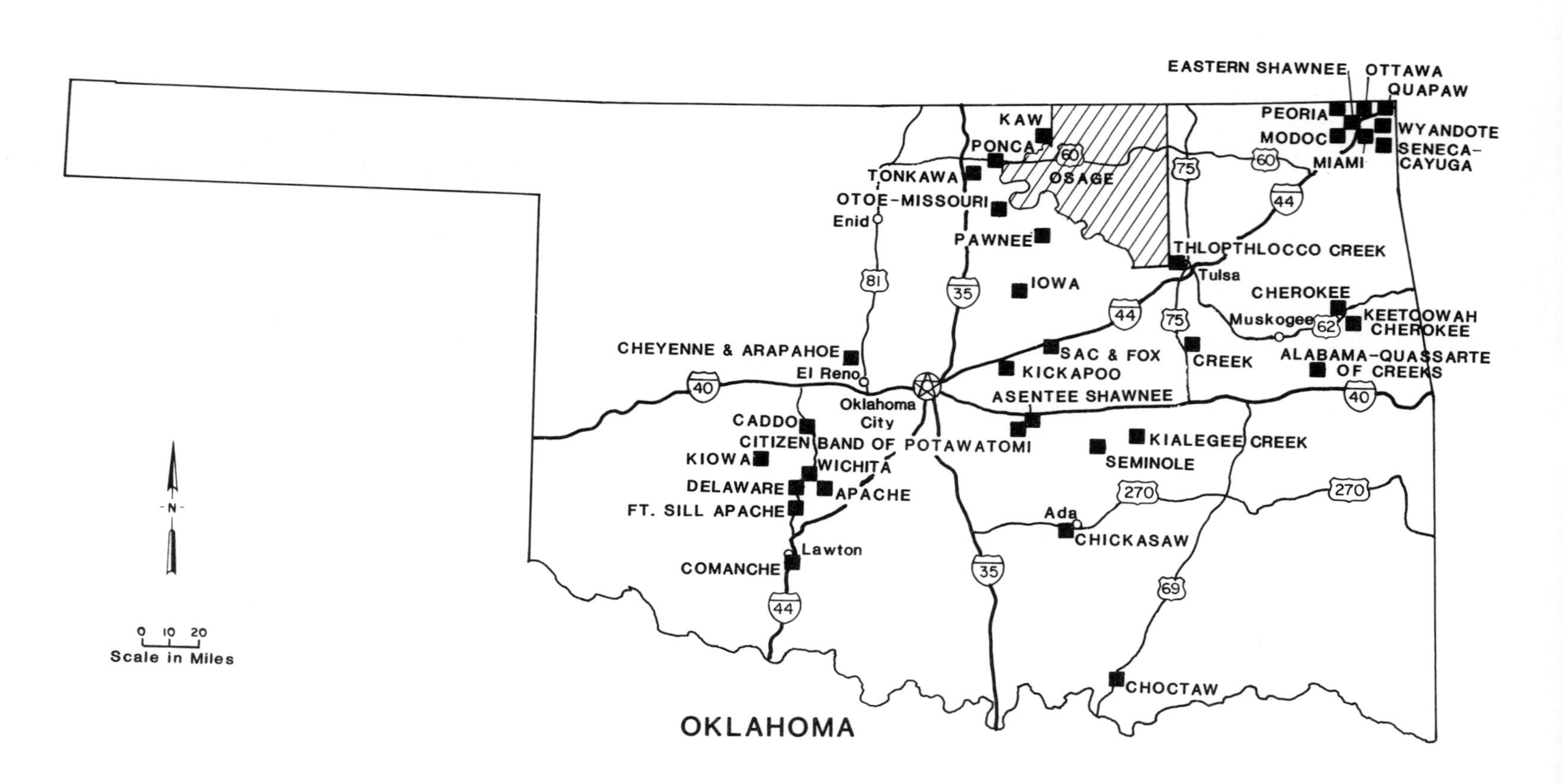
EASTERN SHAWNEE
OTTAWA
QUAPAW
PEORIA
MODOC
WYANDOTE
SENECA-
CAYUGA
MIAMI
KAW
PONCA
OSAGE
TONKAWA
OTOE-MISSOURI
Enid
PAWNEE
THLOPTHLOCCO CREEK
Tulsa
IOWA
CHEROKEE
Muskogee
KEETOOWAH
CHEROKEE
CHEYENNE & ARAPAHOE
SAC & FOX
CREEK
ALABAMA-QUASSARTE
OF CREEKS
El Reno
KICKAPOO
ASENTEE SHAWNEE
Oklahoma
City
CADDO
CITIZEN BAND OF POTAWATOMI
KIALEGEE CREEK
KIOWA
WICHITA
SEMINOLE
DELAWARE
APACHE
FT. SILL APACHE
Ada
CHICKASAW
Lawton
COMANCHE
CHOCTAW
N
0 10 20
Scale in Miles
OKLAHOMA
60
75
44
81
35
62
40
270
69

Thunderbird Entertainment Center. Photo by Stan Labadie. Courtesy of Absentee Shawnee Tribe of Oklahoma.

Absentee Shawnee Tribe of Oklahoma

TRIBAL PROFILE:

The Absentee Shawnee were so named by the U.S. Government when they absented themselves from the Shawnee reservation in Kansas. Now established in central Oklahoma, the Absentee Shawnee Tribe has about 2,600 enrolled members. The tribe holds about 11,600 acres south of the town of Shawnee. Organized under the Indian Welfare Act of 1936, the Absentee Shawnee Tribe is governed by a general council consisting of all enrolled members 18 years and older. The council elects a five member executive committee to manage its government. Tribal programs assist members in housing, medical care, higher education and elder care.

LOCATION:

Shawnee is about 30 miles east of Oklahoma City via I-40, south on US 177.

ADDRESS:

Absentee Shawnee Tribe of Oklahoma
2025 S. Gordon Cooper Drive
P.O. Box 1747
Shawnee, OK 74802
(405) 275-4030

RECREATIONAL OPPORTUNITIES:

Thunderbird Entertainment Center
15700 E. Hwy 9 (at I-35)
Norman, OK
(405) 360-9206
State of the art gaming facility that offers a wide variety of gaming activities including video bingo, casino-style bingo and high stakes bingo. Food service available. Open Thursday from 5:00 p.m. to 1:00 a.m., and continuously from 5:00 p.m. Friday until 1:00 a.m. Monday.

Old Cherokee Capitol, Tahlequah. Courtesy of Sammy Still, Cherokee Nation Photographer.

Cherokee Nation of Oklahoma

TRIBAL PROFILE:

The Cherokee Nation is not a reservation tribe. Its service area comprises 14 counties in northeastern Oklahoma. Removed to Oklahoma from North Carolina in the 1830s, the Cherokee Nation of Oklahoma is governed by a tribal council of 15 members. Preserving Cherokee culture while adapting to changing societies has been a goal of the Cherokee Nation for almost five centuries.

LOCATION:

Seat of tribal government is Tahlequah, southeast of Tulsa, northeast of Muskogee. This region is famed for its numerous recreation areas and reservoirs, as well as state parks. From Muskogee Turnpike, east on US 62.

ADDRESS:

Cherokee Tribe of Oklahoma
P.O. Box 948
Tahlequah, OK 74465
(918) 456-0671

CULTURAL INSTITUTIONS:

Cherokee Arts & Crafts Center
Cherokee Nation Complex
P.O. Box 948
Tahlequah, OK 74465
(918) 456-0511

Arts & Crafts Store
Courthouse Square
Tahlequah, OK 74464
(918) 456-2793
Housed in the Old Cherokee Capitol Building.

Cherokee Heritage Center
Cherokee National Historical Society
(918) 456-6007
Includes complete reconstructed Cherokee village inside traditional timber palisade; tribal members provide tours, and others demonstrate traditional crafts. 3 miles south of Tahlequah on Hwy 62.

Clockwise from top: "Trail of Tears" drama, Cherokee Heritage Theater. Photo by F.W. Marvel. Courtesy of Oklahoma Tourism & Recreation. Baskets at Rural Indian Village, Tsa La Gi Heritage Center. Courtesy of Sammy Still, Cherokee Nation Photographer. Log cabin at Tsa La Gi Heritage Center, also courtesy of Sammy Still.

Special Events:

Cherokee National Holiday
Tahlequah, OK
(918) 456-0671, ext. 212
A celebration of Cherokee culture and tradition, this 5-day festival draws a crowd of 50,000. Activities include parade, pow wow, pageant, rodeo, art exhibit, and arts and crafts sales. Held Labor Day Weekend, Thursday-Monday. Free admission.

Recreational Opportunities:

Located in picturesque Ozark hill country, Tahlequah is growing as a vacation center. Lakes Tenkiller and Ft. Gibson offer much for flat water recreation enthusiasts; the Illinois River, which empties into Lake Tenkiller is one of the state's best canoe streams.

Cherokee Nation's Bingo Outpost
P.O. Box 1000
Roland, OK 74954
(918) 427-7491; (800) 256-2338
High stakes bingo in a 900 seat hall. Exit 325 (US 64), I-40; 7 miles west of Ft. Smith, Arkansas.

Historic Sites:

Tahlequah has been the capital of the Cherokee Nation of Oklahoma since the 1840s. Sites in and around Tahlequah that are listed in the National Register of Historic Landmarks include: Supreme Court Building, Original Cherokee National Prison, Original Capitol and Cherokee Female Seminary.

Cheyenne-Arapaho Tribes

Tribal Profile:

Associated from early times, the Cheyenne and Arapaho tribes were assigned to a common reservation in Oklahoma in 1869. Today the tribes have trust lands of almost 85,000 acres; they are governed by a common tribal business committee composed of 7 members from each of the two tribes. Combined tribal membership is almost 9,400, of whom almost 4,400 live on the Concho Reservation.

Location:

Near the North Canadian River, west of Oklahoma City. Concho is off US 81, about 10 miles north of I-40.

Address:

Cheyenne-Arapaho Tribes
P.O. Box 38
Concho, OK 73022
(405) 262-0345

Special Events:

Jackie Beard Pow Wow
Concho Pow Wow Grounds
(405) 262-8535 or -0345
Indian dancing, arts and crafts. Held in late May or early June.

Cheyenne-Arapaho Summer Fest and Pow Wow
Concho Pow Wow Grounds
Concho, OK
(405) 262-0345 or 745-4120
Indian dancing, arts and crafts, sporting events. Held in early August.

Veteran's Day Pow wow
Geary, OK
Indian dancing, arts and crafts. Held in November.

Recreational Opportunities:

Cheyenne-Arapaho Bingo Enterprises
Box 95
Concho, OK 73022
(405) 262-8245
5 miles north of El Reno, then 1.5 miles southwest.

Cheyenne-Arapaho Watonga Bingo
Watonga, OK 73022
(405) 623-9299
Located 1/2 mile south of 4-way stop in Watonga on US 281.

Chickasaw Nation

TRIBAL PROFILE:

The Chickasaw Nation is one of the non-reservation tribes of Oklahoma; it was removed to Oklahoma from its native land in Mississippi in the late 1830s. The Chickasaw Nation serves tribal members in an 11 county area. Tribal government operates several programs for business development as well as services including health care, education and housing. The tribe owns and operates several bingo operations and convenience stores.

LOCATION:

South Central Oklahoma from the Canadian River to the Red River, the Texas border. Headquarters is Ada, about 35 miles east of I-35 at Exit 74, Pauls Valley.

ADDRESS:

The Chickasaw Nation
520 East Arlington
P.O. Box 1548
Ada, OK 74820
(405) 436-2603

CULTURAL INSTITUTIONS:

Chickasaw Nation Headquarters
Arlington and Mississippi Streets
Ada, OK 74830
(405) 436-2603
Historic pictures and displays; Chickasaw Nation Library is also located here.

SPECIAL EVENTS:

Chickasaw Nation Annual Meeting
Byng Schools
Byng, OK
(405) 436-4734
Activities include State of the Nation address, crowning of Chickasaw princess, arts and crafts show, sports competitions, free lunch. Held in early October.

RECREATIONAL OPPORTUNITIES:

Ada Gaming Center
1500 N. Country Club Rd.
Ada, OK 74820
(405) 436-3740
Complex includes bingo hall, tobacco shop and trading post, the tribal central business services and tribal construction company. Bingo is played Tuesday, Wednesday, Friday and Saturday in this 300 seat hall.

Goldsby Gaming Center
I-35 at Adkins Hill Road
Goldsby, OK
(405) 329-5447
400 seat hall; sessions every day but Monday; matinee on Sunday.

Touso Ishto
Chickasaw Nation Gaming Center
1 Mile Marker, I-35
Thackerville, OK
(405) 276-4229
More than 900 seats; facility includes no-smoking section, food concession, gift shop. Nearest Indian bingo center to Dallas/Fort Worth.

ARCHAEOLOGICAL & HISTORIC SITES:

Office of Cultural Resources
Chickasaw Nation Headquarters
Ada, OK
(405) 436-2603
The Chickasaw Nation has established this department to oversee the acquisition and development of sites important to tribal history. Call for the most current information about sites to tour.

Chickasaw Capitol
Tishomingo, OK
Completed in 1890s, the building is used as the seat for Johnson County. The Chickasaw Nation repurchased it from the state of Oklahoma in 1989, and it will be restored as a cultural center and satellite office for the tribe. This building and a log structure on the site, built as the Chickasaw Nation Capitol in the 1850s, are both listed on the National Register of Historic Landmarks. The log building has been incorporated in a museum operated by the Oklahoma Historical Society.

ACCOMMODATIONS:

Chickasaw Motor Inn
West First and Muskogee
Sulphur, OK 73086
(405) 622-2156
72-room facility with restaurant, club and tobacco shop. The Chickasaw Nation also sponsors bingo here.

Chickasaw Trading Post #1
Rte. 1, Box 8
Davis, OK 73080
(405) 369-5360
On Hwy 7, between I-35 and Chickasaw National Recreation Area (which is entered at Sulphur).

Chickasaw Trading Post #2
1500 N. Country Club Rd.
P.O. Box 1340
Ada, Ok 74820
(405) 436-0444

Choctaw Nation of Oklahoma

TRIBAL PROFILE:

The 10.5 counties that comprise the Choctaw Nation contain some of America's most beautiful scenery and has been home for the Choctaw Nation since the 1830s. The lakes, mountains and forests attract tourists from near and far. The Choctaw Nation of Oklahoma is governed by an elected 12-member tribal council that directs a broad range of social and economic programs to promote the well-being of the tribe.

LOCATION:

Southeastern Oklahoma, from the Canadian River on the north to the Red River and Texas to the south; headquarters in Durant, on US 69/75, near the Texas border.

ADDRESS:

Choctaw Nation of Oklahoma
16th & Locust Streets
Drawer 1210
Durant, OK 74702
(405) 924-8280

SPECIAL EVENTS:

Commemorative Trail of Tears Walk
Skullyville, OK
(405) 924-8280
Commemoration of the forcible removal of the Choctaw Nation from its homeland in Mississippi in 1830. Over 20,000 Choctaw began the journey on the "Trail of Tears," and only 7,000 survived. Re-enactment features a short walk, guest speakers, Indian food and dancing. Free admission. Held 1st Saturday of June.

Choctaw Nation Labor Day Festival
Choctaw Tribal Council Grounds
Tuskahoma, OK
(405) 924-8280
Festival for all ages that includes sports competitions, free musical entertainment, carnival, arts and crafts, exhibition pow wow dancing and stickball, and princess pageant. Draws 100,000 annually; free admission. Friday through Monday, Labor Day weekend.

RECREATIONAL OPPORTUNITIES:

Arrowhead Resort and Hotel
HC 67, Box 5
Canadian, OK 74425
(800) 445-2711 (in-state)
(800) 422-2711
Well known for its beautiful architecture and meticulously kept grounds, this tribally owned facility has almost 100 rooms and parlor suites, and 100 cabins with kitchenettes, as well as conference rooms. Amenities include gift shop, RV sites, boating, playground, recreation programs, game room, swimming pool, tennis, hiking trails and fishing. Resort offers day trips, lake cruises and trail rides.

Choctaw Indian Bingo Palace
3735 Hollis Roberts Road
Durant, OK 74701
(405) 920-0160; (800) 788-BINGO
Friday and Saturday evenings, Sunday afternoon.

Choctaw Council House, Tuskahoma. Photo by F.W. Marvel. Courtesy of Oklahoma Tourism & Recreation.

ARCHAEOLOGICAL & HISTORIC SITES:

Choctaw Council House and Museum: Historic red-brick building, capitol of Choctaw Nation until 1907. Built in 1884, it now houses a museum that exhibits Choctaw artifacts, paintings and photographs. Also has a gift shop. Open 8:00 a.m.-4:00 p.m., Monday-Friday. Tours offered if arranged in advance; donations accepted. For further information contact: Choctaw Museum, Tuskahoma, OK 74574, (918) 569-4465.

Creek (Muscogee) Nation

TRIBAL PROFILE:

The Creek or Muscogee Nation is another one of the non-reservation tribes of Oklahoma, with a jurisdiction of all or part of eight counties. Under a constitution approved in 1979, it is governed by a 31-member tribal council composed of representatives elected from eight districts, led by a principal chief. Tribal government employs about 400 people who contribute to the well-being of tribal members with programs for dental and health care, food, housing, education and environmental protection.

LOCATION:

North central Oklahoma, including Tulsa; Creek Nation capital is Okmulgee, on US 75 between Tulsa and I-40. Checotah is 20 miles south of Muskogee off US 69 and I-40. Eufaula is south of I-40 on US 69.

ADDRESS:

Muscogee Creek Nation
Office of the Principal Chief
P.O. Box 580
Okmulgee, OK 74447
(918) 756-8700

CULTURAL INSTITUTIONS:

Creek Nation Tribal Capitol Complex
Highway 75 at Loop 56
P.O. Box 580
Okmulgee, OK 74447
(918) 756-8700
Complex consists of 5 buildings housing different phases of tribal government, including the Mound building, patterned after an ancient earthen lodge of the early Creeks in Georgia. Tours available daily except holidays on a drop-in basis; groups are encouraged to call ahead to make arrangements.

Pow wow flag ceremony. Courtesy of Gary Robinson, Santa Fe, NM.

Special Events:

Ceremonial Stomp Dances: There are some 16 traditional ceremonial grounds throughout the Creek Nation. Ceremonial Stomp Dances celebrate life, give thanks to the creator and serve as a time of cleansing or purification. Stomp Dances are open to the public; they begin late Friday night, end early Saturday morning and are repeated Saturday night. For details, including exact date (variable), contact Tribal Community Development Officer (918) 756-8700. Held at selected times in summer.

Creek Nation Festival & Rodeo
Creek Nation Complex
In addition to the rodeo, events include Little Olympics, softball tournament (men and women), horseshoe pitching, volleyball, golf and tennis tournaments, parade, arts and crafts exhibits and food concessions. Begins Friday evening and concludes Sunday. Held 3rd weekend of June.

Eufaula Pow Wow
Eastside Ball Park
Eufaula, OK 74432
(918) 689-5066
Indian dancing, raffles, arts and crafts, food, co-ed softball tourney, archery, horseshoes, dominoes, swimming, camping, fishing. Grand Entry Saturday 8 p.m. Admission is free. Held Saturday, Sunday and Monday, Labor Day Weekend.

Recreational Opportunities:

Creek Nation Bingo
81st at Riverside
Tulsa, Ok 74170
(918) 299-8518

Bristow Indian Community Bingo
121 W. Lincoln
Bristow, OK 74010
(918) 367-9168
Thursday and Friday, 5:00 p.m. to midnight.

Checotah Indian Community Bingo
830 N. Broadway
Checotah, OK 74426
(918) 473-5200
300 seat hall; facilities include concessions, handicapped parking, security, and a no-smoking section. $1,000 top prize. Open Wednesday, Thursday, Friday and Monday; 5:00 p.m. to midnight.

Eufaula Indian Community Bingo
806 Forest
Eufaula, OK
(918) 689-9191; -5066 (Community Center Office)
Open Friday, Saturday, Sunday and Tuesday, 5:00 p.m. to midnight.

Okmulgee Creek Nation Bingo
Tribal Capitol Complex
US 75 and Eufaula St.
Okmulgee, OK 74447
(918) 756-8400

ARCHAEOLOGICAL & HISTORIC SITES:

Traditional tribal churches remain in several old Creek communities; contact Tribal Community Development Officer (918) 756-8700 for details.

Two sites of particular note are the **Eufaula Indian Boarding School** and the **Council Oak Tree** in Tulsa.

BUSINESSES & INDUSTRIES:

Creek Nation Senior Citizens Gift Shop
Administration Building, Tribal Complex
Okmulgee, OK 74447
Offers work of Creek Nation crafts people.

Checotah Indian Community Smoke Shop
830 N. Broadway
Checotah, OK 74426
(918) 473-5200
At the Community Center. Drive through window. Open Monday to Saturday, 8:00 a.m. to 6:00 p.m.

Similar smoke shops are found in Bristow, Coweta, Dewar, Eufaula, Glenpool, Hanna, Holdenville, Kellyville, Muskogee, Okemah, Okfuskee, Okmulgee, Weleetka, Wetumka, Wilson and Yardeka.

Eufaula Community Center Gift Shop
700 Block of Forest
Eufaula, OK
(918) 689-5066
Offers a wide range of items, including handmade crafts. Open weekdays and Saturday morning.

ACCOMMODATIONS:

I-40 Inn
Business Hwy 69
(918) 473-2331

Fountainhead Resort Hotel
(918) 689-9173 or (800) 345-6343

Midway Inn
Hwy 69
(918) 473-2381

Fort Sill Apache Tribe of Oklahoma

TRIBAL PROFILE:

The Fort Sill Apache Tribe is composed of members of the Warm Springs Band of Apache and the Chiricahua Apache. This small group of Indians is often referred to as Chief Geronimo's Band of Apache. The Fort Sill Apache Reservation was established by a series of treaties in 1912, 1913 and 1923. About 100 members of the tribe live in the former reservation area, and tribal enrollment is about 350. The tribe has a written constitution and is led by a six-member tribal business committee.

LOCATION:

Southwestern Oklahoma; Apache is about 15 miles south of Anadarko via US 62/281; north of the Fort Sill Military Reservation and Lake Ellsworth. I-44 (Bailey Tpk) is about 10 miles east of Apache.

ADDRESS:

Fort Sill Apache Tribe of Oklahoma
Rte. 2, Box 121
Apache, OK 73006
(405) 588-2314

CULTURAL INSTITUTIONS:

Fort Sill Apache Tribal Headquarters
Apache, OK
The tribe displays the work of its famous member, Allan Houser. 2 sculptures can be viewed inside; 1 is placed in front of the tribal complex.

Geronimo Guardhouse, Fort Sill. Photo by F.W. Marvel. Courtesy of Oklahoma Tourism & Recreation.

Special Events:

Annual Fort Sill Apache Dance for the Mountain Spirits
Apache, OK
Held 3rd weekend in September.

Archaeological & Historic Sites:

Chief Geronimo's Guard-House
Fort Sill Military Reservation and Museum
(405) 351-5123

The famed Chiricahua Apache chief was imprisoned here after the Apache Indian Wars in 1886. The guardhouse where Chief Geronimo spent his last years and his burial place on Chief's Knoll can be seen. Many tribal members, some who were prisoners of war, are buried here. The Fort Sill Museum includes exhibits of tepees and other Indian artifacts. On Hwy 277, 4 miles north of Lawton.

Iowa Tribe of Oklahoma

Tribal Profile:

The Iowa Tribe of Oklahoma, with 430 enrolled members, is organized under the Oklahoma Indian Welfare Act of 1936; its reservation was established in 1890. The tribe holds title to 1,710 acres within Payne, Lincoln, Oklahoma, and Logan Counties. The Iowa Tribe of Oklahoma is directed by a five-member business committee, headed by the tribal chairman. Other Iowa Indians live on the Iowa Reservation on the Kansas/Nebraska border.

Location:

Northeast of Oklahoma City, on the Cimarron River. East of I-35, Tribal Headquarters 3 miles south of Perkins on US 177.

Address:

Iowa Tribal Office
P.O. Box 190
Perkins, OK 74059
(405) 547-2402

CULTURAL INSTITUTIONS:

Bah-Kho-Je Gallery
201 Main
Coyle, OK 73027
(405) 466-3101
On Hwy 33 between I-35 and Perkins. Hosts Iowa Tribe Art Fair during the pow wow in June.

SPECIAL EVENTS:

Iowa Tribal Pow Wow
Iowa Tribal Complex
Traditional pow wow. Friday evening, afternoon and evenings Saturday and Sunday. Free admission. Held over a weekend in late June.

RECREATIONAL OPPORTUNITIES:

Iowa Tribe's Cimarron Bingo Casino
West Freeman Avenue
Perkins, OK 74059
(405) 547-2403
Evenings(405) 547-5352
Open Monday, Wednesday, Friday evenings; Sunday afternoon.

BUSINESSES & INDUSTRIES:

Iowa Tribal Mini Mart
202 Hwy 177 South
Carney, OK 74832
(405) 547-2402
En route to Turner Turnpike (I-44) from Perkins; open every day, 6:00 a.m. to 10:00 p.m.

Kaw Tribe

TRIBAL PROFILE:

The current state of Kansas was the original home of the Kansa or Kaw Tribe; the tribe was relocated to its present area in the 1870s. Today more than 1,390 members are listed on the tribal roll, with about 325 residing near the original Kaw Reservation, which is now on the shores and partially under the waters of Kaw Reservoir, formed in 1976 by damming the Arkansas River. There are 20,000 acres in trust in Key County. Adult members work at various occupations; many tribal members retain ownership of their original allotted lands.

LOCATION:

Northern Oklahoma; Kaw City is 11 miles east of Ponca City and US 77 on Hwy 11.

ADDRESS:

Kaw Nation
698 Grandview
Kaw City, OK 74641
(405) 269-2552

SPECIAL EVENTS:

Kaw Nation Pow Wow
Kaw Nation Pow Wow Club
(405) 269-2552
Contest pow wow with food concessions, arts and crafts, authentic Native American foods. Pow wow grounds are 1/2 mile west of Washunga Bay exit on Kaw Lake. Free admission. Held Friday evening, Saturday and Sunday, in late July, early August.

RECREATIONAL OPPORTUNITIES:

Kaw Nation Bingo
Newkirk, OK
(405) 362-2578
(800) 847-0070 In OK: (800) 722-4640
On River Road, 1.25 miles east of Main Street stoplight in Newkirk.

ACCOMMODATIONS:

Oklahoman
Braman Exit, I-35
(405) 385-2181
Motel with 15 units, restaurant, gift shop and gas station. About 5 miles south of Kansas border.

Osage Tribal Museum. Photo by F.W. Marvel. Courtesy of Oklahoma Tourism & Recreation.

Osage Tribe

TRIBAL PROFILE:

The Osage Indians originally inhabited the lower Missouri River region and hunted the western plains, including their present reservation in Oklahoma. The first treaty with the U.S. was signed in 1825, and the last treaty established their present reservation in 1871. Tribal life in the 20th Century has been affected significantly by the discovery of oil on this land, and the tribe retains the mineral rights to the more than 1 million acres that comprised the original reservation. Today the tribe is reviving its culture through several programs, including classes in Osage language and traditional arts and crafts such as ribbonwork, leatherwork and Osage fingerweave.

LOCATION:

Northeastern Oklahoma; US 60 crosses the reservation from east to west. Pawhuska is southwest of Bartlesville at the junction of US 60 and Hwy 99.

ADDRESS:

Osage Tribe
c/o Osage Agency
P.O. Box 178
Pawhuska, OK 74056
(918) 287-2495

CULTURAL INSTITUTIONS:

Osage Tribal Museum
c/o Osage Agency
600 N. Grandview Ave.
Pawhuska, OK 74056
(918) 287-2495, ext 280
Permanent exhibits include the history, art, government and religion of the tribe; exhibits of contemporary Osage art and culture change regularly. Classes are offered in Osage culture, art and language. Gift shop. Closed Sundays and holidays. Free admission.

SPECIAL EVENTS:

Annual Osage Dances
Osage Indian Villages
(918) 885-2853
Traditional Osage ceremonial dances. Public participation is not permitted, but spectators are welcome. At the 3 Osage Indian villages: Gray Horse, Hominy and Pawhuska. Held different weekends in June.

RECREATIONAL OPPORTUNITIES:

Osage Tribe of Oklahoma Bingo
Indian Camp
Pawhuska, OK 74056
(918) 287-2404

ARCHAEOLOGICAL & HISTORIC SITES:

Superintendent's House
Osage Agency
Listed on the National Register of Historic Places.
Not open to visitors.

Ottawa Tribe

TRIBAL PROFILE:

The Ottawa are of the Algonquian language family that populated the northeastern portion of the continent when European colonization began. They presently live in Michigan and Canada as well as Oklahoma. The tribe was established in Oklahoma during the 1870s; the Ottawa Tribe of Oklahoma belongs to the Inter-Tribal Council of Miami, which organizes some multi-tribal events and operates a gift shop at council headquarters in Miami.

LOCATION:

Northeastern corner of Oklahoma, off I-44 (Will Rogers Turnpike).

ADDRESS:

Ottawa Tribe of Oklahoma
P.O. Box 110
Miami, OK 74355
(918) 540-1536

SPECIAL EVENTS:

Ottawa Celebration & Pow Wow
Homecoming celebration, plus ceremonial baby naming, memorial feasts, traditional games, intertribal dancing and traditional stomp dancing all night. 6 miles southeast of Miami. Free admission. Held Friday, Saturday and Sunday, Labor Day weekend.

ARCHAEOLOGICAL & HISTORIC SITES:

Ottawa Cemetery
Tribal Grounds
Burial site of 12 chiefs of the Ottawa Nation.

Pawnee Tribe

TRIBAL PROFILE:

The Pawnee were relocated to Oklahoma from Nebraska in 1876, and tribal lands were assigned in 1892. The tribe still holds just over 700 acres, and reservation population is about 2,230; tribal membership is 2,408. The Pawnee Tribe was organized under the Oklahoma Indian Welfare Act of 1936 and is governed by an eight-member tribal business council.

LOCATION:

North Central Oklahoma; Pawnee is about 30 miles east of I-35, via US 64. 50 miles west of Tulsa.

ADDRESS:

Pawnee Tribe of Oklahoma
P.O. Box 470
Pawnee, OK 74058
(918) 762-3621

CULTURAL INSTITUTIONS:

Pawnee Tribal Library
Pawnee, OK
(918) 762-2485

Ceremonial Round House
Pawnee, OK
(918) 762-3624
Site of traditional ceremonies, meetings, etc. East of town.

SPECIAL EVENTS:

Pawnee Pow Wow
Pawnee Fair Grounds
(918) 762-3692; -2108
Annual tribal homecoming celebration; honors veterans. Parade July 4th. Activities include 5-mile run, traditional Indian dancing and arts and crafts. Admission is free; 4-day event, begins at 8:00 nightly. Held over 4th of July.

Pawnee Veterans Day Dance
Pawnee Indian Christmas Day Dance
Pawnee Round House
Pawnee, OK
(918) 762-3621
Gatherings, music. Contact the Communications Department for details for these and other dances held throughout the year.

RECREATIONAL OPPORTUNITIES:

Pawnee Tribal Bingo
Roan Chief Center
Pawnee Tribal Reserve
(918) 762-3624; -9904 after 4:30 p.m.
Sessions 5 nights a week; closed Sunday and Wednesday.

ARCHAEOLOGICAL & HISTORIC SITES:

Pawnee Agency: Beautiful old buildings, including tribal headquarters. Built of sandstone block, mostly before 1900. Some are listed on the National Register of Historic Landmarks. About 1 mile east of Pawnee. Contact the Pawnee Tribal Communications Department (918-762-3621) to arrange a tour.

BUSINESSES & INDUSTRIES:

Pawnee Tribal Trading Post
Pawnee, OK
(918) 762-3101
Includes convenience store with gas pumps, smoke shop as well as Pawnee crafts and foods.

ACCOMMODATIONS:

Campground and RV facilities about 1 mile away.

Peoria Tribe of Oklahoma

TRIBAL PROFILE:

The Peoria Tribe of Oklahoma belongs to the Inter-Tribal Council of Miami, which organizes some multi-tribal events and operates a gift shop at council headquarters in Miami.

Peoria Tribe of Oklahoma
P.O. Box 1527
Miami, OK 74355
(918) 540-2535

Ponca Tribe

TRIBAL PROFILE:

Descended from inhabitants of the northern plains, the Ponca Tribe first made a treaty with the U.S. in 1817. Removed to Oklahoma in the 1870s, the Ponca retain almost 1,000 acres in trust. Tribal enrollment is about 2,200, governed under a constitution ratified in 1950; tribal services are shared among the five tribes living in north central Oklahoma.

LOCATION:

Northern Oklahoma. Ponca City is about 15 miles east of I-35, near the Kansas border on US 177; White Eagle, site of tribal headquarters and the fair grounds, is south of Ponca City on US 177.

ADDRESS:

Ponca Tribe
Box 2, White Eagle
Ponca City, OK 74601
(405) 762-8104

SPECIAL EVENTS:

Annual Ponca Pow Wow
White Eagle Park
Ponca City, OK
(405) 762-8104
Traditional event, first held more than 115 years ago; festival with Indian dancing, parade, arts and crafts. South of Ponca City. Held in late August.

RECREATIONAL OPPORTUNITIES:

Ponca Tribe of Oklahoma Bingo
5 miles S. on US 177
Ponca City, OK 74601
(405) 762-8104

Citizen Band of Potawatomi Tribe

TRIBAL PROFILE:

Trust acreage of the Citizen Band of Potawatomi is just over 4,000, mostly allotted to individuals. Tribal membership stands at approximately 14,500, about 1,000 of whom live on the reservation. Tribal government is managed by a five-member business committee. The Potawatomi have a variety of business ventures, the profits from which are used to improve the lives of tribal members.

LOCATION:

Shawnee is about 30 miles east of Oklahoma City via I-40 and south of the interstate on US 177.

ADDRESS:

Citizen Band of Potawatomi
1901 Gordon Cooper Drive
Shawnee, OK 74801
(405) 275-3121

CULTURAL INSTITUTIONS:

Potawatomi Indian Museum and Craft Shop
1901 Gordon Cooper Drive
Shawnee, OK
(405) 275-3121
Indian art work, both traditional and contemporary, and handmade items including beadwork and ribbonwork. Open Monday-Friday, 8:00 a.m.-5:00 p.m.

SPECIAL EVENTS:

Potawatomi Pow Wow
Tribal Complex
Presents pow wow and traditional northern Potawatomi drums, singing and dancing. Arts and crafts. Held last weekend in June.

Recreational Opportunities:

Potawatomi Tribal Bingo
Hardesty Road
Shawnee, OK
(405) 273-2242
High-stakes bingo in an 800 seat hall; 7 nights a week, sessions beginning at 7:30 p.m. 1/4 mile east of US 177 on Hardesty Road.

Fire Lake Golf Course
South Beard Street
Shawnee, OK
(405) 275-4471
Public 18-hole course with pro shop, 70 Yamaha golf carts. Full-line driving range. Restaurant.

Businesses & Industries:

First Oklahoma Bank of Shawnee
130 East MacArthur
Shawnee, OK 74801
(405) 275-8830
Full-service commercial bank with $25 million in assets.

Potawatomi Tribal Convenience Store
Hardesty Road
Shawnee, OK
(405) 275-1480
Cigarettes, gasoline. Next door to the bingo hall.

Quapaw Tribe

Tribal Profile:

The Quapaw Tribe is organized under the Indian Reorganization Act of 1934 and governed by a business committee consisting of a chief and six committee members. There are presently about 2,300 enrolled members of the tribe; the focus of tribal activity is community service operations directed at promoting the well-being of tribal members.

Location:

Near the borders of Oklahoma with Arkansas and Kansas; near I-44 (Will Rogers Turnpike) on US Alt 69.

Address:

Quapaw Tribe of Oklahoma
P.O. Box 765
Quapaw, OK 74363
(918) 542-1853

Special Events:

Quapaw Tribal Pow Wow
Beaver Springs Park
Quapaw, OK
(918) 542-1853
Pow wow nightly, featuring a variety of Indian dancing; Indian arts and crafts on display. Park is 3 1/2 miles south of Quapaw. Free admission. Held for 3 days, at the 4th of July.

Recreational Opportunities:

Quapaw Entertainment Center
Miami, OK
(918) 540-2514
High stakes bingo, Thursday, Saturday and Sunday. O-gah-pah Convenience Store also at this site. On Mushroom Farm Road.

Accommodations:

Hotels and motels in Miami, 13 miles from pow wow grounds; camping at Twin Bridges State Park, 9 miles south of grounds.

Sac and Fox Tribe of Oklahoma

Tribal Profile:

The Sac and Fox Tribes first affiliated in the early part of the 18th Century when they were neighbors in the Great Lakes region. They had settled in Indian Territory by 1870 and had written and adopted a constitution by 1890.

Location:

Northeast quadrant of Oklahoma; Stroud is at the junction of I-44 (Turner Turnpike) and US 377, about half way between Oklahoma City and Tulsa. Tribal headquarters is about 6 miles south of Stroud.

Address:

Sac and Fox Nation
Rte. 2, Box 246
Stroud, OK 74079
(918) 968-3526

Cultural Institutions:

Sac and Fox Tribal Museum
5 miles south of Stroud
(918) 968-3526
Museum displays Sac and Fox history, including such famous tribal members as Black Hawk and Keokuk. Features a memorial and exhibit honoring Jim Thorpe, Olympic champion.

Special Events:

Sac & Fox Annual Pow Wow
Sac & Fox Nation Reservation
Stroud, OK
(918) 968-3526
Indian dancing, arts and crafts. Held mid-July.

Recreational Opportunities:

Indian Country Bingo
2321 N. Stillwater
Stroud, OK 74079
(405) 743-1214

Archaeological & Historic Sites:

The area around tribal headquarters features several sites of interest, some of which are open to the public. Contact tribal headquarters for details.

Businesses & Industries:

Sac and Fox Tribal RV Park
Modern campground with swimming pool, showers, recreational facilities. North of the Cultural Center.

Sac and Fox Tribal Mini-Mart
Architecturally modeled after a traditional Sac & Fox summer lodge; offers groceries as well as arts and crafts.

Seminole Nation of Oklahoma

Tribal Profile:

The Seminole Nation is one of the non-reservation Indian nations of Oklahoma; its people are descendants of those Seminoles who survived the tribe's removal from Florida in the 1830s. The Seminole Nation operates under a constitution approved and ratified in 1969, whereby 14 bands of Seminole Indians each elect three representatives to the tribal council.

Location:

South central Oklahoma, southeast of Oklahoma City; south of I-40. Wewoka is at the junction of US 270 and Ok Hwy 56.

Address:

Seminole Nation of Oklahoma
P.O. Box 1498
Wewoka, OK 74884
(405) 257-6343

Seminole Nation Museum. Photo by F.W. Marvel. Courtesy of Oklahoma Tourism & Recreation.

Cultural Institutions:

Seminole Nation Museum
6th and Wewoka
Wewoka, OK 74884
(405) 257-5580
Exhibits explain Seminole culture and history. Gallery and craft shop feature contemporary and traditional Seminole crafts, including patchwork.

Special Events:

Seminole Nation Days
Mekusukey Mission Grounds
Seminole, OK
(405) 257-6343
Princess contest, traditional dances, parade, feast, stickball, held 2nd weekend of September. Revival evenings during the following week, succeeded by a pow wow during the 3rd weekend of September. Free admission.

Businesses & Industries:

SNOANA Manufacturing
P.O. Box 1498
Wewoka, OK 74884
(405) 257-6287
Tours by appointment.

Seneca-Cayuga Tribe of Oklahoma

Tribal Profile:

One of the Iroquoian Eastern Woodlands tribes relocated to Oklahoma in the 1830s, the Seneca-Cayuga Tribe of Oklahoma operates under a constitution approved and ratified in 1937. The tribe belongs to the Inter-Tribal Council of Miami; there are about 2,500 enrolled members of the Seneca-Cayuga Tribe.

Location:

In the extreme northeast corner of Oklahoma; Tribal headquarters are in Miami, close to I-44 (Will Rogers Turnpike) on US Alt 69.

Address:

Seneca-Cayuga Tribe
P.O. Box 1283
Miami, OK 74355
(918) 542-6609

SPECIAL EVENTS:

Green Corn Feast - Thanksgiving Harvest
Bassett Grove Ceremonial Grounds
Annual ceremonial dances, naming of babies and social dances. Fancy dances of visiting tribes one night. 8 miles northeast of Grove. Free admission. Held in August; generally 1st week.

RECREATIONAL OPPORTUNITIES:

Grove Bingo
Rte. #4, Box 374-50
Grove, OK 74344
(800) 842-0299 (in-state) or
(800) 842-9229
High stakes bingo, open Tuesday, Friday and Saturday evenings; Sunday matinee. Features include a good food concession. On the east side of Lake O' The Cherokee; on Hwy 10 midway between US 60 and Hwy 25.

BUSINESSES & INDUSTRIES:

Lighthouse Restaurant
Grove, OK 74344
Directly across the street from the bingo hall.

Ranch Resort
Grove, OK 74344
Smoke shop, next to Lighthouse Restaurant.

Thlopthlocco Tribal Town

TRIBAL PROFILE:

One of Oklahoma's non-reservation tribes, the Thlopthlocco Tribe operates under a constitution approved and ratified in 1938. The town is managed by a business committee composed of the Tribal Town King and four Town Warriors, elected every four years. Their current enrollment is about 1,500 members, and the tribe is actively pursuing new recreational and business programs.

LOCATION:

East central Oklahoma; about 60 miles east of Oklahoma City, 6 miles east of Okemah, off I-40 at Clearview Exit 227.

ADDRESS:

Thlopthlocco Tribal Town
P.O. Box 706
Okemah, OK 74859
(918) 623-0419

RECREATIONAL OPPORTUNITIES:

Thlopthlocco Bingo
Okemah, OK
(918) 623-0419
Facilities include smoke and gift shop open every day; bingo Tuesday, Wednesday and Sunday. Gift shop features Indian art and jewelry made by tribal members.

United Ketoowah Band of Cherokee

TRIBAL PROFILE:

Incorporated in 1950, the United Ketoowah Band of Cherokee Indians in Oklahoma has about 7,000 members. It is governed by a nine-member council whose members represent nine districts.

LOCATION:

The 14 counties of Northeast Oklahoma that constituted the old Cherokee Nation. Tahlequah is southeast of Tulsa, about 35 miles north of I-40 from the Vian Exit (Hwy 82).

ADDRESS:

United Ketoowah Band of Cherokee Indians in Oklahoma
P.O. Box 746
Tahlequah, OK 74464
(918) 456-5491

CULTURAL INSTITUTIONS:

Cherokee Historical Theater
Tahlequah, OK
(918) 456-6007

Historic Murrell House, near Tahlequah. Photo by F.W. Marvel. Courtesy of Oklahoma Tourism & Recreation.

SPECIAL EVENTS:

National Indian Fiddling Contest
Tahlequah, OK
(918) 456-9678
Old time fiddling; competition from 10:00 a.m. Saturday, in mid-August.

RECREATIONAL OPPORTUNITIES:

Ketoowah Bingo
2450 Muskogee
Tahlequah, OK 74464
(918) 456-8927, -6131
Wednesday and Saturday at 6:00 p.m.

TRIBAL ORGANIZATIONS:

Ketoowah Enterprise Board
P.O. Box 746
Tahlequah, OK
(918) 456-0146

Dancer at American Indian Exposition, Anadarko. Photo by F.W. Marvel. Courtesy of Oklahoma Tourism & Recreation.

Red Earth Celebration, Oklahoma City. Photo by F.W. Marvel. Courtesy of Oklahoma Tourism & Recreation.

Other Oklahoma Tribes

Please contact the following tribes directly for tourism information.

Apache Tribe of Oklahoma
P.O. Box 1220
Anadarko, OK 73005
(405) 247-9493

Caddo Tribe of Oklahoma
P.O. Box 487
Binger, OK 73009
(405) 656-2344

Comanche Tribe of Oklahoma
HC 32, Box 1720
Lawton, OK 73502
(405) 492-4988

Delaware Tribe of Western Oklahoma
P.O. Box 825
Anadarko, OK 73005
(405) 247-2448

Eastern Shawnee Tribe of Oklahoma
P.O. Box 350
Seneca, Missouri 64865
(417) 776-2435

Kickapoo Tribe of Oklahoma
P.O. Box 70
McLoud, OK 74851
(405) 964-2075

Kiowa Tribe of Oklahoma
P.O. Box 369
Carnegie, OK 73015
(405) 654-2188

Miami Tribe of Oklahoma
P.O. Box 1326
Miami, OK 74355
(918) 542-1445 or 542-2890

Modoc Tribe of Oklahoma
P.O. Box 939
Miami, OK 74355
(918) 542-1190

Otoe-Missouria Tribe of Oklahoma
Route 1, Box 62
Red Rock, OK 74651
(405) 723-4434

Peoria Tribe of Oklahoma
P.O. Box 1527
Miami, OK 74355
(918) 540-2535

Wichita and Affiliated Tribes
P.O. Box 729
Anadarko, OK 73005
(405) 247-2425

Oregon

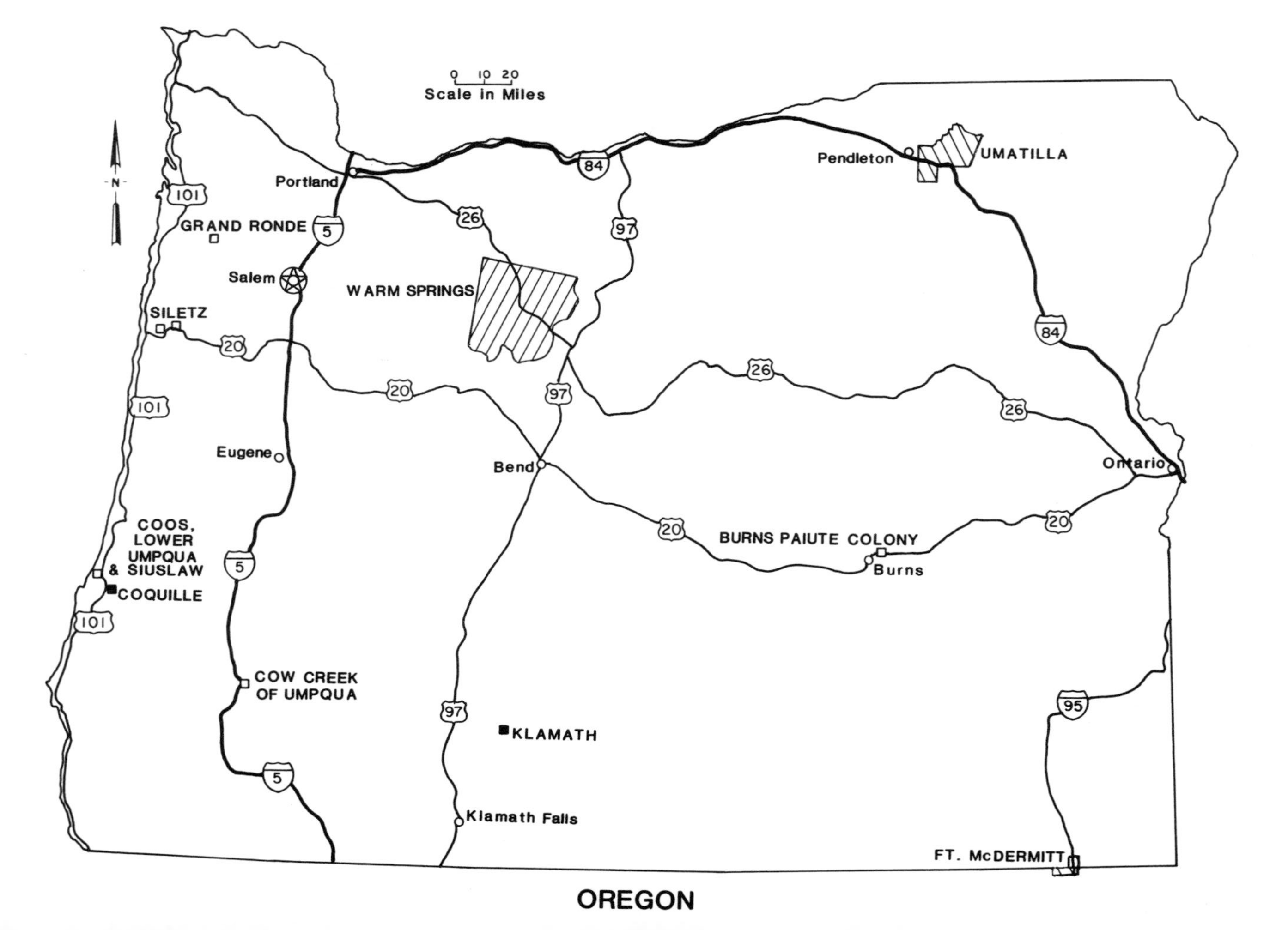
0 10 20
Scale in Miles
N
Portland
84
101
GRAND RONDE
5
26
97
Salem
WARM SPRINGS
SILETZ
20
Pendleton
UMATILLA
84
26
97
101
20
Eugene
Bend
Ontario
COOS, LOWER UMPQUA & SIUSLAW
COQUILLE
101
20
BURNS PAIUTE COLONY
Burns
20
5
COW CREEK OF UMPQUA
97
KLAMATH
95
5
Klamath Falls
FT. McDERMITT

OREGON

Burns Paiute Reservation

TRIBAL PROFILE:

Home to approximately 250 tribal members, Burns Paiute Reservation is in southeastern Oregon. Traditionally fishers and hunters travelling over parts of Idaho, eastern Oregon and eastern Washington, this band of the Paiute Tribe now lives on a reservation covering 11,785 acres just north of the Malheur National Wildlife Refuge. The Paiute were assigned to reservations in 1863; this band of the tribe governs by a five-member council under a constitution approved in 1968.

Burns-Paiute General Council
HC71, 100 Pasigo Street
Burns, OR 97720
(502) 573-2088

Confederated Tribes of Coos, Lower Umpqua, and Suislaw Indians
455 S. 4th Street
Coos Bay, OR 97420
(503)257-5454

Coquille Indian Tribe
P.O. Box 1435
Coos Bay OR 97420
(503) 267-4587

Cow Creek Band of Umpqua Tribe of Indians
2400 Stewart Parkway, Ste. 300
Roseburg, OR 97470
(5030 672-9405

Fort McDermitt Reservation

see Nevada

Grand Ronde Reservation

Tribal Profile:

From 1853 to 1855, treaties were negotiated and ratified with several tribes and bands in Oregon. In 1856, several tribes were relocated to the Grand Ronde area, and the Grand Ronde Reservation was created by Executive Order in 1857. The tribes located here include the Chasta, Kalapuya, Molalla, Rogue River, and Umpqua. The relationship between the tribes and the federal government ceased under the Termination Act of 1954, but the trust relationship was re-established in 1983, and a bill providing for the purchase of 9,811 acres of timberland to serve as a reservation land-base was legislated in 1988. This property forms the nucleus for tribal economic self-sufficiency. The tribes are planning housing, elders' meal site, pow wow grounds and a longhouse.

Location:

Surrounded by national forest in the heart of the Coast Ranges of northwestern Oregon, Grand Ronde is on scenic Hwy 18, east of US 101 and west of Salem.

Address:

Confederated Tribes of Grand Ronde
9615 Grand Ronde Rd.
Grand Ronde, OR 97347
(503) 879-5211

Special Events:

Annual Pow Wow
Grand Ronde Reservation
Thousands come to this celebration featuring dancing, drumming, and food. Saturday 8:00 a.m.-midnight, Sunday 10:00 a.m.-6:00 p.m. Held 3rd weekend in August.

Recreational Opportunities:

Fort Hill RV Park in Willamina offers the nearest camping facilities.

Archaeological & Historic Sites:

Tribal Cemetery: Long the traditional final resting place for the Grand Ronde tribal members. Call for specifics and permission to visit. For further information call: (503) 879-5525.

Historic Train Depot: From the days of the old steam trains, the station is now home to Tribal Social Services and the Alcohol and Drug offices.

Klamath Reservation

Tribal Profile:

Having lived on the 1.8 million acre Klamath Reservation until termination in 1954, the Klamath Tribe was restored to federal recognition 1986. Inhabitants of this region for hundreds of years, the 2,700 Klamath tribal members are working to rebuild their land base after losing their reservation. The tribe has also begun establishing tribal enterprises and now has a timber business -- thinning trees planted after logging operations have been completed in an area. New tribal offices and a cultural center are in the planning stages.

Location:

North of Upper Klamath Lake and the town of Klamath Falls, the Klamath tribal offices are on US 97 in south-central Oregon, about 50 miles north of the California/Oregon border. Chiloquin is on the banks of the Williamson River in the Cascades, surrounded by lakes, national forest, and wildlife refuges.

Address:

The Klamath Tribe
P.O. Box 436
Chiloquin, OR 97624
(503) 783-2219

Cultural Institutions:

Klamath Tribe Museum
Tribal Admin. Office
(503) 783-2219, ext. 162
Changing exhibits of rock tools, baskets, and clothing. Currently displaying a Klamath basket collection, clothing, and beadwork on long-term loan from Harriet Parker, who lived in the Oregon region in the early 1900s. Off Hwy 97.

Special Events:

Annual Klamath All-Indian Basketball Tournament
(800) 783-3093
Teams from all over the U.S. participate in this tournament, claimed the oldest all-Indian basketball tournament in the world. Held in mid-March, spanning 4 days.

Klamath Lake. Photo by John Kirk.

Treaty Days
Klamath, OR
Pow wow, Indian rodeo, parade and arts and crafts are all part of the festivities commemorating the 1986 restoration of tribal status. Held in late August.

Red/White Two-Man Golf Tournament
Harbor Links Golf Course
Klamath Falls, OR
(800) 783-3093
Hosted by the Big Basin Indian Golf Club, the tournament takes place on a 36-hole golf course and includes 2 flights and a women's division. 2-day event; held in mid-June.

Klamath Tribe Sobriety Pow Wow
Chiloquin Big Gym
Big dinner, pow wow, dance contest to bring in the New Year. Meal begins 4 pm. on December 31; pow wow follows, ending approximately 12:45 a.m. on January 1.

Recreational Opportunities:

Fishing and Hunting: Popular throughout the region; state permit required.

Archaeological & Historic Sites:

Scattered around tribal lands are old villages sites, caves and other places of interest that the visitor may see with permission from the tribal office. One cave on former reservation lands was excavated, uncovering sandals carbon-dated 10,000 years in age. Spear points dating back some 14,000 years have also been found in the region.

Accommodations:

Lodgings in Klamath Falls, 27 miles south.

Restrictions and/or Special Considerations:

Archaeological/historic places of interest should remain as they were found; please do not remove any items or leave anything behind.

Siletz Reservation

TRIBAL PROFILE:

Headquartered in the Siletz River Valley of Coastal Oregon, the Confederated Tribes of the Siletz regained their status as a sovereign tribal group in 1977, the first tribe in the state to do so. A coalition of 24 separate tribes and bands, the Siletz has created an economic development commission, STEDCO, to oversee lumbering, industrial properties, the former state fishing hatchery, and Siletz Tribal Smokehouse. Some traditional art forms, such as beadwork and basketry, continue.

LOCATION:

Situated in close proximity to some of the best sport fishing rivers and stream beds. Due west of Corvallis near the coast and US 101, Siletz Reservation is on Logsden Hwy, off Hwy 229, or US 20 at Blodgett.

ADDRESS:

Confederated Tribes of Siletz Indians of Oregon
P.O Box 549
Siletz, OR 97380
(503) 444-2532

CULTURAL INSTITUTIONS:

Siletz Library & Archives
119 E. Logsden Rd., Bldg. II
Siletz, OR 97380
(503) 444-2532

SPECIAL EVENTS:

Pow wows take place throughout the year on the tribal pow wow grounds at Government Hill, near the Tribal Center. Contact the tribal office for dates and times.

Nesika Illahee Pow Wow
Government Hill
Thousands come to celebrate the restoration of the Siletz Tribe to federal recognition, and the return of some reservation lands. Free admission. Held 2nd weekend in August, Friday-Sunday evening.

RECREATIONAL OPPORTUNITIES:

Friday Night Bingo
Government Hill, Tribal Community Bldg.
Siletz, OR
(503) 444-2532
Doors open 5:30 p.m., bingo hours 7:00-10:00 p.m.

BUSINESSES & INDUSTRIES:

Siletz Tribal Smokehouse
P.O. Box 1004
Depoe Bay, OR 97380
(503) 765-2286
(800) 828-4269
Selling seafood fresh from the ocean, including salmon and shellfish, and traditional/honey-smoked salmon and tuna. Store and mail order sales. Gift shop also specializes in Native American crafts, such as beadwork, leatherwork and woodwork by tribal members. Open 10:00 a.m.-5:00 p.m., Monday-Saturday; 10:00 a.m.-3:00 p.m., Sunday.

TRIBAL ORGANIZATIONS:

Siletz Tribal Dancers
P.O. Box 549
Siletz, OR 97380
(503) 444-2532

ACCOMMODATIONS:

Hotels, camping and RV facilities available in Newport, 15 miles southwest.

Photo taken on Umatilla Indian Reservation. Courtesy of Council of Energy Resource Tribes, Photo Files.

Umatilla Reservation

TRIBAL PROFILE:

The Umatilla Reservation covers about 246,000 acres in the foothills of the Blue Mountains. It is home for a coalition of three main tribes, the Umatilla, Cayuse and Walla Walla, and membership of the confederated tribes stands at just under 1,000. The tribes have organized leasing and farming enterprises to manage and develop land and agriculture.

LOCATION:

Situated just east of Pendleton, west of the Umatilla National Forest. I-84 passes through the reservation; take 2nd exit east of Pendleton to reach the main reservation highway.

ADDRESS:

Confederated Tribes of the Umatilla Indian Reservation
P.O. Box 638
Pendleton, OR 97801
(503) 276-3165

SPECIAL EVENTS:

Happy Canyon Pageant
Round-Up Grounds
(503) 276-2553
Indian festival and pow wow. Activities include a night pageant, rodeo, arts and crafts, traditional "prize" dancing and parade. Held in conjunction with the well-known PRCA sanctioned Pendleton Round-Up. Admission charged. Held 2nd full week of September, beginning at 1:00 p.m daily.

Root Festival
Always held in the spring when the roots are at their best. Call or write for date.

RECREATIONAL OPPORTUNITIES:

Mission Bingo
Mission Community Center
Mission Hwy/Old Hwy 30
(503) 276-3873
Play for over $10,000 in cash and prizes every Friday night. Also offer pull tabs, supplies, and concessions. Early bird starts at 6:30 p.m., regular session at 7:00 p.m. 5 miles east of Pendleton on old Hwy 30.

Power boating on the Warm Springs Reservation. Courtesy of John Running.

Warm Springs Reservation

TRIBAL PROFILE:

Created by treaty in 1855, Warm Springs Reservation became home to Wascos and Sahaptin-speaking bands of the Upper and Lower Deschutes. Later, Paiute prisoners of war and their families moved to the 640,000 acre reservation. Today, three tribes, the Wasco, Warm Springs, and Paiute, live in a vibrant community of 3,000 people with a rich and proud heritage. With energy and determination the tribes have developed timber and water resources and numerous enterprises to invest in its community and peoples. Meeting the need for social services, housing, and education are some of the tribes' many goals.

LOCATION:

North-central Oregon on the eastern slopes of the Cascade Range, Warm Springs Reservation is bordered on the east and south by rivers and lakes. US 26 crosses the reservation, 14 miles west of US 97.

ADDRESS:

Confederated Tribes of the Warm Springs Reservation of Oregon
1233 Veteran St.
P.O. Box C
Warm Springs, OR 97761
(503) 553-1161

CULTURAL INSTITUTIONS:

Tribal Culture & Heritage Dept.
(503) 553-1161

Warm Springs Information Center
Hwy 26
(503) 553-1156
Houses a gift shop selling beautifully crafted baskets and baby cradles, among other things.

Warms Springs Museum
Shitike Creek & US 26
(503) 553-1161, ext. 331/338
For over 2 decades the tribes have dreamed of constructing a modern facility to bring alive the story of the Confederated Warm Springs Tribes. Dioramas, multi-media exhibits, illuminated maps and graphics, video recordings and interpretive displays using artifacts collected and stored by the tribes will give the visitor a firsthand experience of ancient songs and languages, and an inside view of a rich and colorful culture, past and present. Scheduled for opening in mid-1993.

SPECIAL EVENTS:

Dances: Held at Kah-Nee-Ta Resort on Sundays throughout the summer months. Also, July 4th celebration, numerous fun runs, mini-marathons, and golf tourneys. Contact the resort for information.

Root Feast
An important traditional occasion. Held in early April.

Root Feast Rodeo
Rodeo Grounds
Warm Springs, OR
Rodeo Grounds off Kah-Nee-Ta Hwy. Held in early April.

Pi Ume Sha Treaty Days Celebration
Pi Ume Sha Grounds
Warm Springs, OR
Thousands flock to this 4-day event to enjoy competitive dancing, drumming, parade, fun run, endurance horse race, stick games, Fry Bread Golf Tournament, All-Indian Rodeo, and more. No admission charged. Usually held 3rd weekend in June.

Pi Ume Sha Treaty Days All-Indian Rodeo
Rodeo Grounds
See Celebration description for details. Saturday and Sunday, 1:30 p.m. Rodeo Grounds are on Kah-Nee-Ta Hwy; fee.

Huckleberry Feast
Warm Springs Reservation
Held in August.

All-Indian Holiday Basketball Tournament
Warm Springs, OR
Held week between Christmas and New Year's.

RECREATIONAL OPPORTUNITIES:

Fishing: Fishing, as well as camping for anglers, permitted by the tribe in the following areas; all other reservation waters are closed to fishing. Contact the tribal office regarding these diverse opportunities for fishing throughout reservation lands, along with details about permits, fees, and regulations.

High Cascade Mountain Lakes: These lakes include Trout, Long, Island, Dark, Boulder, and Harvey Lakes only. Trout fishing. Season April through October.

Deschutes River: Fishing area from the locked gate at the mouth of Dry Creek north 6 miles to Jefferson County Line. Season April through October.

Warm Springs River: From Kah-Nee-Ta village downstream to the Resort Golf Course. Season April 18 through October.

Lake Simtustus: Daily limits. Season April 25 through October.

Metiolus Arm of Lake Billy Chinook: Trout, bass, and Kokanee; daily bag limit. Season March through October.

McQuinn Strip: Lakes and streams in the Strip; no permit required.

Breitenbush Lake Campground: In the High Cascades Mountain Lakes region.

TRIBAL ORGANIZATIONS:

Middle Oregon Indian Historical Society (MOIHS)
2148 Kota St.
P.O. Box C
Warm Springs, OR 97761
(503) 553-1161, ext. 331/338
Established in 1974, its mandate is to "preserve and maintain the culture, artifacts, and lifestyle of the Middle Oregon Indian people" and to construct housing to realize that goal.

BUSINESSES & INDUSTRIES:

Burger Inn
Warm Springs, OR
(503) 553-1206
Fast food.

Chevron Station
Warm Springs, OR
(503) 553-3282

Deschutes Crossing
Warm Springs, OR
(503) 553-1300
Restaurant.

Macy's Market
Warm Springs, OR
(503) 553-1597

KWSO
Warm Springs, OR
(503) 553-1965
Educational radio station.

KTWI & KTWS
Bend, OR
Both are commercial radio stations.

Left, vacationers at the Kah-Nee-Ta Resort, Warm Springs, Oregon. Right, smoking salmon at Kah-Nee-Ta Resort. Photos courtesy of Cappelli, Miles, Wiltz & Kelly, Eugene, Oregon.

Warm Springs Forest Products Industries
Box 810
Warm Springs, OR 97761
(503) 553-1131
Business operations in all phases of wood products production, including logging, sawmill, stud mill, veneer and plywood plant. Tours by prior arrangement.

Enterprises: Warm Springs Power Enterprises, Apparel Industries, Clothing Company, and Rock Crushing; and Tribal Construction Company. Member businesses include DMJ Automotive Garage, 6 logging companies, and a construction company.

ACCOMMODATIONS:

Kah-Nee-Ta Resort
Box Office K
Warm Springs, OR 97761
(503) 553-1112 or (800) 831-0100
Resort offering activities and accommodations to satisfy almost any vacationer's inclination and situated in a region blessed with sunshine 300 days a year. Numerous executive and deluxe rooms, suites and cottages; RV, trailer and camp sites; tepee rentals. Amenities include 2 restaurants, lounge, 2 gift shops, 2 swimming pools, 18-hole golf course, miniature golf course, riding stable, bike paths, river rafting, and fishing.

Rhode Island

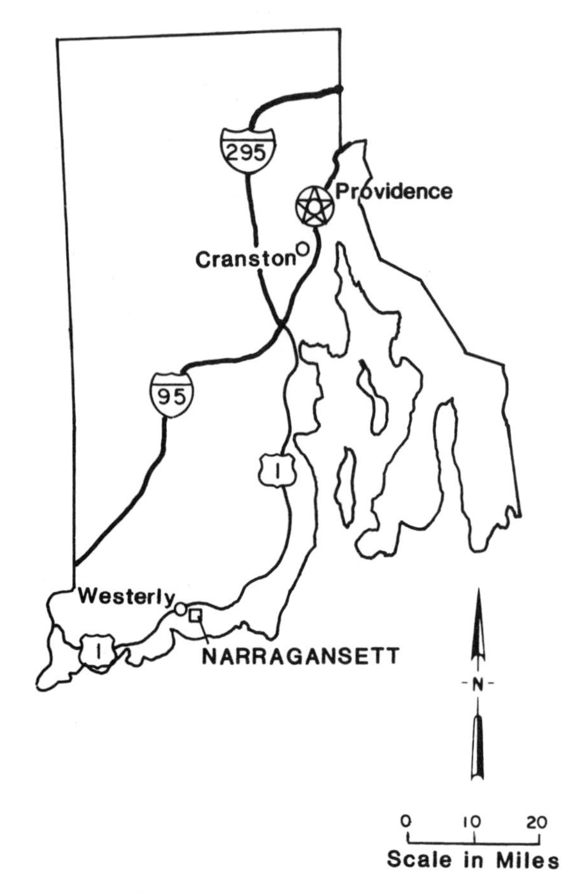

RHODE ISLAND

Narragansett Reservation

TRIBAL PROFILE:

A federally recognized Indian tribe, the Narragansett lives on the 1,800-acre Narragansett Indian Reservation. Tradition is important here; the tribe attempts to follow ancient religion, ceremonies, oral histories and the Circle of the People. Committees, commissions, and departments work to meet the needs of the Narragansett Tribe, as members balance old lifestyles with new, working in such diverse occupations as stone masonry, teaching, fishing, electrical, and ministry.

LOCATION:

Southern Rhode Island, dotted with numerous ponds, swamps, and wildlife refuges. North of Block Island near Ninigret Pond, Charlestown is east off coastal US 1 on Rte. 2.

ADDRESS:

Narragansett Indian Tribe
P.O. Box 268
Charlestown, RI 02813
(401) 364-1100 or (800) 243-6278

CULTURAL INSTITUTIONS:

Narragansett Indian Longhouse
Rte. 2
Charlestown, RI
Presentations, lectures, and tours. Call tribal office for current events or to arrange a tour.

SPECIAL EVENTS:

Annual August Meeting
Narragansett Indian Church Grounds
This Green Corn and Thanksgiving celebration is an historical and traditional religious occasion, and representatives come from tribes throughout the U.S. Activities include drumming, dancing, singing, gathering traditional foods, Indian crafts sales, games, and competition dances, both traditional and fancy for men, women, and children. The Church grounds are off Rte. 2. Held one weekend in mid-August, Noon-6:00 p.m. Admission charged.

Great Swamp Pilgrimage
Held last Sunday in September.

Harvest Thanksgiving Ceremony
Narragansett Indian Longhouse
Hundreds come to this religious celebration and feast of thanksgiving for the harvest. The Longhouse is off Rte. 2. Held 1st Sunday in October, noon-5:00 p.m.

Nickomoh Celebration
Narragansett Indian Longhouse
These ancient observances are held during winter months every year to give thanks and honor ancestors, the Great Creator, and Spirits of Giving and Sharing by observing a gift exchange. This ceremony is an historical part of tribal tradition and is the equivalent of the Christmas holidays. Held one Sunday in December, noon-6:00 p.m.; check with the tribal office for specific date.

New Year Celebration
Narragansett Indian Longhouse
An annual occasion and celebration of thanksgiving for the spring sap runs. Held Sunday in mid-March.

ARCHAEOLOGICAL & HISTORIC SITES:

Many important sites are dispersed throughout Narragansett lands, including burial sites, monuments, signal rocks and crying rocks. Contact John Brown (401-364-9834) for information.

BUSINESSES & INDUSTRIES:

Dove Indian Trading Post
Main Street
Rockville, RI 02873
(401) 539-2094, -2786
Selling jewelry, leatherwork, beadwork, and pottery. Open Monday-Saturday, 7:30 a.m.-5:30 p.m.; closed from 11:30-3:30, Monday-Friday.

Narragansett Indian Arts & Crafts Co-op Board
Narragansett Indian Longhouse
Rte. 2, South County Trail
P.O. Box 268
Charlestown, RI 02813
(401) 364-1100, -9832

South Carolina

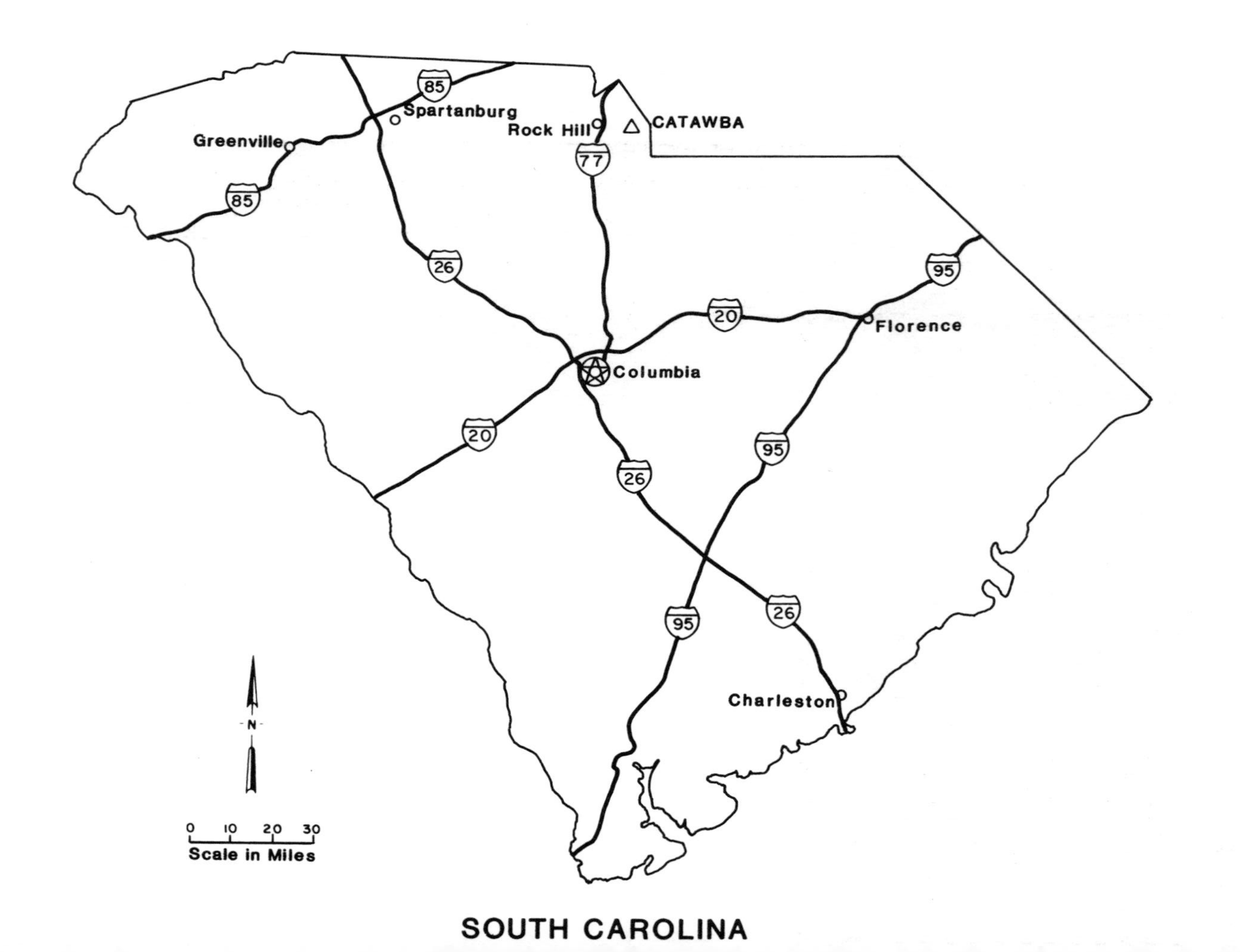

SOUTH CAROLINA

Catawba Reservation

TRIBAL PROFILE:

Catawba is a Siouan tribe that was most populous in the Carolinas. Decimated by smallpox and warfare, the tribe was allotted 15 square miles for a reservation in 1793. Over time the reservation dwindled to 100 acres owned by the tribe, with just over 700 Indian residents. Tribal status was terminated in 1962. At one time highly skilled in pottery and basketry arts, the Catawba Tribe has recently revived pottery production and is also endeavoring to renew basketry and beadwork traditions. Textile factories in the region are the main source of employment for tribal members.

LOCATION:

Just south of the North Carolina border, near I-77.

ADDRESS:

Catawba Tribe
Rte. 3, Box 324
Rock Hill, SC 29730
(803) 324-0259

CULTURAL INSTITUTIONS:

Preservation Committee: Working to sustain and rekindle Catawba culture and traditions.

SPECIAL EVENTS:

Catawba Indian Pow Wow
10 miles southeast of Rock Hill. Held last weekend in November.

BUSINESSES & INDUSTRIES:

Several potters work on the Catawba Reservation; inquire for details at the tribal office.

Sarah Ayers
1182 Brookwood Circle
West Columbia, SC 29169
(803) 794-5436
Noted Catawba potter named "Outstanding Native American Artist," with works in the collections of museums throughout the U.S. Offering ceramic pipes, vases, pitchers, canoes, and other crafts. Approximately 80 miles south of the reservation. Special and mail orders accepted.

South Dakota

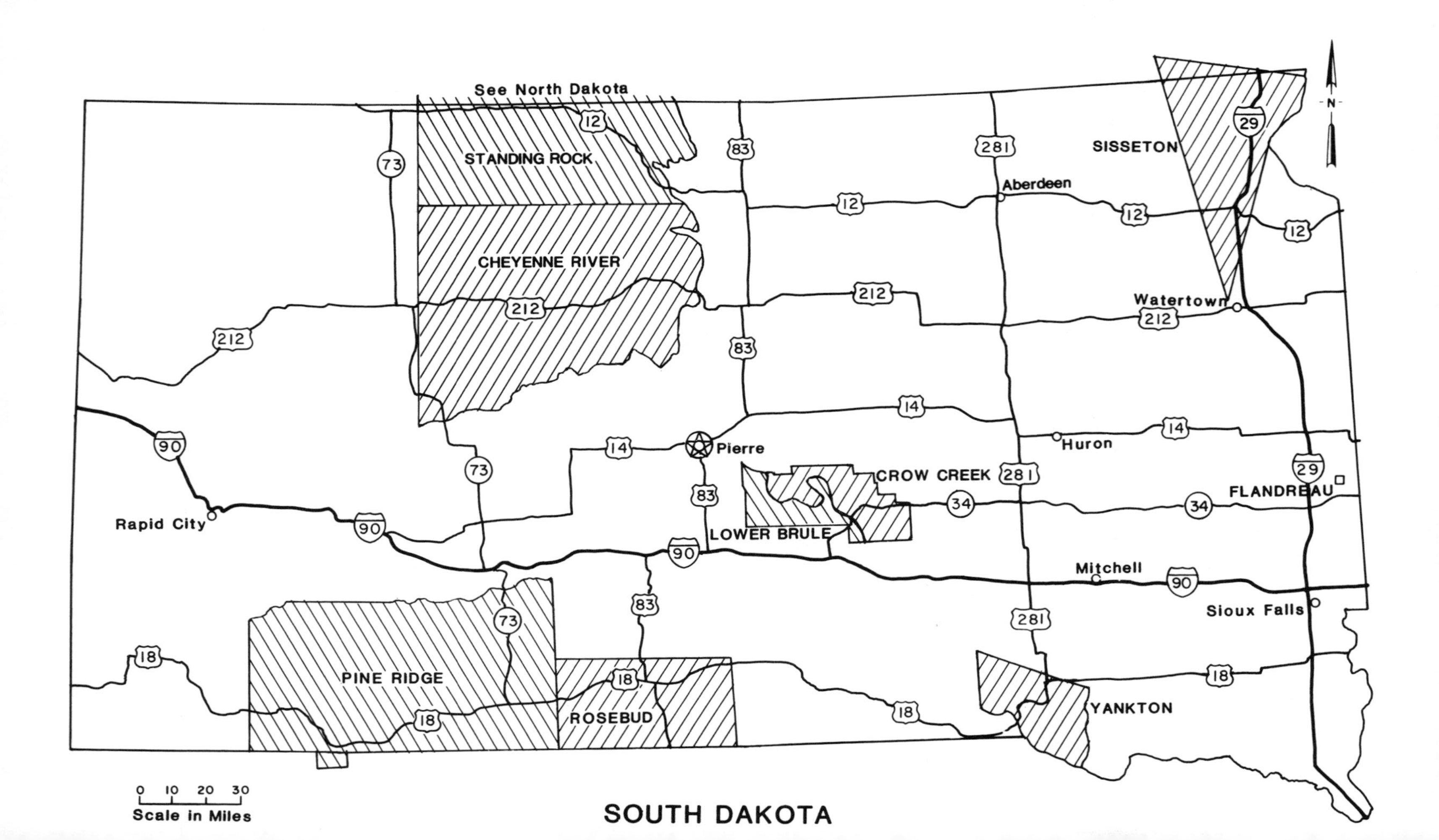

SOUTH DAKOTA

Fred Dubray and the tribal buffalo herd. Courtesy of Helen Clausen, Eagle Butte, SD.

Cheyenne River Sioux Reservation

Tribal Profile:

The Cheyenne River Reservation was established by Act of Congress of 1889. With some of the original allotment now under Lake Oahe, tribal lands measure 1.4 million acres. Living on rolling prairie split by washes, buttes, streams and rivers, the 10,724 member tribe derives from four major bands – the Minnecojou, Sans Arc, Blackfoot, and Two Kettle. Tribal government is dedicated to improving the standard of living and reducing unemployment. Steps made toward this objective include ranching, cable, telephone, construction, and gas enterprises. The Cheyenne River Sioux culture is being rekindled through ancient traditional ceremonies and bilingual, bicultural teaching in the schools.

Location:

Northeast of Badlands National Park in north-central South Dakota, the Cheyenne River Reservation's eastern border is Lake Oahe, formed by damming the Missouri River. US 212 bisects the reservation.

Address:

Cheyenne River Sioux Tribe
P.O. Box 590
Eagle Butte, SD 57625
(605) 964-4155

Cultural Institutions:

H.V. Johnson Cultural Center
Eagle Butte, SD
(605) 964-2542
Displays a pictorial history of the reservation, information on former chiefs, and native art work – mainly beadwork and jewelry.

Special Events:

Contact the Cultural Center with questions or for more information about the following events.

H. V. Johnson Cultural Center Pow Wow
Eagle Butte, SD
This annual pow wow draws 1,500 participants and guests. Admission fee. Held in mid-May.

Left, Tiny Tot Miss Indian. Right, young calf rider at Eagle Butte rodeo. Photos courtesy of Helen Clausen, Eagle Butte, SD.

Iron Lightning Pow Wow
Iron Lightning, SD
Visitors come from all over the world to attend this traditional pow wow, which features horseshoe and softball tournaments and a 10-K memorial run. Held 4th of July weekend.

Red Scaffold Pow Wow
Red Scaffold, SD
Annual pow wow, rodeo, and softball tournament. Held in mid-August.

Cherry Creek Pow Wow
Cherry Creek, SD
Annual pow wow, rodeo, and softball tournament. Held in late August.

Eagle Butte Fair
Eagle Butte, SD
Fair and pow wow feature parades, traditional dancing, carnival, rodeo, Lakota Artists Market, and softball tournament. Held Labor Day weekend. Admission charged.

Recreational Opportunities:

Cheyenne Lounge
Eagle Butte, SD
(605) 964-8271
8-lane bowling alley, pool tables, dances on the weekends, and restaurant.

Fishing & Hunting: Abundant fishing opportunities at the Lake Oahe Reservoir. Boat launches available outside reservation. Hunting of deer, antelope, grouse, and prairie dogs. Camping available throughout the area. Permits and licenses obtainable from Tribal Game, Fish & Parks Dept. (605-964-7812).

Businesses & Industries:

Diamond A Cattle Co.
Hwy 212
Eagle Butte, SD
964-1115
Restaurant serving American-style fare.

Eagle Butte News
(605) 964-2100
Weekly paper reporting local activities and items of interest.

Bison Herd: The tribal bison herd is being bred under the aegis of the Planning Dept. Currently about 400 head of buffalo range on the east end of reservation. Obtain permission to view the herd from the Planning Dept. (605-964-4000).

Accommodations:

Harding Motel
Hwy 212
Eagle Butte, SD
(605) 964-2448

Super-8 Motel
Opening in July 1992; contact the tribal office for details and location.

Crow Creek Sioux Reservation

Tribal Profile:

The Crow Creek Sioux Reservation was established in 1889. It is one of three parcels of land retained by the Sioux after the Treaty of Fort Laramie, whereby all Sioux land east of the Missouri River was ceded to the U.S. government. Today the reservation includes almost 126,000 acres held in trust; there are 3,000 enrolled members of the tribe. Tribal government is under a constitution approved in 1949; it is led by a seven-member council. The reservation is in south-central South Dakota on the eastern shore of the Missouri River, about 15 miles north of I-90 via Hwy 50, at Chamberlain.

Crow Creek Sioux Tribe
P.O. Box 658
Fort Thompson, SD 57339
(605) 245-2221

Flandreau Santee Sioux Reservation

Tribal Profile:

The Flandreau Santee Sioux Reservation was established in 1934; it occupies 2,200 acres with tribal enrollment estimated at 615 members. The reservation is governed by the executive committee of the tribal council under a constitution and bylaws approved and ratified in 1936. Tribal members are economically integrated with the surrounding community.

Location:

Southeastern South Dakota; 45 miles north of Sioux Falls, east of I-29 on Hwy 13 near the Minnesota border.

Address:

Flandreau Santee Sioux Tribe
P.O. Box 283
Flandreau, SD 57028
(605) 997-3891

Special Events:

Flandreau Santee Sioux Wacipi
Pow Wow Grounds
Contest pow wow for men, women and children draws a crowd of about 1,000. Festivities Friday evening through Sunday; Grand Entry Saturday at 1:00 p.m. Pow wow grounds 1.5 miles north of Flandreau on Hwy 13. Small admission fee includes some meals. Held 3rd weekend in July.

Recreational Opportunities:

Royal River Casino
P.O. Box 326
Flandreau, SD 57028
(605) 997-3746
Features slot machines from $.05 to $5, poker machines, blackjack and poker tables. Open 9:00 a.m. to 2:00 a.m. Monday-Thursday and continuously from 9:00 a.m. Friday to 2:00 a.m. Monday.

Businesses & Industries:

First American Mart
Flandreau, SD
(605) 997-9978
Convenience store with gas station.

Flandreau Santee Sioux Gift Shop
At tribal headquarters, featuring items crafted by Flandreau Santee Sioux members, as well as items from tribes in other parts of the country. Open weekdays, 8:00 a.m. to 4:30 p.m.

Accommodations:

First American Inn
RR 3 Box 168
Flandreau, SD 57028
(605) 997-3761 or
(800) 933-3761
Motel with 10 recently remodeled rooms. Not far from the casino.

Lake Traverse Reservation

TRIBAL PROFILE:

Article III of the Treaty of February 19, 1867, created the Lake Traverse Reservation as the assigned homeland for the Sisseton-Wahpeton Sioux Tribe. Today the reservation includes approximately 109,000 acres in trust. The tribal enrollment is approximately 9,300. Tribal government is under a constitution ratified in 1946 and is led by an 18 member tribal council. Located in the northeastern corner of South Dakota, the reservation is crossed by I-29 from north to south. There are several lakes on the reservation.

Sisseton-Wahpeton Sioux Tribe
Rte. 2, Agency Village
Sisseton, SD 57262
(605) 698-3911

Lower Brule Reservation

TRIBAL PROFILE:

The Lower Brule Sioux Reservation was established by Act of Congress in 1889; present trust acreage stands at approximately 130,300 acres. There are about 1,900 enrolled members in the tribe, approximately 1,000 of whom live on the reservation. Tribal government is under a constitution approved in 1935, ratified in 1936, with recent amendments. Tribal government is lead by an 18-member tribal council. Lower Brule is in south central South Dakota, across the Missouri River from the Crow Creek Reservation; adjacent to Fort Pierre National Grassland.

Lower Brule Sioux Tribe
Lower Brule, SD 57548
(605) 473-5561

Pine Ridge Reservation

TRIBAL PROFILE:

The Pine Ridge Reservation covers almost 2.8 million acres, with 1.8 million acres in trust status. Tribal enrollment is estimated at 28,000, with a reservation population of 20,400. The reservation was established in 1889 as home for the Oglala Lakota Nation. The tribe is governed by a 16-member tribal council that is led by a five-member executive committee, under a constitution approved in 1934.

LOCATION:

Southwestern South Dakota; I-90 runs east-west just north of the reservation, a small portion of which extends across the border into Nebraska. Badlands National Park extends into the reservation, which is bordered on the west by Buffalo Gap National Grassland.

ADDRESS:

Oglala Sioux Tribe
P.O. Box H #468
Pine Ridge, SD 57770
(605) 867-5821

CULTURAL INSTITUTIONS:

Oglala Lakota College
P.O. Box 490
Kyle, SD 57752
(605) 455-2321

SPECIAL EVENTS:

The following events are all held in or near Pine Ridge. For detailed directions and information call the tribal office.

Red Cloud Art Show
Held in June.

Badlands of Pine Ridge. Courtesy of Janis Allen, Kadoka, SD.

Pine Ridge Encampment
Held in early May.

Sun Dance
Held in August.

Oglala Nation Pow Wow
Held in August.

RECREATIONAL OPPORTUNITIES:

Pine Ridge Reservation has 3 community bingo operations: Children's Village Community Bingo; Enterprise Bingo, Wounded Knee District; and Pine Ridge Village Bingo. Call the tribe at (605) 867-5281 for specifics as to time, dates and cost.

White Clay Reservoir
Oglala Reservoir
Hunting and fishing on the reservation are excellent; check with the Dam Safety Office at tribal headquarters for the tribal permits and license that are required.

ARCHAEOLOGICAL & HISTORIC SITES:

Badlands: There are many scenic areas of badlands on the reservation.

Wounded Knee Monument: Marks the site of the massacre in 1890 and the burial place of the Sioux families killed there. 6 miles north of the town of Wounded Knee.

TRIBAL ORGANIZATIONS:

Veterans' organizations, particularly the Native American Legion and the Vietnam Veterans Associations and their auxiliaries, are active on the Pine Ridge Reservation. Contact the tribal office to obtain information about events these groups are holding.

ACCOMMODATIONS:

Lodgings available in Pine Ridge at Wolf Creek Motel and in surrounding communities; no owners are tribal members.

Rosebud Reservation

TRIBAL PROFILE:

The Rosebud Reservation, created by the Act of 1889, covers 528,000 acres of trust land abutting the Nebraska border. The Rosebud Sioux Tribe is part of the Teton division of the Sioux. Tribal enrollment stands at over 15,500, many of whom are involved in tribal enterprises such as ranching, manufacturing, and electronics.

LOCATION:

In south-central South Dakota; Mission is at the junction of US 18 and US 83.

ADDRESS:

Rosebud Sioux Tribe
Box 430
Rosebud, SD 57570
(605) 747-2381

CULTURAL INSTITUTIONS:

Buechel Memorial Lakota Museum
St. Francis Mission
St. Francis, SD
(605) 747-2361
Lakota Sioux artifacts, including moccasins, toys, pipe bags, and beaded cradles, Peyote Native American Church gourd fans and staffs. Over 300 items in the collection, with a small portion on display. Open 7 days a week, 9:00 a.m.-6:00 p.m. during summer; October to May by appointment only.

SPECIAL EVENTS:

Annual Rosebud Fair
Rosebud, SD
Pow wow and singing contests, rodeo, softball competition, parade, arts and crafts sales, pageant, historic reenactment, and Indian musical entertainment. Held 4th weekend in August, beginning Friday.

RECREATIONAL OPPORTUNITIES:

Prairie Hills Golf Course
(605) 856-4986
9-hole golf course with lounge. 2 miles south of Mission on US 83.

Ghost Hawk Canyon
Crazy Horse Canyon
Both sites have campsites, picnic areas, outdoor cooking, and fishing.

Camping: There are many other campgrounds throughout the reservation; contact the tribal office for location and details.

ARCHAEOLOGICAL & HISTORIC SITES:

St. Francis Mission: School and mission built by Jesuits and Franciscan nuns in 1886, replaced around 1916 after the buildings burned down.

Old College Building: Standing since early 1900s; originally served as BIA offices. West of Tribal Building.

BUSINESSES & INDUSTRIES:

Paul Szabo Studio
P.O. Box 360
Mission, SD
(605) 856-4548
Silver, gold, bone and horn jewelry; wholesale and retail. Appointment only.

Rosebud Sioux Ranch
(605) 747-2381
A tribal ranching enterprise.

ACCOMMODATIONS:

Maverick Motel
Mission, SD
(605) 856-4560

Yankton Reservation

Tribal Profile:

The Yankton Sioux Reservation was established by treaty in 1858 in the area traditionally occupied by the Yankton Sioux Tribe. While the reservation is spread over about 400,000 acres, tribal lands are just over 37,000 acres. About 3,100 of the 5,800 members of the tribe live on the reservation. The governing body is a nine-member tribal business and claims committee, elected under a constitution approved in 1963. Primary source of tribal income was farm leases until 1991, when the tribe opened its casino. Additional economic development projects recently undertaken include a moccasin factory and a hotel.

Location:

Southeastern South Dakota, bordering the Missouri River and the state of Nebraska. South of I-90; access from US 18 and US 281.

Address:

Yankton Sioux Tribe
P.O. Box 248
Marty, SD 57361
(605) 384-3804, -3641

Special Events:

Fort Randall Pow Wow
Lake Andes, SD
Annual pow wow drawing a crowd of 2,000; in addition to traditional drumming and dancing, features 2 meals daily, lots of camping, ball games, horseshoe tournaments and fishing. Free admission. Held 1st full weekend in August.

Recreational Opportunities:

Fort Randall Casino
Rte. 1, Box 100
Lake Andes, SD 57356
(605) 487-7871
Includes 200 seat bingo hall guaranteeing $500 blackout, blackjack and poker tables, slot machines; open 24 hours daily, 7 days a week.

Archaeological & Historic Sites:

For detailed directions and information on visiting these sites, call the tribal office at (605) 384-3804.

Struck-by-the-Ree Monument
Greenwood, SD
Memorial to the famous warrior and chief.

Tyrannosaurus Rex Dig
Marty, SD

Accommodations:

Motels in Lake Andes, Pickstown and Wagner.

Texas

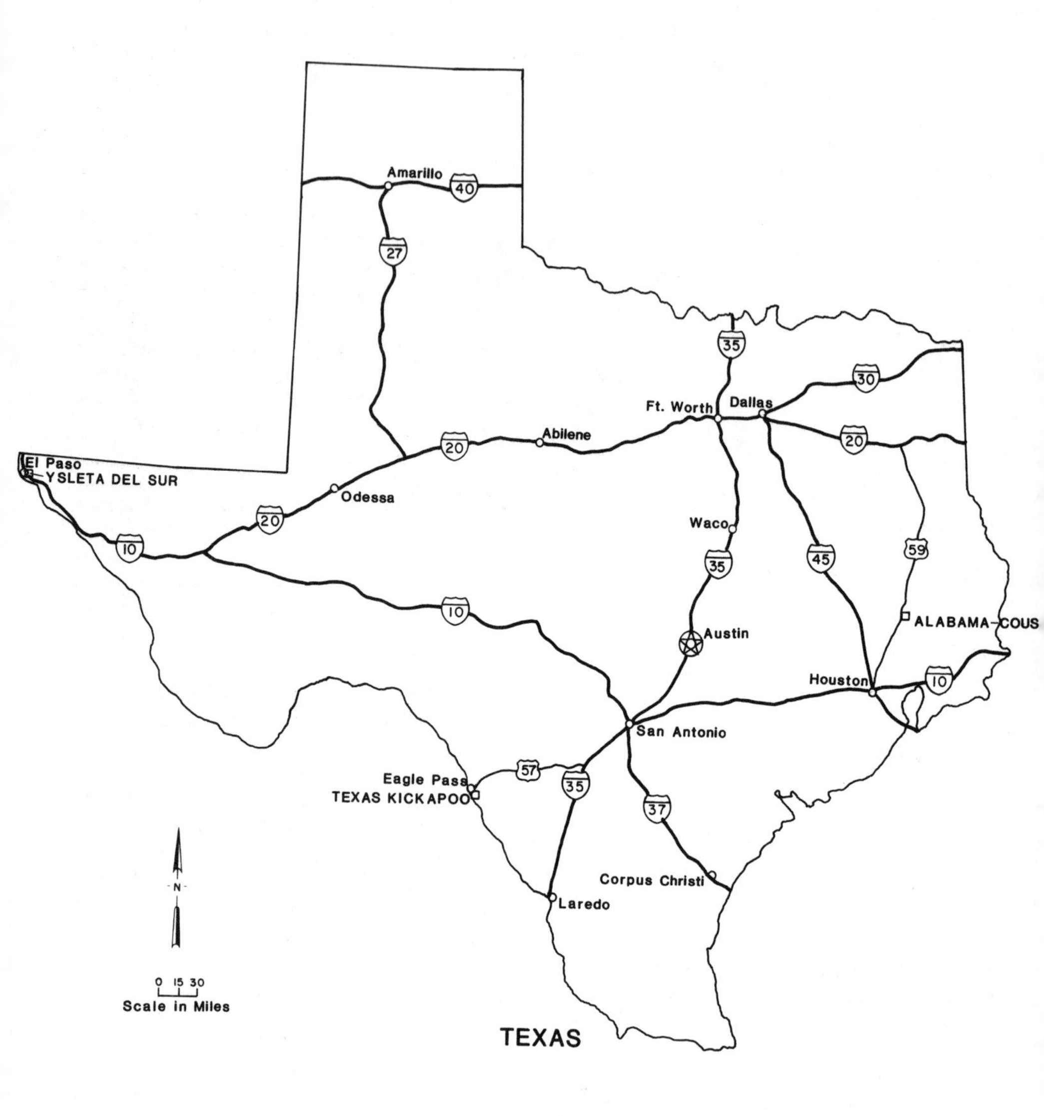
Amarillo
40
27
35
30
Ft. Worth
Dallas
20
Abilene
El Paso
YSLETA DEL SUR
Odessa
Waco
10
45
59
35
ALABAMA-COUS
Austin
Houston
San Antonio
Eagle Pass
TEXAS KICKAPOO
57
37
N
Corpus Christi
Laredo
0 15 30
Scale in Miles

TEXAS

Alabama-Coushatta Reservation

TRIBAL PROFILE:

Of Muskogean lineage and members of the Upper Creek Confederacy in their original homeland, now called Alabama, the Alabama and Coushatta Tribes came to Texas in the 1700s. The reservation was created in 1854 with the purchase of 1,280 acres of land by the Texas legislature and was enlarged by another 3,071 acres in 1926 by the state and federal governments and placed under state trusteeship. Additional land has been acquired by the tribe since that time, and the Alabama-Coushatta have focused considerable energy on tourism, captivating the public imagination today.

LOCATION:

Northeast of Houston and surrounded by virgin pine forests known as the Big Thicket, the Alabama-Coushatta Reservation is east of I-45 off US 190.

ADDRESS:

Alabama-Coushatta Tribe
Rte. 3, Box 640
Livingston, TX 77351
(409) 563-4391 or (800) 444-3507

CULTURAL INSTITUTIONS:

Visitors & Information Center
Activities, cultural institutions, and tours all operating March-May and September-November: Friday-Saturday 10:00 a.m.-5:00 p.m., Sunday 12:30-5:00 p.m.; June-August 10:00 a.m.-6:00 p.m., Sunday 12:30-6:00 p.m. Group tours available on Thursdays and Fridays.

Museum of Alabama and Coushatta
Dioramas dramatizing and detailing history of the Alabama and Coushatta tribes. Behind gift shop.

Living Indian Village
Living history museum featuring basket making, weaving, beadwork and arrowheads; crafts and food preparation demonstrations, and a guided walking tour.

SPECIAL EVENTS:

Annual Pow Wow
Reservation Ballpark
Contestants come to vie for prizes in 8 different categories. The occasion draws hundreds of people to watch the dancing and enjoy the arts and crafts show. Entry fee. Held 1st weekend in June.

Indian Dancers
Tribal Dance Square
Cultural dances take place on weekends during the spring and fall months – March-May and September-November. Check for times at the Visitors & Information Center.

RECREATIONAL OPPORTUNITIES:

Big Thicket Wilderness Tours: Guided tours through this incredible wilderness area to see rare species of trees, plants, and wild animals.

Indian Country Tours: Excursions on open-air buses take the traveller back in time to early pioneer days in East Texas when the Alabama-Coushatta first settled here; depicting examples of traditional styles of Indian homes, campsites, and hunting grounds.

Indian Chief Train: All-aboard for Big Thicket Country and scenic vistas of the reservation.

Lake Tombigbee: Wide range of camping and outdoor sports possibilities: primitive camp sites, tent sites, full RV hook-ups, cabins, area lighting, picnic tables, fire rings, drinking water; fishing, swimming, hiking and nature trails all on or around glistening 26-acre, fully stocked Lake Tombigbee. Year round.

BUSINESSES & INDUSTRIES:

Tribal Enterprise (gift shop)
(409) 563-4391 or (800) 392-4794 (in-state)
Products offered include pine needle baskets, grass basketry, beadwork, vests, ribbon shirts, and pottery. Open March-November, 10:00 a.m.-5:00 p.m., Tuesday-Saturday; 12:30-5:00 p.m. Sunday. Mail order accepted.

Inn of Twelve Clans Restaurant
(409) 563-4391, ext. 203
Serving American-style dishes, Indian fry bread and tacos, and Light and healthful foods. Hours: Monday-Thursday 11:00 a.m.-5:00 p.m., Friday-Sunday until 6:00 p.m.

Service Center
Park Rd. 56, Hwy 190
Convenience store, gas station, and laundromat.

ACCOMMODATIONS:

Lodgings in Livingston and Woodville, 17 miles to the west and east respectively.

Texas Kickapoo Reservation

TRIBAL PROFILE:

The Kickapoo Traditional Tribe of Texas recently received federal recognition. As a result, the tribe is in the process of acquiring lands and will organize tourism opportunities when other needs have been addressed. Eagle Pass is on the Rio Grande River and the U.S. border with Mexico, on US 277.

ADDRESS:

Kickapoo Traditional Tribe of Texas
P.O. Box 972
Eagle Pass, TX 78853
(512) 773-2105

Ysleta Del Sur Pueblo Reservation

TRIBAL PROFILE:

Originally living in New Mexico, the Ysleta del Sur Pueblo Indians were moved by the Spanish to Texas in the 1680s. The tribe built Ysleta Mission, still part of tribal lands. The Tigua Indians have retained many of their customs of tribal government, religion and ceremony, and lifestyle. Based on these considerations, the Pueblo was officially recognized by the federal government in 1987. Today, approximately 804 Tigua Indians live on about 97 acres. Tribal enterprise, including park concessions and fees, is the main contributor to the tribal income.

LOCATION:

The city of El Paso is on the Mexico border, a few miles south of New Mexico in west Texas. Ysleta del Sur Pueblo adjoins the Rio Grande River south of El Paso, across the border from Zaragosa, Mexico. From I-10, 3.5 miles via Zaragosa Rd.; left on Alameda, then right on Old Pueblo Rd.

ADDRESS:

Ysleta Del Sur Pueblo
122 South Old Pueblo Rd.
El Paso, TX 79936
(915) 859-7913

CULTURAL INSTITUTIONS:

Tigua Cultural Center
122 South Old Pueblo
El Paso, TX 79936
(915) 859-3916
Includes a restaurant, gift shop, and Indian shops; it has a self-guided tour of Indian pottery, jewelry, and artifacts from tribal and mission history.

SPECIAL EVENTS:

St. Anthony's Feast Day
Ysleta Mission
(915) 858-6934
A feast and pow wow celebrating the Virgin Guadalupe (Mary). Dancing throughout the day; dinner is offered. Held on June 13. Free.

Ysleta Street Festival
Ysleta Mission Grounds
(915) 858-6934
A celebration of Ysleta's multi-cultural heritage featuring over 100 booths with Southwestern foods, arts and crafts. Top-name entertainment, both national and local talent, play throughout this 3-day extravaganza. Held in early August. Admission charged.

Indian Dancing
Cultural Center
Contact the tribal office for dates and times of dances and ceremonies. Held throughout the summer.

Indian Bread Baking
Cultural Center
Weekly basis.

ARCHAEOLOGICAL & HISTORIC SITES:

Mission San Antonio de los Tiguas: Ysleta Mission is the first built in the area, dating from 1691, and is listed as the 2nd oldest continuously used church in the U.S. It is behind the Cultural Center. There are 2 sister missions within a 5-mile radius: San Elizario Presidio Chapel and Socorro Mission. All 3 missions are on the National Register of Historic Places and are on the Mission Trail; brochures at the Cultural Center.

BUSINESSES & INDUSTRIES:

Tigua Restaurant
122 Old South Pueblo
(915) 859-3916

Wyngs Restaurant & Spirits
122 Old South Pueblo
El Paso, TX
(915) 858-1033

ACCOMMODATIONS:

Many hotels and motels available in the El Paso area.

Utah

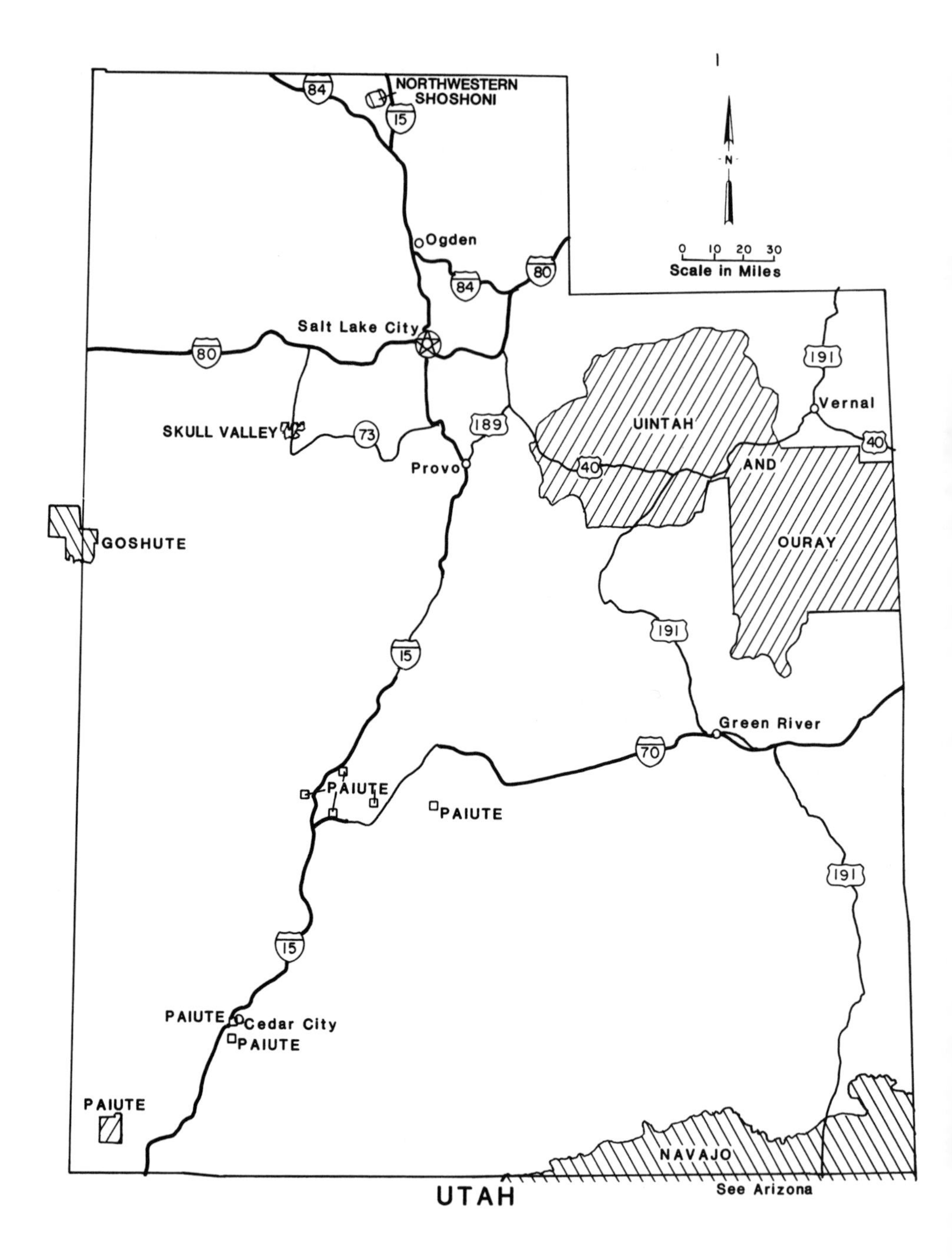
NORTHWESTERN
SHOSHONI
84
15
Ogden
84
80
0 10 20 30
Scale in Miles
N
Salt Lake City
80
191
Vernal
40
SKULL VALLEY
73
189
UINTAH
Provo
40
AND
GOSHUTE
OURAY
191
15
Green River
70
PAIUTE
PAIUTE
191
15
PAIUTE
Cedar City
PAIUTE
PAIUTE
NAVAJO
See Arizona

UTAH

Goshute Reservation

Tribal Profile:

The Goshute Indian Reservation was established by treaty in 1863; the Confederated Tribes operate under a corporate charter ratified in 1941 that established a five-member council. The tribe numbers about 400. The reservation is 60 miles south of Wendover, spanning Utah's border with Nevada; it is reached via US Alt 93 in Nevada.

Address:

Confederated Tribes of the Goshute Reservation
P.O. Box 6104
Ibapah, UT 84034
(801) 234-1136

Navajo Reservation

see Arizona

Paiute Indian Tribe of Utah

Tribal Profile:

The Paiutes have lived in the area now organized into Utah, Arizona, Nevada and California for hundreds of years. Divided into five bands in the late 1800s, the Paiute Tribes in Utah were terminated by the federal government in 1954; recognition was restored in 1980. The constitution of the Paiute Indian Tribe of Utah was approved in 1981; tribal membership is approximately 580.

Location:

Southwestern Utah; tribal offices are in Cedar City, approximately 250 miles south of Salt Lake City on I-15. Near Zion National Park.

Address:

Paiute Indian Tribe of Utah
600 N. 100 East
Cedar City, UT 84720
(801) 586-1112

Special Events:

Annual Restoration Gathering and Pow Wow
Cedar City, UT
Commemorates the reinstatement and federal recognition of the Utah Paiutes in 1980. Activities include princess pageant, softball tournament, parade, Paiute cultural activities, pow wow. Free admission. Held 2nd weekend in June, beginning Friday evening.

Businesses & Industries:

Paiute Fabric Products
P.O. Box 9
Kanosh, UT 84637
(801) 759-2434

Skull Valley Reservation

Tribal Profile:

The Skull Valley Band of Goshute Indians, which numbers 105, has about 17,500 acres in trust in Tooele County. The band has a traditional form of government with most powers reserved to the general council, consisting of all adult members. Limited authority is delegated to a three-member Skull Valley Executive Committee. A large portion of the Skull Valley Reservation is under lease to a company that maintains a rocket motor test site owned by the band.

Address:

Skull Valley Band of Goshute Indians
c/o Uintah and Ouray Agency
P.O. Box 130
Fort Duchesne, UT 84026
(801) 722-2406; leave a message

Uintah and Ouray Reservation

Tribal Profile:

The Uintah and Ouray Reservation was established by Executive Order of 1861, setting aside the Uintah Valley for three bands of Ute Indians: Uintah, Uncompahgre and Whiteriver. Presently the tribe and its members own approximately 2.2 million acres, and another 2 million acres lie within the reservation boundaries. Enrolled membership of the tribe is about 3,130. It is governed by a six member tribal business committee on which each band has two seats. The committee leads a government employing about 400, which is aggressively involved in the development, improvement and growth of the tribe's economy and associated infrastructures. Tribal industry includes agriculture, forestry and mineral resource development.

Location:

Scenic northeastern Utah between Vernal and Provo. Fort Duchesne is on US 40, 23 miles from the airport in Vernal. The southern portion of the reservation is east of the Green River as it flows through Desolation Canyon.

Address:

Uintah and Ouray Ute Tribe
P.O. Box 130
Fort Duchesne, UT 84026
(801) 722-5141

Cultural Institutions:

Ute Tribal Museum
Library and Audio Visual Center
Fort Duchesne, UT
At the Bottle Hollow Resort Complex.

Special Events:

Bear Dance
Fort Duschesne, UT
Traditional dance and feast celebrating spring and the emergence of the bear from hibernation. General public invited. Held Memorial Day Weekend.

Sun Dance
Sun Dance Grounds
The Sun Dance was given to the Ute by their relatives, the Shoshone, during the 19th century and holds an important place in the tribe's religious life. Cameras, sound and video recording equipment are not permitted at the ceremony. Approx 10 miles north of Fort Duchesne, 4 miles east of Neola, 4 miles south of Whiterocks. Held twice annually for 3 or 4 days in July and August.

Pow Wow Celebration
Fort Duchesne, UT
Dancers and singers come from all over the U.S. to participate in this pow wow. Festivities include Indian Market Days, handgame tournament, and all-Indian rodeo. At the junction of US 40 and Hwy 88. Held for 4 days, 1st week of July.

Recreational Opportunities:

Utah wilderness offers awesome canyons, petroglyphs, rapid rivers, mountain meadows and alpine trails.

Businesses & Industries:

Chapoose Rivers & Trails
P.O. Box 141
Fort Duchesne, UT 84026
(801) 722-4735, -2072
Outfitters offering whitewater adventures in Desolation Canyon. 3 to 7 day trips mix the excitement of rafting with creature comforts, including delicious dutch-oven cooking. May through early October.

Ute Bulletin
P.O. Box 400
Fort Duchesne, UT 84026
(801) 722-5141, ext. 243 or 244
Tribal newspaper.

Ute Indian Machining and Manufacturing
Produces custom made parts, machined parts, machine tool manufacturing, fabricated sheet metal items, precision metal shipping containers, electronic assembly work, wood shipping and storage containers, and drill bit sharpening.

Accommodations:

Bottle Hollow Inn and Conference Center
P.O. Box 190
Fort Duchesne, UT 84026
(801) 722-5141, -3941
Offers a unique opportunity to enjoy first-class accommodations and dramatic scenery, and to learn about the Ute Indian culture. Amenities include convention facilities; restaurant serving Indian, Mexican and Chinese food; swimming pool; and a private lake stocked with trout and bass, featuring beaches, waterskiing and boating. On US 40 west of Fort Duchesne.

Florence Creek Lodge
P.O. Box 141
Fort Duchesne, UT 84026
(801) 722-4735
Nestled at the confluence of Florence Creek and the Green River, on the historic site of the ranch owned by Jim McPherson, sometime outfitter for Butch Cassidy and the Sun Dance Kid. 10 rooms, meals offered; reservations required. Open May-November.

Virginia

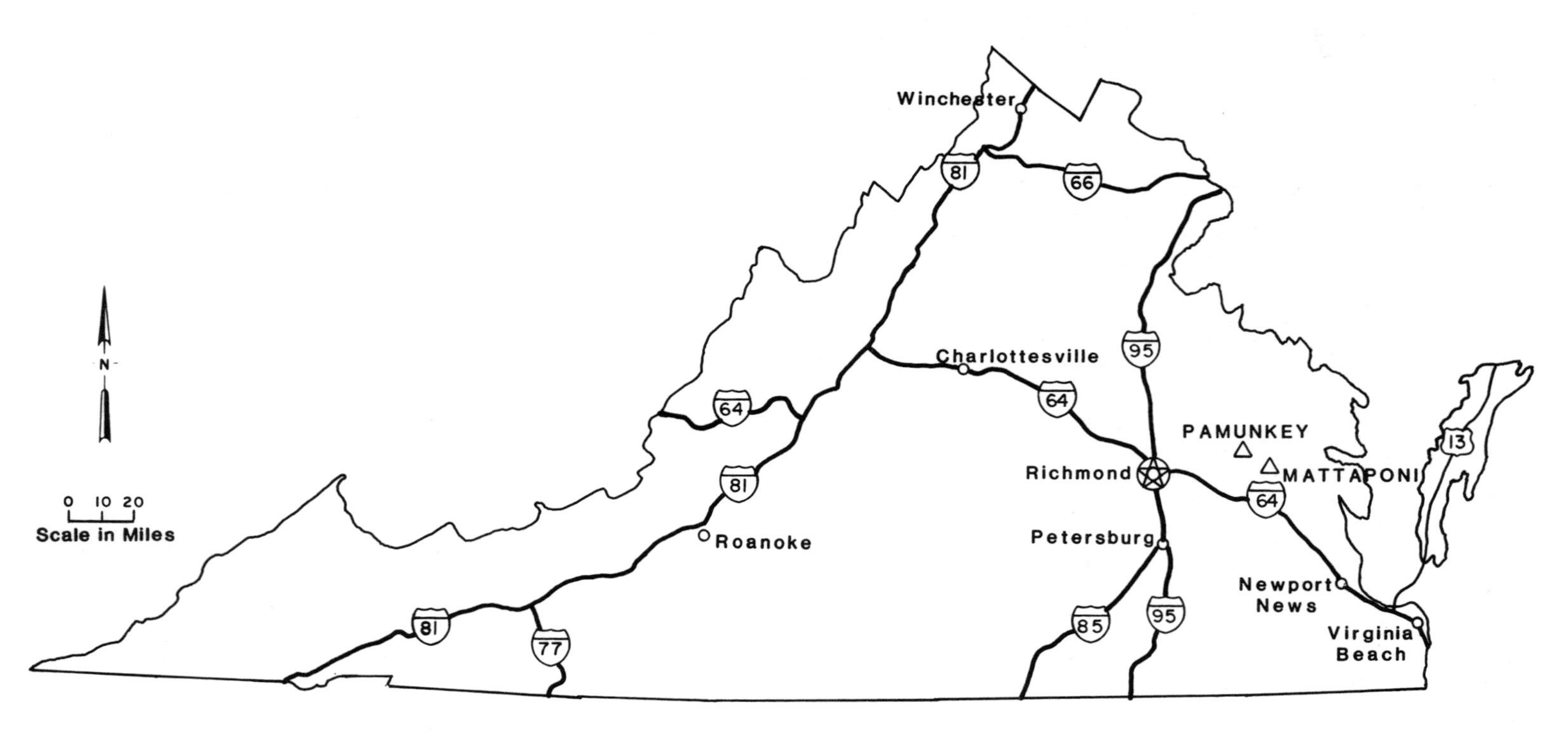
Winchester
81
66
Charlottesville
95
64
64
PAMUNKEY
MATTAPONI
Richmond
81
Roanoke
Petersburg
64
13
Newport
News
Virginia
Beach
81
77
85
95
N
0 10 20
Scale in Miles

VIRGINIA

Mattaponi Reservation

TRIBAL PROFILE:

The Mattaponi Indians were part of the Powhatan Confederacy, the alliance of Algonquian tribes under Chief Powhatan in Virginia when Captain John Smith arrived in 1607. The Mattaponi Indian Reservation is one of the oldest reservations in the U.S., sharing that status with the Pamunkey Reservation near by. The tribe was recognized by the colonial Virginia House of Burgesses and the Crown of England in 1658, and they have retained the rights and status from that date forward. The reservation was established in 1658; today it covers a small portion of the original land title, less than 200 acres, and is home to 75 tribal members.

Chief Webster "Little Eagle" Custalow. Courtesy of Mattaponi Tribe.

LOCATION:

On the Mattaponi River just above its confluence with the Pamunkey River in east-central Virginia, due east of Richmond. Accessible from I-64 and US 360, West Point is at the junction of Hwy 33 and Hwy 30. Reservation lands lie 13 miles north of West Point on Hwy 625.

ADDRESS:

Mattaponi Tribe
Box 255, Rte. 2
West Point, VA 23181
(804) 769-2194

CULTURAL INSTITUTIONS:

Mattaponi Museum
West Point, VA
(804) 769-2229
Archaeologists have come from all over the U.S. to examine this impressive collection of original Indian artifacts. Open Saturday and Sunday all year; hours vary. Call ahead for arrangements to see the museum at other times, and for information about the historical tour. Picnic areas nearby.

RECREATIONAL OPPORTUNITIES:

Camping on the reservation is by appointment only.

BUSINESSES & INDUSTRIES:

Minne-Ha-Ha Educational Trading Post
Box 255, Rte. 2
West Point, VA 23181
(804) 769-2194
Handmade pottery, beadwork, and other Indian crafts for sale; custom work done by request. The educational features of the trading post include programs on pottery, Indian dances and songs, and past and present lifestyle of the Mattaponi. By appointment only.

River of High Banks Craft Shop
Rte. 2, Box 270
West Point, VA 23181
(804) 769- 4711
Mattaponi artisan offering pottery, beadwork, masks, and sculpture. By appointment only.

ACCOMMODATIONS:

Washington Burgess Inn
P.O. Box 492
West Point, VA 23181
(804) 843-2100

Pamunkey Reservation

Tribal Profile:

Once part of the Powhatan Confederacy, the alliance of Virginia Algonquian tribes under Chief Powhatan, the Pamunkey Tribe has been governed by a tribal council and chief since 1607. The Pamunkey Reservation is one of the oldest in the U.S., sharing that standing with nearby Mattaponi Reservation. Assisted by the State of Virginia, Pamunkey started the Pottery School in the 1930s; it has been headquarters for the Pamunkey Potter's Guild since then. Envisioned as a way to develop pottery as a source of income and to help the tribe through the Great Depression, the school fosters this traditional craft.

Location:

On the Pamunkey River above its confluence with the Mattaponi River in east-central Virginia, due east of Richmond and less than 50 miles from Chesapeake Bay. Accessible from I-64 and US 360, King William is on Hwy 30. Reservation lands lie south of King William on Hwy 632.

Address:

Pamunkey Indian Reservation
Rte. 1, Box 787
King William, VA 23086
(804) 843-2851

Cultural Institutions:

Pamunkey Indian Museum
Box 2050
King William, VA 23086
(804) 843-4792
Collections of original artifacts and replicas portraying the history of the Pamunkey people from the ice age to the present. Craft shop offers beautifully crafted traditional pottery and other handcrafted items.

Pottery School
Pamunkey Reservation
(804) 843-4792

Businesses & Industries:

Pamunkey Pottery & Crafts Trading Post
Rte. 1
King William, VA 23086
(804) 843-4792
Selling pottery, beadwork and toys. Open 9:00 a.m.-5:00 p.m. Monday-Saturday, Sunday 1:00-6:00 p.m. Northeast of Richmond on US 360, south on Hwy 30 and secondary Rte. 633; adjacent to the museum.

Washington

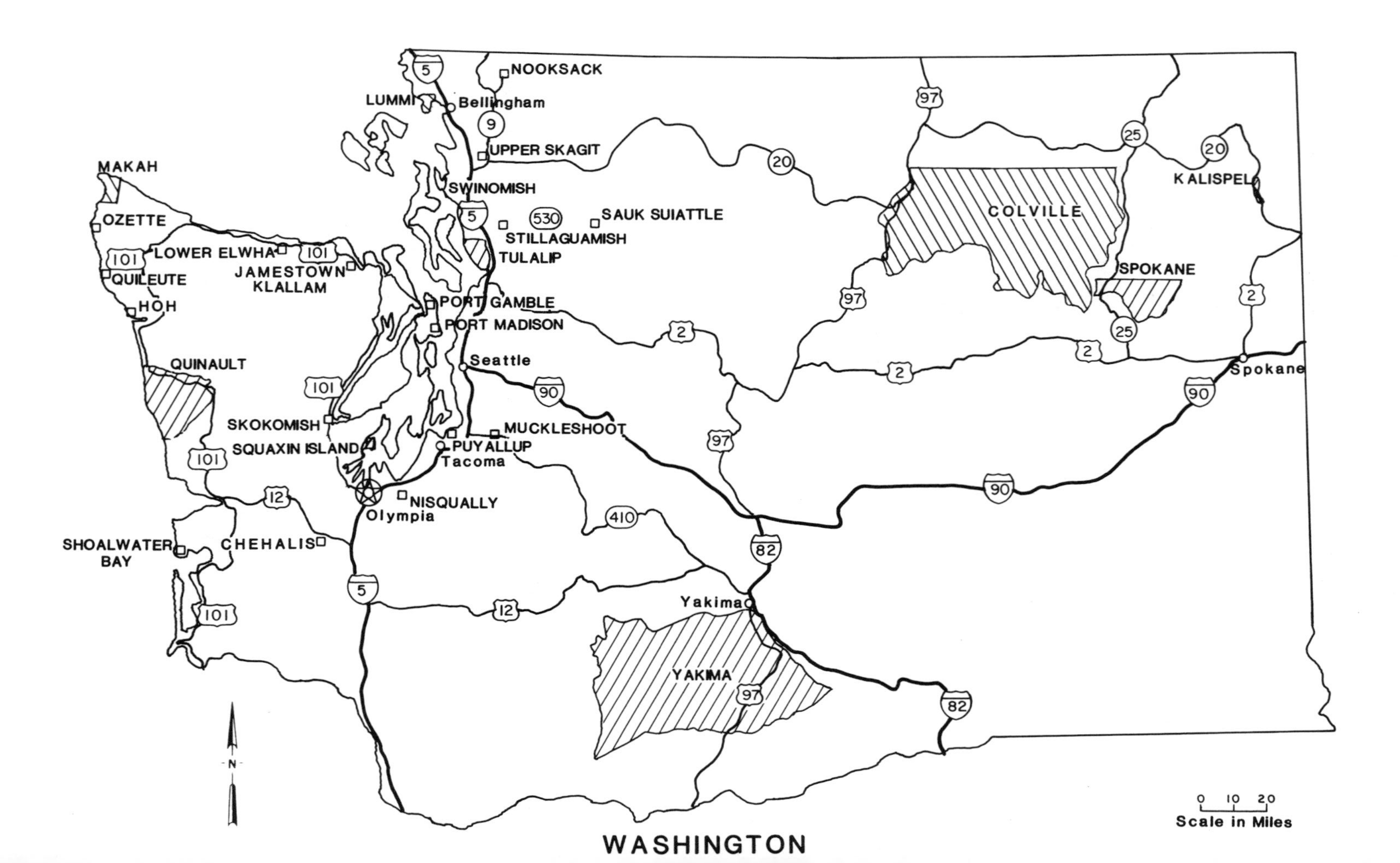
NOOKSACK
LUMMI
Bellingham
UPPER SKAGIT
MAKAH
SWINOMISH
OZETTE
SAUK SUIATTLE
STILLAGUAMISH
LOWER ELWHA
TULALIP
JAMESTOWN KLALLAM
QUILEUTE
HOH
PORT GAMBLE
PORT MADISON
Seattle
QUINAULT
SKOKOMISH
MUCKLESHOOT
SQUAXIN ISLAND
PUYALLUP
Tacoma
NISQUALLY
Olympia
SHOALWATER BAY
CHEHALIS
COLVILLE
KALISPEL
SPOKANE
Spokane
Yakima
YAKIMA
N
0 10 20
Scale in Miles

WASHINGTON

Chehalis Reservation

Tribal Profile:

Established by Executive Order in 1864, the Chehalis Reservation was originally home to Chehalis, Chinook Clatsop, and Cowlitz Indian bands. The Chehalis Tribe was part of the Coastal Indian culture of the Pacific Northwest, and Chehalis Indian culture centered around the abundant fish and forests. A tribal constitution was approved in 1939, providing for the election of a five-member business committee to direct tribal affairs. The Confederated Tribes of the Chehalis Reservation have approximately 2,600 acres of trust and individually-owned lands, home to 200 Indian residents; tribal enrollment is over 500.

Location:

Southwestern Washington; reservation extends along US 12 south of the Olympic Peninsula and the state capital, Olympia. West of I-5 on US 12.

Address:

Chehalis Community Council
P.O. Box 536
Oakville, WA 98568
(206) 273-5911

Special Events:

Tribal Day Celebration
Held in May.

Recreational Opportunities:

Fishing & Hunting: Chehalis Reservation is sandwiched between US 12 and the Chehalis River. Contact the Tribal Office for information regarding camping, hunting, and fishing.

Chehalis Bingo
Oakville, WA 98568
(206) 273-8066
Check for scheduling and games available.

Accommodations:

Lodgings nearby in Centralia, 17 miles east of Oakville.

Colville Reservation

Tribal Profile:

The bands comprising the Confederated Tribes of Colville are the Colville, Entiat/Chelan, Lake, Methow, Moses Columbia, Nespelem, Nez Perce, Okanogan, Palouse, Sanpoil, Senijextee, Skitswish, and Wenatchee. The reservation spans over 1.3 million acres in a small segment of the territory originally inhabited by these Plateau Indians – the uplands of Idaho, eastern Oregon, and eastern Washington. The tribes approved a constitution on April 19, 1938, and the confederated tribes, over 7,700 enrolled members, are governed by a 14-member business council.

Location:

In north-central Washington, the reservation is bound on 3 sides by the Columbia and Okanogan Rivers, and on the fourth by Colville National Forest. Scenic Hwy 21 splits the reservation north-south; scenic Hwy 155 passes through Nespelem and Omak.

Address:

Colville Confederated Tribes
P.O. Box 150
Nespelem, WA 99155
(509) 634-4711

The Columbia River crossing Indian country. Courtesy of Council of Energy Resource Tribes, Photo FIles.

CULTURAL INSTITUTIONS:

Colville Museum & Gallery
516 Birch St.
Coulee Dam, WA
(509) 633-0751
Exhibits authentic village and fishing scenes, native art, traditional cedar baskets, coins and metals, pre-1860s Russian trade beads, and ancient artifacts. Gift shop sells moccasins, beaded ware, turquoise jewelry, T-shirts, and both current and out-of-print books on the Colville Tribe. Hours: Monday-Saturday, 10:00 a.m.-6:00 p.m.; Sunday, noon-5:00 p.m. Small admission charge.

SPECIAL EVENTS:

Throughout late spring, summer, and fall the Confederated Tribes hold pow wows, Indian dances, and numerous other activities. Contact the tribal office for particulars.

July 4th Encampment
Nespelem, WA

RECREATIONAL OPPORTUNITIES:

Outdoor sporting opportunities are abundant on the reservation, particularly in the Coulee Dam Recreation Area and on the Columbia River. There are also several lakes, smaller rivers and forests. Tribal lands cross the Kettle River Range. Contact the tribal office for information regarding camping, hunting, boating, and fishing.

ARCHAEOLOGICAL & HISTORIC SITES:

Chief Joseph Memorial: Burial site of the famous Nez Perce leader. In Nespelem, WA.

St. Mary's Mission: Just above Omak Lake, on the east side of Okanogan River in the northwestern portion of the reservation.

Jamestown Klallam Reservation

TRIBAL PROFILE:

The foundation of the Klallam Tribe's land base was laid in 1874 with the purchase of a 200-acre plot of land. Named after the tribal chief Lord James Balch, the Jamestown settlement of the Klallam Indians is integral to the stability and continuity of the tribe. Other land has been added since the original acquisition. Since federal recognition came on February 10, 1981, the Klallam have been working steadily toward greater independence, augmented by the formation of JKT Development, Inc. Arts publishing, offering limited edition prints, is a recent addition to tribal enterprise.

LOCATION:

Northeastern corner of the lush Olympic Peninsula, at the edge of the Olympic National Forest. The tribal center is on Old Blyn Hwy, off US 101 and 7 miles east of Sequim.

ADDRESS:

Jamestown Klallam Tribe
305 Old Blyn Hwy
Sequim, WA 98382
(206) 683-1109

CULTURAL INSTITUTIONS:

Jamestown Klallam Library
Blyn, WA
(206) 683-1109
Indian arts, history, culture, and legend constitute the main holdings.

RECREATIONAL OPPORTUNITIES:

Campsites and RV facilities in East Sequim Bay State Park, 3 miles west of the tribal center.

ARCHAEOLOGICAL & HISTORIC SITES:

Several sites of historic significance, such as the Hazel Sampson Homestead and Jamestown Cemetery where tribal chief Lord James Balch is buried, are on the reservation. Communicate with the tribal office for details and permission to visit.

BUSINESSES & INDUSTRIES:

Native Expressions Art Gallery
Tribal Center
Sequim, WA 98382
(206) 683-1109, ext. 12
Offers representation of Northwest Coast native art, featuring mostly local artisans.

Dungeness Oyster House
Sequim, WA
Selling fresh oysters, crab, smoked salmon and clams. Open year round.

ACCOMMODATIONS:

Sequim Bay Lodge (Best Western)
Sequim, WA 98382
4 miles west of the tribal center.

RESTRICTIONS AND/OR SPECIAL CONSIDERATIONS:

Some areas are off-limits to visitors; please contact the tribal office for specifics.

Kalispel Reservation

TRIBAL PROFILE:

Drawn to this region by the abundant fish and forest harvest, the Kalispel Tribe of Indians was part of the Plateau Indian culture. Following a treaty agreement of 1855, the Kalispel moved to their present reservation. Approximately 100 tribal members live on the 4,629 acre Kalispel Reservation; tribal enrollment is 190.

LOCATION:

Northeastern Washington, north of Spokane; surrounded by national forest. The western boundary of the reservation follows the Pend Oreille River. Usk and Cusick are on scenic Hwy 20.

ADDRESS:

Kalispel Tribe of Indians
P.O. Box 39
Usk, WA 99180-0039
(509) 445-1147

SPECIAL EVENTS:

Barter Fair
Cusick, WA
(509) 445-1112
Indian pow wow held the 3rd weekend in May and the last weekend in September.

Buffalo Bar-B-Que
Cusick, WA
(509) 445-1112
Barbecue and contest dancing. Held 1st weekend in August.

RECREATIONAL OPPORTUNITIES:

Salish Campground: Amenities include a boat launch, RV hook-ups, and campsites. Request permits for fishing from the tribal office; arrangements for camping should be made in advance. Open seasonally.

BUSINESSES & INDUSTRIES:

Kalispel Case Line
P.O. Box 267
Cusick, WA 99119
(509) 445-1121
Manufacturing protective aluminum cases for guns, cameras, bows.

ACCOMMODATIONS:

Lodgings in nearby Newport, south of Usk on Hwy 20.

Lummi Reservation

TRIBAL PROFILE:

The Muckl-te-oh or Point Elliot Treaty of January 22, 1855, marked the creation of the Lummi Reservation. Over 7,000 acres comprise the reservation, home for 1,300 tribal members; estimated enrollment is 3,200 members. The Lummi are active in land and coastal development endeavors and in developing and maintaining weaving and other cottage industry.

LOCATION:

10 miles east of Bellingham in northwestern Washington, not far from the Canadian border. The San Juan Islands, as well as many other state and national recreation areas and parks, are nearby. Off I-5, Hwy 540.

ADDRESS:

Lummi Indian Nation
2616 Kwina Road
Bellingham, WA 98226
(206) 734-8180

CULTURAL INSTITUTIONS:

Lummi Museum
In the planning stages.

Northeast Community College
2522 Kwina Road
Bellingham, WA 98226
(206) 676-2772

SPECIAL EVENTS:

Lummi Stommish (Water Festival)
Stommish Grounds
Hales Passage, Lummi View Drive
Tribes from all over Washington and Canada compete in canoe races. Indian arts and crafts are sold, barbecue salmon dinners offered, and Indian dances performed. Held the 2nd or 3rd weekend in June, depending upon the tides, from 10:00 a.m.-3:00 p.m.

RECREATIONAL OPPORTUNITIES:

Lummi Casino
2559 Lummi View Drive
Bellingham, WA 98226
(206) 758-7559
Offers poker and blackjack. Restaurant in the building. Off I-5, Exit 260 (Slater Rd.) to Haxton Way, travel south 8 miles to the casino. Open 24 hours, 7 days a week.

BUSINESSES & INDUSTRIES:

Indian Isabelle's Indian Workshop
4435 Haxton Way
Ferndale, WA 98248
(206) 734-5216
Selling baskets, jewelry, and knit clothing. Special orders accepted. Hours 11:00 a.m.-5:00 p.m., Monday-Friday.

Fran & Bill James, Lummi Indian Craftsmen
2043 Lummi View Rd.
Ferndale, WA 98248
(206) 758-2522
Fashioning Northwest Coast Salish wool blankets and cedar bark baskets from natural materials. Some special orders and mail order accepted.

TRIBAL ORGANIZATIONS:

Lummi Indian Weavers

ACCOMMODATIONS:

There are many lodgings throughout the region, some of the closest to Lummi Reservation are:

Best Western Heritage Inn
151 E. McCloud Ave.
Bellingham, WA 98226
(206) 647-1912

Best Western Lakeway Inn
714 Lakeway Dr.
Bellingham, WA 98226
(206) 671-1011

The Hampton
3985 Bennett Dr.
Bellingham, WA
(206) 676-7700

Makah Reservation

TRIBAL PROFILE:

The Makah Reservation is the western-most Indian reservation in the lower 48 states. Created by treaty in 1855 and subsequently amended and enlarged, the 24,526 acre reservation is home to over 800 of the 1,869 tribal members. Many traditional occupations such as fine basket weaving, wood carving, and harvesting sea and forest life are still important to the tribe. Forestry contributes greatly to income today, and the tribe is developing housing, mineral, and other tribally based ventures. The Makah Tribe has no linguistic association with any other tribe in the U.S.

Ozette Indian Reservation, 12 miles south on Cape Alava, is a small and remote region with an old hunting village. Although it is no longer inhabited, the Makah consider it part of tribal lands.

LOCATION:

On the northwestern tip of the Olympic Peninsula on Cape Flattery and Koitlah Point, across the Strait of San Juan de Fuca from Vancouver, B.C. Scenic Hwy 112 follows the coast and ends at the Makah Reservation.

ADDRESS:

Makah Tribal Council
P.O. Box 115
Neah Bay, WA 98357
(206) 645-2205

CULTURAL INSTITUTIONS:

Makah Cultural and Research Center
P.O. Box 95
Neah Bay, WA 98357
(206) 645-2711, -2712
Displays archeological materials, thousands of years old, from the Ozette dig; it also runs cultural programs for the tribe. Some Makah wares are for sale; price list available by mail. Open daily, 10:00 a.m.-5:00 p.m., June through September 15; closed Monday and Tuesday, September 16 through May.

SPECIAL EVENTS:

Makah Days
Neah Bay, WA
Street fair and festival; includes war canoe races, salmon bake and barbecue, traditional and modern games, parade, arts and crafts, Indian musical entertainment, and various sporting events. Free admission. Held in late August.

RECREATIONAL OPPORTUNITIES:

Makah Tribal Bingo
Neah Bay, WA
(206) 645-2201, ext 412
Lucky 7 Jackpot, Write Your Own Bingo, and pull tabs. Bingo hours 7:00-10:00 p.m., doors open 5:00 p.m. Next to the tribal center.

Thunderbird Resort & RV Park
Neah Bay, WA
(206) 645-2540

Camping is limited to the town of Neah Bay most of the year, although a small campground is open on the ocean from June through August. Contact the Cultural Center for details.

ACCOMMODATIONS:

Makah Motel
Neah Bay, WA
(206) 645-2366

Muckleshoot Reservation

TRIBAL PROFILE:

The Muckleshoot Reservation was established by Executive Order in 1857. Part of the Coastal Indian culture of the Pacific Northwest who built their lives around abundant water and forest resources, the Muckleshoot Indians now live on 1,188 acres in the foothills of the spectacular Cascade Mountains.

LOCATION:

Northeast of Tacoma and slightly north of Lake Tapps; Hwy 164 passes through much of the Muckleshoot Indian Reservation. Accessible from I-5 via Hwy 167.

ADDRESS:

Muckleshoot Indian Tribe
39015 172nd Avenue S.E.
Auburn, WA 98002
(206) 939-3311

SPECIAL EVENTS:

Seniors Pow Wow
Muckleshoot Tribal Gymnasium
This event is attended by 2 to 8 drum groups and Indian dancers, drawing hundreds of spectators from throughout the area. Arts and crafts show part of the occasion. Held the 3rd Saturday evening every month.

RECREATIONAL OPPORTUNITIES:

Muckleshoot Indian Bingo
2602 Auburn Way South
Auburn, WA 98002
(800) 358-3118 (in-state) or (206) 735-2404
Offering Megabingo, Pull Tabs, Jackpots, Superjackpots and Bonanza. Gift Shop features handcrafted Indian arts and crafts. Open 7 days a week, 3 sessions daily. Closed Thanksgiving and Christmas.

Left, carvings grace the Muckleshoot Tribal Retirement Home. Right, Mt. Rainier from the Muckleshoot Reservation. Photos courtesy of Raymond W. Loloff.

ARCHAEOLOGICAL & HISTORIC SITES:

St. Clair's Catholic Mission: The second oldest church in the state, awaiting historical site status. Pending renovation, only the outside can be viewed. Next to the tribal administration building.

BUSINESSES & INDUSTRIES:

Muckleshoot Tribal Enterprises Gift Shop
16527 S.E. 392nd St.
Auburn, WA 98002
(206) 833-3920
Featuring a selection of Indian sweaters, handcrafted drums, Northwest Indian carvings, beaded, silver and turquoise jewelry, liquor and tobacco products. Open 7 days a week; hours vary.

Nooksack Reservation

TRIBAL PROFILE:

Federal recognition for the Nooksack Tribe came in 1973; in 1974 individual members applied for family homesteads of 160 acres per family along the Nooksack River. At this time, approximately 2,000 acres are held in trust for the 1,200 tribal members. In 1990, the tribe incorporated 7 acres of riverfront, and another 40 acres have been purchased for a recreation complex, which will include a bingo and gaming casino, restaurant, motel, and RV park. The main source of tribal income is commercial salmon, halibut, and shellfish harvesting.

LOCATION:

Northwestern Washington; Deming is on the Nooksack River, 13 miles east of Bellingham and I-5, on scenic Hwy 542 (Mt. Baker Hwy), near its junction with Hwy 9.

ADDRESS:

Nooksack Tribal Council
5048 Mt. Baker Hwy
P.O. Box 157
Deming, WA 98244
(206) 592-5176

RECREATIONAL OPPORTUNITIES:

Nooksack Bingo & Gaming Casino opening soon. Contact the tribal office for details.

Fishing & Camping: With several miles of tribal lands on Nooksack River shores, fishing and camping opportunities abound. Contact the tribal office or Fisheries Patrol for permits and information.

BUSINESSES & INDUSTRIES:

Deming Liquor Store
Deming Self-Serve
5065 Mt. Baker Hwy
Deming, WA 98244
(206) 592-5864
Deming Liquor Store and Self-Serve share a building with separate entrances. Self-Serve is a convenience store, also selling Nooksack arts and crafts, such as small drums, wood carvings, jewelry.

Smokeshop and Trading Post
5048 Mt. Baker Hwy
Deming, WA 98244
(206) 592-5397

ACCOMMODATIONS:

Circle F Bed & Breakfast
Squalicum Ranch
2399 Mt. Baker Hwy
Bellingham, WA 98226
(206) 733-2509
Cozy turn-of-the-century farmhouse tucked away on over 300 acres of private wooded trails and open pasture. Offers modest rates. Fly fishing on Squalicum Lake. 3 miles east of Deming.

Port Madison Reservation

TRIBAL PROFILE:

Port Madison Reservation covers 8,012 acres on a spit of land overlooking Puget Sound. Created as part of the Point Elliot Treaty in 1855, the reservation was enlarged by Executive Order in 1864. This is the headquarters of the 1,500 member Suquamish Tribe, which was drawn to this area by the abundance of fish and timberland that were the foundation for its rich religious and cultural traditions. Totem pole construction is one expression of that culture still visible on the reservation. Its beautiful location and famous agate beach make the reservation popular with sightseers.

LOCATION:

West of Puget Sound, across from Seattle. Hwy 16, connecting with I-5 in Tacoma, travels up coastal islands and intersects Hwy 3 or 303, near Suquamish. Ferry shuttles between Seattle and Winslow (1/2 hour), then Hwy 305 to Suquamish.

ADDRESS:

Suquamish Tribe
P.O. Box 498
Suquamish, WA 98392
(206) 598-3311

CULTURAL INSTITUTIONS:

Suquamish Tribal Museum
P.O. Box 498
(206) 598-3311

After showing on the European continent, "The Eyes of Chief Seattle" has come home to the Suquamish Tribal Museum. This exhibit interprets the history and culture of the Suquamish through photographs, artifacts, and quotations; other displays include woven baskets, a dugout canoe, tools, fishing equipment, and an audio-visual program. Museum also houses a gift shop selling traditional style Suquamish/Puget Sound Salish products, such as baskets and wooden carvings. Special orders welcomed; send for mail order information.

SPECIAL EVENTS:

Chief Seattle Days
Downtown Suquamish
Includes a competition pow wow, dugout canoe races, salmon bake, vendors, and ceremony at Chief Seattle's grave site. No admission fee. Starts Friday evening at 6:00, Saturday 10:00 a.m to 11:00 pm.; Sunday till 6:00 p.m. 3rd weekend of August.

ARCHAEOLOGICAL & HISTORIC SITES:

Old Man House: The site of the original Suquamish village with a park and small replica/construction of the house, along with an information post. South of Suquamish.

ACCOMMODATIONS:

Evergreen Motel
Poulsbo, WA
(206) 779-3921

Fishing on the Olympic Peninsula. Courtesy of John Running.

Quileute Reservation

TRIBAL PROFILE:

The Quileute Indians were part of the Coastal Indian culture of the Pacific Northwest. Whaling and sea travel, along with fish and forest products, are all part of tribal economy and culture. The Quinault Treaty of 1855 specified creation of the Quileute Reservation, and it was established by Executive Order in 1889. It comprises 800 acres in a protected harbor on the Pacific Ocean; commercial and sports fishing, as well as summer recreation, are important to tribal income. The Quileute Tribe has 800 enrolled members.

LOCATION:

On the coast of the Olympic Peninsula, surrounded by the Olympic National Park. US 101 is about 12 miles inland from the coast at Forks; just north is Rte. 110 heading directly to La Push.

ADDRESS:

Quileute Tribal Council
P.O. Box 279
La Push, WA 98350-0279
(206) 374-6163

CULTURAL INSTITUTIONS:

Quileute Tribal School
La Push, WA

Sunset on the Quileute Reservation. Courtesy of John Running.

Special Events:

Quileute Days
La Push, WA
Hundreds of people come to celebrate the Quileute heritage and culture. Activities include bone games, canoe races, children's games, sports, and fireworks. Admission is free. Held 1st weekend in July.

Businesses & Industries:

Boatlauncher Restaurant
(206) 374-9700
Open May to November; hours vary seasonally.

Accommodations:

La Push Ocean Park Resort
(206) 374-5409
Cabins, camping, RV hookups and motel units available. Reservations made well in advance are recommended. Open year-round.

Shoreline Resort
(206) 374-5267, -6488
Offering cabins and RV hookups. Advance booking recommended. Open year-round.

Columbia River borders the Spokane Reservation. Courtesy of Council of Energy Resource Tribes, Photo Files.

Spokane Reservation

TRIBAL PROFILE:

This region has long been home to the Spokane Tribe, and the 155,000 acre Spokane Indian Reservation was created in the 1881. Tribal membership stands at 2,100. An elected five-member business council governs the reservation. Forestry is the main source of income with the Spokane Indian Reservation Timber Enterprise managing sales of over 1 million board feet of timber per year. A treatment plant for preserving lumber, along with the new tribal sawmill, adds to the economic well-being of the tribe. The southwestern region recreational resort project is underway, planned to take advantage of the tribe's 44 miles of shoreline on Lake Roosevelt. Houseboats will be available at on the new marina.

LOCATION:

Northeastern Washington; the Spokane and Columbia Rivers and the Coulee Dam Recreation Area mark the southern and western boundaries of the reservation. Hwy 25 runs through the eastern portion of the reservation.

ADDRESS:

Spokane Tribe
P.O. Box 100
Wellpinit, WA 99040
(509) 258-4581

CULTURAL INSTITUTIONS:

Museum
Spokane Tribe Community Center
Displays of clothing, arrowheads, mortars and pestles, axe heads, and baskets, among others items. Expansion is in the planning stages.

SPECIAL EVENTS:

Spokane Indian Days
Fairgrounds
Wellpinit, WA
Thousands attend this pow wow to enjoy the war dancing – contest dancing for all age categories – arts and crafts booths, concessions, hand games, card games, modern dancing, exhibits, and arcade games. Festivities continue 24 hours a day throughout the Labor Day weekend.

RECREATIONAL OPPORTUNITIES:

Spokane Tribal Bingo
Chewelah, WA
(509) 935-6167
High stakes bingo activities include megabingo, one game per session; Pick 6 Lotto video machines; and video pull tabs. Hours Saturday and Sunday noon-9:00 p.m., Monday 5:30-10:00 p.m.

Fishing Sites: Facilities with pit toilets and picnic tables on the shore of **Lake Roosevelt** can be reached by boat. **Fort Spokane National Park** on the western side of the lake has a boat launch. **Roosevelt, Turtle, and Benjamin Lakes** provide excellent fishing.

Obtain fishing permits from the Parks Dept. (509-258-4482) or the Law & Order Dept. (509-258-4569).

BUSINESSES & INDUSTRIES:

Mc Coy's Marina
Lake Roosevelt
Selling bait tackle, beer, snacks, gas.

Tribal Trading Post
Wellpinit, WA
(509) 258-7121
Grocery and general store. Hours 8:00 a.m.-6:00 p.m., Monday-Friday; 10:00 a.m.-4:00 p.m. Saturday-Sunday.

Eagle Feather Sawmill
Wellpinit, WA

Spokane Tribal Fish Hatchery
(509) 258-7297
5 miles east of Wellpinit.

Spokane Tribal Wood Products
Wellpinit, WA
(509) 258-7431
Making pressure-treated wood products.

ACCOMMODATIONS:

Most convenient lodgings situated in Loon Lake, 22 miles east, and Davenport 20 miles south.

Squaxin Island Reservation

TRIBAL PROFILE:

The Treaty of Medicine Creek was signed in 1854, bringing together the Sa-heh-wa-mish, Squaxin, S'Homamish, Stehchass, T'Peeksin, and Squi-aitl bands of Indians from the Puget Sound to form the Squaxin Island Tribe. Today tribal enrollment stands at approximately 500 members, headquartered on a 2,000 acre reservation. Salmon and shellfish have always been an important part of tribal culture, as well as hunting the abundant wildlife. Management of the considerable natural resources contributes much to tribal prosperity.

LOCATION:

Among the inlets of the southern Puget Sound, the reservation is at the base of the Olympic Peninsula not far from Olympic National Park. Via US 101 from I-5, just north of Olympia, Washington's capital city.

ADDRESS:

Squaxin Island Tribe
S.E. 70 Squaxin Lane
Shelton, WA 98584
(206) 426-9781

RECREATIONAL OPPORTUNITIES:

Squaxin Island Bingo
Old Tribal Center
(206) 427-1440; or 426-3442
Offering progressive $1,000 bingo Wednesday-Saturday; Sundays guaranteed jackpot. Doors open Wednesday-Friday and Sunday at 6:00 p.m., Saturday at noon. Behind the Trading Post.

SPECIAL EVENTS:

Sa-heh-wa-mish
Mason County Fairgrounds
Shelton, WA
(206) 426-9781
Indian pow wow and art fair with Indian dancing competition, drum and singing competition, bone

games, salmon bake, Indian foods, and arts and crafts. Admission charged. Camping and RV hook-up available during the festival at the fairgrounds. Held weekend in mid-June.

BUSINESSES & INDUSTRIES:

Hartstene Oyster Company
Island Enterprises
(206) 426-3442
Check in advance for tour availability.

Kamilche Trading Post
McCleary, WA
(206) 426-5254
Convenience store and Indian arts and crafts. Exit US 101 onto Hwy 108.

ACCOMMODATIONS:

Lodging in Shelton, 6 miles north; Olympia 20 miles south.

Upper Skagit Reservation

TRIBAL PROFILE:

One of the many Coast Salish tribes from the Puget Sound region, the 580 member Upper Skagit Tribe originated from five extended villages along the Skagit River. Traditional salmon fishing forms the tribe's community and economic base, and salmon are the source of traditional stories, songs, and literature. Family groups still gather in seasonal encampments along the river to angle from skiffs. Tribal members are actively involved in issues with regional and national significance such as water rights, fisheries, and environmental protection.

LOCATION:

About 70 miles north of Seattle on the Skagit River. The modern village and community facilities are east of I-5 on scenic Hwy 20; the tribe owns 63 acres of commercial property along I-5.

ADDRESS:

Upper Skagit Indian Tribe
2284 Community Plaza
Sedro-Wooley, WA 98284
(206) 856-5501

CULTURAL INSTITUTIONS:

The tribe is developing a tourist activity center along I-5 that will incorporate a permanent historical/archaeological exhibit.

RECREATIONAL OPPORTUNITIES:

Traditional Indian Salmon Fishing: A popular activity along the scenic Skagit River, the 6th largest river in the U.S., from July through September. Part of the catch includes wild king, silver, pink, and steelhead salmon. Late September is the time to view thousands of spawning salmon.

Skagit River: Listed as a U.S. wild/scenic river, is the winter home of 400 bald eagles. Some fishing is allowed during their nesting season. Check with the tribe for permit information and season details.

There are abundant opportunities for outdoor activities such as wilderness and sub-wilderness hiking, whitewater and eagle float trips, downhill and cross-country skiing, ocean fishing, clamming, and crabbing. Please call the tribe for details.

ARCHAEOLOGICAL & HISTORIC SITES:

Closed to the public at this time. Contact the tribal office for information.

BUSINESSES & INDUSTRIES:

Upper Skagit Fisheries Department
(206) 856-5501

Upper Skagit Cedar Gift Factory
(206) 856-5501
Northwest tribal designs.

ACCOMMODATIONS:

Skagit Valley abounds with camping clubs, state and federal parks, and bed and breakfast lodgings.

Courtesy of Yakima Indian Nation.

Yakima Reservation

TRIBAL PROFILE:

Created by treaty on June 9, 1855, the Yakima Reservation covers 1.6 million acres of land on the eastern slopes of the glorious Cascade Range. Comprised of 14 tribes and bands, the Yakima were traditionally hunters and fishermen with highly developed basketry techniques. Today they pursue numerous enterprises and industries; forestry, agriculture, and ranching constitute the main livelihood for the Yakima Nation. Tribal membership stands at about 8,186.

LOCATION:

In mountainous country adjacent to two wilderness areas, the possibility for outdoor sports seems limitless in this region, summer or winter. South and west of Yakima in south-central Washington, just off I-82; US 97 runs through the reservation.

ADDRESS:

Confederated Tribes and Bands of the Yakima Indian Nation
P.O. Box 151
Toppenish, WA 98948
(509) 865-2255

CULTURAL INSTITUTIONS:

Yakima Nation Cultural Heritage Center
Toppenish, WA
(509) 865-2800
Houses gift shop, unique museum with historical dioramas of the Yakima, Indian history library, theater and restaurant. Museum admission fee; open daily 10:00 a.m.-6:00 p.m.

Many Toppenish buildings display an array of historical, authentic murals depicting people or legends of the Yakima Nation.

Special Events:

Contact the Cultural Center (509-865-2800, ext. 751) for information, exact location and times of activities.

Annual Washington's Birthday Pow Wow
Toppenish, WA
Held in mid-February.

Annual Speelyi-Mi Arts & Crafts Trade Fair
Cultural Center
Toppenish, WA
Held in mid-March.

Annual Yakima Nation All-Indian Men's Basketball Tourney
Wapato, WA
Held in late March.

Black Lodge Pow Wow
White Swan, WA
Held in late March.

Celilo Wyam Pow Wow
Celilo, WA
Held in mid-April.

Annual Rock Creek Root Feast & Pow Wow
Rock Creek, WA
Held in mid-April.

Granger Cherry Festival & Parade
Granger, WA
Held in early May.

Central Washington Junior Livestock Show
Toppenish, WA
Held in early May.

Mid Columbia Pow Wow
Celilo, WA
Held in early May.

Annual Satus Longhouse Pow Wow
Satus, WA
Held in early May.

Zillah Community Day & Parade
Zillah, WA
Held in early May.

Annual Weaseltail Memorial & Pow Wow
White Swan, WA
Held in late May.

Annual Mural In A Day
Toppenish, WA
Well-known artisans come to create a painting on the side of a pre-selected Toppenish town building. A food fair and arts and crafts sales round out the occasion. Held in early June.

Annual Yakima Nation Cultural Center Anniversary Pow Wow
Toppenish, WA
A parade, pow wow, all-Indian rodeo, and competition dancing. Commemorates Treaty of 1855, leading to the consolidation of 14 tribes and bands to form the Yakima Nation. Free admission; event hours vary daily. Held 1st weekend in June, Thursday through Sunday.

White Swan All-Indian Rodeo
White Swan, WA
A pow wow is also part of the activities. Held in early June.

Annual Tiinowit International Pow Wow
Sundome, WA
Featuring hundreds of native dancers from tribes throughout the US and Canada; a superb craft market; and special international guests. Celebrating the Treaty of 1855. Held in early June. Admission charged.

Annual Toppenish Pow Wow & Rodeo
Toppenish, WA
Pioneer Fair and Indian Village, as well as pow wow and rodeo events. Held in early July.

Zillah Old Fashioned 4th Fireworks
Zillah, WA
Held on July 4th.

Annual Scalper's Invitational All-Indian Softball Tourney
Wapato, WA
Held in July.

Annual Eagle Spirit Pow Wow
Satus, WA
Held in late August.

Wapato Harvest Festival & Parade
Wapato, WA
Held in early September.

Annual National Indian Days Celebration & Pow Wow
White Swan, WA
Held in mid-September.

Northwest Indian Summer Celebration
White Swan, WA
Held in early October.

Mid Columbia River Pow Wow
Celilo, WA
Held in late October.

Annual Veteran's Day Pow Wow
Toppenish, WA
Held in mid-November.

Zillah Old Fashioned Christmas
Zillah, WA
Held in early December.

Toppenish Christmas Festival & Santa Express
Toppenish, WA
Held in mid-December.

Christmas Pow Wow
Wapato, WA
Held on December 25.

New Year's Day Pow Wow
White Swan, WA
Held in December 31.

RECREATIONAL OPPORTUNITIES:

There are camping and RV sites next to the Culture Center.

ARCHAEOLOGICAL & HISTORIC SITES:

Many legendary sites important to the Yakima people, including rock formations and painted rocks, are scattered throughout the reservation and Cascade region. Check with the Cultural Center for further information and directions.

BUSINESSES & INDUSTRIES:

Heritage Inn Restaurant
Yakima Nation Cultural Center
(206) 865-2551
Serving a wide variety of foods to delight the palate, including buffalo steaks, salmon, fried bread, and homemade pies. Open daily.

Mt. Adams Furniture Factory
(509) 575-4434
Tours should be set up in advance with the Sales Department.

ACCOMMODATIONS:

Motels in close proximity to the reservation in Yakima.

Other Washington Reservations

Please contact the following reservations directly for tourism information.

Hoh Tribal Business Council
HC 80, Box 917
Forks, WA 98331-9304
(206) 374-6582

Lower Elwha Tribal Community Council
1666 Lower Elwha Road
Port Angeles, WA 98362-9518
(206) 452-8471

Nisqually Indian Community Council
4820 She-Nah-Num Dr. SE
Olympia, WA 98503-9199
(206) 456-5221

Port Gamble Community Council
P.O. Box 280
Kingston, WA 98346-0999
(206) 297-2646

Puyallup Tribal Council
2002 E. 28th Street
Tacoma, WA 98404-4996
(206) 597-6200

Quinault Indian Nation Business Committee.
P.O. Box 189
Taholah, WA 98587-0189
(206) 276-8211

Sauk-Suiattle Tribal Council
5318 Chief Brown Lane
Darrington, WA 98241-9421
(206) 435-8366

Shoalwater Bay Tribal Council
P.O. Box 130
Tokeland, WA 98590-0130
(206) 267-6766

Skokomish Tribal Council
N. 80 Tribal Center Road
Shelton, WA 98584-9748
(206) 426-4232

Stillaguamish Board of Directors
3439 Stoluckquamish Lane
Arlington, WA 98223-9056
(206) 652-7362

Swinomish Indian Tribal Community
P.O. Box 817
LaConner, WA 98257-0817
(206) 466-3163

Tulalip Board of Directors
6700 Totem Beach Road
Marysville, WA 98270-9694
(206) 653-4585

Wisconsin

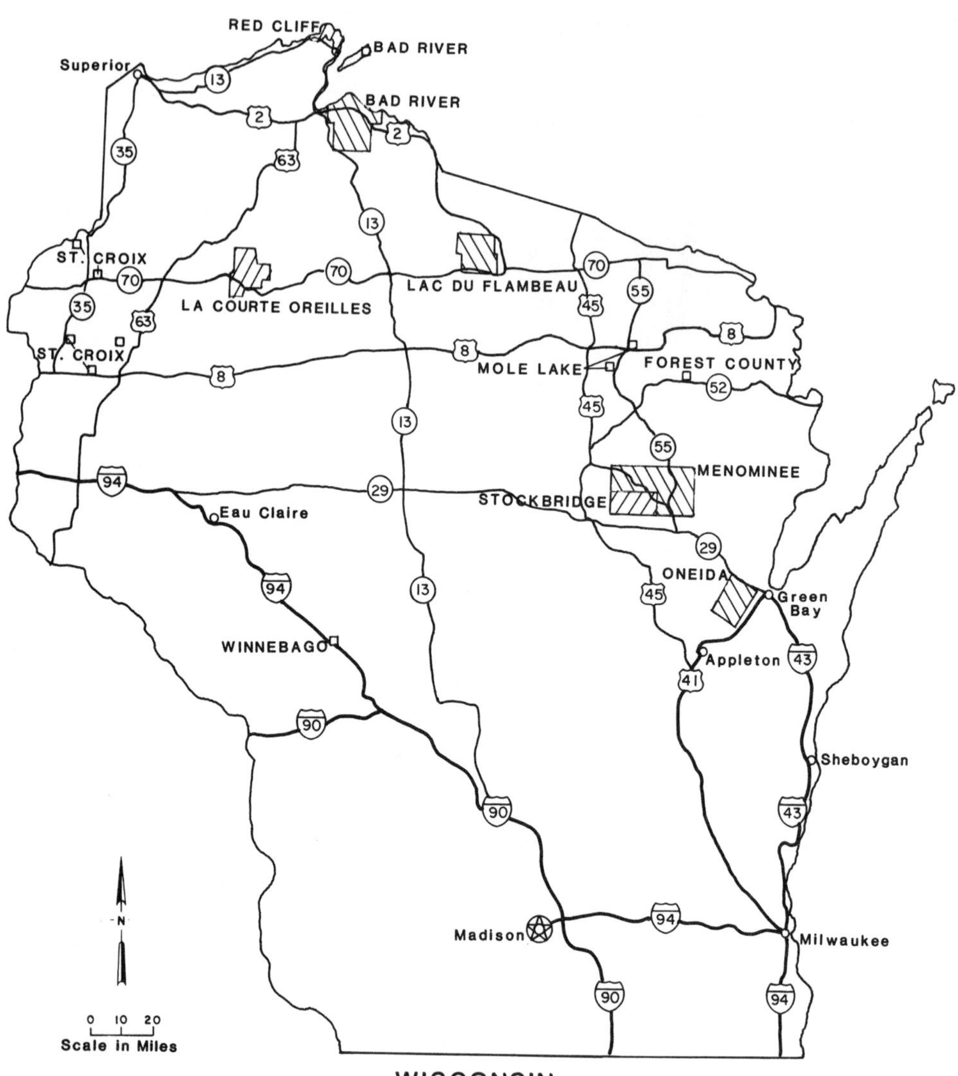
RED CLIFF
BAD RIVER
Superior
13
BAD RIVER
2
2
35
63
13
ST. CROIX
70
70
LAC DU FLAMBEAU
70
55
45
LA COURTE OREILLES
35
63
8
ST. CROIX
8
MOLE LAKE
FOREST COUNTY
8
52
45
13
55
MENOMINEE
94
29
STOCKBRIDGE
Eau Claire
29
ONEIDA
94
13
45
Green Bay
WINNEBAGO
Appleton
43
41
90
Sheboygan
90
43
N
94
Madison
Milwaukee
90
94
0 10 20
Scale in Miles

WISCONSIN

Ricing. Photo by Amoose. Courtesy of the Great Lakes Indian Fish & Wildlife Commission.

Bad River Reservation

TRIBAL PROFILE:

Established by treaty in 1854, Bad River Reservation is home to almost 1,700 members of the 5,000 member Bad River Band of Lake Superior Chippewa Indians. Tribal lands cover 55,000 acres by Lake Superior and almost 200 acres on Madeline Island in extreme northern Wisconsin. Much of the area is forested, with wetlands, farmlands and communities making up the remainder. The seven-member Bad River Tribal Council oversees tribal enterprises and services. In addition to its gaming enterprise, the tribe operates a logging operation and a fish hatchery.

LOCATION:

Northern Wisconsin, on Lake Superior; scenic US 2 traverses the northern portion of the reservation in this region rich with sporting opportunities; 100 miles of river flow through the reservation to the lake.

ADDRESS:

Bad River Band of Lake Superior Chippewa Indians
P.O. Box 39
Odana, WI 54861
(715) 682-7111

CULTURAL INSTITUTIONS:

Living Center Heritage Complex
US 2
Odana, WI
Museum, educational arts and crafts center, and ceremonial hall used for traditional tribal rites and festivals. Archives open to the public in the summer.

SPECIAL EVENT:

Manomin Pow Wow
Held 3rd weekend in August.

RECREATIONAL OPPORTUNITIES:

Bad River Gaming Complex
(715) 682-7111
Includes a bingo hall offering high stakes bingo and casino featuring blackjack, slot machines and much more, housed in a traditional-style log building. US 2, 10 miles east of Ashland.

KaKagon Sloughs: 7,000 acre wetland where wild rice is harvested each August.

Lake Superior Shoreline: 17 miles of natural beauty.

Forest County Potawatomi Reservation

Tribal Profile:

Forest County Reservation covers 11,692 acres in a checkerboard band across central Nicolet National Forest in Forest, Marinette, and Oconto Counties. The reservation is home to 460 members of this band of the Potawatomi; tribal membership stands at 783. The Executive Tribal Council governs under a constitution adopted in 1982. Some tribal ventures include a bingo facility, smoke shop, construction company, and a logging operation.

Location:

Northeastern Wisconsin near the Michigan border and due north of Oshkosh; tribal lands can be reached via Hwy 32, off Hwy 64.

Address:

Forest County Potawatomi Community of Wisconsin
P.O. Box 346
Crandon, WI 54520
(715) 478-2903

Recreational Opportunities:

Forest County Potawatomi Reservation has a bingo operation. Call the tribe at (715) 478-2903 for specifics as to time, dates and cost.

Lac Courte Oreilles Reservation

Tribal Profile:

The Lac Courte Oreilles Band of Lake Superior Chippewa Indians of Wisconsin occupies a part of its traditional homeland. The Treaty of La Pointe in 1854 established specific territorial rights for the Lac Courte Oreilles people, including allocation of the approximately 48,000 acre reservation. Of the 5,800 tribal members, about 3,000 live on or near the reservation today. The Lac Courte Oreilles Band has experienced tremendous business growth over the past several decades, and tribal enterprises include a logging and sawmill business, auto repair and gas station, health facility and a community college.

Location:

Northwestern Wisconsin, about 90 miles south of Duluth, Minnesota. Hayward is at the junction of US 63 and WI 27.

Address:

Lac Courte Oreilles Ojibwa Tribe
Rte. 2, Box 2700
Hayward, WI 54843
(715) 634-8934

Cultural Institutions:

Lac Courte Oreilles College
(715) 634-4790
Open for tours; has displays of Indian artifacts and traditional beadwork.

Special Events:

Anishinabeway Conference
Held 3rd week in June.

Honor of the Earth Pow Wow
On the reservation, 11 miles SE of Hayward. Held 3rd weekend of July.

Protect the Earth Festival
Held Labor Day Weekend.

Veteran's Pow Wow
Held in November.

New Year's Eve Pow Wow
Held December 31.

Top, Honor of the Earth Pow Wow. Right, LCO Commercial Center. Courtesy of Lac Courte Oreilles Planning Dept.

RECREATIONAL OPPORTUNITIES:

Lac Courte Oreilles Casino
Hayward, WI
Noon to midnight, daily.

Lac Courte Oreilles Bingo Parlor
Hayward, WI
Monday through Thursday, from 6:30 p.m., Sunday afternoon.

ARCHAEOLOGICAL & HISTORIC SITES:

St. Francis Solanus Mission
(715) 634-8934

BUSINESSES & INDUSTRIES:

Lac Courte Oreilles Cranberry Marsh
(715) 945-2459
36 acre farm; open for tours during seasonal harvest.

WOJB Radio Station
100,000 watt FM radio station, an affiliate of National Public Radio.

LCO Commercial Center
Includes grocery store, video rental shop, general merchandise store, restaurant and Quick Stop gas station.

Lac du Flambeau Reservation

TRIBAL PROFILE:

The Lac du Flambeau Reservation is part of the Lakeland area tourist region of northern Wisconsin and abuts Chequamegon National Forest and Northern Highlands State Forest. The reservation covers approximately 98,000 acres which is a combination of private and trust lands; tribal lands abound with water and forest life. The reservation is home to about 2,400 persons year round, but the population nearly triples during the summer tourist season. The reservation was established by treaty in 1854 for this band of the Chippewa and included three townships, later expanded. The main occupations of the Lac du Flambeau Tribe are tribal government jobs, labor in local factories, forest firms, resorts, tourism and some harvesting of seasonal crops.

LOCATION:

Near the Michigan border in north-central Wisconsin, Lac du Flambeau is crossed by Hwys 70 and 47, accessed from US 2, US 8 and US 51.

ADDRESS:

Lac du Flambeau Band of
Lake Superior Chippewa Indians
P.O. Box 67
Lac du Flambeau, WI 54538
(715) 588-3303

CULTURAL INSTITUTIONS:

Lac du Flambeau Museum
Lac du Flambeau, WI
(715) 588-3333
Open May through October, 10:00 a.m. to 4:00 p.m., Monday through Friday; until 7:00 p.m. on Tuesday pow wow nights. Drop-in visitors welcome during other months on Monday, Wednesday, and Friday.

Lac du Flambeau Indian Bowl and Authentic Village
Lac du Flambeau, WI 54538

Lac du Flambeau Tribal Library
Lac du Flambeau, WI 54538

SPECIAL EVENTS:

Exhibition Pow Wows
Pow Wow Grounds
Every Tuesday night June through August. Contact the tribal office or museum for details.

Bear River Pow Wow
Pow Wow Grounds
Hundreds of dancers participate in this annual event. Food and arts and crafts sales. Held weekend after July 4th.

RECREATIONAL OPPORTUNITIES:

Lac du Flambeau Bingo
Lac du Flambeau, WI 54538
Contact the tribal office for schedule.

Lake of the Torches Casino
Lac du Flambeau, WI 54538
Contact the tribal office for details regarding gaming opportunities and hours of operation.

Lac du Flambeau Campground and Marina
(715) 588-3303, -3103
RV facilities and bait shop.

Outdoor Sports: Lac du Flambeau is billed as the "Vacation Capital of the North", with 158 spring-fed lakes, sandy shores, and groves of birch and pine. Snowmobiling, camping, hunting, fishing, and other water sports are all possibilities; contact the tribal office.

BUSINESSES & INDUSTRIES:

The Lac du Flambeau Tribe owns and operates a fish hatchery, an enterprise that manufactures electrical components and lumber operations, as well as the LDF Ojibwe Mall and Grocery Store, Tribal Gas Station and a real estate leasing enterprise.

Wa-Swa-Gon Arts & Crafts
P.O. Box 477
Lac du Flambeau, WI 54538
(715) 588-7636
Offering beadwork, birch bark items, moccasins, fingerweaving, traditional and ceremonial outfits, and carvings. Hours: 9:00 a.m.-4:00 p.m., Monday through Friday, Memorial Day through Labor Day.

Ready for dinner at Menominee Logging Camp Museum. Courtesy of the Menominee Tribe.

Menominee Reservation

TRIBAL PROFILE:

The Menominee Indians are an Algonquian speaking tribe that has lived in what is now Wisconsin for about 5,000 years. Roughly 3,900 out of the 6,400 tribal members of the Menominee Tribe occupy this reservation of approximately 235,000 acres, most of which is intensively managed timberland. The land is scenic, with an abundance of lakes, streams and wildlife.

LOCATION:

Northeastern Wisconsin, east of Wausau, near Shawano. Both Hwy 47 and 55 pass through Menominee lands. The reservation boundaries are those of Menominee County.

ADDRESS:

Menominee Tribe of Wisconsin
P.O. Box 397
Keshena, WI 54135
(715) 799-5100

CULTURAL INSTITUTIONS:

Menominee Logging Camp Museum
Neopit, WI
(715) 799-3757
Guides explain the thousands of old logging artifacts during tour of 7 log buildings, including bunk house, cook shanty, wood butcher's shop and blacksmith shop, all dating from the start-up of the tribe's timber enterprise early in the 20th century. Next to the Wolf River, 1-1/4 mile north of Keshena at the junction of Hwy 47 and county road VV, just south of Neopit. Open daily except Monday, May through mid-October. Small fee.

Top, shooting the rapids on Wolf River. Bottom, Menominee Nation Casino. Photos courtesy of the Menominee Tribe.

Special Events:

Veterans Memorial Day Pow Wow
Woodland Bowl
(715) 799-4324
The Bowl, a natural amphitheater, accommodates this annual gathering. Held Memorial Day weekend. Near Keshena, WI.

Annual Menominee Nation Contest Pow Wow
Woodland Bowl
This annual event attracts visitors from throughout North America. Activities include senior citizen honor ceremony, princess selection, arts and crafts exhibits and sales, food concessions featuring traditional Indian foods, competitions in traditional dress and dance. Small admission fee. Held 1st weekend in August.

Recreational Opportunities:

Menominee Nation Casino
Keshena, WI 54135
(715) 799-4606
Over 20,000 square feet, Las Vegas style games. Full service bar, security, lighted parking. Open 1:00 p.m., 7 days a week, 364 days a year.

Menominee Tribal Bingo
P.O. Box 397
Keshena, WI 54135
(800) 421-3077 or (715) 799-4495
A full range of food concessions available, snacks to a full meal; no alcohol allowed. Security provided. Bus tours welcome; accommodates over 400 people. Sessions held daily except Sunday. Adjacent to the casino.

Smokey Falls Rafting
P.O. Box 247
Keshena, WI 54135
(715) 799-4945
White water rafting on the Wolf River, 15 miles north of Keshena. Wolf River drops 900 feet as it winds through 59 miles of the Menominee Reservation. Long run about 5 1/2 hours, short run about 1 hour. Reasonable fee; reservations required.

Rafting on the Wolf River must be done through a business owned by a tribal member.

Smokey Falls: The main falls give the area its name, with constant mist created by water cascading down a 40-foot drop. Can be viewed from an island accessible via a foot bridge. Granite and white water rapids, about 9 miles north of Keshena.

Wolf River Dells: Spectacular canyon with a picnic area, refreshments and souvenirs. North of Smokey Falls.

Archaeological & Historic Sites:

Spirit Rock: Legend says the disappearance of this natural stone monument will signal the extinction of the Menominee. Historic marker at site; north of Keshena on Hwy 55.

Businesses & Industries:

Menominee Tribal Enterprises (M.T.E.)
Neopit, WI 54150
(715) 756-2311
In business since 1908, M.T.E. is a modern, well-equipped logging and lumber manufacturing plant. M.T.E limits cut to 25 million feet annually and plants trees to replace the cut, ensuring products for the future.

Menominee Tribal Supermarket and Smokeshop
Keshena

Restrictions and/or Special Considerations:

Hunting, fishing and access to tribal land are exclusive rights of Menominee tribal members and are protected by federal law.

Oneida Reservation

Tribal Profile:

The Oneida Nation was a member of the Iroquois Confederacy, formed in the 1500s, comprised of the Cayuga, Mohawk, Oneida, Onondaga and Seneca Tribes. This band of the Oneida Tribe removed to Wisconsin from New York in the 1820s, having sold much of its lands or lost them through war and unscrupulous land deals. A reservation in Wisconsin was established by treaty in 1838. The Oneida Reservation constitutes 2,900 acres with the population on or near tribal lands totalling approximately 4,900 enrolled members; tribal enrollment is 10,300. Oneida is a proud and progressive tribe, self-determined, caring for its people from the cradle to the grave. This attention takes the form of programs that include Headstart, child care, career training, the Oneida Healthworks Fitness Center, a senior citizen center offering dinners, and a transit system.

Location:

Eastern Wisconsin, 7 miles west of Green Bay, with portions of the suburbs surrounding the reservation. Hwy 54 passes east-west through Oneida.

Address:

Oneida Tribe
P.O. Box 365
Norbert Hill Center, 3000 Seminary Rd.
Oneida, WI 54155
(414) 869-2214

Cultural Institutions:

Oneida Library
(414) 869-2210
Lending library.

Oneida Nation Museum
Box 365
886 Double E Rd.
Oneida, WI 54155
(414) 869-2768
Exhibits present an overall view of the Iroquois with an emphasis on the Oneida, including displays of Indian ceremonial attire, dioramas, and activities room. A reconstructed stockaded village features a full-size replica of an Oneida longhouse, life-skills demonstrations, and medicinal herb garden. Guided tours. Gift shop. Open 9:00 a.m.-5:00 p.m. Mon-Sat, May-September; closed Sat and Sun, October-April. Admission charged.

Oneida Tribal School
Oneida, WI

Special Events:

Oneida Annual Pow Wow
Norbert Hill Center
Oneida, WI
Traditional Oneida dances and a competition pow wow form the main part of the festivities which also feature arts, crafts and Indian foods sales. Grand entry Friday and Saturday 1:00 p.m. and 5:00 p.m., Sunday 1:00 p.m. only. 7 miles west of Green Bay off Hwy 54. Admission cost. Held 4th of July weekend.

Oneida Championship Fall Pow Wow
Norbert Hill Center
Oneida, WI
Held in October.

Recreational Opportunities:

The Oneida Nation sponsors 4 to 5 fun runs throughout the year, drawing top-name participants. Contact tribal office for times and dates.

Oneida Bingo & Casino
Division of First American Games
Irene Moore Activity Center
Hwy 172
Green Bay, WI
(800) 472-4263 (in-state) or (800) 238-4263
Offering blackjack, slot machines, and video poker, as well as bingo. Call for schedule of activities and games.

Big Green Lotto
(800) 472-4263 (in-state) or
(800) 238-4263
Lottery drawn every Wednesday night, Cash 3 drawn daily. Tickets sold at a variety of locations; call for details.

Businesses & Industries:

Oneida Cannery, Oneida Healthworks Fitness Center, Oneida Research and Technology Center, Comprehensive Health Center, and Oneida Printing are some of the enterprises undertaken by the Oneida Nation.

Oneida One-Stops
Oneida Reservation
Four convenience stores offering discount cigarettes, video gaming, and gas. One store contains the largest walk-in humidor in the area and sells gourmet coffees.

ACCOMMODATIONS:

Radisson Inn Green Bay
2040 Airport Dr.
Green Bay, WI 54313
(415) 494-7300 or (800) 333-3333
Premium hotel with 202 rooms, specialty suites and executive rooms. Features Shenandoah Restaurant and Purcell's Lounge on the premises, as well as swimming pool, sauna, hot tub, exercise room. The Inn is in a wooded area with hiking trails and a pond. Conference facilities include The Great Lakes Complex, accommodating up to 650 people, and an auditorium that will hold 120. Next to the Oneida Casino and across from Austin Straubel Airport.

Red Cliff Reservation

TRIBAL PROFILE:

Red Cliff Reservation is the home of the Red Cliff Band of Lake Superior Chippewa Indians, one of several bands of Ojibwa (Chippewa) Indians living in Wisconsin, Minnesota, Michigan and Canada. Trust acreage for the reservation is almost 8,000 acres; reservation population is about 1,500, with tribal enrollment nearly 3,000. The Reservation is governed by a nine-member tribal council under a constitution adopted in 1936. Tribal businesses include construction and fisheries.

LOCATION:

Northern tip of the Bayfield peninsula, on Lake Superior; reached via Hwy 13 from Ashland or Superior. Adjacent to the Apostle Islands.

ADDRESS:

Red Cliff Tribe
P.O. Box 529
Bayfield, WI 54814
(715) 779-5805

CULTURAL INSTITUTIONS:

Buffalo Art Center
Bayfield, WI
(715) 779-3755

SPECIAL EVENTS:

Annual Red Cliff Traditional Pow Wow & Home Coming
(715) 779-3700
A sharing of traditional heritage: songs, dancing, crafts and food; traditional games and children's activities. 3 miles north of Bayfield on Hwy 13. Small admission fee. Held Friday evening through Sunday afternoon, 1st weekend of July.

Contact the Red Cliff Tribal Council for information about other cultural events and programs occurring on the reservation throughout the year.

RECREATIONAL OPPORTUNITIES:

Red Cliff Recreational Complex and Isle Vista Casino
Bayfield, WI 54814
(715) 779-3739
Latest in gaming fun, including blackjack tables, variety of slots, pull tabs. Afternoon and evening Big Bucks Bingo.

Red Cliff Lanes
Bayfield, WI
(715) 779-3700
Hosting family bowling outings.

Red Cliff Marina and Campground: 40 sites with water and electrical service, along with hiking and boating. On Lake Superior; fee.

Apostle Islands National Lakeshore: Hiking and ski trails; at the northern boundary of the reservation.

ARCHAEOLOGICAL & HISTORIC SITES:

La Pointe Indian Cemetery
Madeline Island, WI

St. Croix Reservation

Tribal Profile:

The St. Croix Chippewa live on this 1,943 acre reservation created by proclamation of the Secretary of the Interior in 1938. Reservation lands are held in trust for the 759 members and are home to 1,288 Indians. Most employment is seasonal work, including hospitality, guiding and forestry.

Location:

On a small lake north of Eau Claire in northwest Wisconsin, St. Croix Reservation is in segments; the largest is on Hwy 70.

Address:

St. Croix Chippewa Indians of Wisconsin
P.O. Box 287
Hertel, WI 54845
(715) 349-2195

Recreational Opportunities:

St. Croix Reservation has a bingo operation. Call the tribe at (715) 349-2195 for specifics as to time, dates and cost.

Sokaogon Chippewa Community (Mole Lake)

Tribal Profile:

After signing a treaty in 1854, the chief of the Mole Lake Band selected tribal lands in the heart of a region abundant with wild rice, a Chippewa food staple. However, the land rights of the Sokaogon Band were not resolved until the Indian Reorganization Act was passed in 1934. The smallest of the Wisconsin reservations with just under 2,000 acres, Mole Lake is headquarters for approximately 1,600 enrolled members of the Mole Lake Band of Sokaogon Chippewa; about 400 tribal members live on the reservation. Sources of income for the tribe include bingo and casino operations, and a smoke shop. The tribe expects to expand cultural restoration projects and environmental planning, utilizing the profits from gaming operations.

Location:

Northeastern Wisconsin; just west of the Forest County Reservation, Mole Lake Reservation is on Hwy 55 northeast of Wausau.

Address:

Sokaogon Chippewa Community
Mole Lake Band
Rte. 1, Box 625
Crandon, WI 54520
(715) 478-2604

Recreational Opportunities:

Grand Royale Casino
Hwy 55
Crandon, WI 54520
(715) 478-2604
Blackjack, video games and slot machines. Open Noon to 3:00 a.m. every day.

Regency Resort Casino
Hwy 55
Crandon, WI 54520
(715) 478-2604
Blackjack, video games and slot machines, open noon to 3:00 a.m. every day. Across the highway from Grand Royale.

Mole Lake Bingo Hall
Crandon, WI 54520
(715) 478-2604
High stakes bingo on Monday, Tuesday, Friday, Saturday and Sunday.

Archaeological & Historic Sites:

Battle of Mole Lake Historical Marker

Businesses & Industries:

Mole Lake Smoke Shop

Stockbridge Reservation

TRIBAL PROFILE:

The Treaty of February 11, 1856, and the Proclamation of the Secretary of the Interior on March 19, 1937 established a reservation for the Stockbridge (Mahican) and Munsee Tribes. Initially a 23,040 acre portion of the Menominee Reservation was appropriated for these tribes; however, the land on Lake Winnebago was ceded in exchange for the present 15,602 acre property many miles north. The Mahicans are originally from Massachusetts, having migrated west to New York and later removed with other tribes to Wisconsin. Today tribal membership stands at 1,595, with over half living on reservation lands. Forestry is integral to the economic well-being of the tribe, and other enterprises are in the planning stages.

LOCATION:

Northeastern Wisconsin, immediately south of the Menominee Reservation. Accessed via Hwy 289, on a county road.

ADDRESS:

Stockbridge Munsee Community
Rte. 1
Bowler, WI 54416
(715) 793-4111

RECREATIONAL OPPORTUNITIES:

Stockbridge-Munsee Bingo: Call the tribe at (715) 793-4111 for specifics as to time, dates and cost.

Winnebago Reservation

TRIBAL PROFILE:

Over 4,200 acres are held in trust for this band of the Winnebago Tribe, scattered over Shawano, Marathon, Clark, Wood, Adams, Juneau, Monroe, Jackson, LaCrosse, and Crawford Counties. Originally living near Winnebago Lake and Green Bay, much of the tribe was moved to three different states over a period of 12 years before returning to Wisconsin and refusing to move again. Now reservation population exceeds 2,700 and tribal membership stands at 3,918, many of whom are involved in tribally owned businesses: three bingo operations and four smoke shops. The Winnebago are considering expanding tribal enterprise to include a retail mall, hotel, convenience stores, candy factory, and day care.

LOCATION:

Southwest Wisconsin; north of I-94, adjacent to Black River State Forest.

ADDRESS:

Wisconsin Winnebago
P.O. Box 311
Tomah, WI 54660
(608) 372-4147

RECREATIONAL OPPORTUNITIES:

Ho-Chunk Bingo
Lake Delton, WI
(608) 356-9268
Contact for scheduling of games.

The Winnebago Tribe also operates Rainbow Falls Bingo and Sands Bingo. Call the tribe at (608) 372-4147 for specifics as to time, dates and cost.

Wyoming

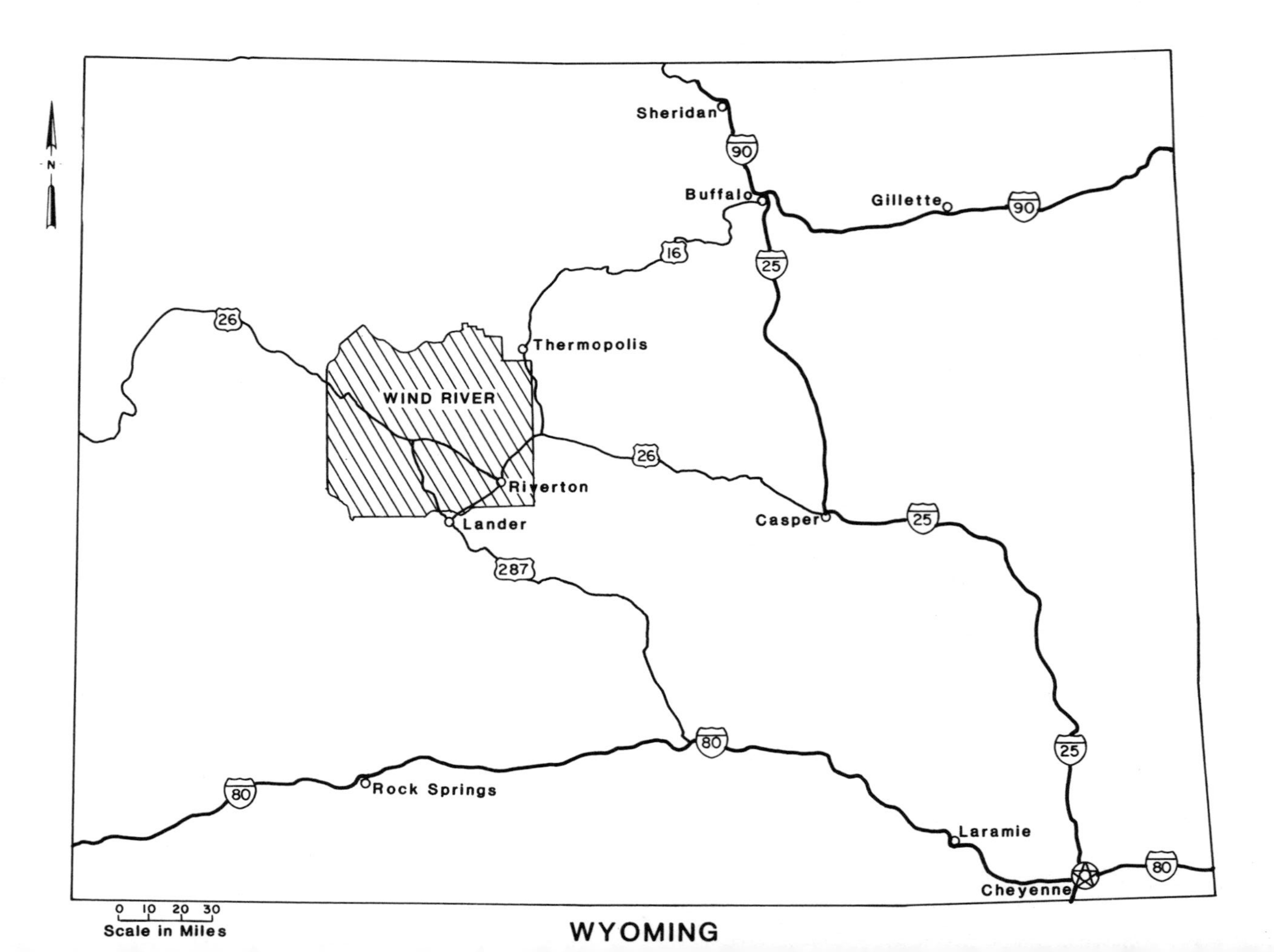
N
Sheridan
90
Buffalo
Gillette
90
16
25
26
Thermopolis
WIND RIVER
26
Riverton
Lander
Casper
25
287
80
25
80
Rock Springs
Laramie
Cheyenne
80
0 10 20 30
Scale in Miles
WYOMING

Wind River in the Rockies. Courtesy of Catherine Vandemoer.

Wind River Reservation

The Wind River Reservation is Wyoming's only Indian reservation and covers almost 2 million acres in the beautiful west-central portion of the state. It was established in 1863 for the Shoshone, who were joined by the Arapahoe in 1878. The reservation is shared by the Shoshone and Arapahoe tribes; both tribes maintain separate business councils and operate a joint business council. The tribes preserve disparate activities and traditions, material for this guide was obtainable only from the Shoshone Tribe.

Shoshone Tribe

Tribal Profile:

Placed on the Wind River Reservation by treaty in 1863, today the Shoshone Tribe is mainly involved in ranching and forestry, together with some coal mining. The tribe, now approximately 5,000 members, is fostering a resurgence in traditional ceremonies and dances, as well as arts and crafts including quill and bead work.

Location:

The proximity of Wind River to the Rocky Mountains and the Continental Divide, as well as Yellowstone and Grand Teton National Parks, makes the reservation a natural stopping-off point. North of Lander on US 287; reached from I-80 via US 287 or US 191 and Hwy 28.

Address:

Arapahoe Tribe
P.O. Box 217
Fort Washakie, WY 82514
(307) 332-6120

Eastern Shoshone Tribe
P.O. Box 538
Fort Washakie, WY 82514
(307) 332-3532

Awaiting his turn -- young Arapahoe dancer. Courtesy of Debra Thunder, Northern Arapahoe.

Cultural Institutions:

Shoshone Tribal Cultural Center
P.O. Box 1008
Fort Washakie, WY 82514
(307) 332-9106

Special Events:

For scheduling and dates of annual dances and ceremonies, call or write to the Tribal Cultural Center.

Treaty Day Recognition
Fort Washakie Pow Wow Grounds
Fort Washakie, WY
Commemorates the 1868 treaty between the Eastern Shoshone and the United States. Events are scheduled throughout the day beginning with the Treaty Day Recognition, followed by Indian games, style show, feast and Indian dancing. Free admission. Held in late June.

Shoshone Indian Days and Rodeo
Fort Washakie, WY
(307) 332-9106
Indian festival and pow wow following the Treaty Day. Events include competition Indian dancing, games, giveaways, and a feast sponsored by the Shoshone Entertainment Committee. Admission is free; held in late June.

Recreational Opportunities:

Rocky Acres RV Facilities
c/o Shoshone Tribe
P.O. Box 358
Fort Washakie, WY 82514
RV facilities, hookups and showers. Also sells reservation fishing permits. Off US 287, 7 miles north of Lander.

Archaeological & Historic Sites:

Fort Washakie Historic District: Contact the tribal cultural center for information regarding a guided walking tour, or a 19-site self-guided walking tour of the district. Two notable monuments on the tour honor Sacajawea and Chief Washakie.

Businesses & Industries:

R.V. Greeves Art Gallery
Fort Washakie, WY
(307) 332-3557
Primarily stone and bronze sculptures by local artisans.

Warm Valley Arts and Crafts
P.O. Box 358
Fort Washakie, WY
(307) 332-7330
Native made gifts and crafts.

Shoshone Tribal Service
#3 North Fork Road
Fort Washakie
(307) 332-2906
Reservation information, gas and a deli.

Tribal Organizations:

Shoshone Entertainment Committee
P.O. Box 538
Fort Washakie, WY 82514

Organizes and schedules the many annual traditional dances and ceremonies.

Accommodations:

Hotels and motels in Lander and Riverton.

Mountain lake. Courtesy of Catherine Vandemoer.

Appendix I
Location of Tribes, Bands and Communities by State and Reservation or Community

Tribe	State	Reservation, Rancheria, or Community
Absentee Shawnee	Oklahoma	Shawnee, OK
Alabama	Texas	Alabama-Coushatta Reservation
Algonquian	Virginia	Mattaponi, VA
Apache	Arizona	Camp Verde Reservation Ft. Apache Reservation Ft. McDowell Reservation San Carlos Apache Reservation Tonto Apache Reservation
	New Mexico	Jicarilla Apache Reservation Mescalero Apache Reservation
	Oklahoma	Ft. Sill Apache Reservation
Arapaho	Oklahoma Wyoming	Concho, OK Wind River Reservation
Arikara	North Dakota	Ft. Berthold Reservation
Assiniboine	Montana	Ft. Belknap Reservation Ft. Peck Reservation
Bannock	Idaho	Ft. Hall Reservation
Blackfeet	Montana	Blackfeet Reservation
Cachil Dehe	California	Colusa Rancheria
Cahuilla	California	Agua Caliente Reservation Los Coyotes Reservation
Catawba	South Carolina	Catawba Reservation*
Cayuga	Oklahoma	Miami, OK
Cayuse	Oregon	Umatilla Reservation
Chasta	Oregon	Grand Ronde Reservation
Chehalis	Washington	Chehalis Reservation
Chemehuevi	California Arizona	Chemehuevi Reservation Colorado River Reservation
Cherokee	North Carolina Oklahoma	Cherokee Reservation Tahlequah, OK
Cheyenne	Oklahoma Montana	Concho, OK Northern Cheyenne Reservation

Tribe	State	Reservation, Rancheria, or Community
Chickasaw	Oklahoma	Ada, OK
Chinook	Washington	Chehalis Reservation
Chippewa (aka Ojibwa)	Michigan	Bay Mills Reservation Grand Traverse Reservation Isabella Reservation Lac Vieux Desert Reservation L'Anse Reservation Sault Ste. Marie Reservation
	Minnesota	Bois Forte (Nett Lake) Reservation Fond du Lac Reservation Grand Portage Reservation Leech Lake Reservation Mille Lacs Reservation Red Lake Reservation White Earth Reservation
	Montana	Rocky Boy's Reservation
	North Dakota	Turtle Mountain Chippewa Reservation
	Wisconsin	Bad River Reservation Lac Courte Oreilles Reservation Lac du Flambeau Reservation Red Cliff Reservation St. Croix Reservation Mole Lake Reservation
Chitimacha	Louisiana	Chitimacha Reservation
Choctaw	Mississippi Oklahoma	Choctaw Reservation Durant, OK
Chuckchansi	California	Picayune Rancheria
Chumash	California	Santa Ynez Reservation
Clatsop	Washington	Chehalis Reservation
Cocopah	Arizona	Cocopah Reservation
Colville	Washington	Colville Reservation
Concow	California	Round Valley Reservation
Coos	Oregon	Coos Bay, OR
Coquille	Oregon	Coos Bay, OR
Couer D'Alene	Idaho	Coeur D'Alene Reservation
Coushatta	Louisiana Texas	Coushatta Reservation* Alabama-Coushatta Reservation
Cowlitz	Washington	Chehalis Reservation
Cree	Montana	Rocky Boy's Reservation

Tribe	State	Reservation, Rancheria, or Community
Creek	Alabama	Poarch Creek Reservation
	Oklahoma	Okmulgee, OK
Crow	Montana	Crow Reservation
Dakota (aka Lakota, Nakoda or Sioux)	Minnesota	Shakopee Reservation
		Lower Sioux Community
		Prairie Island Sioux Reservation
		Upper Sioux Community
	Montana	Ft. Peck Reservation
	Nebraska	Santee Sioux Reservation
	North Dakota	Devils Lake Sioux Reservation
		Standing Rock Sioux Reservation
	South Dakota	Cheyenne River Sioux Reservation
		Crow Creek Sioux Reservation
		Flandreau Santee Sioux Reservation
		Lake Traverse Reservation
		Lower Brule Reservation
		Pine Ridge Reservation
		Rosebud Reservation
		Yankton Reservation
Entiat/Chelan	Washington	Colville Reservation
Fox	Kansas	Sac & Fox Reservation
	Oklahoma	Stroud, OK
	Iowa	Sac & Fox Settlement (Reservation)
Goshute	Utah	Goshute Reservation
		Skull Valley Reservation
Gros Ventre	Montana	Ft. Belknap Reservation
Haliwa-Saponi	North Carolina	Haliwa-Saponi Reservation*
Hassanamisco-Nipmuc	Massachusettes	Hassanamisco Reservation*
Havasupai	Arizona	Havasupai Reservation
Hidatsa	North Dakota	Ft. Berthold Reservation
Hopi	Arizona	Hopi Reservation
Houma	Louisiana	Golden Meadow, LA
Hualapai	Arizona	Hualapai Reservation
Hupa	California	Hoopa Valley Reservation
Iowa	Kansas	Iowa Reservation
	Oklahoma	Iowa Reservation
Iroquois	New York	Allegany Reservation
		Oneida Reservation
		Onondaga Reservation
		Tuscarora Reservation

Tribe	State	Reservation, Rancheria, or Community
Kalapuya	Oregon	Grand Ronde Reservation
Kalispel	Washington	Kalispel Reservation
Kansa (aka Kaw)	Oklahoma	Kaw City, OK
Karuk	California	Karuk Reservation
Kaw (See Kansa)		
Kickapoo	Kansas Texas	Kickapoo Reservation Texas Kickapoo Reservation
Klallam	Washington	Jamestown Klallam Reservation
Klamath	Oregon	Klamath Reservation
Kootenai	Idaho Montana	Kootenai Reservation Flathead Reservation
Kumeyaay	California	Sycuan Reservation
Lake	Washington	Colville Reservation
Lower Descutes	Oregon	Warm Springs Reservation
Lower Umpqua	Oregon	Coos Bay, OR
Luiseno	California	LaJolla Reservation Soboba Reservation
Lummi	Washington	Lummi Reservation
Mahican	Wisconsin	Stockbridge Munsee Reservation
Makah	Washington	Makah Reservation
Maliseet, Houlton Band of	Maine	Houlton, ME
Mandan	North Dakota	Ft. Berthold Reservation
Mashantucket	Connecticut	Mashantucket Pequot Reservation
Mashpee-Wampanoag	Massachusetts	Mashpee-Wampanoag Reservation*
Mattaponi	Virginia	Mattaponi Reservation*
Me-Wuk	California	Chicken Ranch Rancheria Tuolemne Rancheria
Menominee	Wisconsin	Menominee Reservation
Mesquakie (See Fox)		
Methow	Washington	Colville Reservation
Mi-Wuk	California	Trinidad Rancheria
Miccosukee	Florida	Miccosukee Reservation
Micmac	Maine	Houlton and Presque Isle, ME

Tribe	State	Reservation, Rancheria, or Community
Mission Indians	California	Barona Reservation Cabazon Reservation Viejas Reservation La Jolla Reservation Los Coyotes Reservation Pala Reservation Rincon Reservation Santa Ynez Reservation Santa Ysabel Reservation Soboba Reservation Sycuan Reservation
Mohave	Arizona California	Ft. McDowell Reservation Ft. Mojave Reservation
Mohawk	New York	St. Regis Mohawk Reservation
Mojave	California	Ft. Mojave Reservation
Molalla	Oregon	Grand Ronde Reservation
Moses Columbia	Washington	Colville Reservation
Muckleshoot	Washington	Muckleshoot Reservation
Munsee	Wisconsin	Stockbridge Munsee Reservation
Muscogee (aka Creek)	Alabama Oklahoma	Poarch Creek Reservation Okmulgee, OK
Narragansett	Rhode Island	Narragansett Reservation
Navajo	Arizona New Mexico	Navajo Reservation Alamo Navajo Reservation Cañoncito Navajo Reservation Ramah Navajo Reservation
Nespelem	Washington	Colville Reservation
Nez Perce	Idaho Washington	Nez Perce Reservation Colville Reservation
Nomlachi	California	Round Valley Reservation
Nooksack	Washington	Nooksack Reservation
Ojibwa (See Chippewa)		
Okanogan	Washington	Colville Reservation
Omaha	Nebraska	Omaha Reservation
Oneida	New York Wisconsin	Oneida Reservation Oneida Reservation
Onondaga	New York	Onondaga Reservation

Tribe	State	Reservation, Rancheria, or Community
Osage	Oklahoma	Osage Reservation
Osakiwug (See Fox)		
Ottawa	Michigan Oklahoma	Grand Traverse Reservation Miami, OK
Paiute	California Nevada Oregon	Ft. Bidwell Reservation Ft. Independence Reservation Duck Valley Reservation Fallon Colony & Reservation Ft. McDermitt Reservation Las Vegas Colony & Reservation Lovelock Colony & Reservation Moapa River Reservation Pyramid Lake Reservation Reno-Sparks Colony Summit Lake Reservation Walker River Reservation Yerington Colony & Reservation Burns Paiute Reservation
Palouse	Washington	Colville Reservation
Pamunkey	Virginia	Pamunkey Reservation*
Papago (See Tohono O'odham)		
Passamaquoddy	Maine	Indian Township Reservation Pleasant Point Reservation
Paughusett	Connecticut	Paughusett Golden Hill Reservation*
Pawnee	Oklahoma	Pawnee Reservation
Pend d'Oreilles	Montana	Flathead Reservation
Penobscot	Maine	Penobscot Reservation
Peoria	Oklahoma	Miami, OK
Pequot	Connecticut	Mashantucket Pequot Reservation Paucatuck Eastern Pequot Reservation*
Pima-Maricopa	Arizona	Gila River Reservation Salt River Reservation
Pit River	California	Round Valley Reservation
Pomo	California	Coyote Valley Rancheria Robinson Rancheria Round Valley Reservation Sherwood Valley Rancheria
Ponca	Nebraska Oklahoma	Lake Andes, South Dakota Ponca Reservation

Tribe	State	Reservation, Rancheria, or Community
Potawatomi	Kansas	Potawatomi Reservation
	Michigan	Hannahville Reservation
		Huron Potawatomi Reservation*
		Potawatomi Reservation*
	Oklahoma	Citizen Band of Potawatomi Reservation
	Wisconsin	Forest County Potawatomi Reservation
Pueblo	New Mexico	Acoma Pueblo
		Cochiti Pueblo
		Isleta Pueblo
		Jemez Pueblo
		Laguna Pueblo
		Nambe Pueblo
		Picuris (San Lorenzo) Pueblo
		Pojoaque Pueblo
		Sandia Pueblo
		San Felipe Pueblo
		San Ildefonso Pueblo
		San Juan Pueblo
		Santa Ana Pueblo
		Santa Clara Pueblo
		Santa Domingo Pueblo
		Taos Pueblo
		Tesuque Pueblo
		Zia Pueblo
		Zuni Pueblo
	Texas	Ysleta del Sur Pueblo
Quapaw	Oklahoma	Quapaw, OK
Quechan	Arizona	Ft. Yuma Reservation
Quileute	Washington	Quileute Reservation
Rogue River	Oregon	Grand Ronde Reservation
S'Homamish	Washington	Squaxin Island Reservation
Sac (See Fox)		
Sahaptin	Oregon	Warm Springs Reservation
Sa-heh-wa-mish	Washington	Squaxin Island Reservation
Salish	Montana	Flathead Reservation
	Washington	Upper Skagit Reservation
San Luiseno	California	La Jolla Rancheria
		Rincon Rancheria
Sanpoil	Washington	Colville Reservation
Schaghticoke	Connecticut	Schaghticoke Reservation*

Tribe	State	Reservation, Rancheria, or Community
Seminole	Florida	Big Cypress Reservation Brighton Reservation Dania Reservation Hollywood Reservation Immokalee Reservation Miccosukee Reservation
	Oklahoma	Wewoka, OK
Seneca	New York	Allegany Reservation Cattaraugus Reservation Oil Springs Reservation Tonawanda Seneca Reservation
	Oklahoma	Seneca-Cayuga Tribe, Miami, OK
Senijextee	Washington	Colville Reservation
Shasta	California	Quartz Valley Reservation
Shawnee	Oklahoma	Shawnee, OK
Shinnecock	New York	Shinnecock Reservation*
Siletz Confederacy of 24 tribes	Oregon	Siletz Reservation
Shoshone	Idaho	Ft. Hall Reservation
	Nevada	Duck Valley Reservation Duckwater Shoshone Reservation Ely Indian Colony Fallon Colony & Reservation Ft. McDermitt Reservation Te Moak Reservation, (*includes the Battle Mountain Colony, Elko Band Colony, South Fork Band Colony, and the Wells Band Colony*) Yomba Shoshone Reservation
Sioux (See Dakota)		
Skitswish	Washington	Colville Reservation
Spokane	Washington	Spokane Reservation
Squaxin	Washington	Squaxin Island Reservation
Squi-aitl	Washington	Squaxin Island Reservation
Stehchass	Washington	Squaxin Island Reservation
Suislaw	Oregon	Coos Bay, OR
Suquamish	Washington	Port Madison Reservation
Sycuan	California	Sycuan Reservation
T'Peeksin	Washington	Squaxin Island Reservation
Tache	California	Santa Rosa Rancheria

Tribe	State	Reservation, Rancheria, or Community
Tachi	California	Santa Rosa Rancheria
Thlopthlocco	Oklahoma	Okemah, OK
Tigua	Texas	Ysleta del Sur Pueblo
Tiwa (See Pueblo)		
Tohono O'odham (aka Papago)	Arizona	Ak Chin Reservation Gila Bend Reservation San Xavier Reservation
Tolowa	California	Big Lagoon Rancheria Trinidad Rancheria
Tonawanda (See Seneca)		
Towa (See Pueblo)		
Tunica-Biloxi	Louisiana	Tunica-Biloxi Reservation
Tuscarora	New York	Tuscarora Reservation
Uintah	Utah	Uintah & Ouray Reservation
Umatilla	Oregon	Umatilla Reservation
Umpqua	Oregon	Coos Bay, OR Grand Ronde Reservation
Uncompahgre	Utah	Uintah & Ouray Reservation
Unkechauge	New York	Poospatuck Reservation* Shinnecock Reservation*
Upper Descutes	Oregon	Warm Springs Reservation
Upper Klamath	California	Quartz Valley Reservation
Upper Skagit	Washington	Upper Skagit Reservation
Ute	Colorado Utah	Ute Mountain Reservation Southern Ute Reservation Uintah & Ouray Reservation
Wailaki	California	Round Valley Reservation
Walla Walla	Oregon	Umatilla Reservation
Wampanoag	Massachusettes	Mashpee-Wampanoag Reservation* Wampanoag Reservation
Warm Springs	Oregon	Warm Springs Reservation
Wascos	Oregon	Warm Springs Reservation

Tribe	State	Reservation, Rancheria, or Community
Washoe	California Nevada	Woodsford Colony Carson Indian Colony Dresslerville Colony Reno-Sparks Colony Stewart Colony
Wenatchee	Washington	Colville Reservation
Whiteriver	Utah	Uintah & Ouray Reservation
Winnebago	Nebraska Wisconsin	Winnebago Reservation Winnebago Reservation
Wintun	California California	Colusa Rancheria Rumsey Rancheria
Yakima	Washington	Yakima Reservation
Yaqui	Arizona	Pacua Yaqui Reservation
Yavapai	Arizona	Camp Verde Reservation Ft. McDowell Reservation Yavapai-Prescott Reservation
Yokut	California	Santa Rosa Rancheria Tule River Reservation
Yuki	California	Round Valley Reservation
Yuman	Arizona	Ft. Yuma Reservation
Yurok	California	Big Lagoon Rancheria Trinidad Rancheria Resighini Rancheria

*** Denotes State Reservations.**

Appendix II
Pow Wow Directory by State and Month

Listed by states and months with the tribal office, organization, or contact's pertinent information to assist you with any questions you may have regarding the pow wow. This is not a complete listing of all pow wows held throughout the country. Call the tribe or Indian community that you are seeking information on for current dates and status of the local pow wows.

Alabama

November

Poarch Band of Creeks Pow Wow
Poarch Band of Creeks
Route 3, Box 243A
Atmore, AL 36502
(205) 368-9136

Arizona

Pueblo dances are held throughout the year. For a schedule of upcoming events, contact:

Hopi Cultural Center
P.O. Box 67
Second Mesa, AZ 86043
(602) 734-2401

January

Kachina Dances
Hopi Cultural Center
P.O. Box 67
Second Mesa, AZ 86043
(602) 734-2401

Kachina dances are held from mid-winter through summer. Contact cultural center for details.

February

O'odham Tash Indian Celebration
Tohono O'odham Nation
P.O. Box 837
Sells, AZ 85634
(602) 383-2221

March

Mul-Chu-Tha Community Fair
Gila River Indian Community
P.O. Box 97
Sacaton, AZ 85247
(602) 562-3311

April

Cocopah Festivities Day
Cocopah Tribal Council
P.O. Bin G
Somerton, AZ 85350
(602) 627-2102

Holy Week Ceremonies
Pascua Yaqui Tribal Council
7474 S. Camino de Oeste
Tucson, AZ 85746
(602) 883-2838

Native American Student Association Pow Wow
Arizona State University
Tempe, AZ 85287
(602) 965-9011

Spring Roundup All-Indian Rodeo
White Mountain Apache Tribal Council
P.O. Box 700
Whiteriver, AZ 85941
(602) 338-4346

May

San Carlos Tribal Fair
San Carlos Apache Tribe
P.O. 0
San Carlos, AZ 85550
(602) 475-2361

June

Elderfest
White Mountain Apache Tribal Council
P.O. Box 700
Whiteriver, AZ 85941
(602) 338-4346

July

Navajo Rodeo
Navajo Nation Tourism Office
P.O. Box 663
Window Rock, AZ 86515
(602) 871-6436

White Mountain Native American Festival and Indian Market
Chamber of Commerce
Pinetop-Lakeside, AZ 85935
(602) 367-4290

August

Snake Dance
Hopi Cultural Center
P.O. Box 67
Second Mesa, AZ 86043
(602) 734-2401

September

Apache Tribal Fair
White Mountain Apache Tribe
P.O. Box 700
Whiteriver, AZ 85941
(602) 338-4346

Navajo Nation Fair
Navajo Nation Tourism Office
P.O. Box 663
Window Rock, AZ 86515
(602) 871-6436

Peach Festival
Havasupai Tribal Office
P.O. Box 10
Supai, AZ 86435
(602) 448-2961

White Mountain Tribal Fair & Rodeo
White Mountain Apache
Tribal Council
P.O. Box 700
Whiteriver, AZ 85941
(602) 338-4346

National Indian Days Pow Wow
Colorado River Tribes
Parker, AZ
(602) 669-9211

October

Arizona State Fair
Phoenix Fairgrounds
Phoenix, AZ

Northern Navajo Fair, Shiprock
Navajo Nation Tourism Office
P.O. Box 663
Window Rock, AZ 86515
(602) 871-6436

November

Veteran's Day Rodeo
San Carlos Apache Tribal Council
P.O. Box 0
San Carlos, AZ 85550
(602) 475-2361

California

January

Annual Native American Film Festival
Southwest Museum
234 Museum Dr.
Highland Park
Los Angeles, CA 90041
(213) 221-2164

Indian Ceremonial Show & Pow Wow
Civic Auditorium
Santa Monica, CA
(213) 430-5112

March

Agua Caliente Indian Market
Agua Caliente Tribal Council
960 E. Tahquitz Canyon Way #106
Palm Springs, CA 92262
(619) 325-5673

April

San Francisco Annual Pow Wow
American Indian Studies Dept
San Francisco State University
1600 Holloway
San Francisco, CA
(415) 338-1111

May

Cupa Days
Pala Tribal Office
P.O. Box 43
Pala, CA 92059
(619) 742-3784

Festival at the Lake
Lake Merritt, Oakland
News of Native California
P.O. Box 9145
Berkeley, CA 94709
(415) 549-3564

Malki Museum Fiesta & Pow Wow
11795 Fields Road
Banning, CA 92220
(714) 849-7289

San Juan Bautista American Indian Art Show
San Juan Bautista Mission
Contact Reyna's Gallerias: (408) 623-2379

Stanford University Pow Wow
Native American Students Assn
P.O. Box 2990
Stanford, CA 94305
(415) 723-4078

June

Corpus Christi Festival
Pala Tribal Office
P.O. Box 43
Pala, CA 92059
(619) 742-3784

Indian Day Big Time
Yosemite National Park
P.O. Box 577
Yosemite, CA 95389
(209) 372-0283

Indian Fair Days
Museum of Man
1350 El Prado
Balboa Park
San Diego, CA 92101
(619) 239-2001

July

Gathering Day
Wassama Roundhouse
State Historic Park
Ahwahnee, CA
(209) 822-2332

Hupa Rodeo
Hupa Tribe
P.O. Box 1245
Hoopa, CA 95546
(916) 625-4110

Kule Loklo Native Amer. Celebration
Point Reyes National Seashore
Kule Loklo Miwok Indian Village
Point Reyes, CA 94956
(415) 663-1092

August

Sierra Mono Museum Indian Fair
Sierra Mono Museum
P.O. Box 275
North Fork, CA 93643
(209) 877-2115

September

California Indian Days
State Indian Museum
2618 K Street
Sacramento, CA 95816
(916) 324-0971

Colorado River Tribes Fair
and Indian Days
Colorado River Tribal Council
P.O. Box 23-B
Parker, AZ 85344
(602) 669-9211

San Juan Bautista American Indian Art Show
San Juan Bautista Mission
Contact Reyna's Gallerias: (408) 623-2379

November

American Indian Film Festival
Palace of Fine Arts
San Francisco, CA
(415) 563-6504

Colorado

May

Bear Dance
Southern Ute Tribal Council
P.O. Box 737
Ignacio, CO 81137
(303) 563-4525

June

Bear Dance
Ute Mountain Ute Tribe
General Delivery
Towaoc, CO 81334
(303) 565-3751

September

Southern Ute Fair
Southern Ute Tribal Council
P.O. Box 737
Ignacio, CO 81137
(303) 563-4525

Florida

August

Labor Day Pow Wow
C.B. Smith Park
Pembroke Pines, FL
(305) 476-7672

December

Miccosukee Arts and Crafts Fair
Miccosukee Tribal Council
P.O. Box 440021
Tamiami Station
Miami, FL 33144
(305) 223-8380

Seminole Fair
Seminole Tribal Council
6073 Sterling Road
Hollywood, FL 33024
(305) 584-0400

Idaho

March

Epethes Pow Wow
Nez Perce Tribe
P.O. Box 305
Lapwai, ID 83540
(208) 843-2253

May

Warriors Memorial Pow Wow
(Honoring Chief Joseph)
Nez Perce Tribe
P.O. Box 305
Lapwai, ID 83540
(208) 843-2253

Coeur d'Alene Pow Wow
Coeur d'Alene Tribal Council
Plummer, ID 83851
(208) 274-3101

August

Looking Glass Pow Wow
Nez Perce Tribe
P.O. Box 305
Lapwai, ID 83540
(208) 843-2253

Shoshone-Bannock Indian Festival
and Rodeo
Shoshone-Bannock Tribes
P.O. Box 306
Fort Hall, ID 83203
(208) 238-3700

October

Four Nations Pow Wow
Nez Perce Tribe
P.O. Box 305
Lapwai, ID 83540
(208) 843-2253

Maine

August

Ceremonial Day
Pleasant Point Passamaquoddy
P.O. Box 343
Perry, ME 04667
(207) 853-2551

Minnesota

March

Heart of the Earth Survival Schools Pow Wow
Minneapolis Convention Center
1301 Second Avenue South
Minneapolis Minnesota
(612) 331-8862

May

Memorial Day Pow Wow
Minnesota Chippewa Tribe
P.O. Box 217
Cass Lake, MN 56633
(218) 335-2252

June

Nett Lake Pow Wow
Nett Lake Reservation Business Committee
P.O. Box 16
Nett Lake, MN 55772
(218) 757-3261

White Earth Pow Wow
White Earth Chippewa Tribe
P.O. Box 418
White Earth, MN 56591
(218) 983-3285

July

Fond du Lac Pow Wow
Fond du Lac Business Committee
105 University Road
Cloquet, MN 55720
(218) 879-4593

August

Grant Portage Rendezvous Days
Grand Portage Chippewa Tribe
P.O. Box 428
Grand Portage, MN 55605
(218) 476-2279

Ni-Mi-Win Celebration
Spirit Mountain
Duluth, MN
(218) 628-2891

September

Labor Day Pow Wow
Minnesota Chippewa Tribe
P.O. Box 217
Cass Lake, MN 56633
(218) 335-2252

Mah-Kato Pow Wow
Mdewakanton Club
P.O. Box 3608
Mankato, MN 56001
(507) 389-6125

Mississippi

July

Choctaw Fair
Choctaw Tribe
P.O. Box 6010
Philadelphia, MS 39350
(601) 656-5251

Montana

February

Fort Belknap Mid-Winter Fair
Fort Belknap Community Council
R.R. 1, Box 66
Fort Belknap Agency
Harlem, MT 59526
(406) 353-2205

June

Red Bottom Celebration
Badlands Celebration
Fort Peck Executive Board
P.O. Box 1027
Poplar, MT 59255
(406) 768-5155

July

Fort Kipp Celebration
Iron Ring Celebration
Wadopana Celebration
Fort Peck Executive Board
P.O. Box 1027
Poplar, MT 59255
(406) 768-5155

Milk River Indian Days
Fort Belknap Tribal Office
Route 1, Box 66
Harlem, MT 59526
(406) 353-2205

North American Indian Days
Blackfeet Tribal Council
P.O. Box 850
Browning, MT 59417
(406) 338-7522

Northern Cheyenne Fourth of July Pow Wow
Northern Cheyenne Tribal Council
P.O. Box 128
Lame Deer, MT 59043
(406) 477-8283

Arlee Fourth of July Pow Wow
Confederated Salish and Kootenai Tribal Council
P.O. Box 278
Pablo, MT 59855
(406) 675-2700

Elmo Standing Arrow Pow Wow
Confederated Salish and Kootenai Tribal Council
P.O. Box 278
Pablo, MT 59855
(406) 675-2700

August

Oil Discovery Celebration
Fort Peck Executive Board
P.O. Box 1027
Poplar, MT 59255
(406) 768-5155

Crow Fair
Crow Tribal Council
P.O. Box 159
Crow Agency, MT 59022
(406) 638-2601

Birney Pow Wow
Northern Cheyenne Tribal Council
P.O. Box 128
Lame Deer, MT 59043
(406) 477-8283

Rocky Boys Pow Wow
Chippewa Cree Tribe
Rocky Boy Route, Box 544
Box Elder, MT 59521
(406) 395-4282

Nevada

June

Red Mountain Indian Pow Wow
Fort McDermitt Indian Reservation
P.O. Box 457
McDermitt, NV 89421
(702) 532-8259

July

Shoshone-Paiute Fourth of July Pow Wow
Shoshone-Paiute Tribal Council
P.O. Box 219
Owyhee, NV 89832
(702) 757-3161

October

Pyramid Lake Pow Wow and Indian Rodeo
Pyramid Lake Paiute Tribe
P.O. Box 256
Nixon, NV 89424
(702) 686-5626

New Mexico

Pueblo dances are held throughout the year. For a schedule of upcoming events, contact:

Indian Pueblo Cultural Center
2401 12th Street, NW
Albuquerque, NM 87102
(505) 843-7270

Eight Northern Indian Pueblos Council
P.O. Box 969
San Juan Pueblo, NM 87566
(505) 852-4265

January

San Ildefonso Feast Day
San Ildefonso Day
P.O. Box 315-A
Santa Fe, NM 87501
(505) 455-2273

March

San Jose Feast Day
Laguna Pueblo
P.O. Box 194
Laguna, NM 87026
(505) 552-6654

April

Institute of American Indian Arts Pow Wow
1369 Cerrillos Road
Santa Fe, NM 87501
(505) 988-6281

Gathering of Nations Pow Wow
University of New Mexico Arena
Albuquerque, NM
(505) 836-2810

May

San Felipe Feast Day
San Felipe Pueblo
P.O. Box A
San Felipe, NM 87001
(505) 867-3381

San Juan Feast Day
San Juan Pueblo
P.O. Box 1099
San Juan, NM 87566
(505) 852-4400

Santa Cruz Feast Day
Taos Pueblo
P.O. Box 1846
Taos, NM 87571
(505) 758-8626

June

San Antonio Feast Day
Sandia Pueblo
P.O. Box 6008
Bernalillo, NM 87004
(505) 867-3317

San Juan Feast Day
Taos Pueblo
P.O. Box 1846
Taos, NM 87571
(505) 758-8626

July

Little Beaver Rodeo and Pow Wow
Jicarilla Apache Tribe
P.O. Box 507
Dulce, NM 87528
(505) 579-3242

Mescalero Festival
Mescalero Apache Tribe
P.O. Box 176
Mescalero, NM 88340
(505) 671-4495

San Buenaventura Feast Day
Cochiti Pueblo
P.O. Box 70
Cochiti, NM 87041
(505) 465-2244

Santa Ana Feast Day
Santa Ana Pueblo
Star Route, Box 37
Bernalillo, NM 87004
(505) 867-3301

Taos Pueblo Pow Wow
Taos Pueblo
P.O. Box 1846
Taos, NM 87571
(505) 758-8626

August

Intertribal Indian Ceremonial
P.O. Box 1
Church Rock, NM 87311
(505) 863-3896

Our Lady of Assumption Feast Day
Zia Pueblo
General Delivery
San Ysidro, NM 87053
(505) 867-3304

San Lorenzo Feast Day
Picuris Pueblo
P.O. Box 127
Penasco, NM 87553
(505) 587-2519

Santa Clara Feast Day
Santa Clara Pueblo
P.O. Box 580
Espanola, NM 87532
(505) 753-7326

September

Jicarilla Apache Fair
Jicarilla Apache Tribe
P.O. Box 507
Dulce, NM 87528
(505) 759-3242

San Agustin Feast Day
Isleta Pueblo
P.O. Box 10
Isleta, NM 878022
(505) 869-3111

San Esteban Feast Day
Acoma Pueblo
P.O. Box 309
Acomita, NM 87034
(505) 552-6604

San Geronimo Feast Day
Taos Pueblo
P.O. Box 1846
Taos, NM 87571
(505) 758-8626

Stone Lake Fiesta
Jicarilla Apache Tribe
P.O. Box 507
Dulce, NM 87528
(505) 759-3242

October

San Francisco Feast Day
Nambe Pueblo
P.O. Box 117-BB
Santa Fe, NM 87501
(505) 455-2036

November

San Diego Feast Day
Jemez Pueblo
P.O. Box 100
Jemez, NM 87024
(505) 834-7359

San Diego Feast Day
Tesuque Pueblo
Route 11, Box 1
Santa Fe, NM 87501
(505) 983-2667

December

Our Lady of Guadalupe Feast Day
Jemez Pueblo
P.O. Box 100
Jemez, NM 87024
(505) 834-7359

Our Lady of Guadalupe Feast Day
Pojoaque Pueblo
Route 11, Box 71
Santa Fe, NM 87501
(505) 455-2278

Shalako
Zuni Pueblo
P.O. Box 339
Zuni, NM 87327
(505) 782-4881

New York

May

The Turtle Pow Wow
Native American Center for the Living Arts
25 Rainbow Mall
Niagara Falls, NY 14303
(716) 284-2427

September

Iroquois Indian Festival
Schoharie Museum of the Iroquois
P.O. Box 158
N. Main Street
Schoharie, NY 12157
(518) 234-8319

Mountain Eagle Indian Festival
Hunter Mountain Festivals
P.O. Box 295
Hunter, NY 12442
(518) 263-4223

Shinnecock Pow Wow
Shinnecock Reservation
Route 27A
Southampton, NY 11968
(516) 283-3776

North Carolina

June

Cherokee Pow Wow
Eastern Band of Cherokee Indians
P.O. Box 455
Cherokee, NC 28719
(704) 497-2771

September

American Indian National Arts Exposition
46 Haywood Street
Asheville, NC 28801
(704) 252-3880

North Dakota

July

Mandaree Pow Wow
Three Affiliated Tribes
P.O. Box 220
New Town, ND 58763
(701) 627-4781

Sisseton-Wahpeton Pow Wow
Sisseton-Wahpeton Tribal Council
COP Box 689
Sisseton, ND 57262
(701) 698-3911

August

Little Shell Pow Wow
Three Affiliated Tribes
P.O. Box 220
New Town, ND 58763
(701) 627-4781

Standing Rock Pow Wow
Standing Rock Sioux Tribal Council
P.O. Box D
Fort Yates, ND 58538
(701) 854-7231

September

Turtle Mountain Labor Day Pow Wow
Turtle Mountain Tribal Council
P.O. Box 900
Belcourt, ND 58316
(701) 477-6451

United Tribes International Pow Wow
Bismarck Civic Center
Bismarck, ND
(701) 255-3285

Oklahoma

May

Oklahoma Indian Heritage Days Celebration
Miami Tribal Office
P.O. Box 1326
Miami, OK 74355
(918) 540-2890

June

Cheyenne-Arapaho Pow Wow
Cheyenne-Arapaho Tribe
P.O. Box 38
Concho, OK 73022
(405) 262-0345

Osage Tribal Ceremonial Dances
Osage Tribal Council
c/o Osage Tribal Agency
Pawhuska, OK 74056
(918) 287-4622

Potawatomi Pow Wow
Citizen Band of Potawatomi
1901 S. Gordon Cooper Dr.
Shawnee, OK 74801
(405) 275-3121

July

Comanche Pow Wow
Comanche Tribal Office
P.O. Box 908
Lawton, OK 73502
(405) 274-3444

Kiowa Fourth of July Pow Wow
Kiowa Tribe
P.O. Box 369
Carnegie, OK 73015
(405) 654-2300

Otoe-Missouria Pow Wow
Otoe-Missouria Tribe
Route 1, Box 62
Red Rock, OK 74651
(405) 723-4434

Pawnee Pow Wow
Pawnee Tribe
P.O. Box 470
Pawnee, OK 74058
(918) 762-3624

Quapaw Pow Wow
Quapaw Tribe
P.O. Box 765
Quapaw, OK 74363
(918) 542-1853

Sac and Fox Pow Wow
Sac and Fox Tribal Office
Route 2, Box 246
Stroud, OK 74079
(918) 968-3526

August

American Indian Exposition
P.O. Box 908
Anadarko, OK 73005
(405) 274-2733 or 274-6651

Caddo Pow Wow
Tribal Complex
Binger, OK
(405) 656-2344

Ottawa Pow Wow
Ottawa Tribe
P.O. Box 110
Miami, OK 74355
(918) 540-1536

Ponca Indian Fair and Pow Wow
Ponca Tribe
Route 6, Box 2
Ponca City, OK 74601
(405) 762-8104

Wichita Tribal Pow Wow
Wichita Tribe
P.O. Box 729
Anadarko, OK 73005
(405) 274-2425

Cherokee National Holiday
Cherokee Heritage Center Grounds
Tahlequah, OK
(918) 456-0671

September

Choctaw Nation Labor Day Festivities
Choctaw Nation of Oklahoma
P.O. Drawer 1210
Durant, OK 74702
(405) 924-8280

Annual Fort Sill Apache
Tribe Celebration
Arrowhead Resort & Hotel Pow Wow Grounds
Canadian, Oklahoma
(918) 339-2711

Seminole Nation Days
Seminole Nation
P.O. Box 1498
Wewoka, OK 74884
(405) 257-6287

Annual Labor Day Pow Wow
Eastside Ball Park
Eufaula, OK
(981) 689-5066

Wyandotte Tribe Annual Pow Wow
Sycamore Valley Recreation Area
Wyandotte, OK
(918) 678-2297

October

Cherokee Fall Festival
Cherokee Nation of Oklahoma
P.O. Box 948
Tahlequah, OK 74465
(918) 456-0671

Chickasaw Nation Annual Day
Chickasaw Nation of Oklahoma
P.O. Box 1548
Ada, OK 74820
(405) 436-2603

Five Civilized Tribes Art Show
Five Civilized Tribes Museum
Agency Hill, Honor Heights Dr.
Muskogee, OK 74401
(918) 683-1701

Comanche War Dance
Cache, OK

December

Christmas Exhibition of Contemporary Indian Arts and Crafts
Southern Plains Indian Museum
P.O. Box 749
Anadarko, OK 73005
(405) 475-6221

Oregon

February

Lincoln's Birthday Pow Wow
Warms Springs Tribal Council
P.O. Box C
Warm Springs, OR 97761
(505) 553-1161

May

Warm Springs Treaty Days
Warm Springs Tribal Council
P.O. Box C
Warm Springs, OR 97761
(503) 553-1161

August

Nesika Illahee Pow Wow
Confederated Tribes of Siletz
Indians of Oregon
P.O. Box 549
Siletz, OR 97380
(503) 444-2532

September

Pendleton Roundup
Pendleton, OR
(800) 524-2984

October

Mid-Columbia River Pow Wow
Celilo Village, OR
(503) 298-1559

South Dakota

June

Oglala Lakota College Graduation Pow Wow
Oglala Lakota College Activities Committee
P.O. Box 490
Kyle, SD 57752
(605) 455-2321

July

Black Hills and Northern Plains Indian Exposition
Black Hills Pow Wow Association
P.O. Box 1476
Rapid City, SD 57709

Flandreau Santee Sioux Traditional Pow Wow
P.O. Box 283
Flandreau, SD 57028
(605) 997-3891

August

Cherry Creek Pow Wow
Cheyenne River Sioux Tribe
H.V. Johnston Cultural Center
P.O. Box 590
Eagle Butte, SD 57625
(605) 964-2542

Crow Creek Pow Wow
P.O. Box 50
Fort Thompson, SD 57339
(605) 245-2221

Fort Randall Pow Wow
Yankton Sioux Tribal Office
P.O. Box 248
Marty, SD 57361
(605) 384-3804

Lower Brule Pow Wow
P.O. Box 187
Lower Brule, SD 57548
(605) 473-5561

Oglala Nation Pow Wow and Rodeo
Oglala Sioux Tribe
P.O. Box H
Pine Ridge, SD 57770
(605) 867-5821

Rosebud Fair and Rodeo
Rosebud Tribal Office
P.O. Box 430
Rosebud, SD 57570
(605) 747-2381

Wazi Paha Oyate Festival
Oglala Lakota Community College
P.O. Box 490
Kyle, SD 57752
(605) 455-2321

September

Cheyenne River Labor Day Pow Wow
Cheyenne River Sioux Tribal Council
P.O. Box 590
Eagle Butte, SD 57625
(605) 964-4155

Utah

April

Bear Dance
Uintah and Ouray Tribal Council
P.O. Box 190
Fort Duchesne, UT 84026
(801) 722-5141

June

Northern Ute Pow Wow and Rodeo
Uintah and Ouray Tribal Council
P.O. Box 190
Fort Duchesne, UT 84026
(801) 722-5141

Washington

January

Mason School Pow Wow
1/5
2812 North Madison
Tacoma, WA
(206) 596-1139

May

Chehalis Tribal Day Celebration
Chehalis Community Council
Howanud Rd.
Oakville, WA 98568
(206) 273-5911

Satus Longhouse Pow Wow
Yakima Nation Cultural Center
P.O. Box 151
Toppenish, WA 98948
(509(865-2800

University of Washington Pow Wow
Seattle, WA
(206) 543-9082

Tinowit International Pow Wow, Treaty Days
Celebration and Rodeo
Yakima Nation Cultural Center
P.O. Box 151
Toppenish, WA 98948
(509) 865-2800

July

Chief Taholah Days
Quinault Tribal Council
P.O. Box 189
Taholah, WA 98587
(206) 276-8211

Colville Fourth of July Pow Wow
Colville Tribe
P.O. Box 150
Nespelem, WA 99155
(509) 634-4711

Toppenish Pow Wow, Rodeo and Pioneer Fair
Yakima Nation Cultural Center
P.O. Box 151
Toppenish, WA 98948
(509) 865-2800

August

Chief Seattle Days
Suquamish Tribe
P.O. Box 498
Suquamish, WA 98392
(206) 598-3311

Makah Festival
Makah Tribal Council
P.O. Box 115
Neah Bay, WA 98357
(206) 645-2205

Omak Stampede Days
Colville Tribe
P.O. Box 150
Nespelem, WA 99155
(509) 634-4711

September

Puyallup Pow Wow
Puyallup Tribal Council
2002 E. 28th Street
Tacoma, WA 98404
(206) 597-6200

Spokane Indians Labor Day Pow Wow
Spokane Tribe
P.O. Box 100
Wellpinit, WA 99040
(509) 258-4581

Yakima Pow Wow
Yakima Nation Cultural Center
P.O. Box 151
Toppenish, WA 98948
(509) 865-2800

Annual National Indian Days Celebration
White Swan Pavilion
White Swan, WA

Wisconsin

July

Bear River Pow Wow
Lac du Flambeau Tribal Council
P.O. Box 67
Lac du Flambeau, WI 45438
(715) 588-3303

Honor the Earth Pow Wow
Lac Courte Oreilles Tribe
Route 2, Box 2700
Hayward, WI 54843
(715) 634-8934

Oneida Pow Wow
Oneida Museum
P.O. Box 365
Oneida, WI 54155
(414) 869-2768

August

Land of the Menominee Pow Wow
Woodland Bowl
Menominee Indian Tribe
P.O. Box 397
Keshena, WI 54135
(715) 799-5100

Manomin Celebration
Bad River Chippewa Tribal Office
P.O. Box 39
Odanah, WI 54861
(715) 682-7111

October

14th Annual Autumn Pow Wow
University of Wisconsin-Milwaukee
Union Ballroom
Milwaukee, WI

Wyoming

June

Big Wind Pow Wow
Shoshone Business Council
Northern Arapaho Business Council
Fort Washakie, WY 82514
(307) 332-4932

Plains Indian Museum Pow Wow
Buffalo Bill Historical Center
P.O. Box 1000
Cody, WY 82414
(307) 587-4771

Shoshone Indian Days Pow Wow and Rodeo
Shoshone Business Council
Fort Washakie, WY 82514
(307) 332-4932

July

Ethete Pow Wow and Rodeo
Northern Arapaho Business Council
P.O. Box 396
Fort Washakie, WY 82514
(307) 332-6120

Appendix III
Photo and Map Credits

(Listed alphabetically by state and by contributor/s)

R.P. Anderson
Tempe, AZ
Arizona
46

Arizona Office of Tourism
Phoenix, AZ
Arizona
13,22,41,45

Gila River Arts & Crafts
Sacatan, AZ
Arizona
19,42

Navajoland Tourism Office
Window Rock, AZ
Arizona
27,33,34,35,39

Mark Nohl
New Mexico Economic & Tourism
Santa Fe, NM
Arizona
37,38

Susan L. Phelps
Shingle Springs, CA
Arizona
25

Billie D. Rogers
Littleton, CO
Arizona
31,36

John Running
Flagstaff, AZ
Arizona
43

Sheraton Resort
Prescott, AZ
Arizona
48

Candi L. Stasiek
McHenry, Ill.
Arizona
14

Sunrise Resort/Chaco Mohlerl
Tucson, AZ
Arizona
15

Sunrise Resort/John Canally
Tucson, AZ
Arizona
16

Susan J. Worthman
Mountain View, CO
Arizona
23

Steve Baldy
Arcata, CA
California
51,60

California Office of Tourism
Sacramento, CA
California
59,67

Dianna Muraski
Springville, CA
California
56,71,80

Sycuan Gaming Center
El Cajon, CA
California
79

Verona M. Worthman
San Diego, CA
California
68,69,74,76

Dale W. Anderson
Aztec, NM
Colorado
86,88

Jeff Andrew
Frisco, CO &
Colorado Tourism Board
Denver, CO
Colorado
87

Chris Ribera
Ignacio, CO
Colorado
85

Foxwood Bingo & Casino
Ledyard, CT
Connecticut
91

Andexler Photography
Fort Lauderdale, FL
Florida
95,98

Bill Held
Hialeah, FL
Florida
97

Lee Tiger & Associates
Miami, FL
Florida
98

Chief Joseph Foundation
Spalding, ID
Idaho
104

John Running
Flagstaff, AZ
Idaho
102

Nez Perce National Historical Park
Spalding, ID
Idaho
104

Iowa Tribe of Kansas & Nebraska
White Cloud, KS
Kansas
113

Chris Ribera
Ignacio, CO
Kansas
115

Coushatta Tribe of Louisiana
Elton, LA
Louisiana
120

Grand Traverse Band of
Ottawa & Chippewa Indians
Economic Development Authority
Suttons Bay, MI
Michigan
136

Michigan State Travel Bureau
Lansing, MI
Michigan
138

Amoose (Ray Moore)
Great Lakes Indian Fish & Wildlife Commission
Odanah, WI
Minnesota
146,148,149,
150,152

John Running
Flagstaff, Arizona
Minnesota
143

Kelsey/MBCI Communications
Philadelphia, MS
Mississippi
155,156

C.S.K.T. Wildland Recreation Program &Flathead Tribe
Pablo, MT
Montana
163

Dale Becker & C.S.K.T. Wildland Recreation Program
Pablo, MT
Montana
164

Council of Energy Resource Tribes
Denver, CO
Montana
159,160

Hardin Photo Service
Hardin, MT
Montana
161,162

Harvey King
Harlem, MT
Montana
166,167

Wotanin Wowapi Newspaper
Poplar, MT
Montana
169

Nevada Commission on Tourism
Carson City, NV
Nevada
180,182,183,185,188

Acoma Pueblo Tourist Center
Acoma, NM
New Mexico
193

Dale W. Anderson
Aztec, NM
New Mexico
199,200

Inn of the Mountain Gods
Mescalero, NM
New Mexico
206

Mark Nohl/New Mexico Economic & Tourism Development Office
Santa Fe, NM
New Mexico
202,208,213,214,215,217,219,
222,223,225,226,227,228

Jim Pierce
Denver, CO
New Mexico
210

Gary Robinson
Santa Fe, NM
New Mexico
201

Ski Apache Resort
Ruidoso, NM 88345
New Mexico
205

Byran Vigil
Dulce, NM
New Mexico
200

Bill Winfield
Cochiti Lake, NM
New Mexico
196

St. Regis Mohawk Tribal Council
Hogansburg, NY
New York
236

Richard Hill
Santa Fe, NM
New York
231,233,238,240,241

Cherokee Travel & Promotion
Cherokee, NC
North Carolina
245,246,247

Turtle Mountain Band of Chippewa Indians
Belcourt, ND
North Dakota
253,255,256,

Stan Labadie & Absentee Shawnee Tribe
Shawnee, OK
Oklahoma
259

Fred W. Marvel
Oklahoma Tourism & Recreation Deptartment
Oklahoma City, OK
Oklahoma
261,265,268,278,
270,276,279,280

Gary Robinson
Santa Fe, New Mexico
Oklahoma
266

Sammy Still
Cherokee Nation of Oklahoma
Tahlequah, OK
Oklahoma
260,261

John Running
Flagstaff, AZ
Oregon
288

Cappelli, Miles, Wiltz & Kelly & Osborn
Eugene, OR
Oregon
290

Council of Energy Resources Tribes
Denver, CO
Oregon
287

John Kirk
Klamath Falls, OR
Oregon
285

Helen Clausen
Eagle Butte, SD
South Dakota
301,302

Janis Allen
Kadoka, SD
South Dakoa
305

Mattaponi Tribe
Virginia
323

Council of Energy Resource Tribes
Denver, Colorado
Washington
328,337

Raymond W. Loloff
Denver, CO
Washington
333

John Running
Flagstaff, AZ
Washington
335,336

Yakima Indian Nation
Confederated Tribes and Bands
Toppenish, WA
Washington
340

Amoose (Ray Moore)
Great Lakes Indian Fish &
Wildlife Commission
Odanah, WI
Wisconsin
347

Lac Courte Oreilles
Planning Dept.
Hayward, WI 54843
Wisconsin
349

Menominee Tribe
Keshena, WI
Wisconsin
351,352

Debra Thunder
Casper, WY
Wyoming
362

Catherine Vandemoer
Denver, CO
Wyoming
361,363

Maps For All 33 States
Raymond W. Loloff
CERT
Denver, CO

The Navajo Nation Map
Cal Nez
Salt Lake City, UT
Arizona
28-29

Index

D

E

F

G

H

N

O

P

R

S

T

V

W

Y

Z